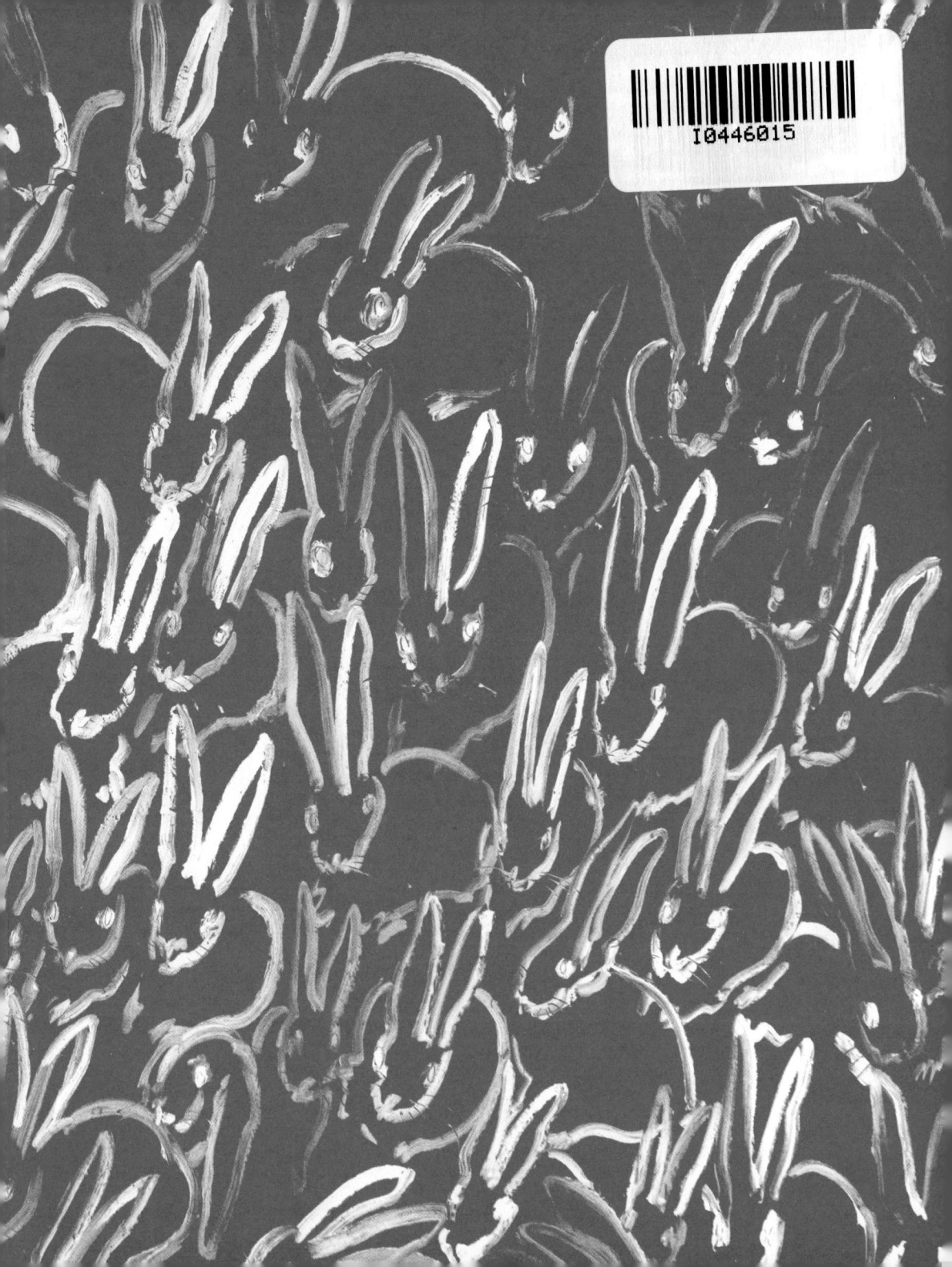

First published in 2018 by

G Editions
500 Seventh Avenue, 8th Floor
New York, New York 10018

www.geditions.com
media@geditions.com

First edition, 2018

Library of Congress Cataloging-in-Publication data is
available from the publisher.

Hardcover edition ISBN 978-1-943876-56-3

Art Director Pau Garcia
Associate Art Director Jonay Cogollos

Printed and bound in China
10 9 8 7 6 5

BITTY
BUNNIES

BITTY
BUNNIES

Hunt Slonem

Foreword
John Berendt

Essay
Bruce Helander

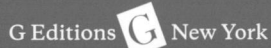
G Editions **G** New York

Contents

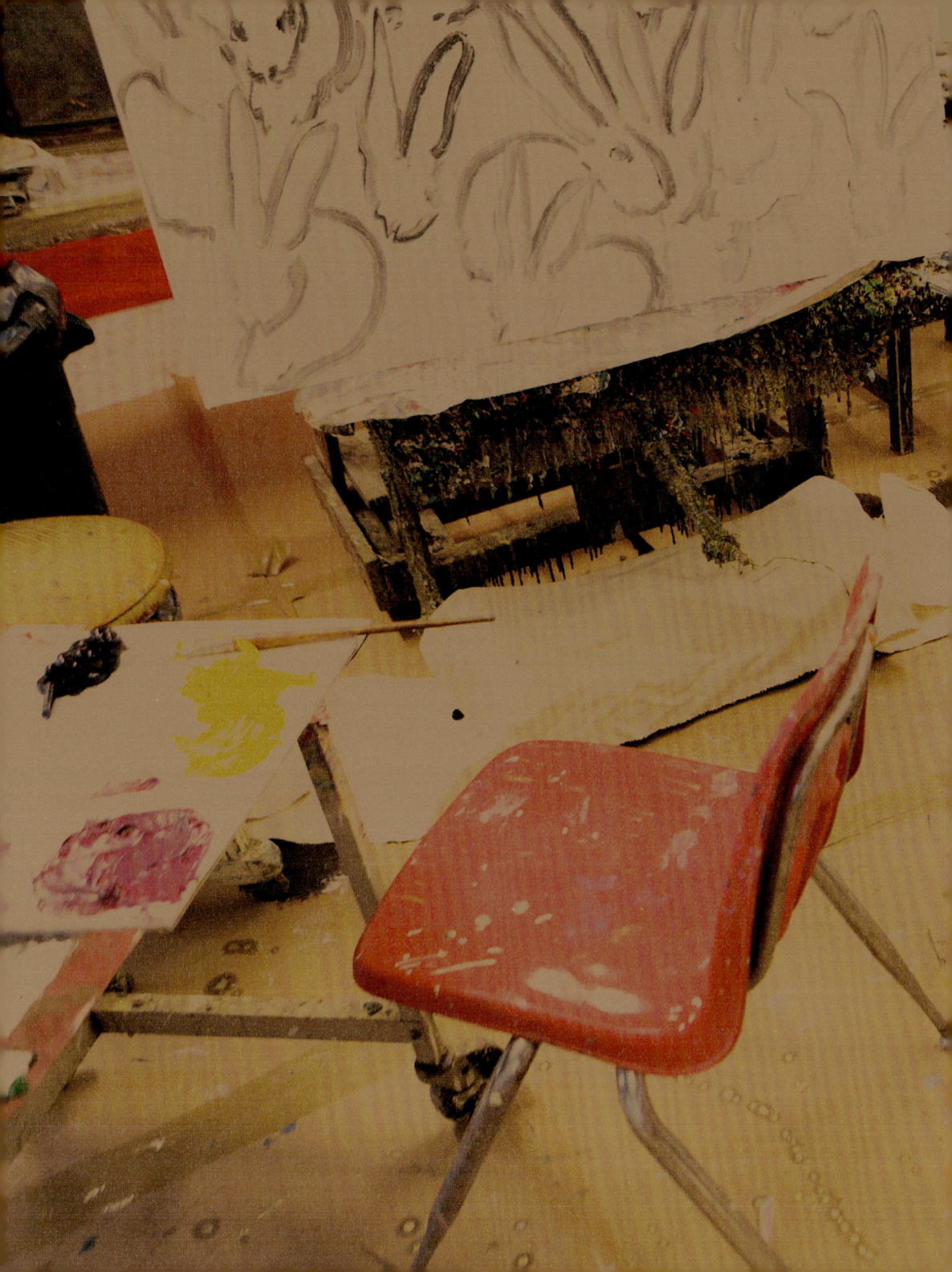

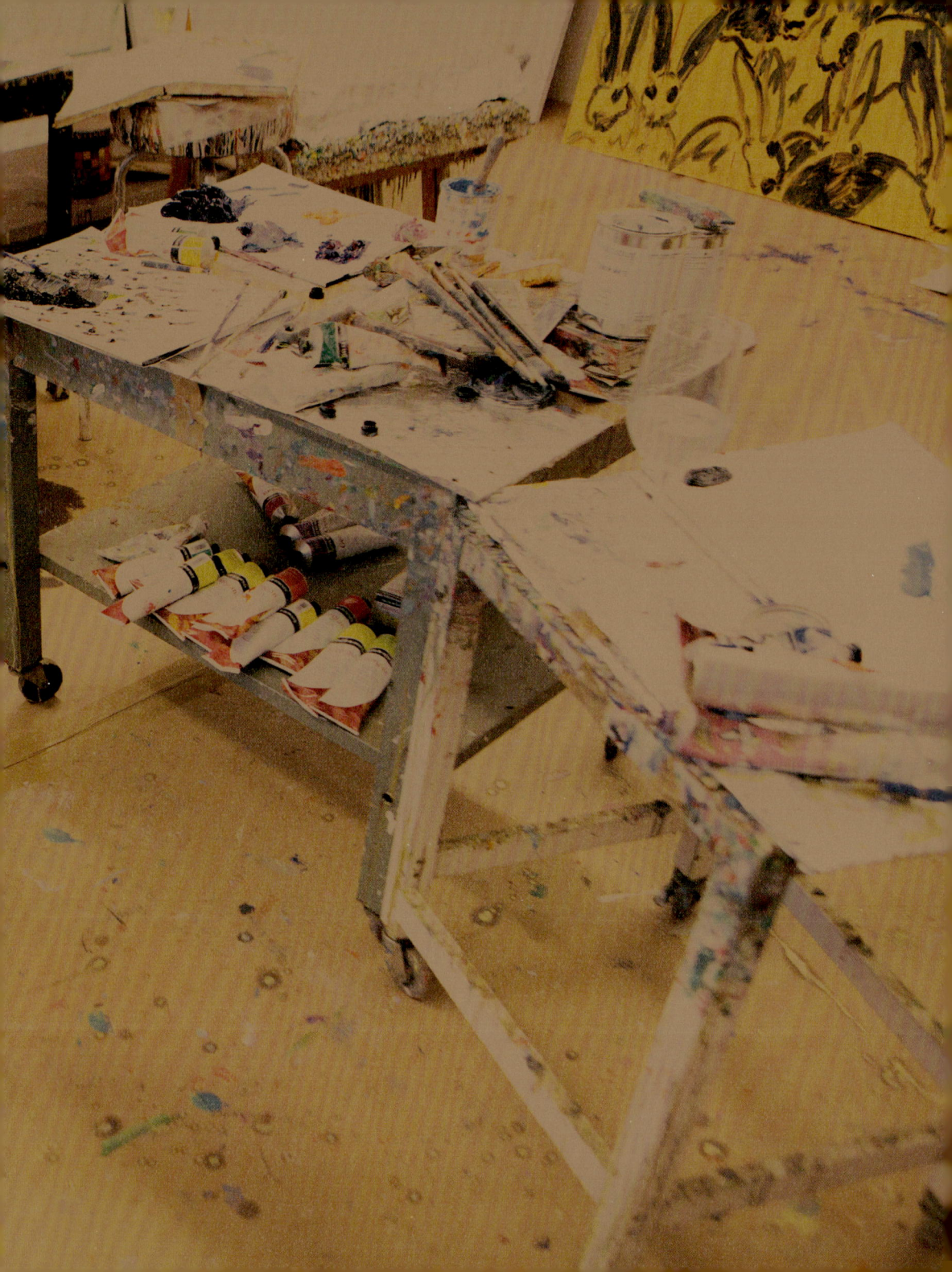

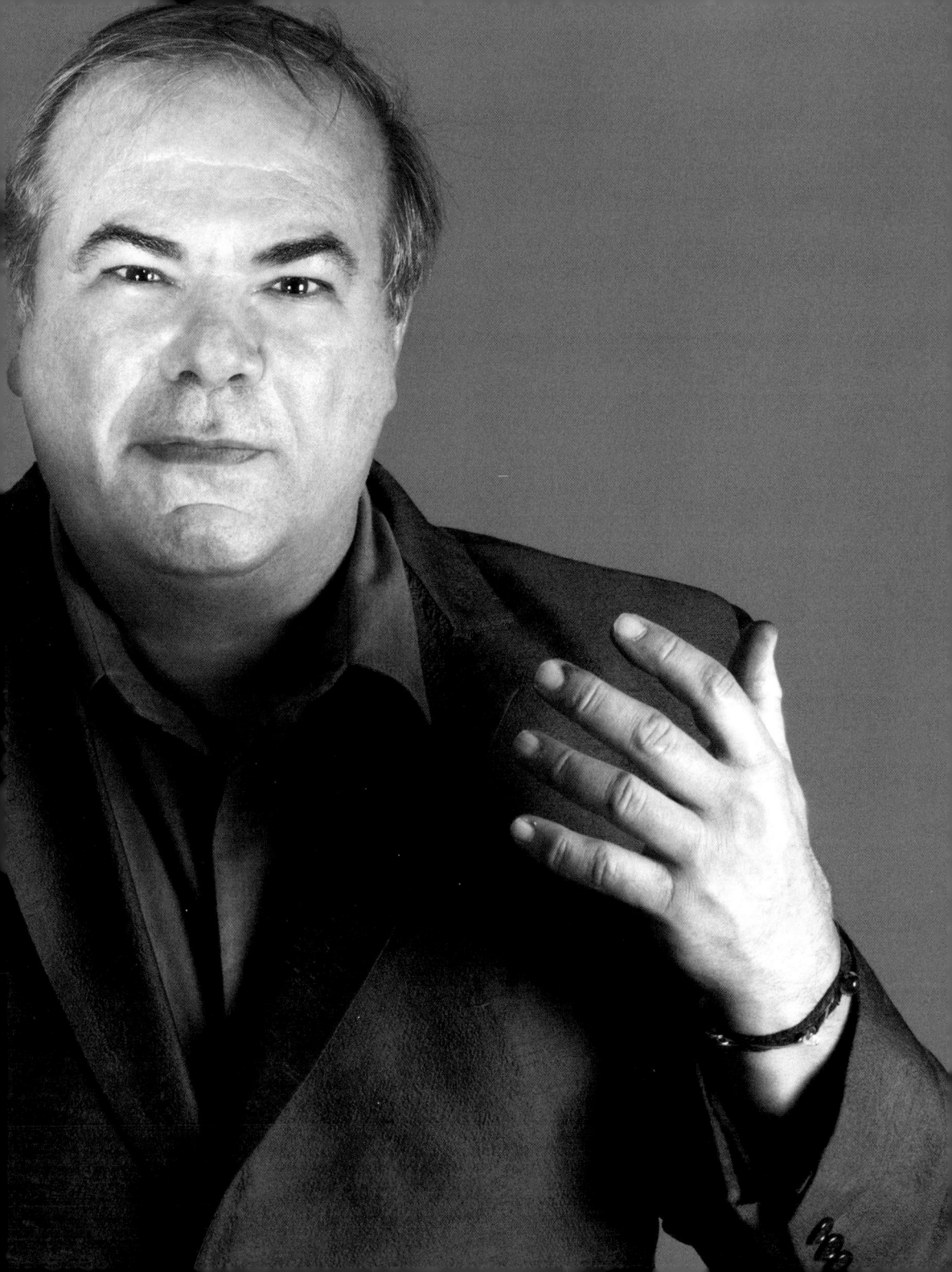

Foreword
Warming Up
John Berendt

Every morning, upon rising—even before he's had his first cup of coffee or called any of his psychic advisors—Hunt Slonem performs his daily warm-ups.

He approaches his work table where a stack of small rectangular panels awaits. Some of the panels are made of wood, some of Masonite. Slonem has prepped them with plain colors the night before, but otherwise they are blank. He squeezes a glob of black paint onto his pallet and works it into a smooth paste with his brush. In the course of the next half hour he will populate all the panels with rabbits.

Slonem paints rabbits in outline, applying quick broad strokes that resemble calligraphy as much as they do rabbits.

These paintings are what he calls his warm-ups. They are the artistic equivalent of calisthenics in which he flexes his painting apparatus to establish control over the colors, shapes and textures that flow from his mind's eye through his arm, hand and brush to the painted surface.

I dropped in on Slonem at his Manhattan studio one morning not long ago while he was in the middle of his warm-ups. He had already completed seven rabbits, three on white backgrounds, one on green, two on blue, and one on red.

"Hans Hofmann was my inspiration for this," he said, referring to the abstract expressionist who was one of his earliest and most significant influences. "He used to start the day by doing a series of small paintings to warm up. He painted abstractions. I paint rabbits."

"Why rabbits?" I asked.

"I was in a Chinese restaurant a few years ago," he said, "and on the back of the menu there was a chart of the Chinese zodiac, designating the years that fall under each sign. It was while I was eating a spring roll that I discovered I was born in the Year of the Rabbit. That means I'm supposed to have a compassionate nature, which I think I do. But even if I hadn't been born in a year of the rabbit, I might have chosen rabbits for my morning warm ups, because I've always loved them. As a child, I kept rabbits as pets. I used to dream about them. I still do, in fact."

Hunt Slonem
Photographed by
Paul Solberg

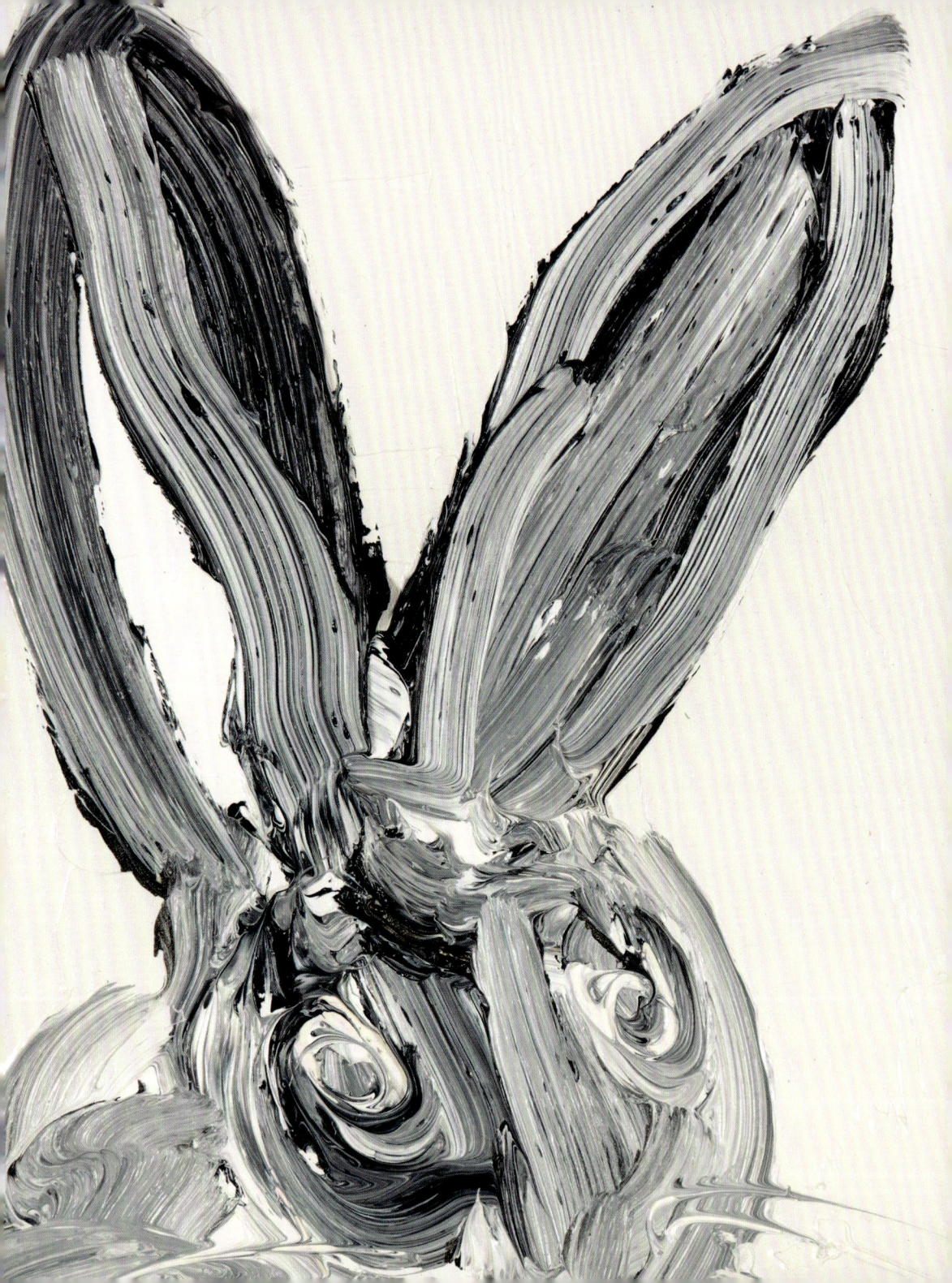

He noticed my skeptical expression.

"Really, I do. I like their dynamism and their independence. They can hold a pose without moving for hours, and then suddenly dart away as if propelled by a coiled spring."

Slonem admitted that there was more to his rabbit habit than pure aesthetics. "What appeals to me most," he said, "is their mystical quality. In my childhood, I was enchanted by the White Rabbit, who leads Alice down the rabbit hole into Wonderland and an altered state. That's always been important to me, the idea of altered states. When I'm painting, I sometimes feel as though I'm somewhere else, observing reality from an outside perspective."

From where? The moon perhaps? According to several cultures, a mystical rabbit lives on the moon. The Chinese say that, seen from earth, the dark spots on the moon look like a rabbit. This moon-based rabbit is in the act of grinding herbs to make an elixir of life, and therefore he stands for immortality.

"Rabbits represent fertility too," said Slonem, "and God knows they've earned it. Somebody once calculated that a couple of rabbits, producing six bunnies once a month (half of them female), can start a production run that will reach into the billions within six years."

"In a small way, it's the same with my rabbits. I never know how many I'll end up painting on a given day. I'm constantly surprised. After a while they take on a life of their own. I've done as many as fifty or sixty in a given day. If you're going to paint multiples, though, it seems right to do it with rabbits. In New Orleans, when the Ogden Museum mounted an exhibition of my work, they had a grouping of a hundred rabbits. At home I've covered whole walls with them."

Which rabbits in the history of art mean the most to Slonem?

"John Tenniel's illustrations for *Alice in Wonderland* were formative for me, especially the White Rabbit and the March Hare. It helps, of course, that both of them were completely mad. Albrecht Dürer's watercolor *Young Hare* is a masterpiece I never tire of looking at. I've painted some of my rabbits from the same perspective, but that's where the similarity ends. Our techniques are worlds apart. Dürer was incredibly painstaking and detailed. For a good portion of *Young Hare*, he used a brush with a single bristle in it. That's certainly how he painted the whiskers. I make the whiskers by using the other end of the brush. I carve the wooden handle to a sharp point and then scratch the whiskers in, one by one."

Slonem was putting the finishing touches on his tenth rabbit. He was all warmed up now, and done with rabbits. It was time for a cup of coffee, and then a call to his psychic for some mystical advice on the day at hand.

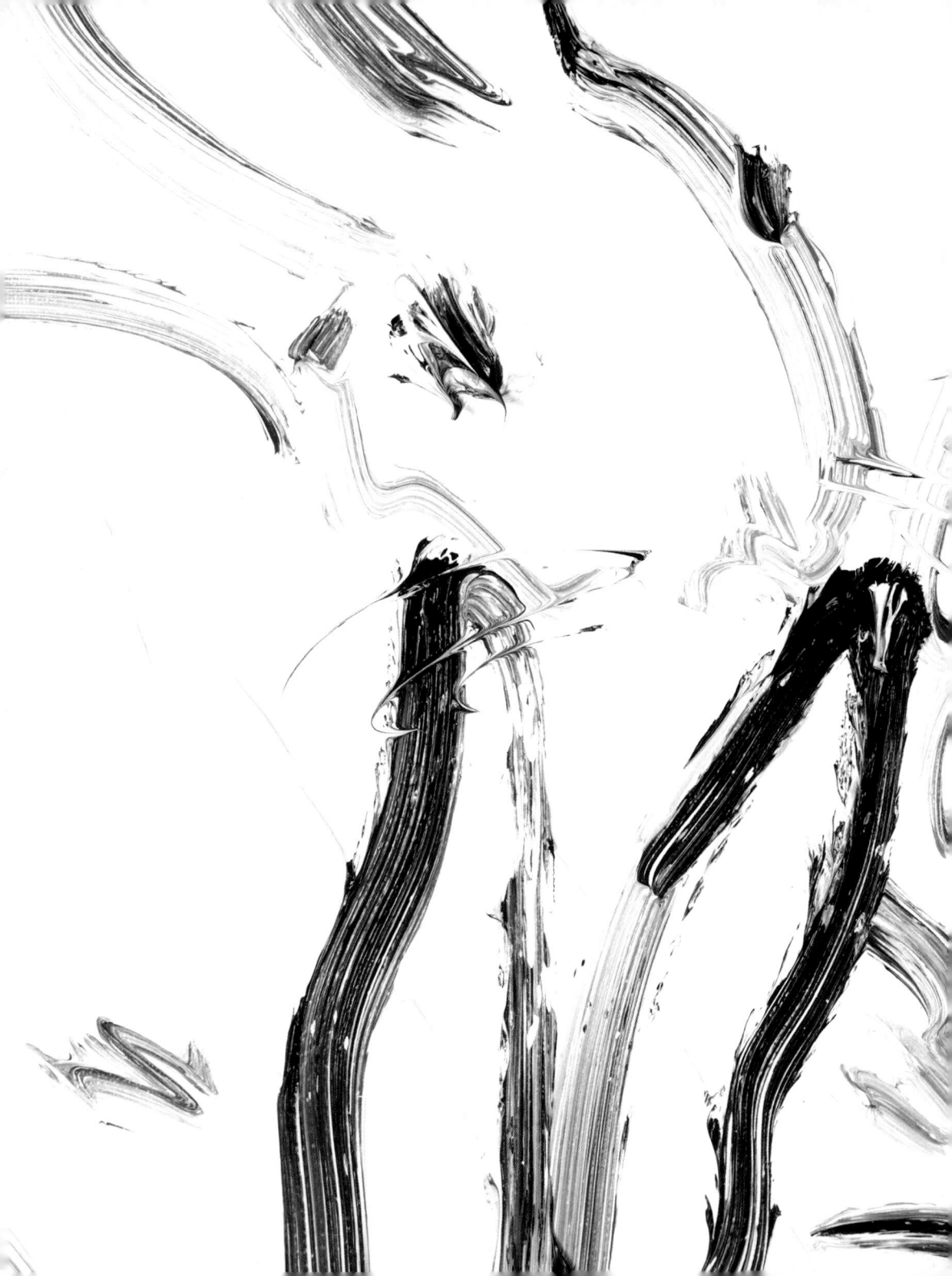

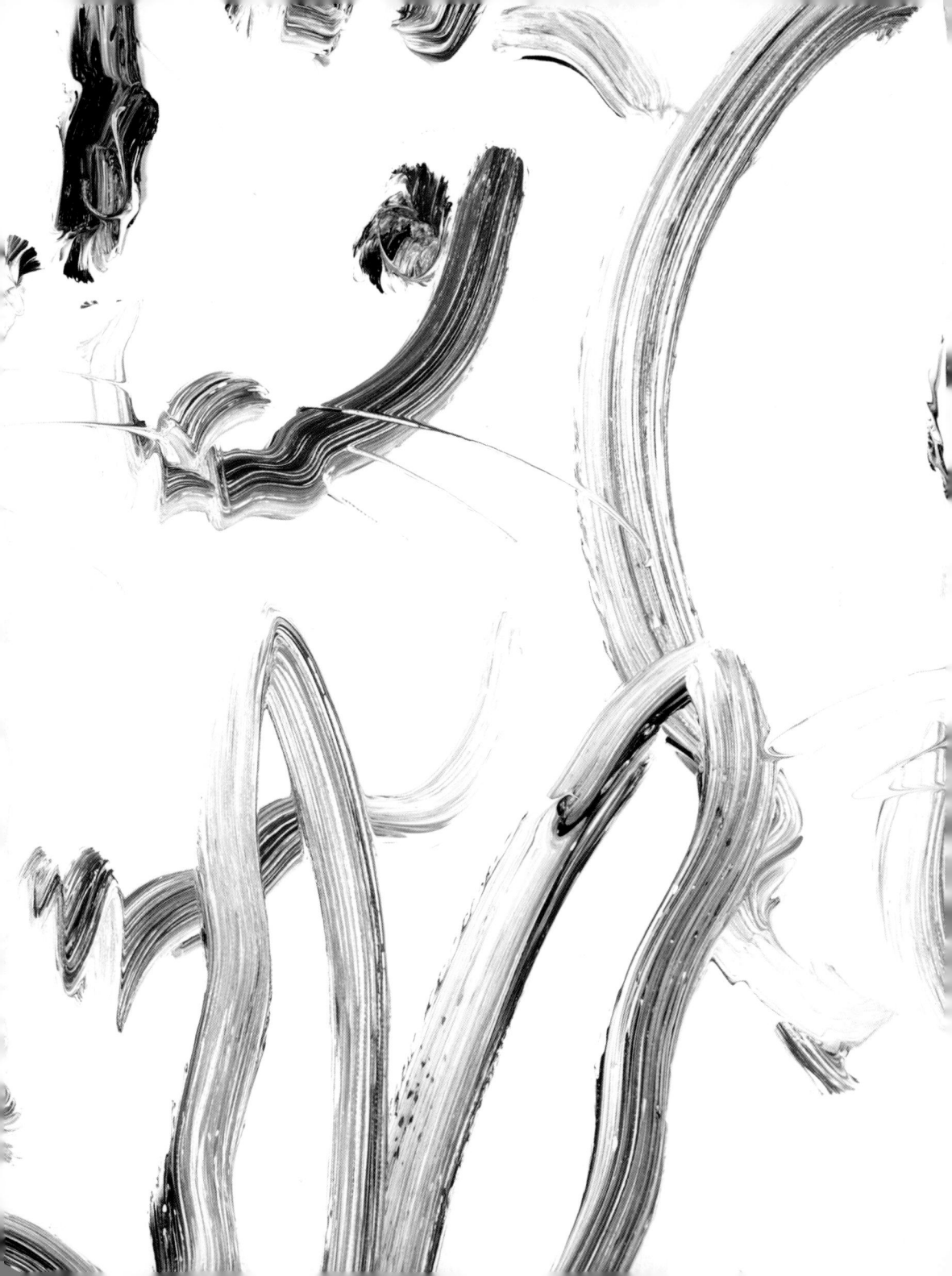

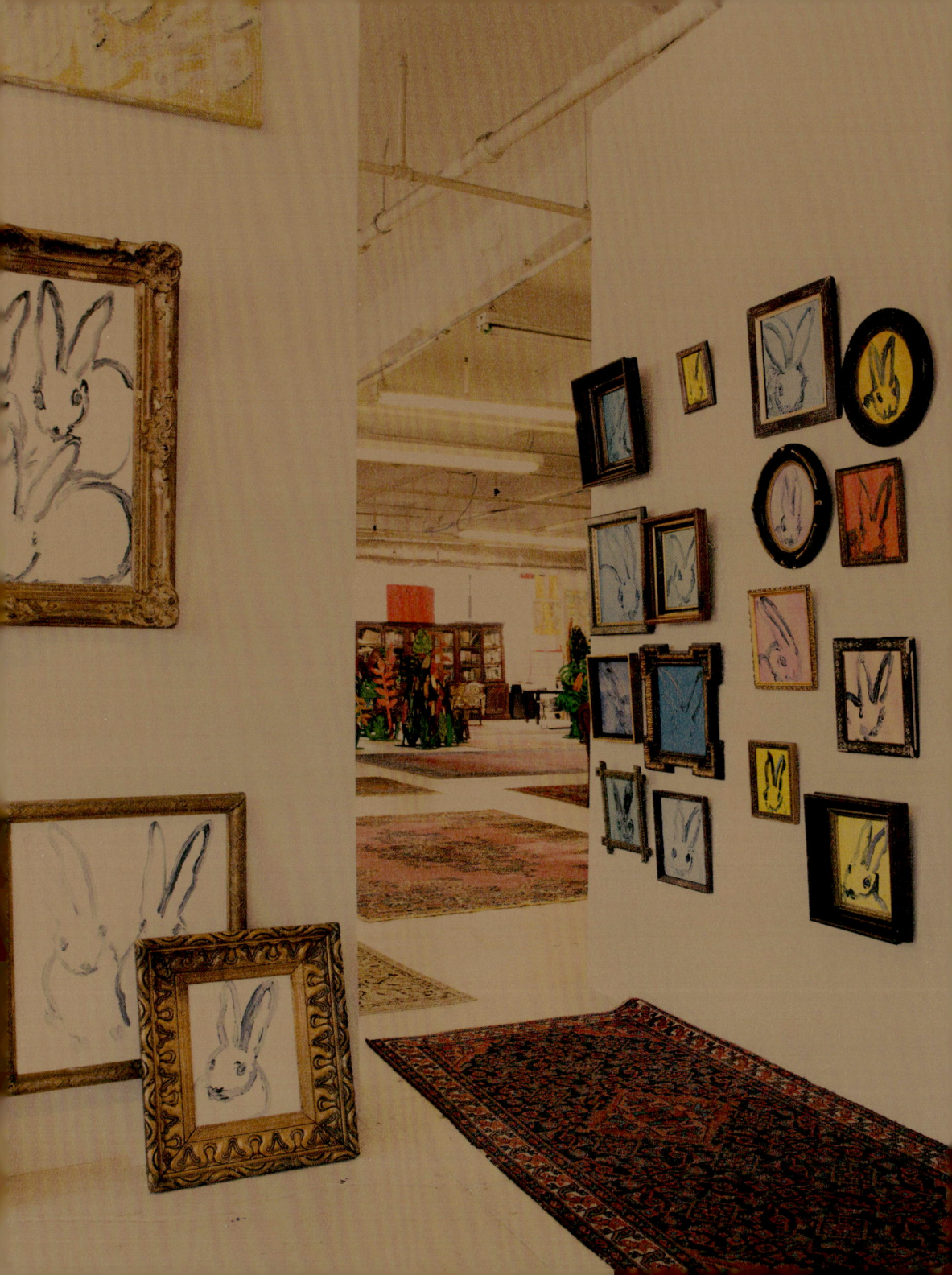

Essay
Quantum Lepus
The Bunny Paintings of Hunt Slonem

Bruce Helander
Edited by Susan Hall

The first time that I met Hunt Slonem, it was a freezing afternoon on the Lower East Side of New York in February, 1986. I still remember pressing the door buzzer while looking up at his loft window as big snowflakes gently fell from the sky onto my shoulders, like feathers tossed into the air. Little did I realize that this wintry, auspicious occasion would be connected somehow to the artist's favorite models, and that I would come to know this talented painter of birds and other beautiful beasts. After being let into the foyer and still gazing upward, a cast iron door opened, and suddenly a heavenly glow of light spilled out, illuminating a towering figure standing at the top of a staircase that lead to a surprising urban sanctuary filled with a flock of welcoming winged creatures. Over time, this friendship proved to be productive for both of us and prompted an ongoing appreciation of his style and working methods, which in turn facilitated a continuing investigation of his paintings. Through this familiarity with his art, I have been fortunate to have curated museum exhibitions of Hunt's work (the most recent being a show of bunny paintings at the Coral Springs Museum of Art in 2010) and have had the opportunity to write extensively about him. My distinct impression after the first studio walk-through was that there was a clear connection to a fraternity of gestural painters whose concentrated manifestations of a specific theme, like Morandi's bottles and cans, Monet's water lilies, or Dine's bathrobes done over and over again, gained them an exceedingly knowledgeable and logically intimate perspective on the endless variety of interpretations available to them. The end result is a magical, precise, abstract narrative that is produced through accurate and painstaking observation.

So, intense awareness with one's subject matter—whether it be a sensuous, innocent nude figure from John Currin, a thoroughbred horse by Deborah Butterfield, an autumn grove of abstracted trees by Wolf Kahn, or a classic rabbit engraving by Albrecht Dürer—admiration and intense examination of a certain entity or item are the building blocks here that artists, especially like Hunt Slonem, learn to gently harness, with intuitive repetitive gestures eventually forming an identifiable and natural signature.

Although over the years Slonem has become most recognized for his bird paintings, he has a keen interest in a variety of wildlife, from monkeys to bunnies. Perhaps it was the rabbits that inhabited his childhood yard in Kittery, Maine, that made an indelible impression on Hunt Slonem and now manifests itself in his illustrious career. Those who know him well see a soft-spoken, calm, thoughtful and contemplative individual that unsurprisingly would find the sweet disposition of the rabbit comforting and appropriate to his own sensibility. Rabbits have been around for a long time, and their use as "models" by artists is well known. Hunt likes to call the works "Bunnies," which seems to give them particular characteristics and makes the whole series more enjoyable. After all, it was Bugs Bunny, chomping on a carrot and asking "What's up, Doc?" who pleased audiences for generations with his wit, speed and penchant for trouble. Arthur Burdett Frost (1851-1908), the creator of Uncle Remus and the Brer Rabbit, whose pictures "breathed the breath of life into these amiable brethren of wood and field," gave a bunny a human slant, with dialogue to match; he declared the common American hare a star. The creatures that came alive before animation was invented all have a character dialect from the "cotton plantations of middle Georgia" before Emancipation. Thus the author was able to preserve the stories dear to Southern children as far as possible and utilize a friendly bunny that spoke in a form that served to maintain the quaint humor of the era.

The use of a bunny as a theme has a distinct and cheerful charm of its own. Rabbits have been around forever. They are small, sensitive mammals in the family Leporidae of the order Lagomorpha, found in several parts of the world. There are dozens of classifications, from the European rabbit, cottontail and Amami rabbit (a revered and endangered species in Japan), to others that are called pikas and hares; Hunt's furry subjects are loved and recognized throughout the planet. Rabbits are social animals, and as pets can find their companionship with a variety of creatures, including humans.

There are a plethora of rabbit classifications that appear in these pages that have some pretty provocative images attached to them. There's the Bushman Rabbit (*Bunolagus monticularis*) and the Volcano Rabbit (*Romerolagus diazi*), or you can gamble on the Dice's Cottontail (*Sylvilagus dicei*) and a host of other breeds whose tails or paws are supposed to bring good luck. A lot of these creatures get their names from the habitat they call home, such as the Marsh Rabbit, the Mountain Cottontail, the Desert Cottontail (*Sylvilagus audubonii*), and the Central African Rabbit (*Poelagus marjorita*). It has been not only the rich variety of breeds that has attracted the artist to his perpetual documentation and abstraction of bunnies (or bunny rabbits as they are affectionately known—especially domesticated rabbits), but that these enchanting animals often are used as a symbol of fertility or rebirth, and have long been associated with spring, as the "Easter Bunny." The species' role as a prey animal also lends itself as a symbol of innocence (and another

Easter connection). But further, rabbits frequently are portrayed as symbols of playful sexuality, which also relates, paradoxically, to the human perception of both their purity and their promiscuity, as well as its reputation as a prolific breeder. In Aztec mythology, a pantheon of four hundred rabbit gods known as Centzon Totochtin, led by Ometotchtli or Two Rabbit, represented fertility, wild parties and drunkenness. The infamous, ready-for-service Playboy Bunny, invented by the pipe-smoking, bathrobe-wearing Hugh Hefner, wore a skimpy company uniform, complete with long satin ears and a big, round, fluffy white tail and supported by legs wearing fishnet stockings and high heels. The other connotations described above, including "playful sexuality," soft skin and a perception of servitude, made the human bunny-girl fit perfectly into the bachelor pad as an objet d'art, complete with "Bunny Bread" toasted on the side table and rabbit ears atop the TV.

In fact, in addition to being an animal with delightful markings that has a precedent for attracting artists from Leonardo da Vinci to Barry Flanagan, who also were intrigued by their quiet, calm temperament and a noble ability to comfortably stay still while being "captured" on canvas or in bronze, there is a lengthy history of folklore connected to the bunny rabbit. In Central Africa, "Kalulu" is widely known for his tricky character and getting the better of bargains at the market. In Asian culture, the rabbit is pictured everywhere, including as one of the Lunar New Year's celestial animals in the Chinese zodiac and in Vietnamese mythological stories that celebrate a rabbit's virtue and youthfulness.

There are lead roles for the rabbit in global traditions from Jewish folklore and Korean myths to those of Native Americans and Central Africans, with a shared theme of the belief that the rabbit bestows good fortune on all who gaze upon his face—as well as some imaginative tips on propagation. And if you get into a bit of trouble over subliminal motivation that tempts participation in this extra-curricular bunny hop, you also might try an outdated pregnancy test, which was based on the idea that a rabbit would die if injected with a pregnant woman's urine (not true). So there are plenty of non-visual connotations to the ordinary bunnies that make them interesting subjects to reproduce, since enthusiastic reproduction by the bunnies has a sense of pride all its own. Anthropomorphized rabbits have appeared in a host of works of film, literature, and technology, notably in the popular novel *Watership Down* by Richard Adams, which also became a movie, and in Beatrix Potter's Peter Rabbit stories, along with the more contemporary film, *Who Framed Roger Rabbit*.

Hunt Slonem's now familiar series of single white rabbit portraits (also serendipitously connected to the White Rabbit and the March Hare from Lewis Carroll's *Alice's Adventures in Wonderland*, and in subsequent rock lyrics famously belted out by Grace Slick of Jefferson Airplane) have taken their place in history and continue to aggressively multiply in a variety of manifestations, symbolizing good luck and producing a spiritual calm in all directions. Slonem also presents ironic comparisons: innocence and lust; naivety and experience; good and evil. The artist has created his own unique brand of hip-hop iconology, and the bunny paintings have developed over time into well-orchestrated and amusing depictions at all angles of a rabbit's silky smooth silhouette, drawn skillfully, simply and swiftly using a paintbrush loaded with black paint laid over a wet thicket of white zinc oxide on board. At its completion, the artist turns the top of his brush handle over to scratch out a few whiskers and perhaps an engraved definition of the pensive eyes.

The humble pleasure offered by these minimal but accurate portrayals of a hare to a harem is that they are rather lovely to look at. The initial development and completion of a characteristic Slonem bunny picture is really quite basic, and is the secret to their spontaneity and ultimate success; his instinctive painting can be connected to the lyrical brushstrokes of de Kooning and the black and white compositions of Franz Kline, or the soft, connective, geometric lines of Brice Marden. For a past review where I wrote enthusiastically about William de Kooning's painting exhibition at L&M Arts, titled "Dutch Boy Paints," I had the opportunity to privately explore for hours the identifiable qualities of disparate marks deliberately dancing across a canvas. It was after seeing this show and de Kooning's recent Museum of Modern Art survey that I began to ponder the obvious parallels of Slonem's quick studies of cottontails with the grand masters of abstraction and their collective ability to begin without a plan, but with a sense of the direction and adventure each work might take. Slonem provides the viewer with a combination of modest painted strokes to develop a handsome composition that fills the four sides of his small, intimate and uncomplicated portraits on board in the same way that Franz Kline perfectly filled out a classic composition, whether it was on the square pages from a telephone book or an oversized canvas waiting to come alive. A closer look at these artists reveals a remarkable facility to manipulate swirling lines into a final predictable configuration. The difference here is that Slonem makes gestures that have a recognizable shape, as opposed to freewheeling exploration devoid of a narrative hint, with the exception of de Kooning's decipherable application of ruby red lips to his series of abstracted women.

Hunt Slonem has the remarkable skill to mix and match living things that have an inherent aptitude to demonstrate integrity and intelligence with a pleasing aesthetic common denominator. The artist has such a firsthand knowledge and familiarity with his models, many of whom he lives with; they share space on his shoulder, or in the case of a baby bunny, nap in his lap as he paints. His thick lines, dispersed in all directions to form a cohesive, clear picture, are what make a Slonem artwork so unique and exciting; patterns also are a natural for this artist. Rhythmic order, as in nature itself, and the interaction of species allow the artist to continue on an endless journey of documentation and exploration that seems well-defined, fresh and articulated with an appreciative eye and a seasoned brush. In the painting *Whisper* (2008), the artist demonstrates again what an exceptional perspective he has on his recurring themes, and that his expanded canvas, like the universe itself, momentarily captures and then releases a delightful image that has transferred its spirit to canvas, immortalizing and celebrating the species in perpetuity.

Ultimately Hunt takes the best dramatic choices from the past and twists and turns his idiosyncratic painted forms into a present-day theatre of cuddly creatures that are seriously fun and handsomely made. Slonem has stuck with his remarkable passion for painting the bunnies and birds (and a small menagerie of other pets) that he has lived with for over thirty years, making very few sidesteps from this well-traveled path, and it has allowed him to carry on sharpening his skills as an abstract painter of living things in nature. I think he would be perfectly happy to paint his fluffy or feathered sidekicks forever.

Slonem's bunny paintings presented in this book are outstanding and dramatic; so confident and accurate, yet loose and abstract. This remarkable balance is consistent throughout and offers the viewer a rare, collective retrospective bound with an indelible impression and perhaps a new way of observing rabbits as regal subjects posing patiently and distinctively, as if silently and unofficially ruling over the artist's studio. As you hop from page to page, the qualitative consistency of his dignified, furry subjects, coupled with the charm of their simple, painterly inventiveness, strike an engaging and enjoyable assembly of adorable creatures that remain original and appealing.

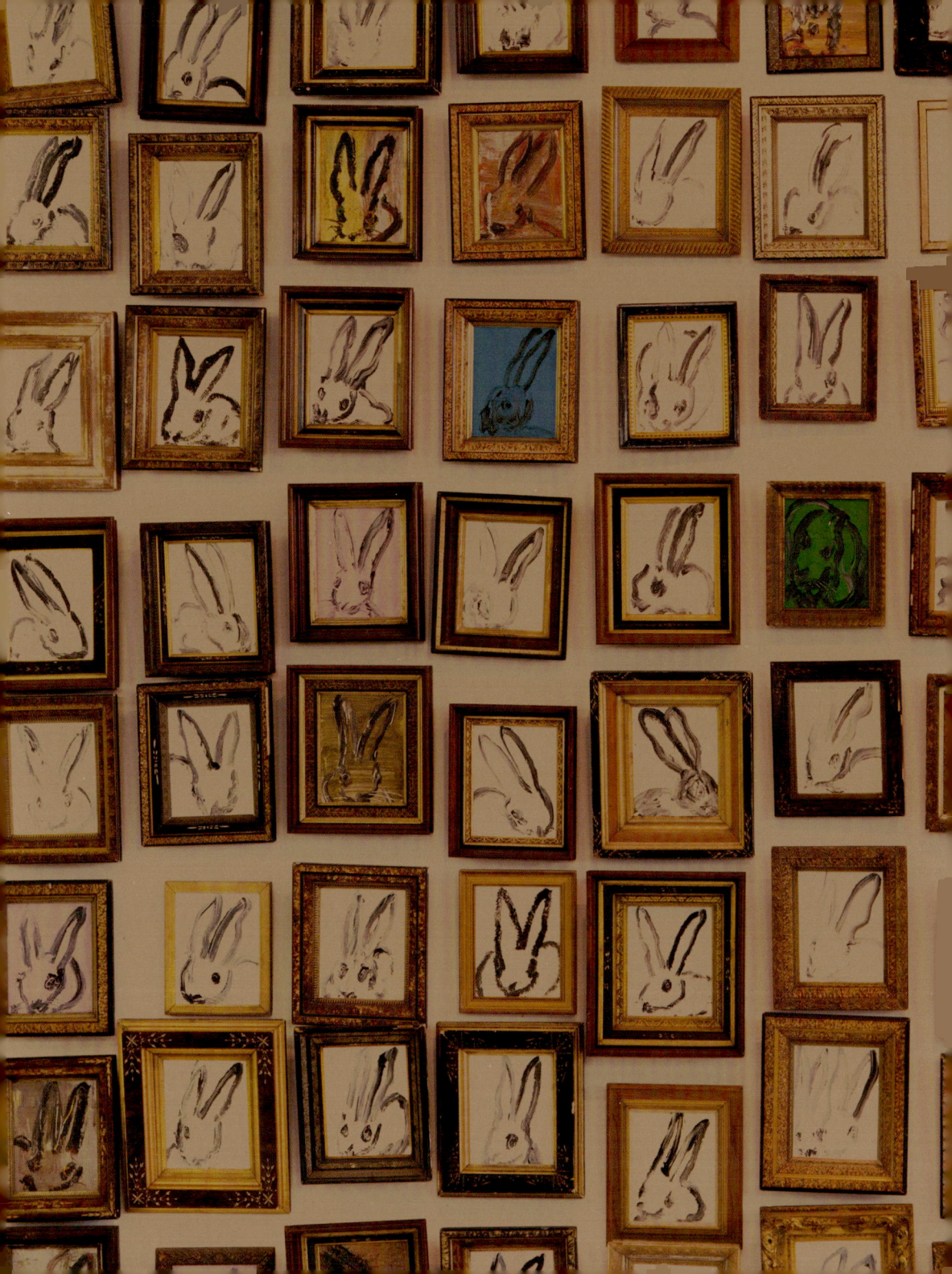

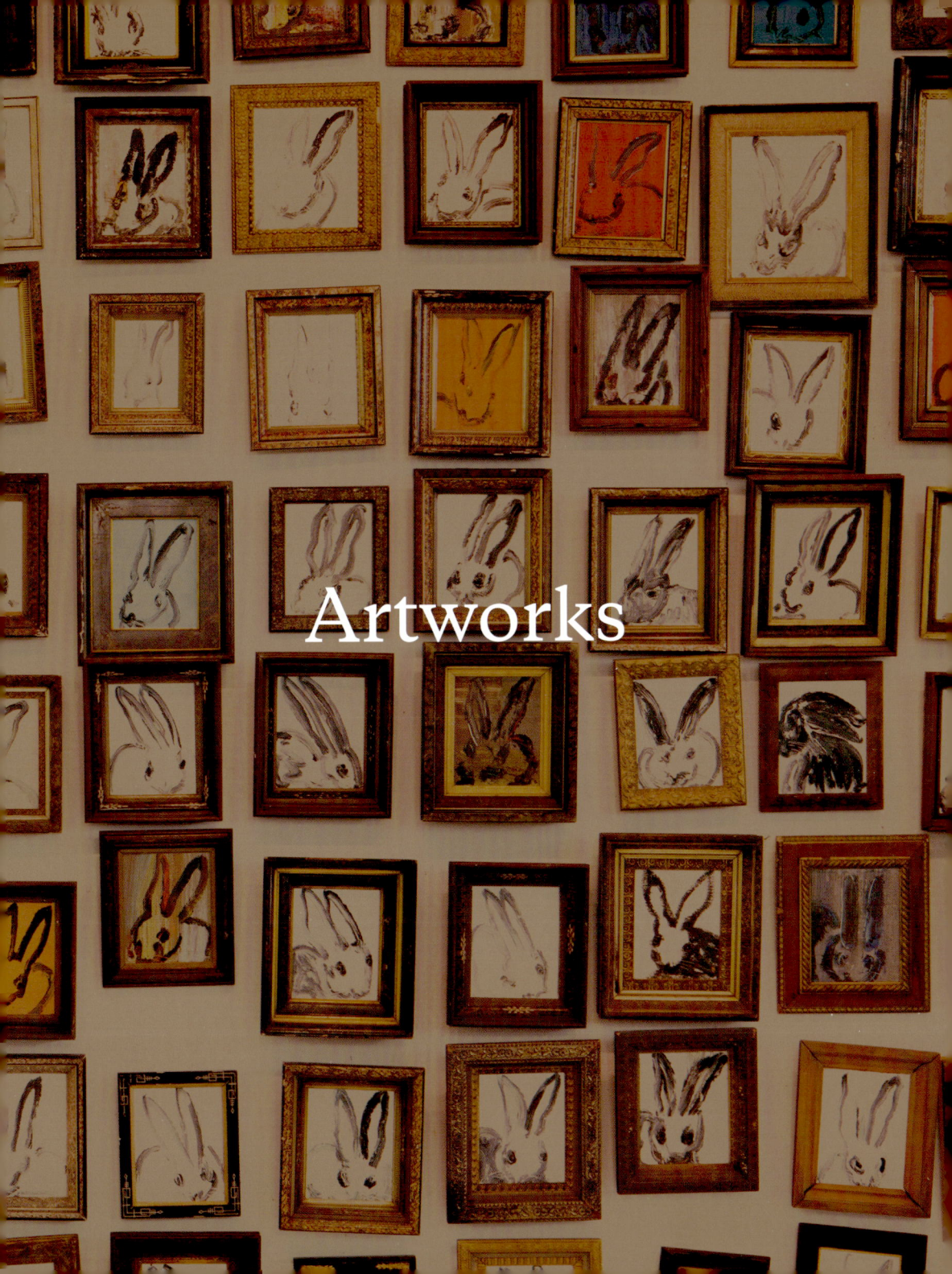

Artworks

24

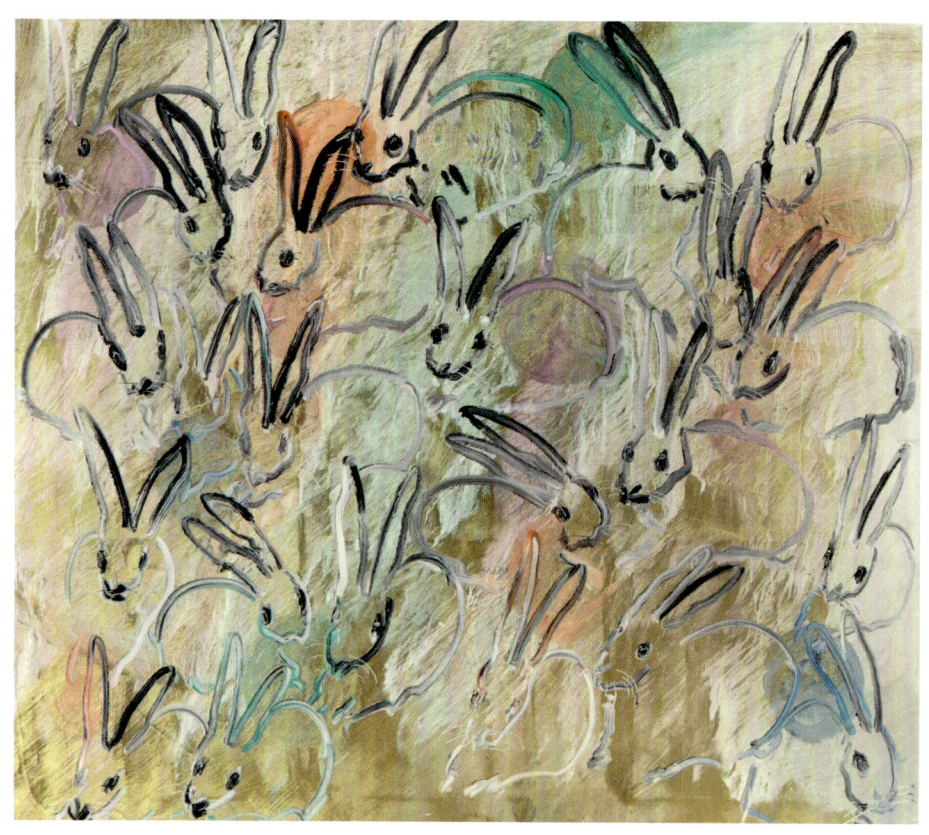

CHINENSIS 3
2013
OIL ON CANVAS
72" X 84"

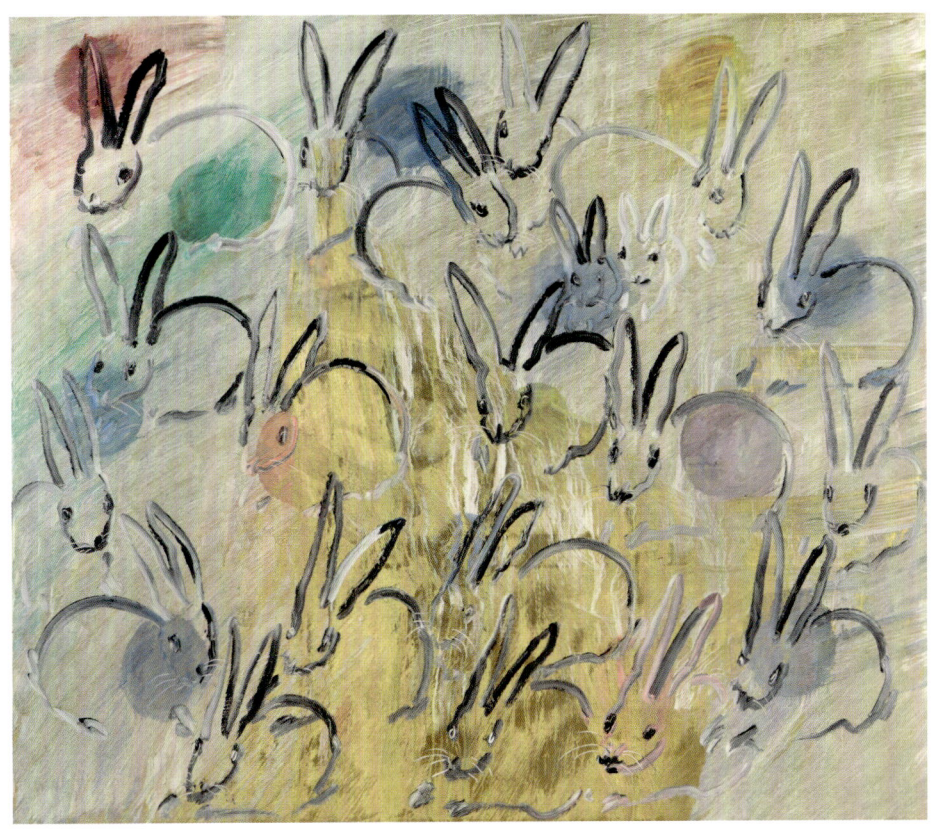

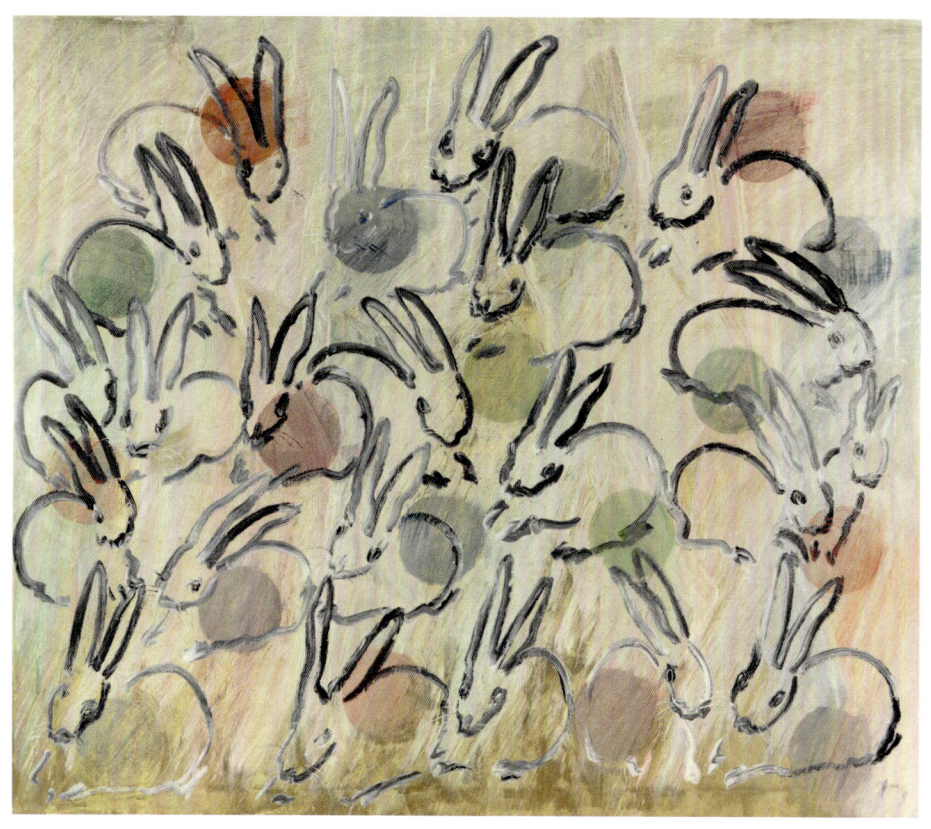

CHINENSIS
2012
OIL ON CANVAS
72" X 84"

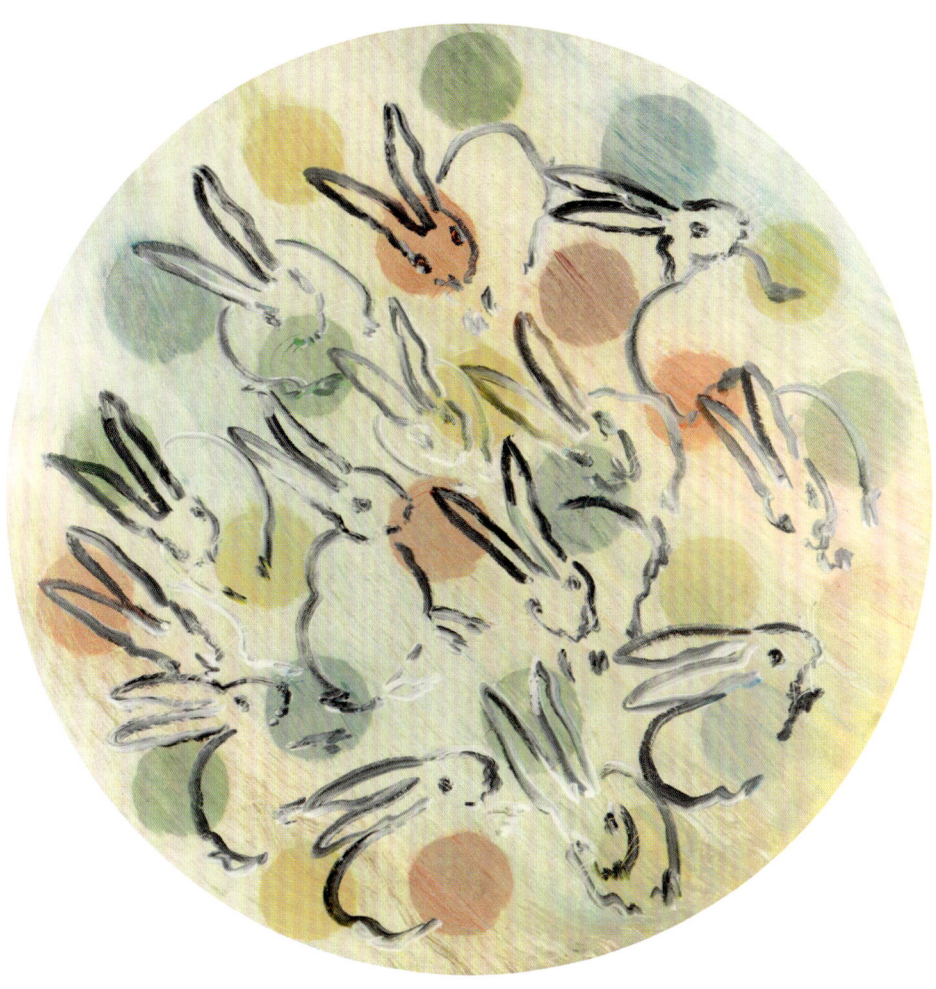

TONDO
2012
OIL ON CANVAS
72 INCH DIAMETER

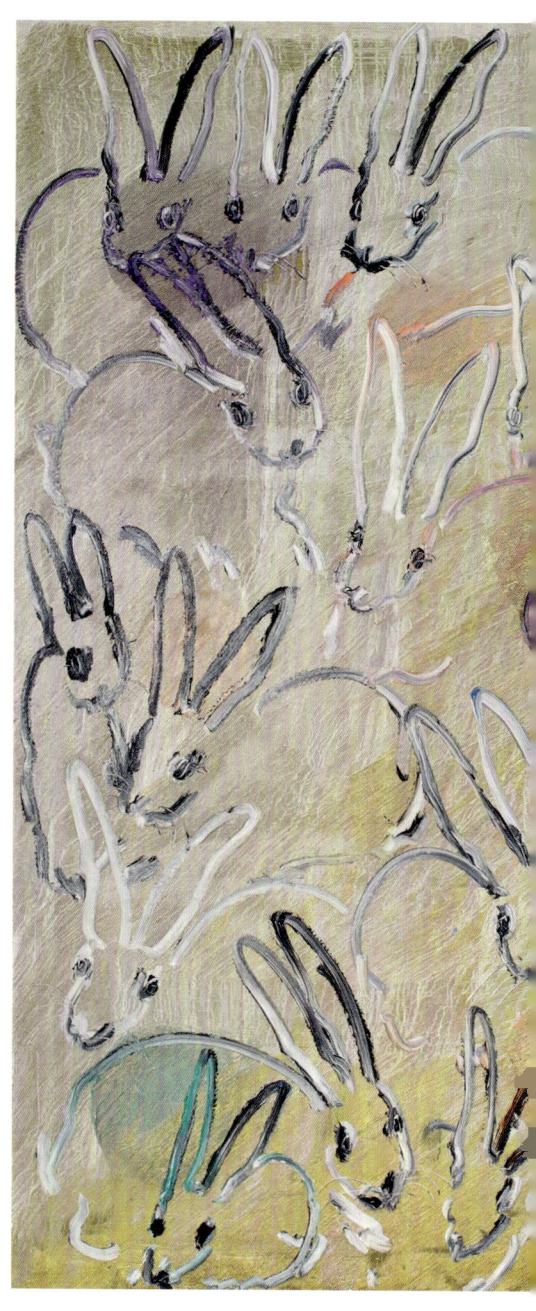

EASTER SUNDAY
2013
OIL ON CANVAS
77" X 101"

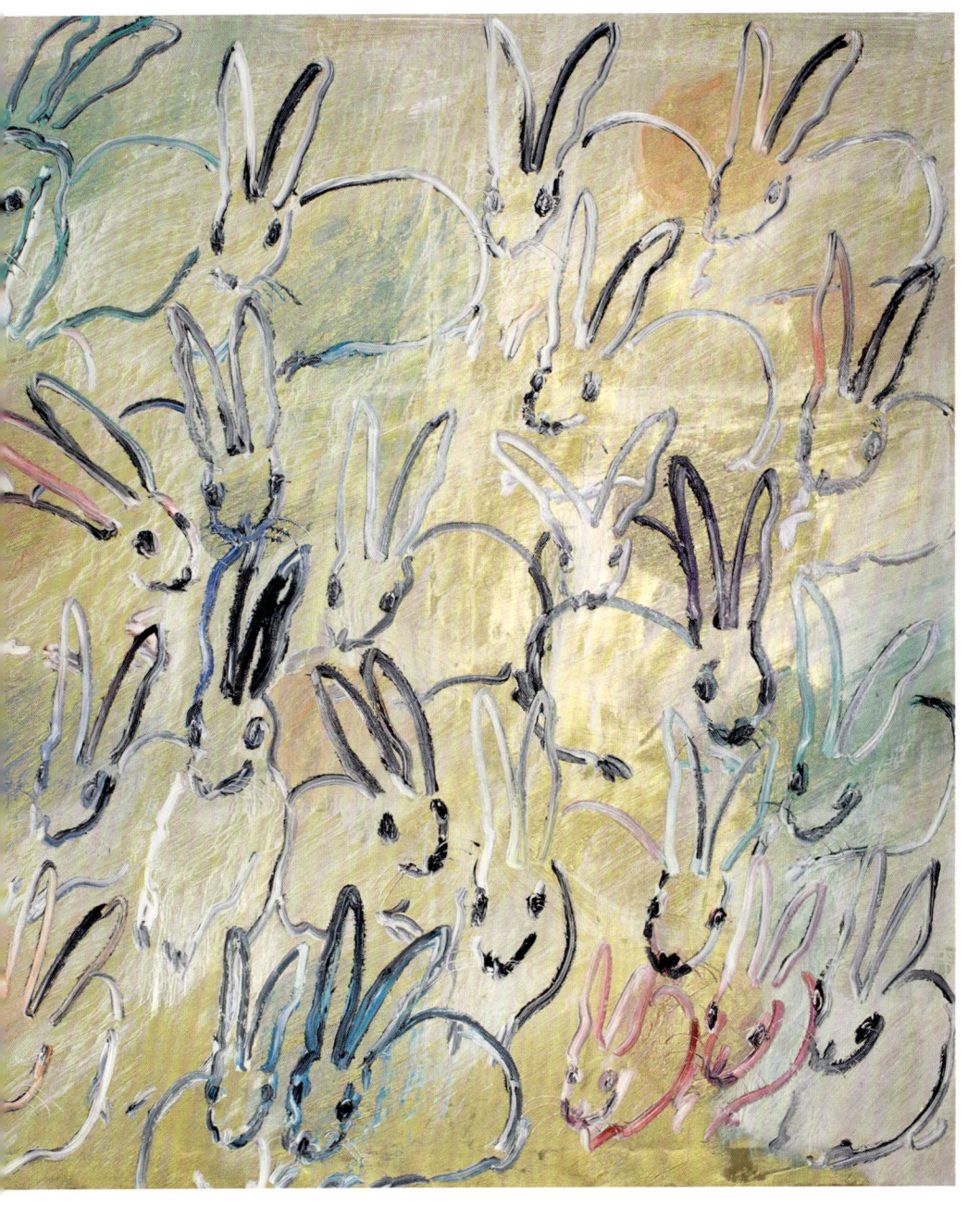

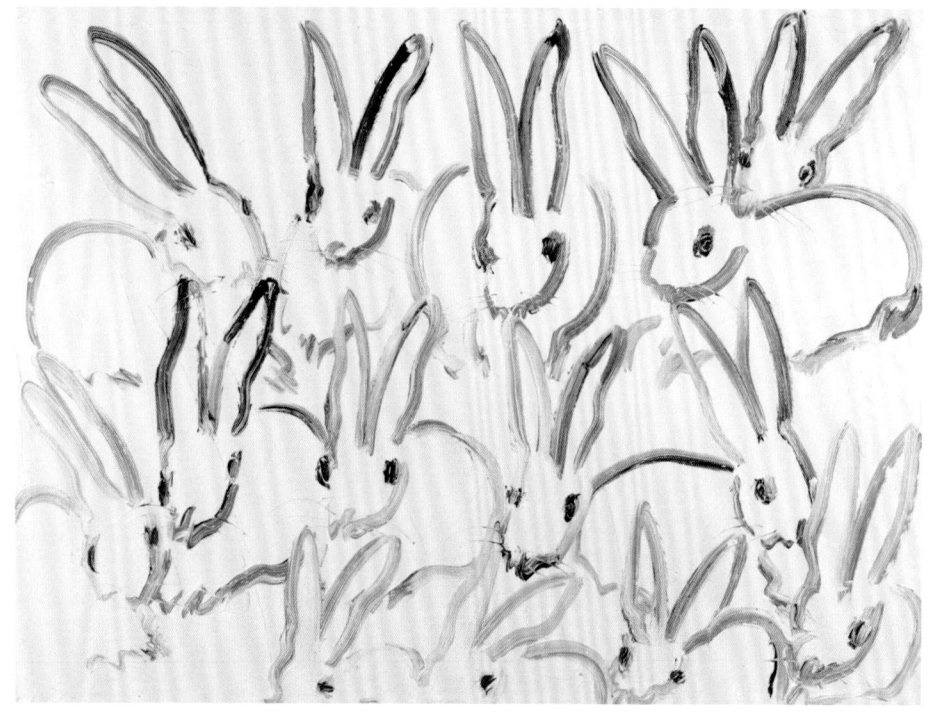

HUTCH
2012
OIL ON CANVAS
36" X 48"

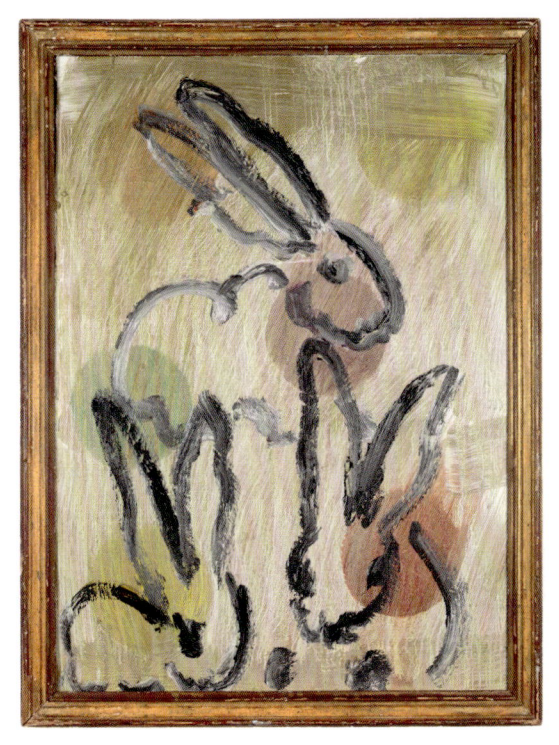

CHINENSIS
2012
OIL ON WOOD
30" X 22"

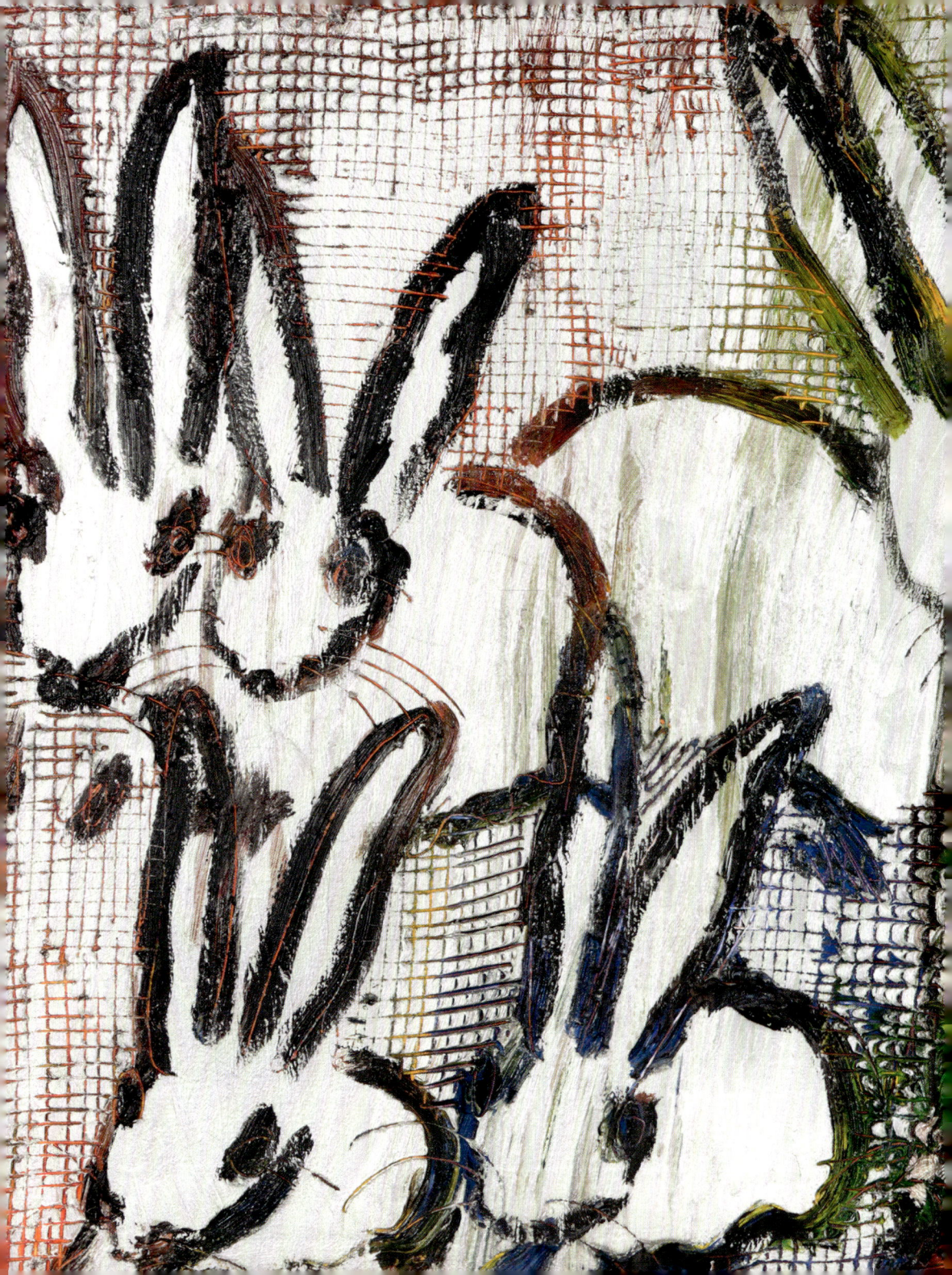

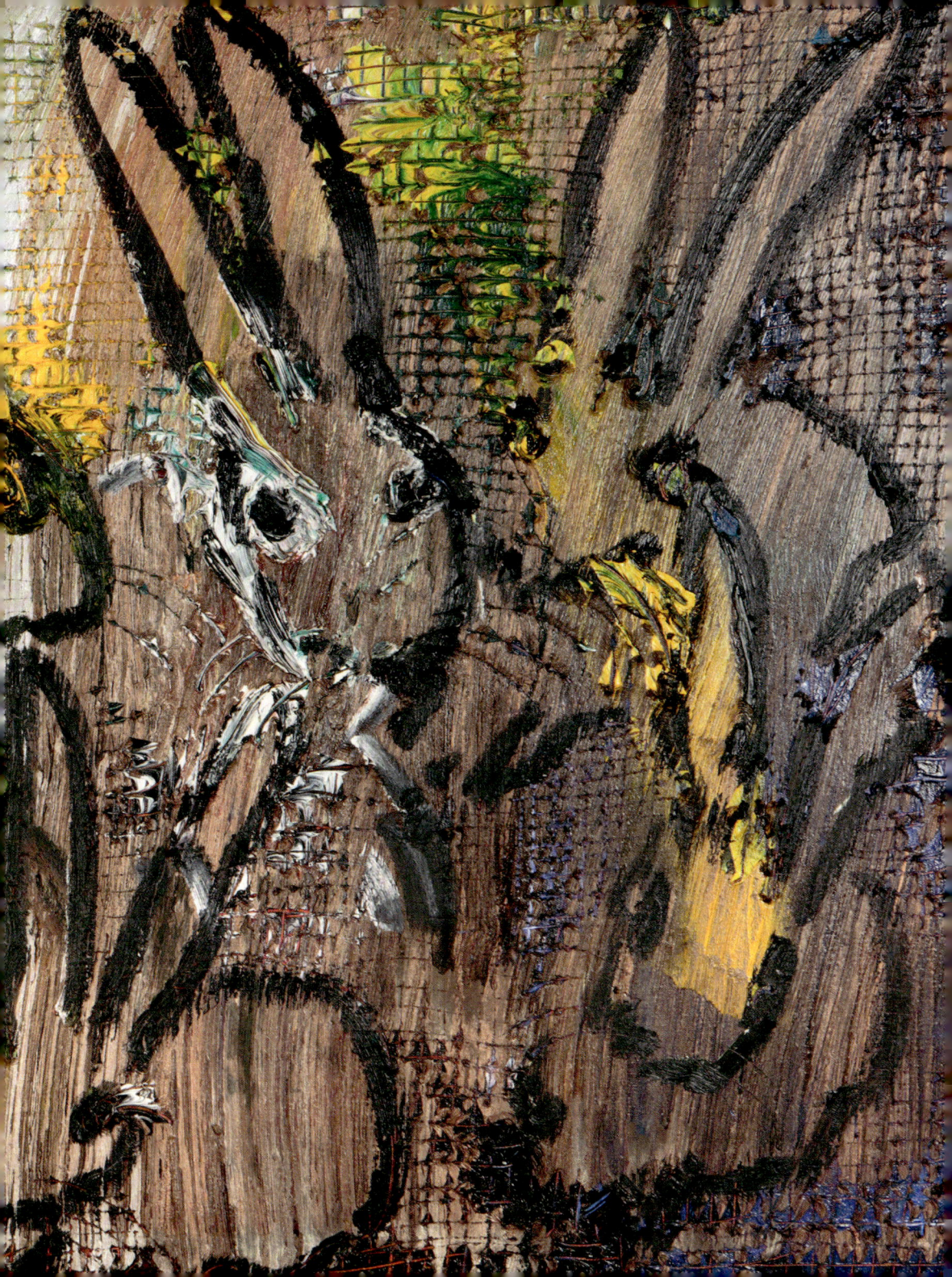

OUTING 3
2013
OIL ON CANVAS
30" X 48"

RUTH & JANET
2013
OIL ON WOOD
23" X 17.5"

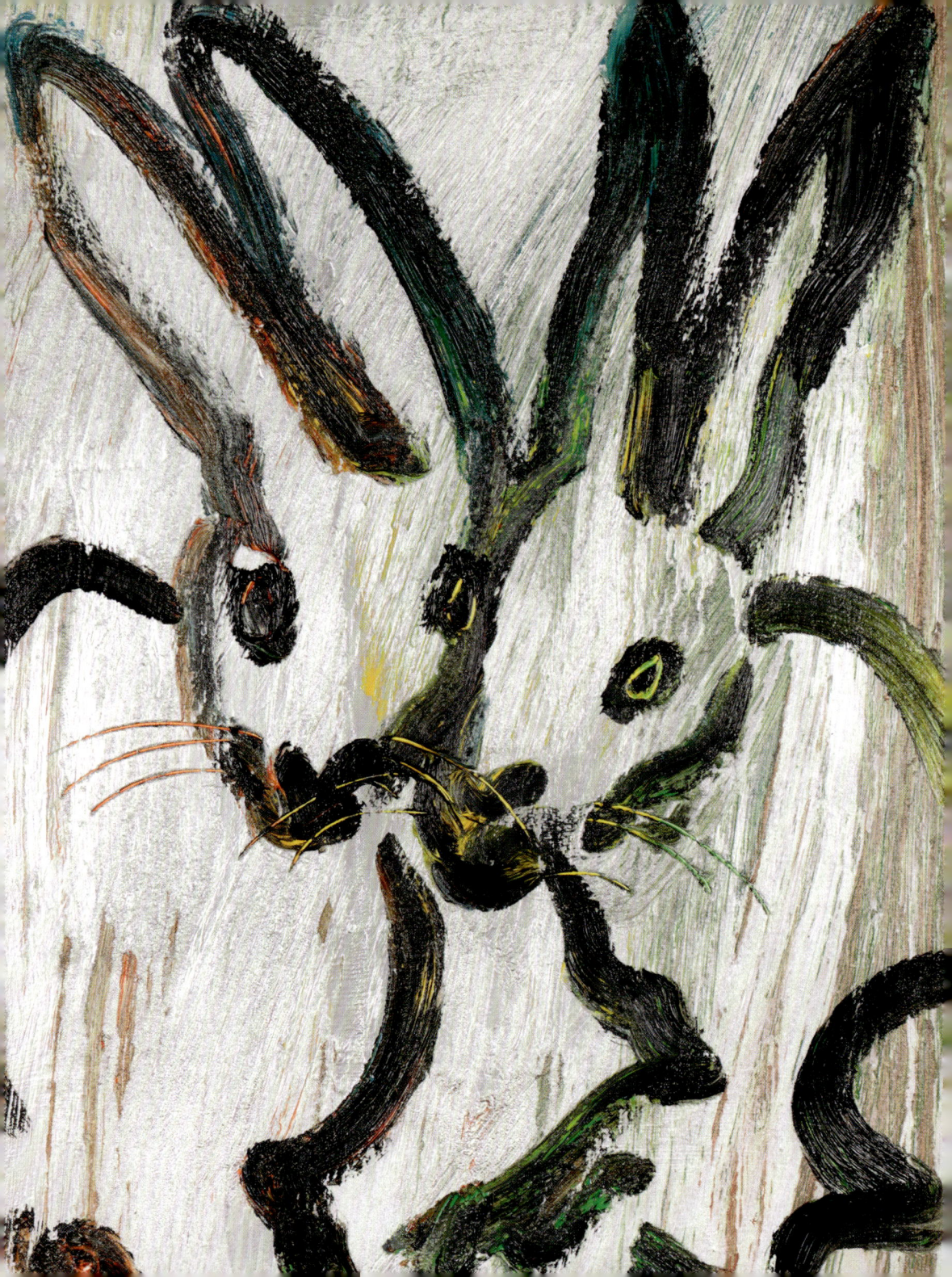

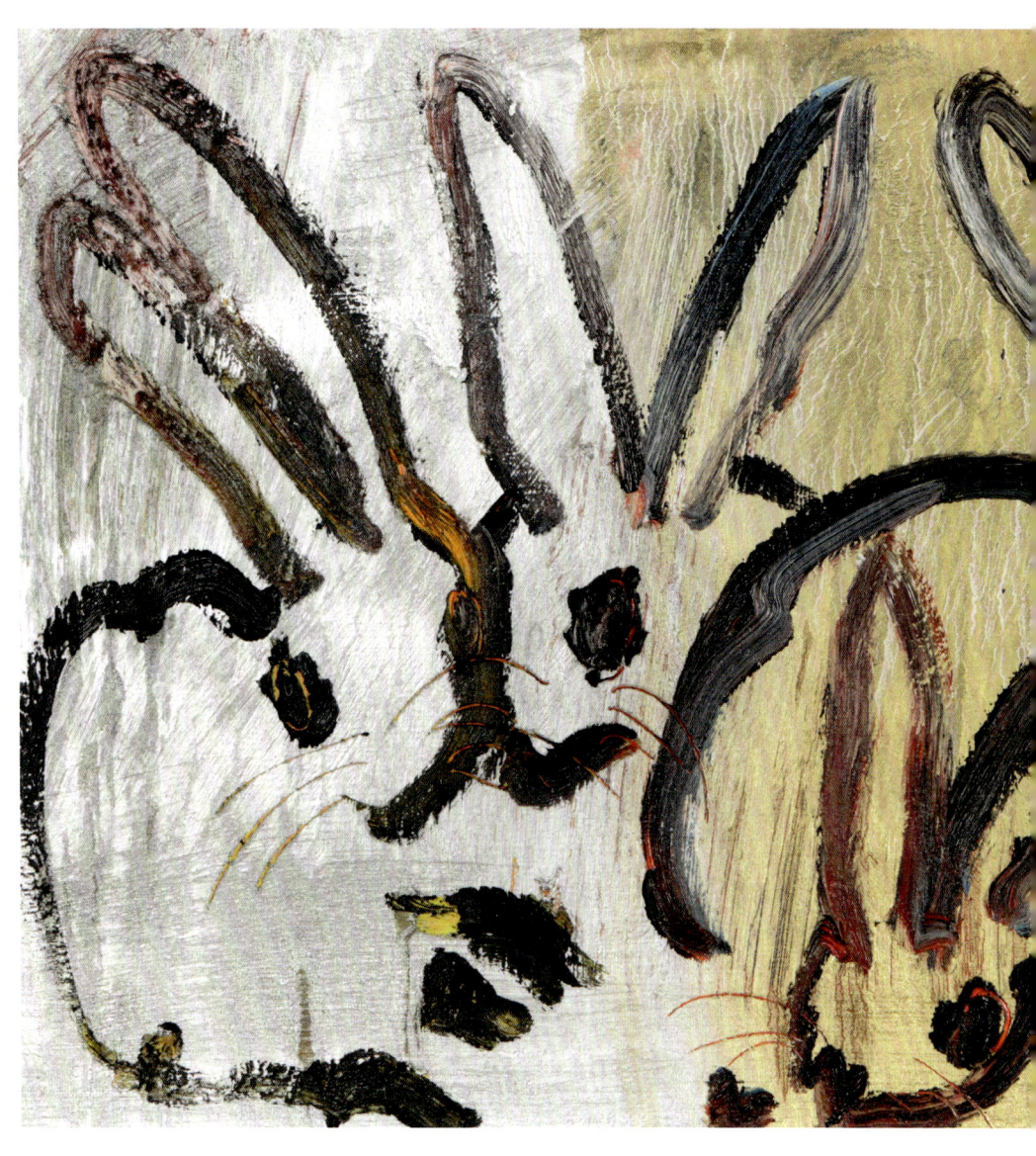

CONCERT
2013
OIL ON CANVAS
30" X 22"

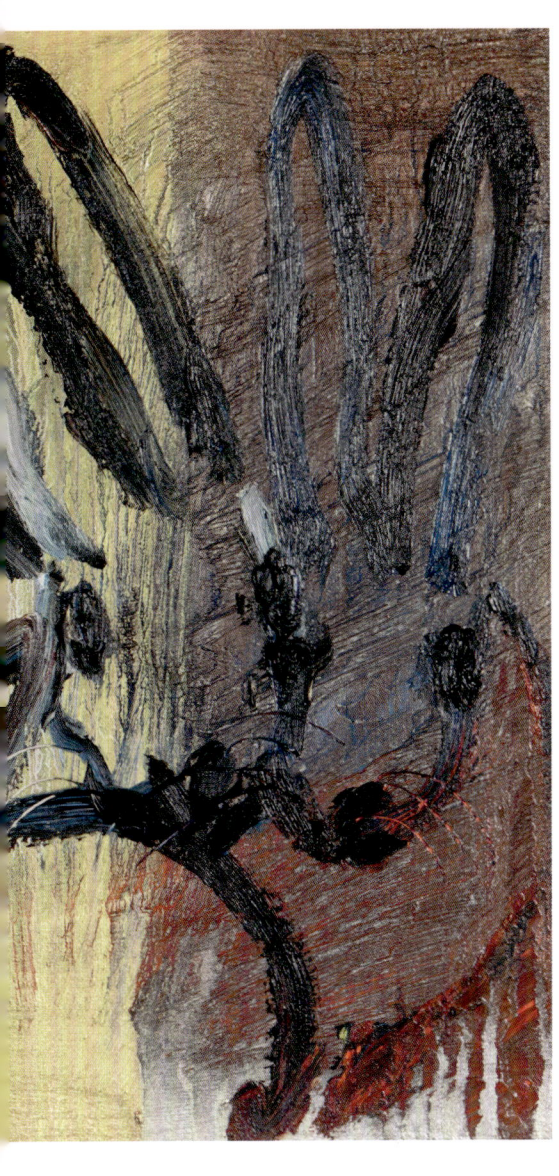

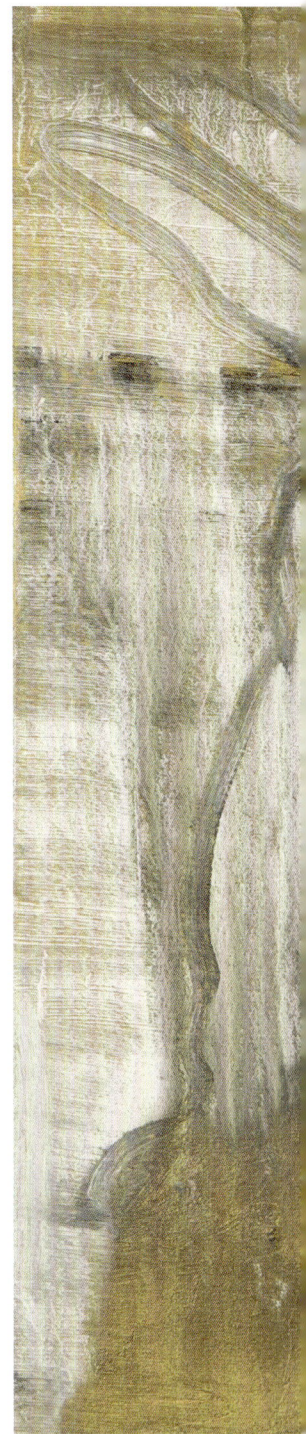

38

HUTCH
2012
OIL ON CANVAS
93" X 133"

HIDDEN AGENDA
2012
OIL ON CANVAS
37" X 17"

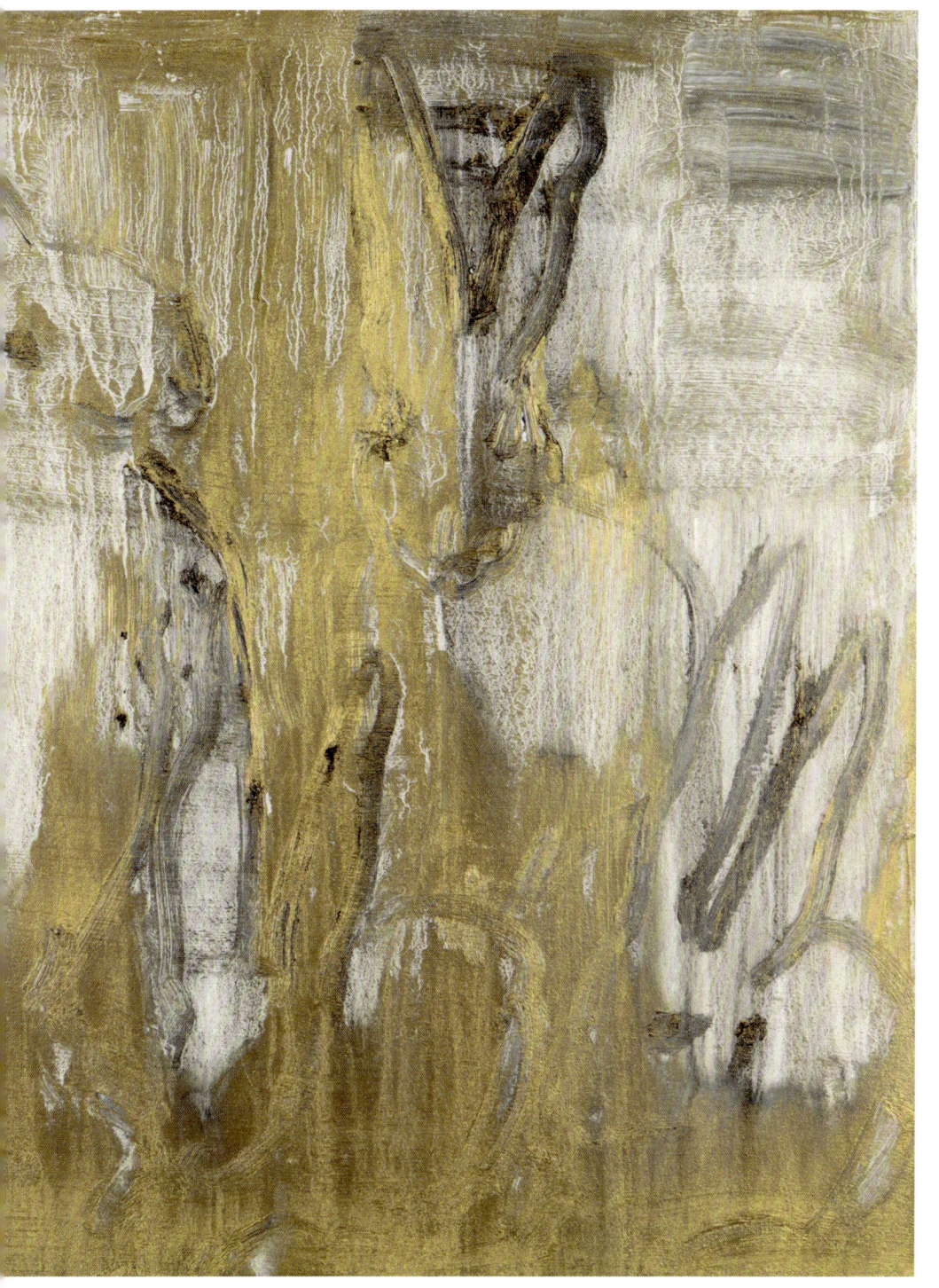

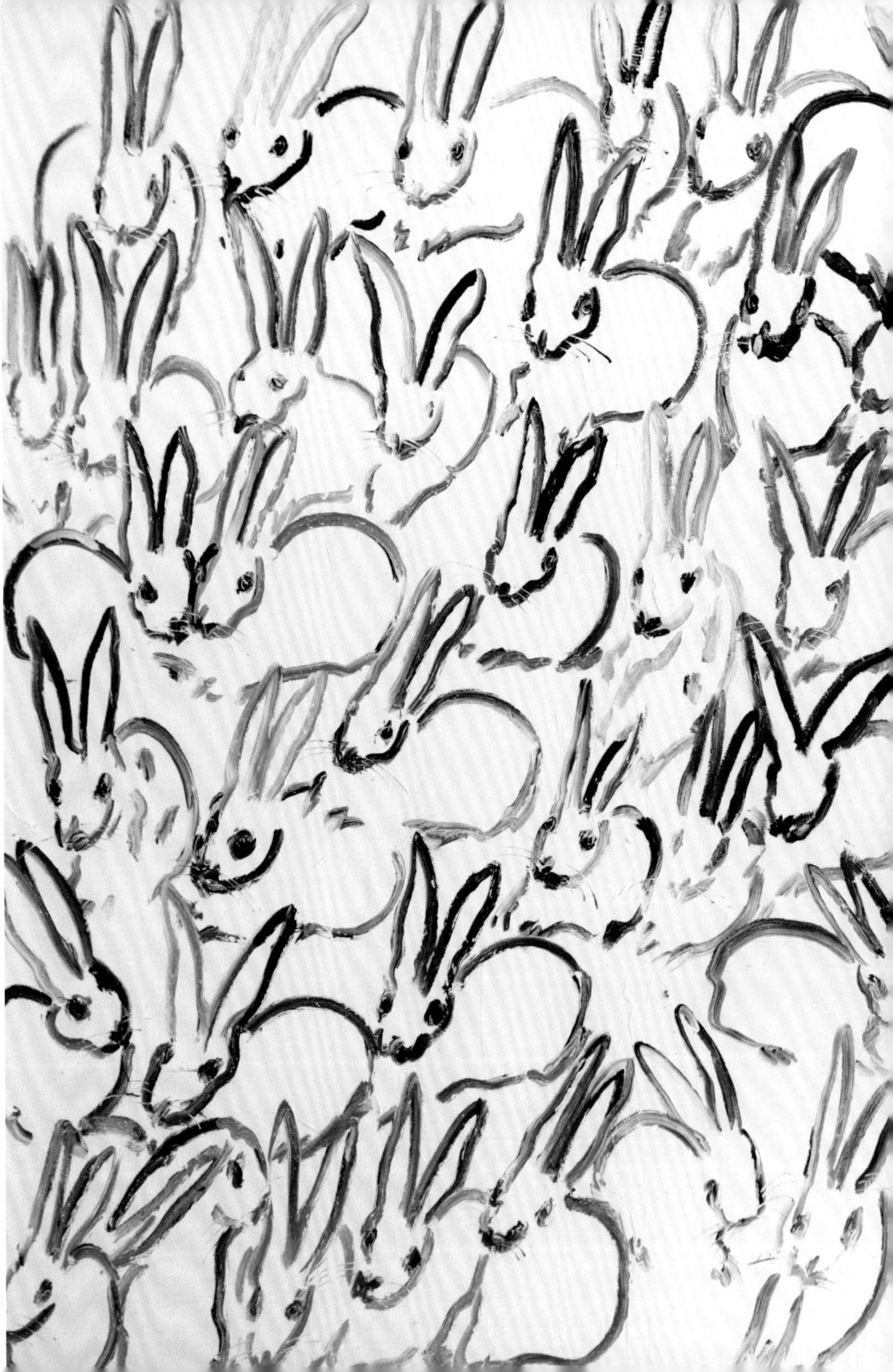

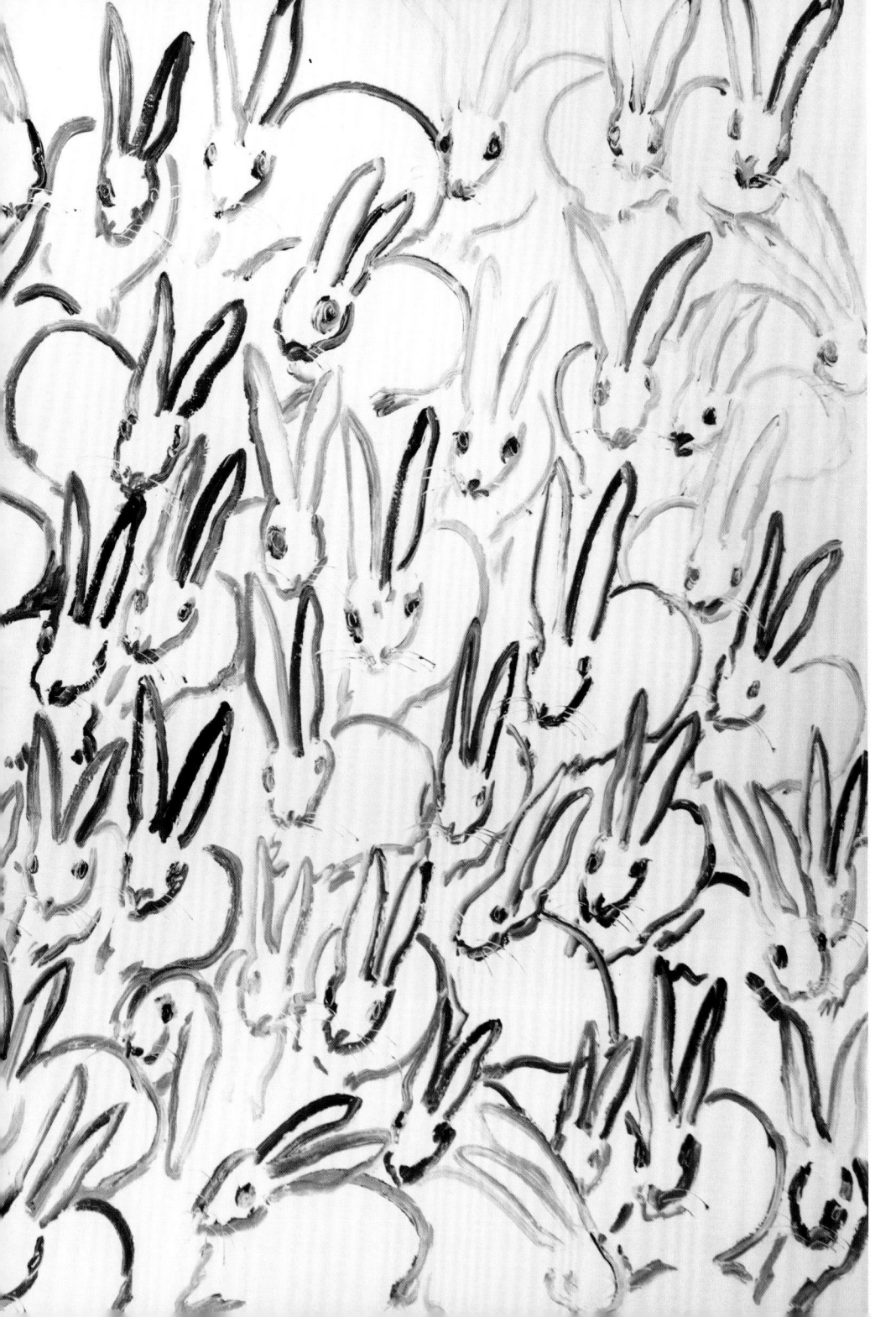

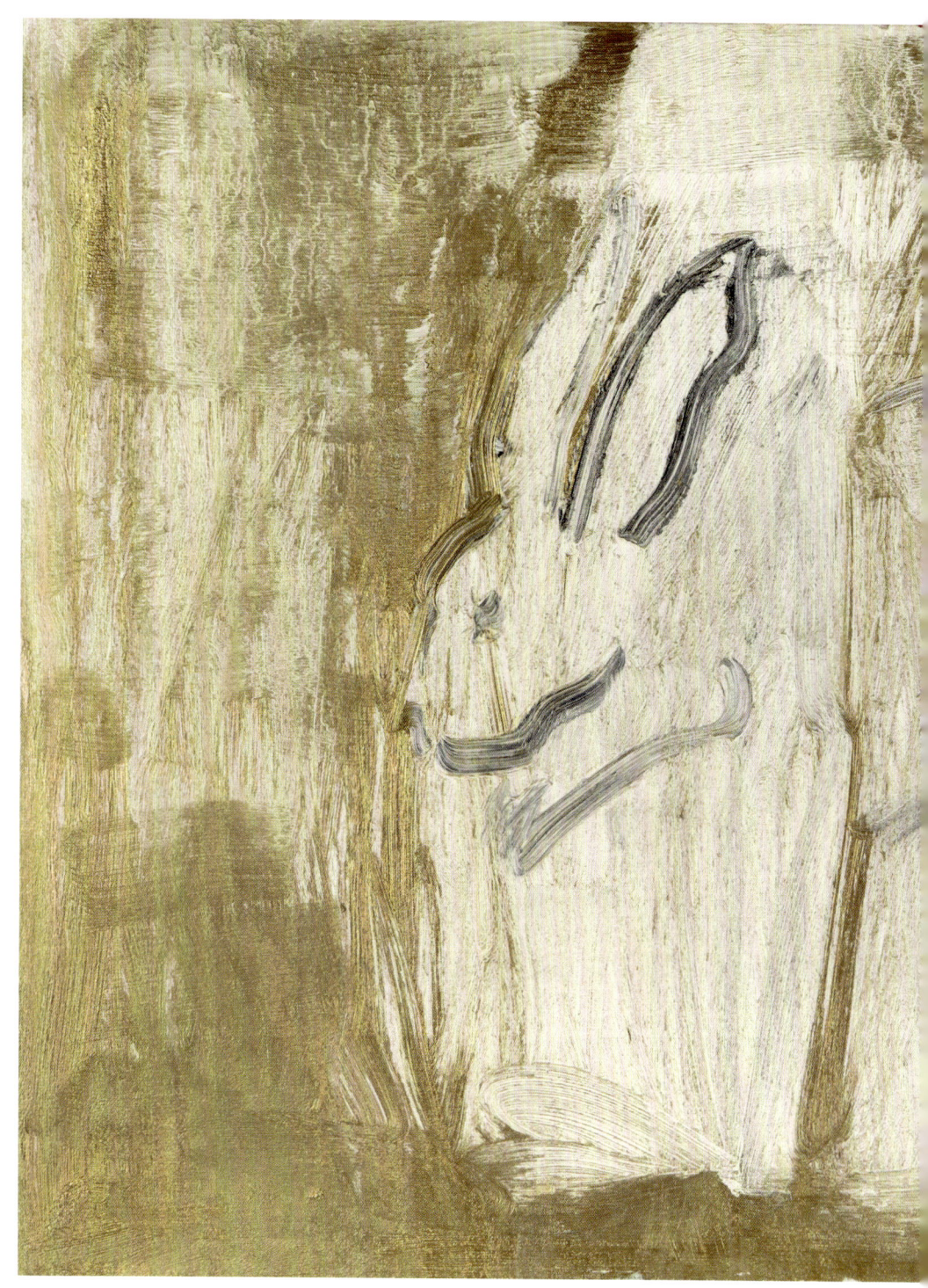

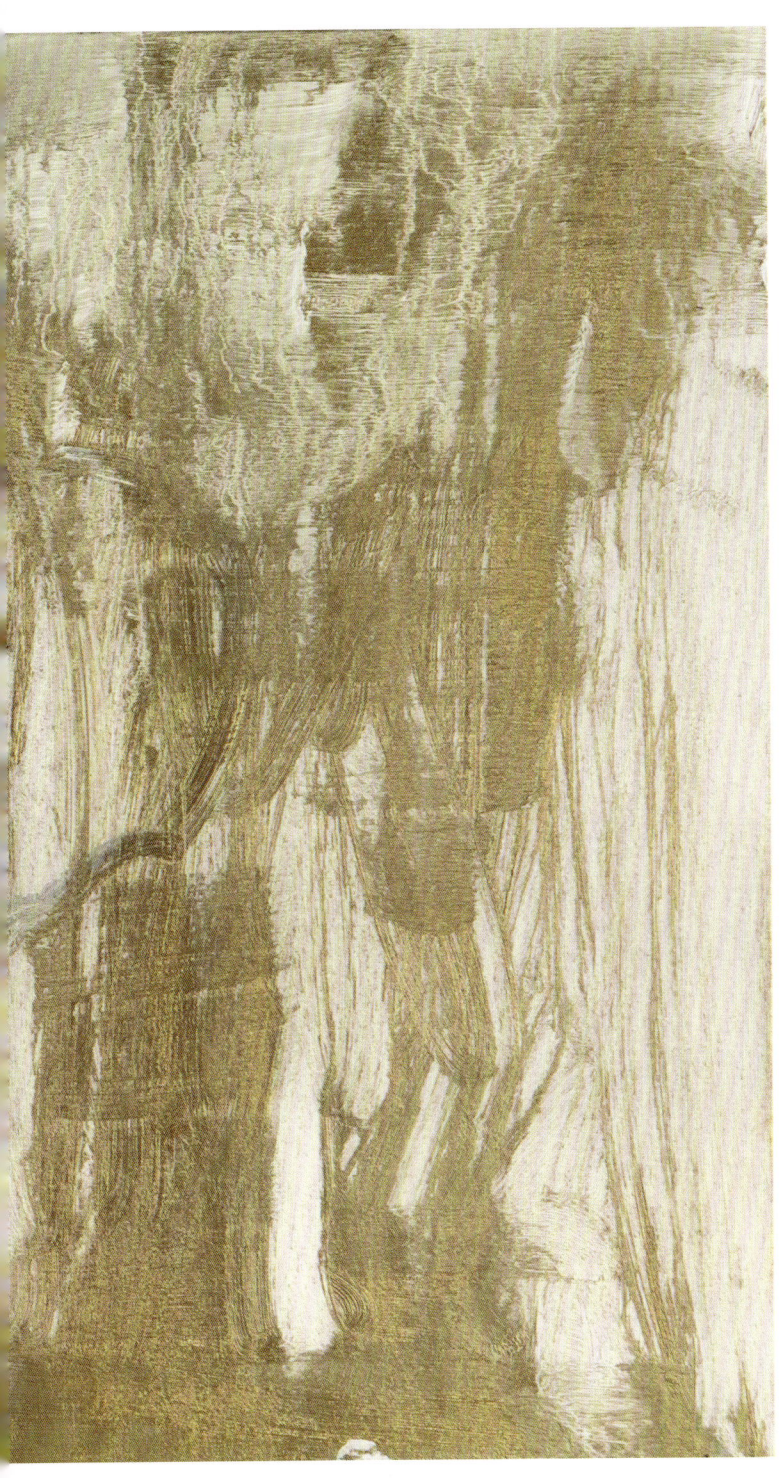

NICOLE
2011
OIL ON CANVAS
30" X 40"

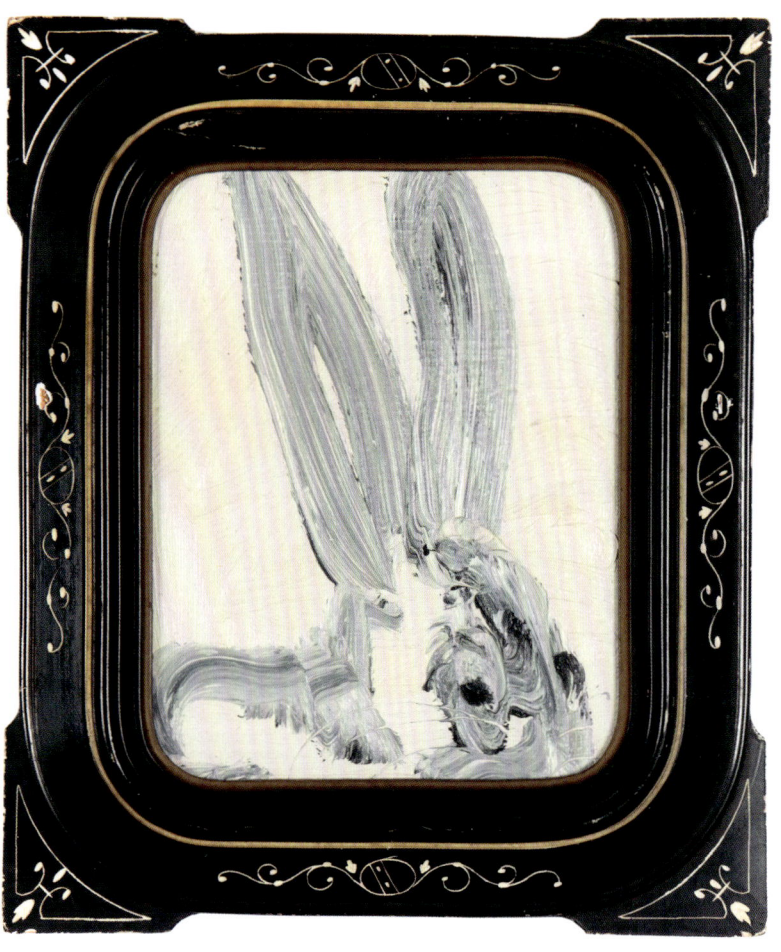

ANN
2012
OIL ON WOOD
10″ X 8″

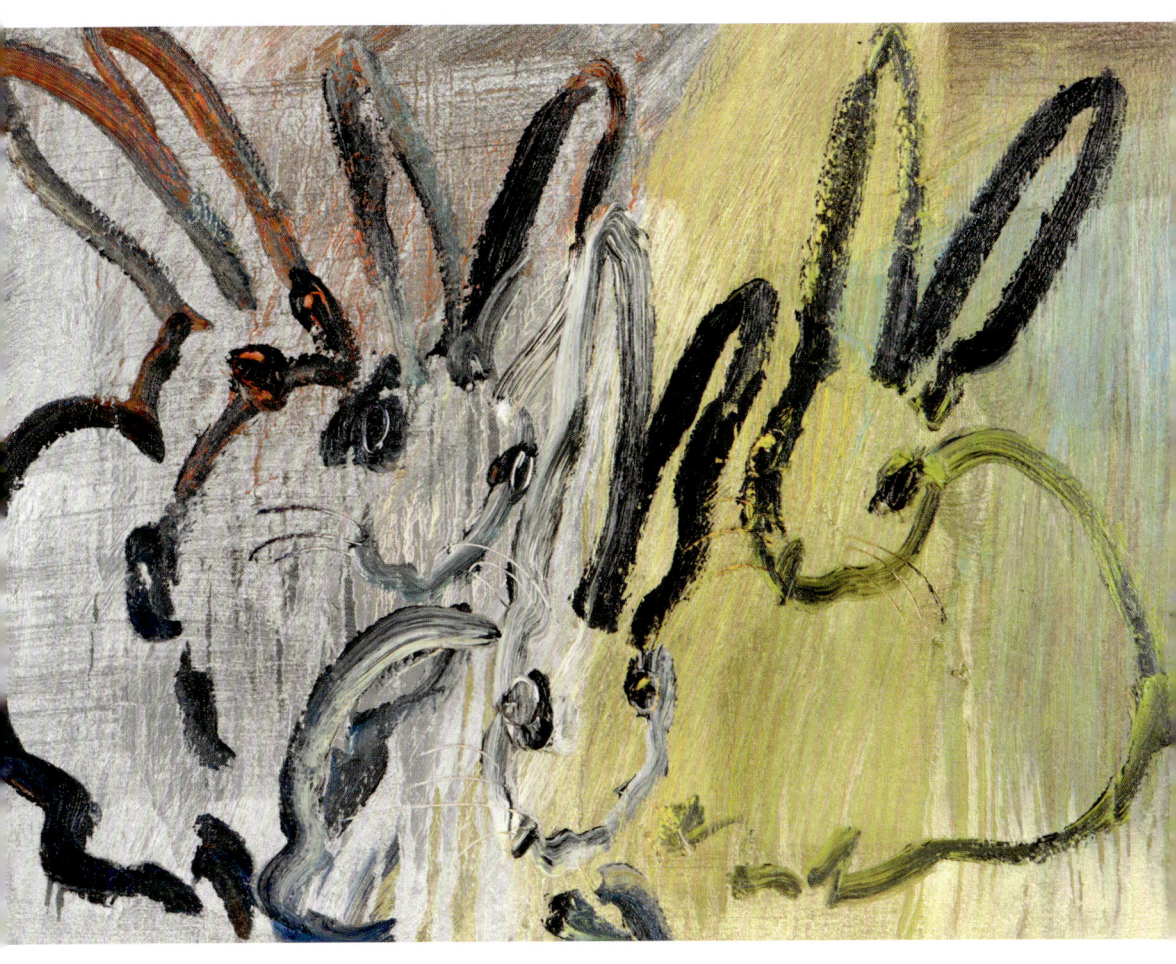

STANDARD
2013
OIL ON CANVAS
30" x 40"

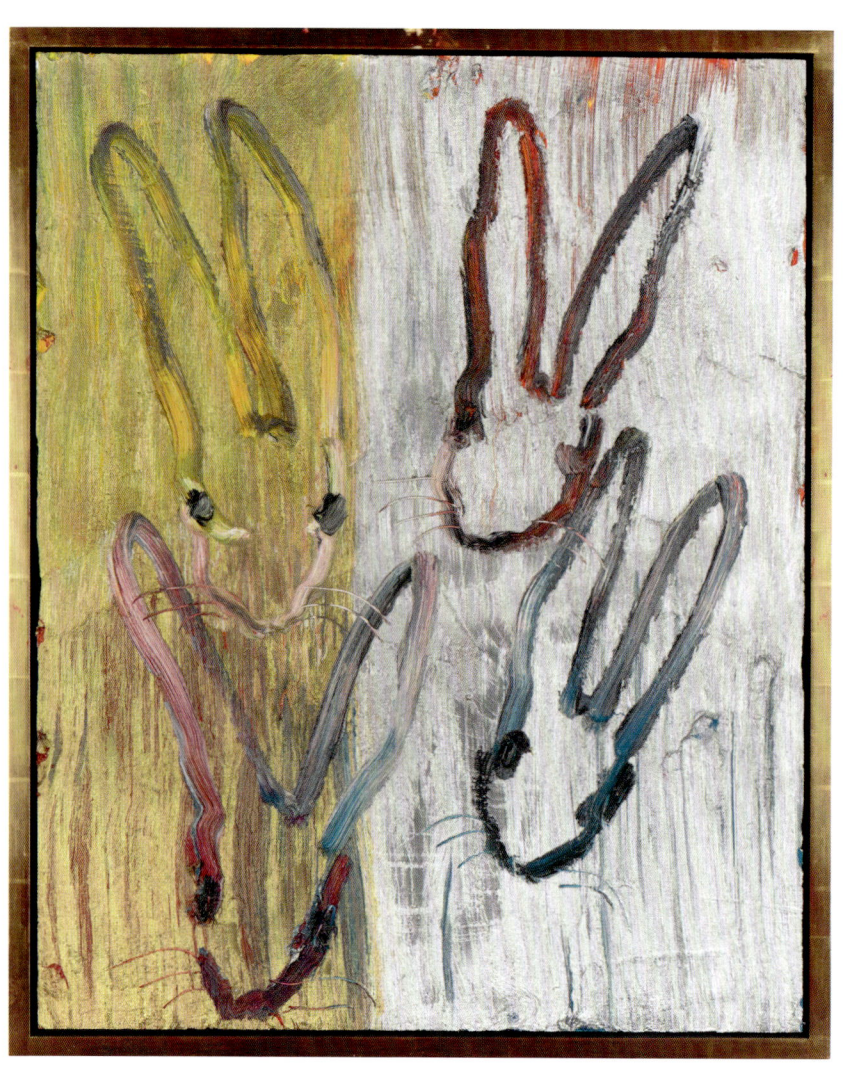

THE HELP
2011
OIL ON WOOD
31" X 25"

PATRICK
2013
OIL ON WOOD
10" X 8"

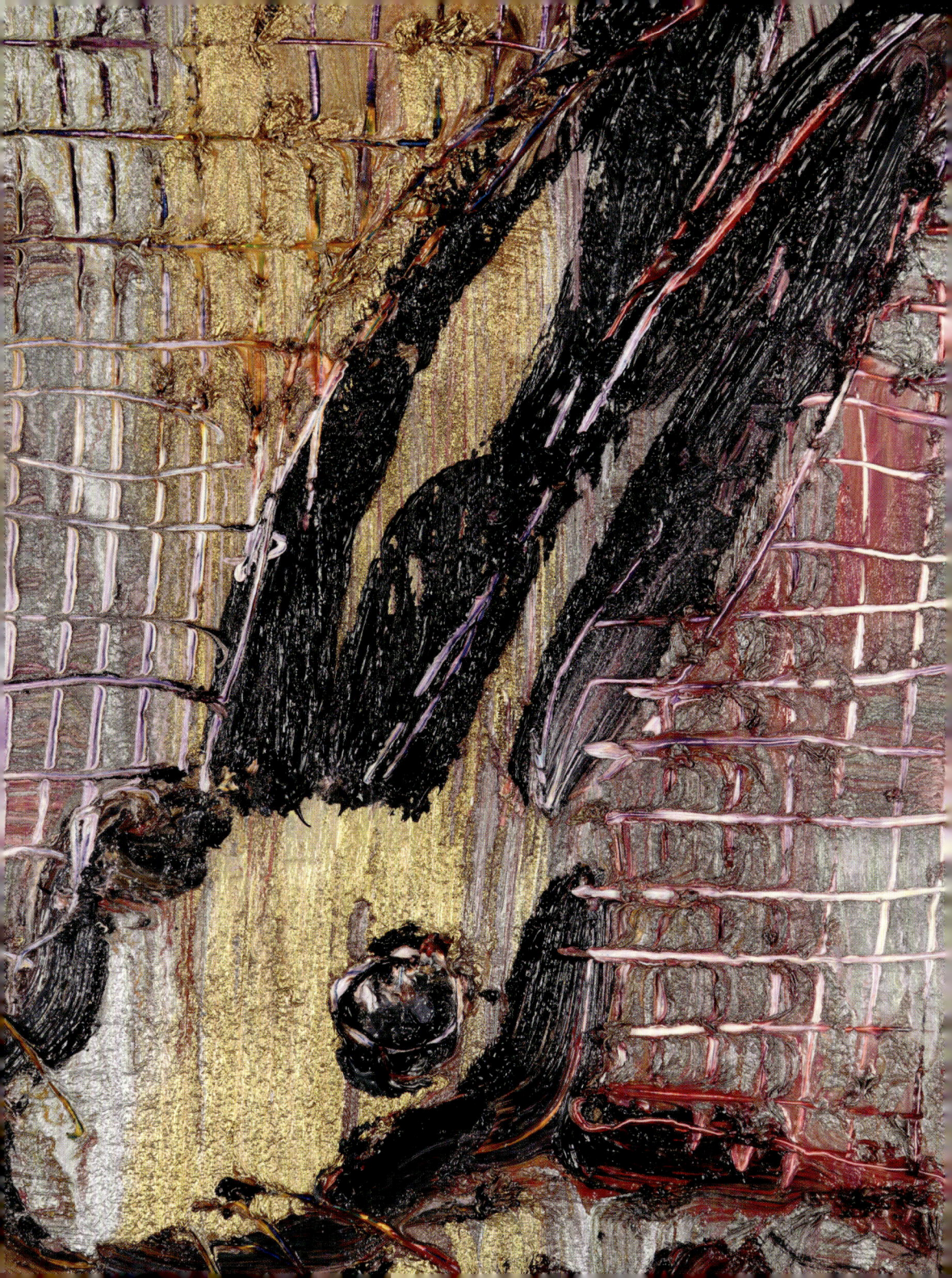

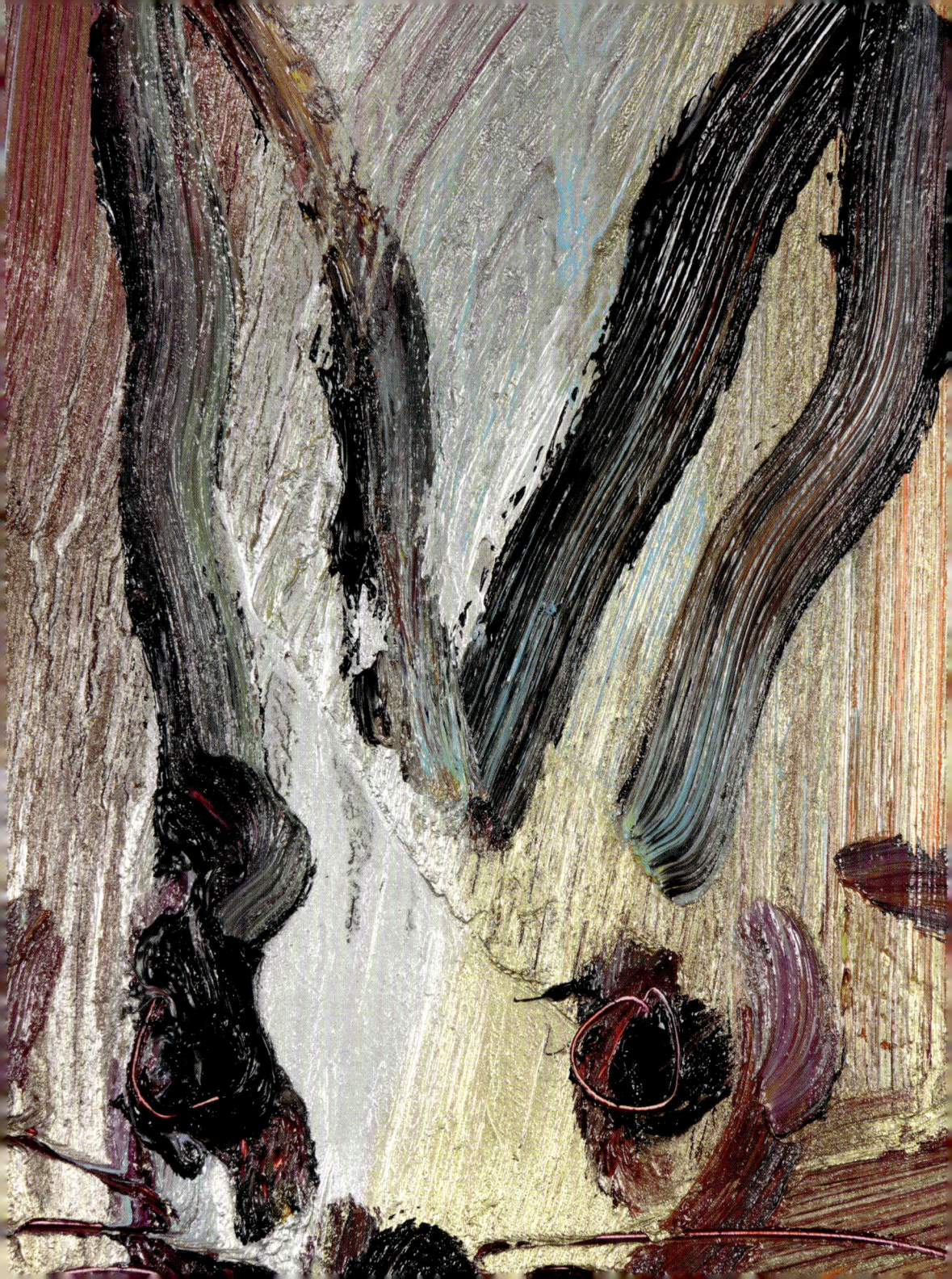

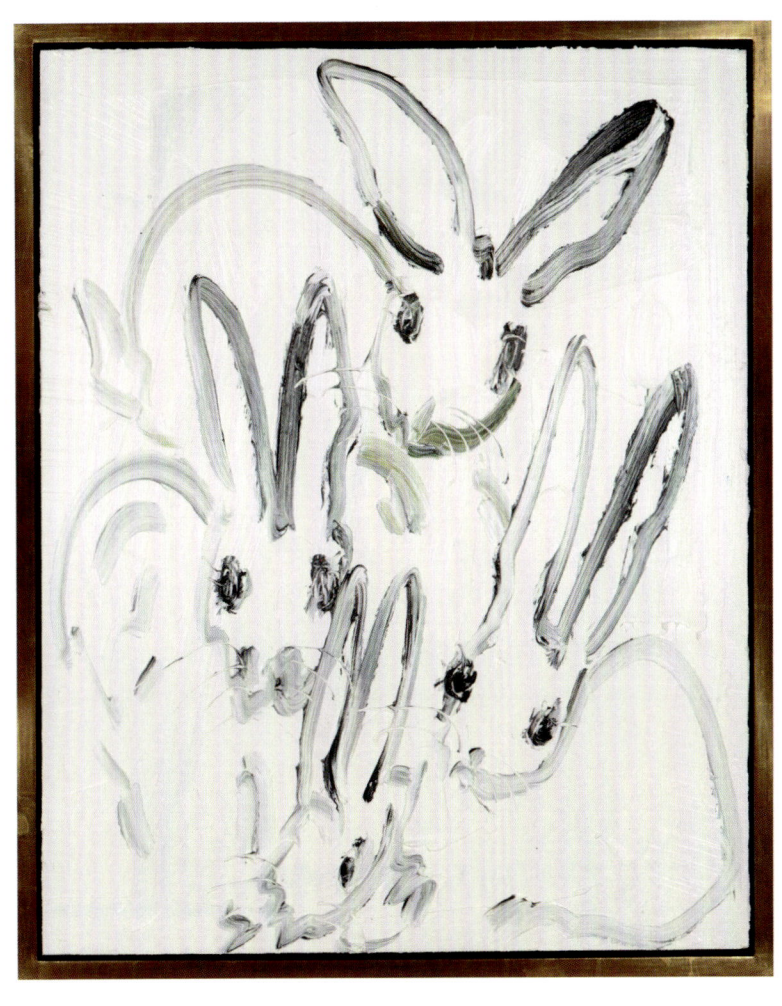

VIVIEN
2013
OIL ON WOOD
10" X 8"

NATCHEZ
2013
OIL ON WOOD
30" X 24"

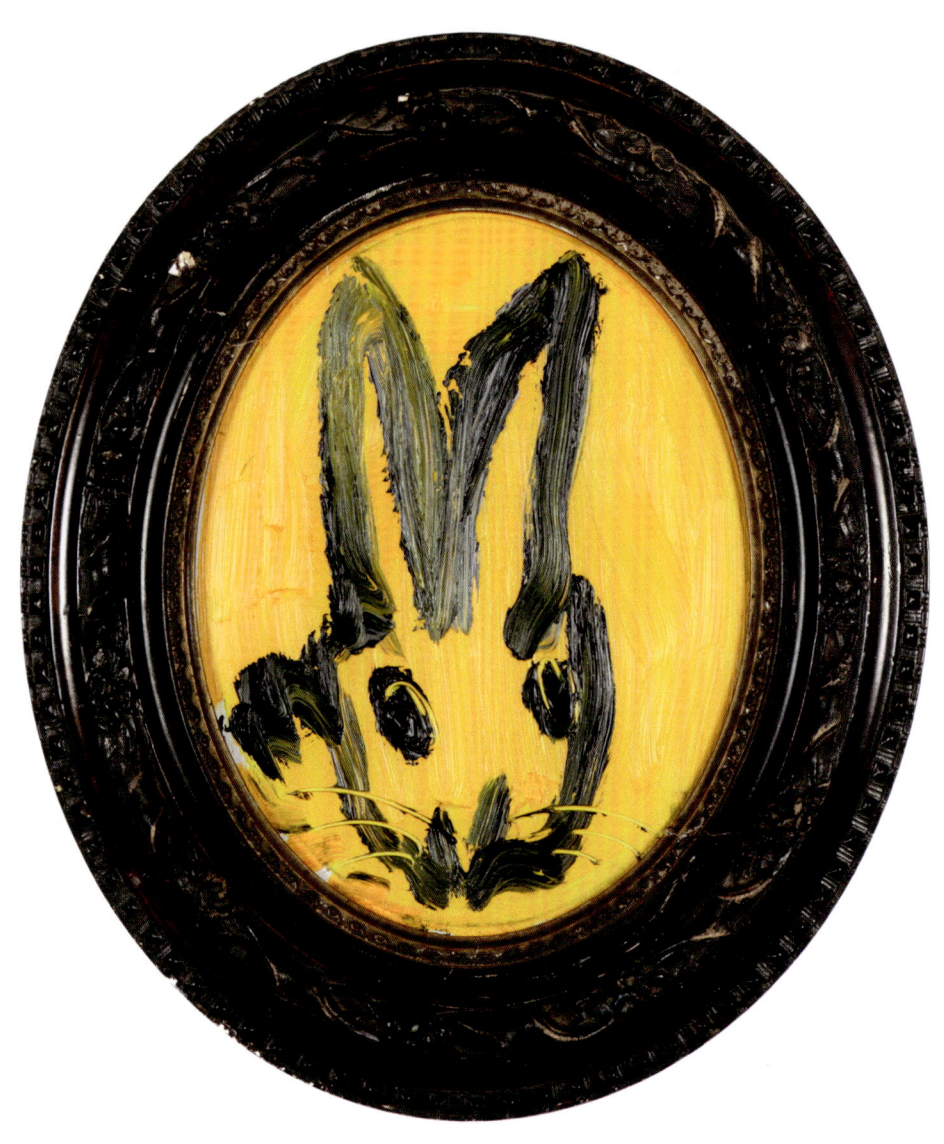

50

VICTORIA
2012
OIL ON WOOD
10" X 8"

LINDA
2013
OIL ON WOOD
10" X 8"

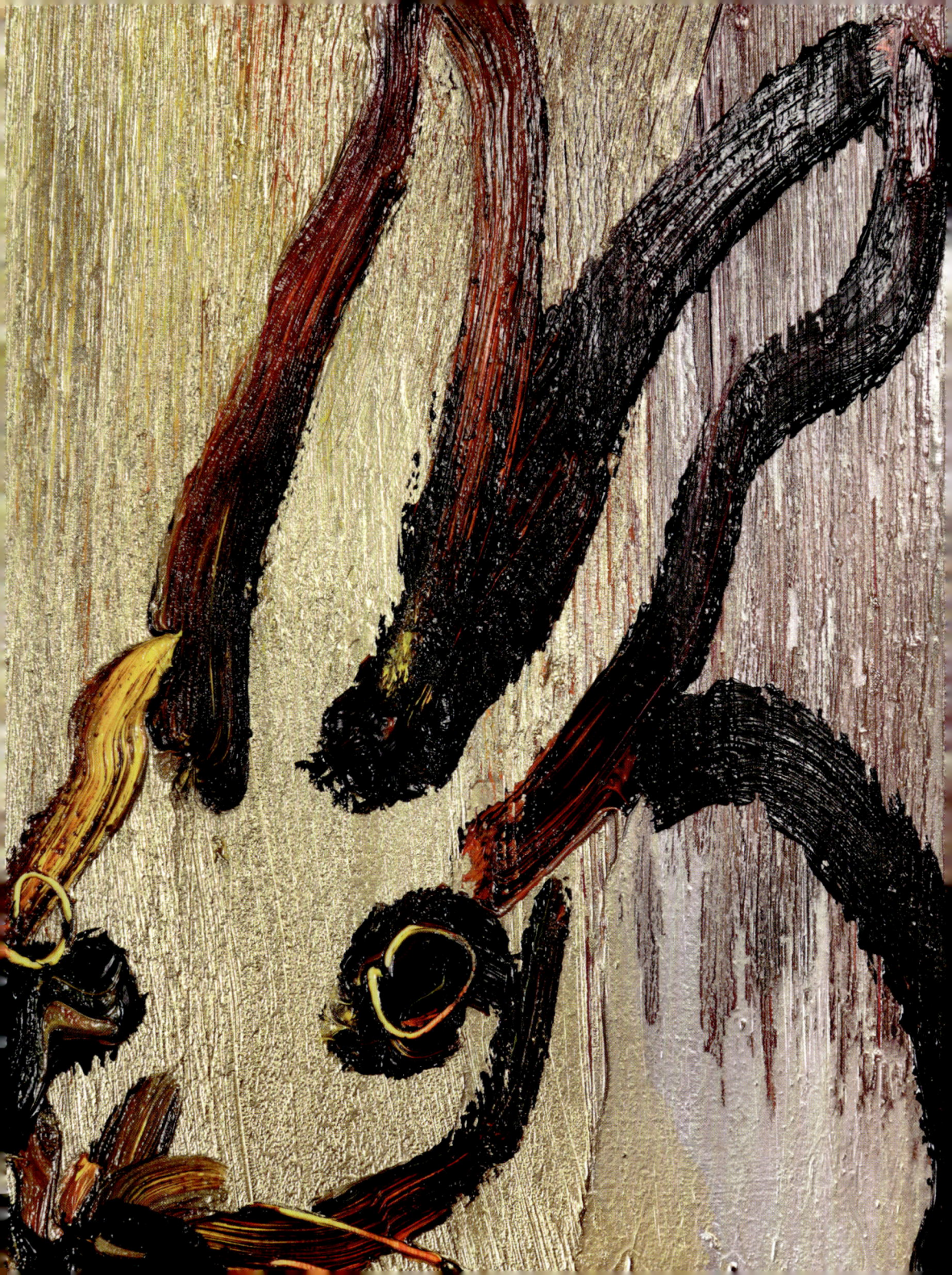

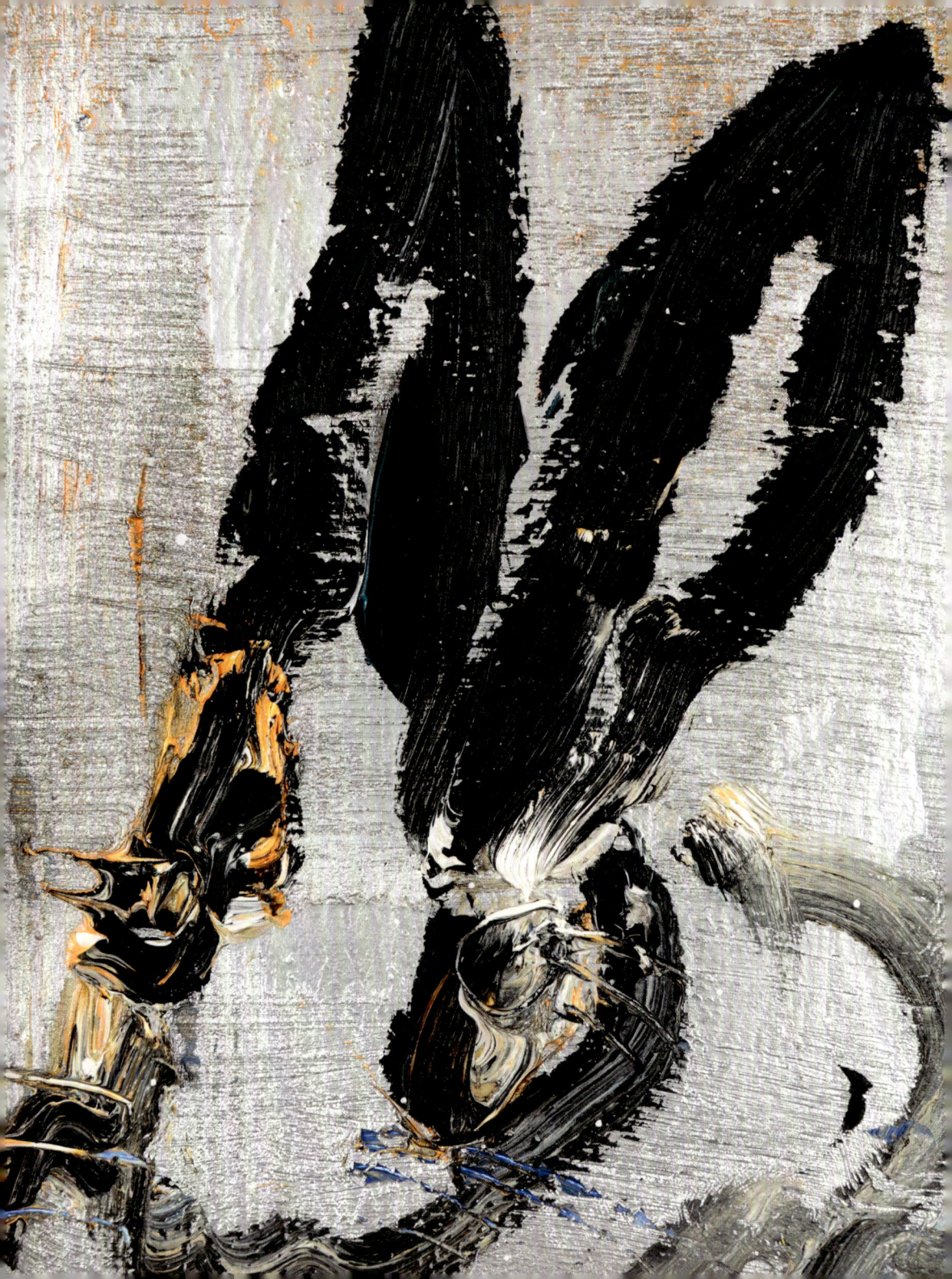

TED
2012
OIL ON WOOD
10" X 8"

54

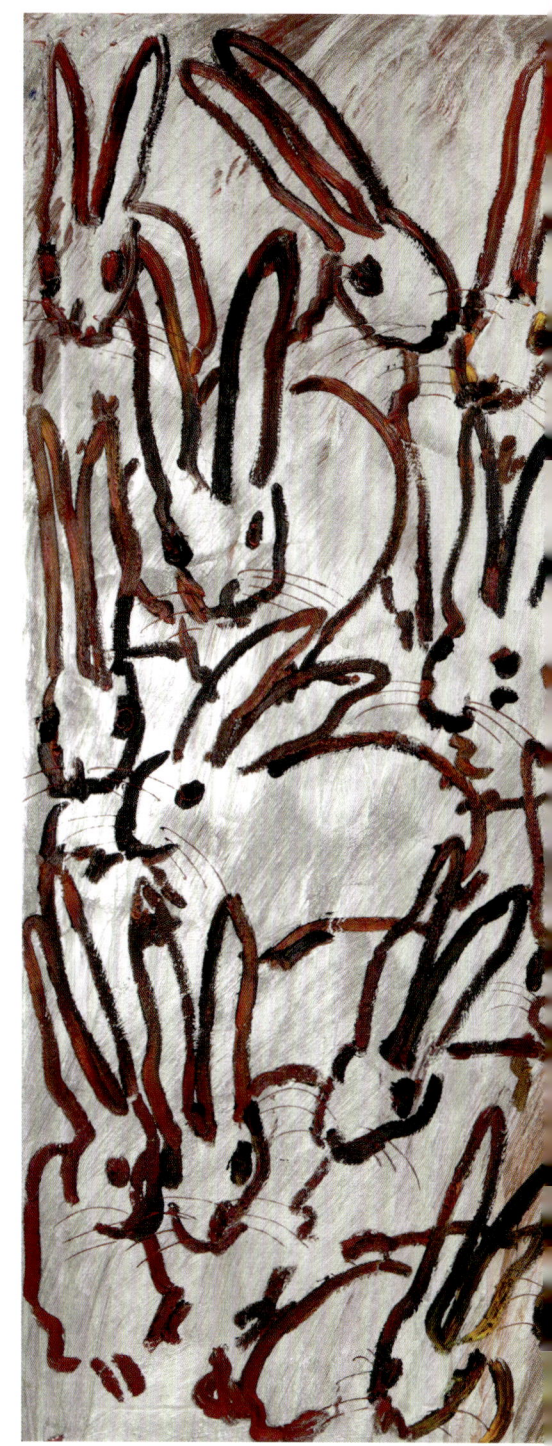

RED SEA
2012
OIL ON CANVAS
72" x 84"

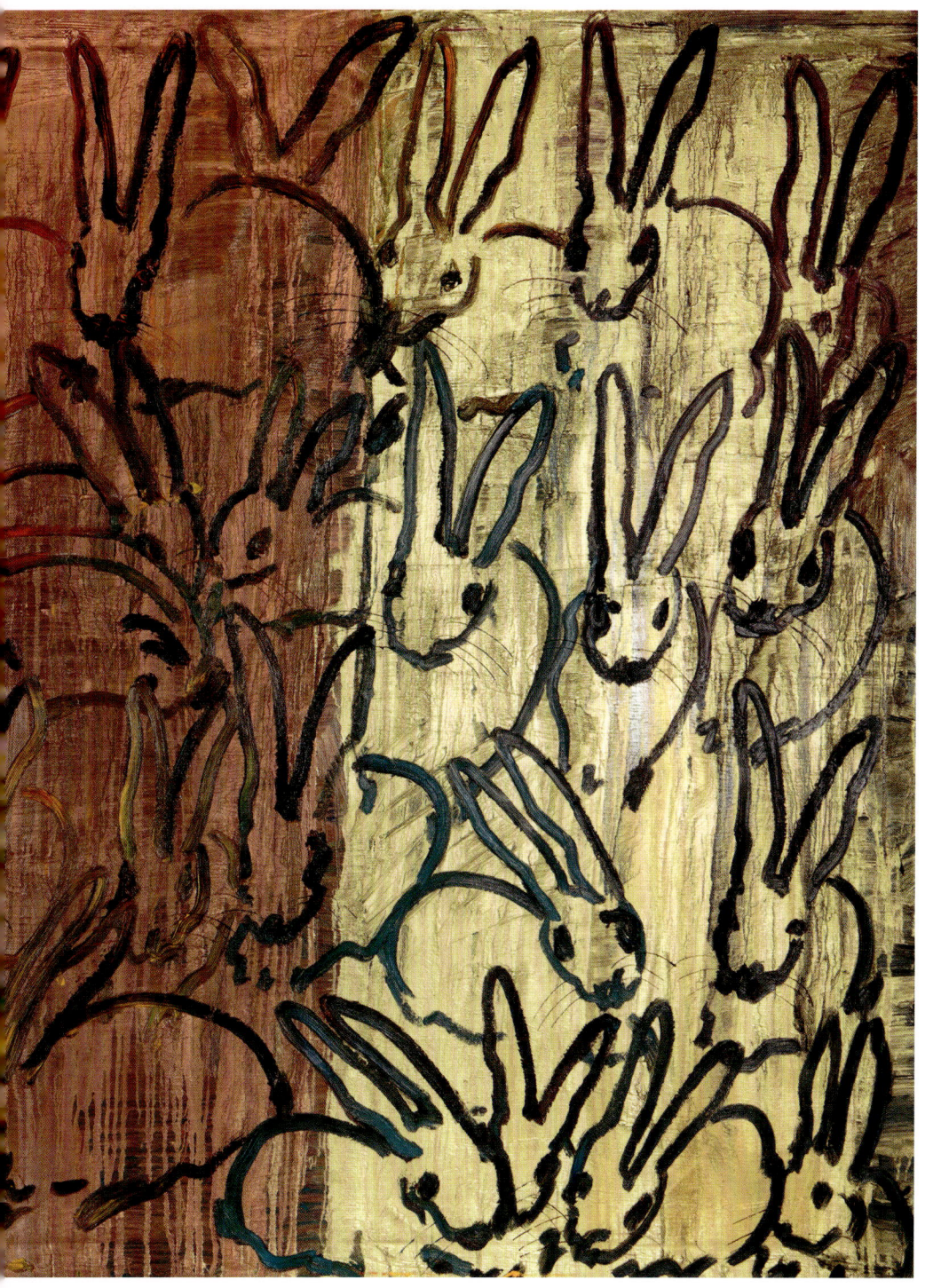

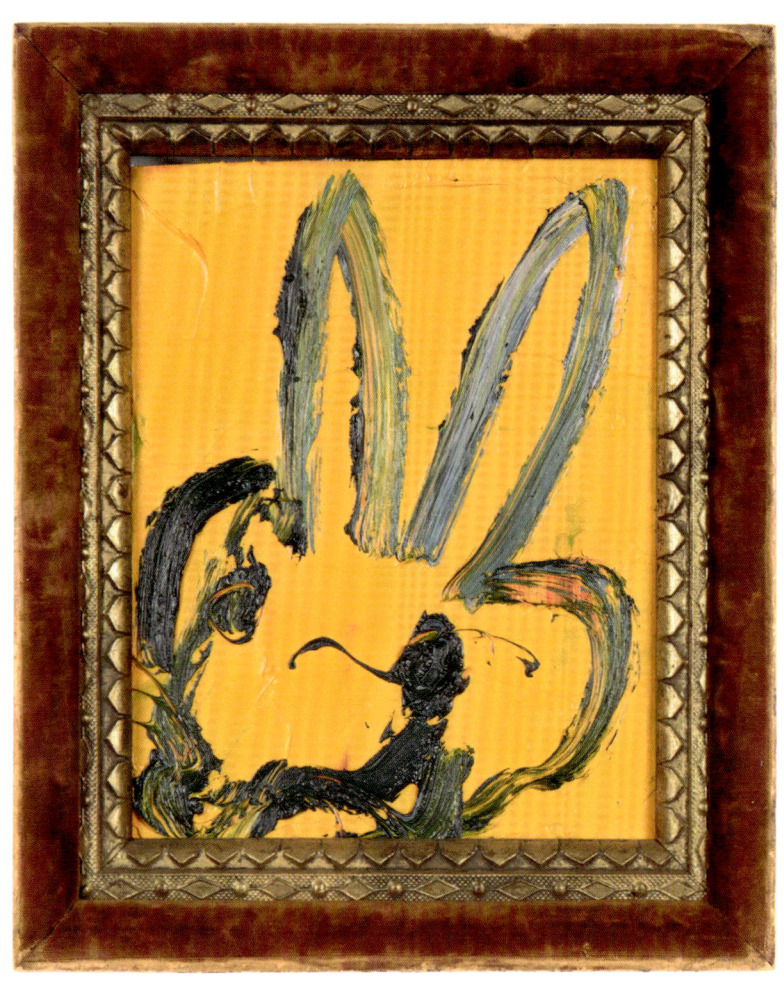

RED VELVET
2013
OIL ON WOOD
10" x 8"

COLBY
2013
OIL ON WOOD
20" x 16"

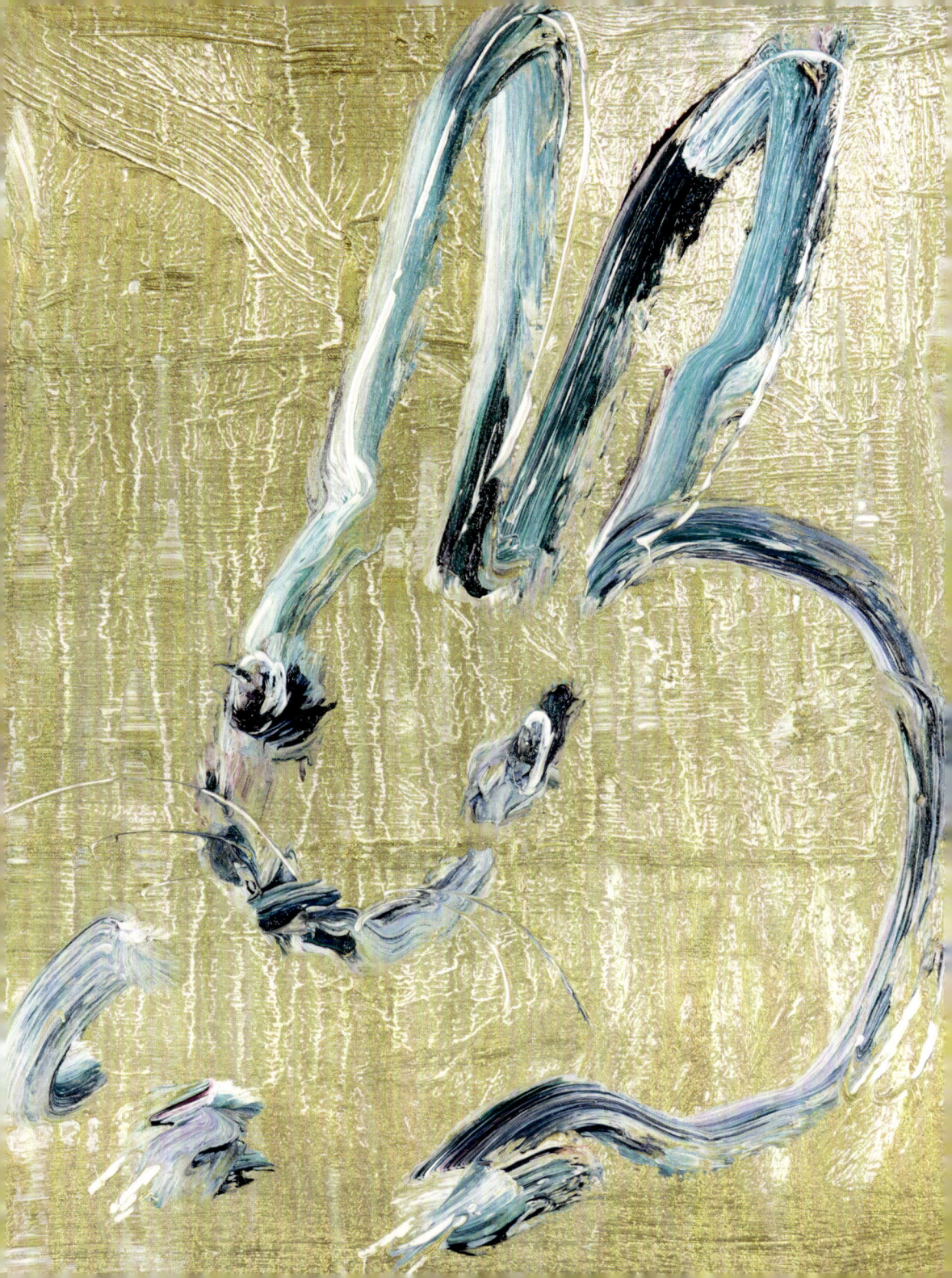

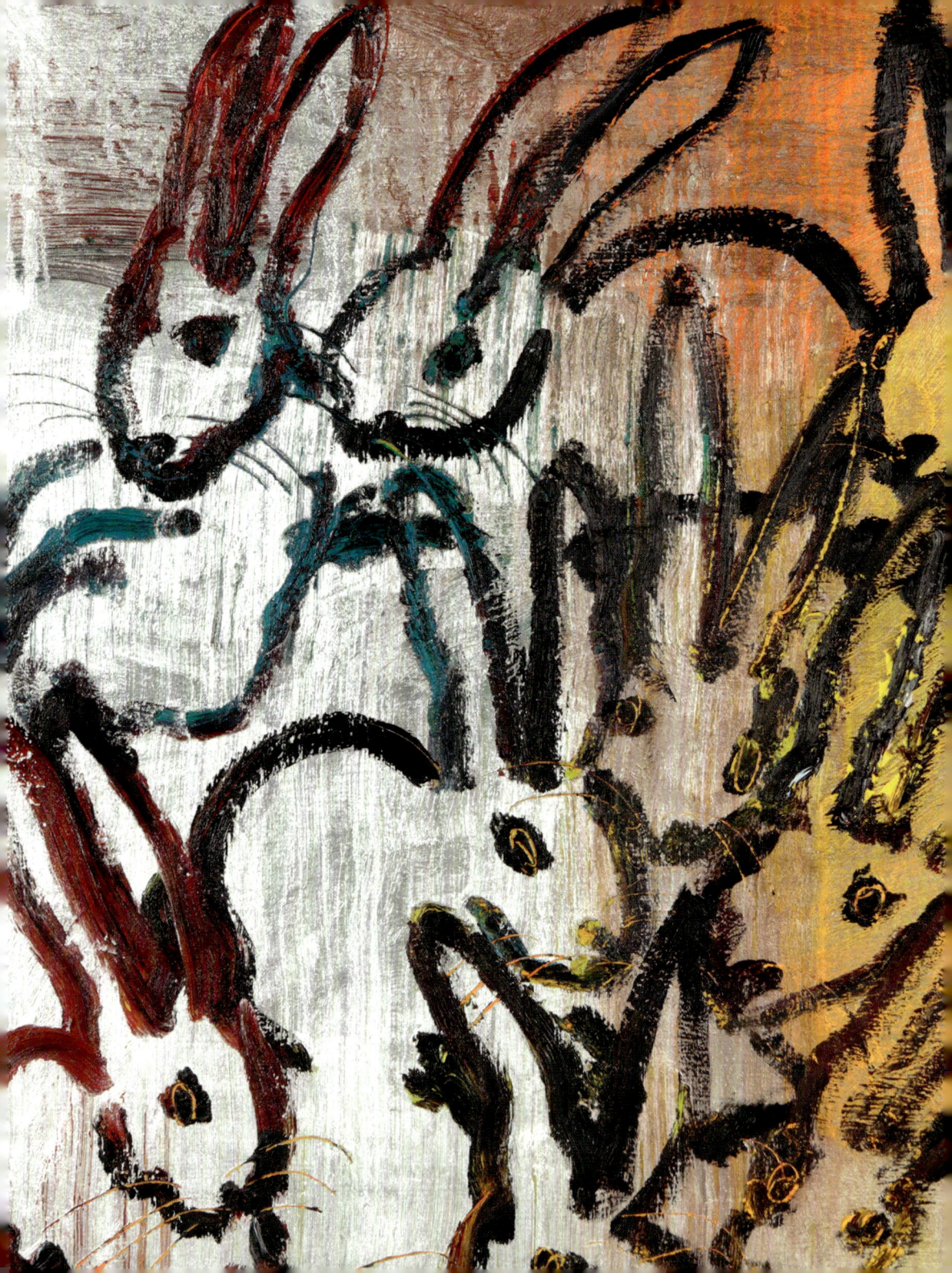

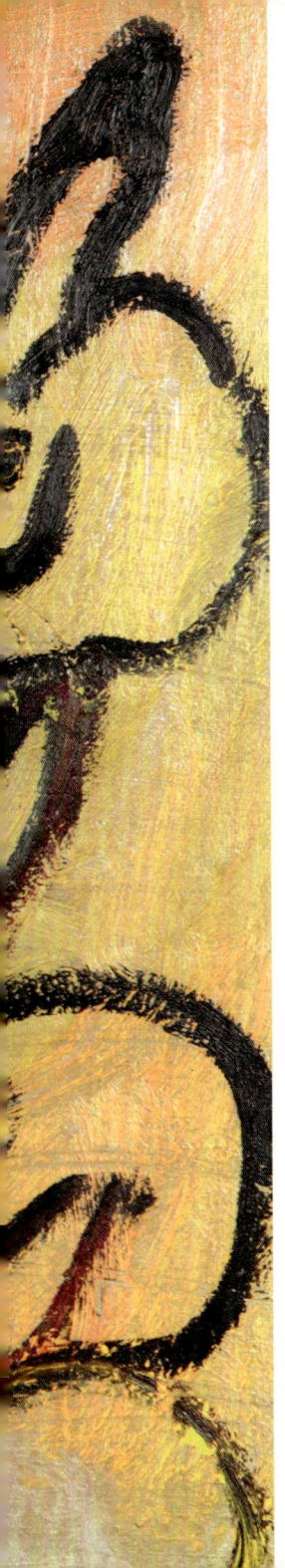

59

AVERY ISLAND
2012
OIL ON CANVAS
37" X 37"

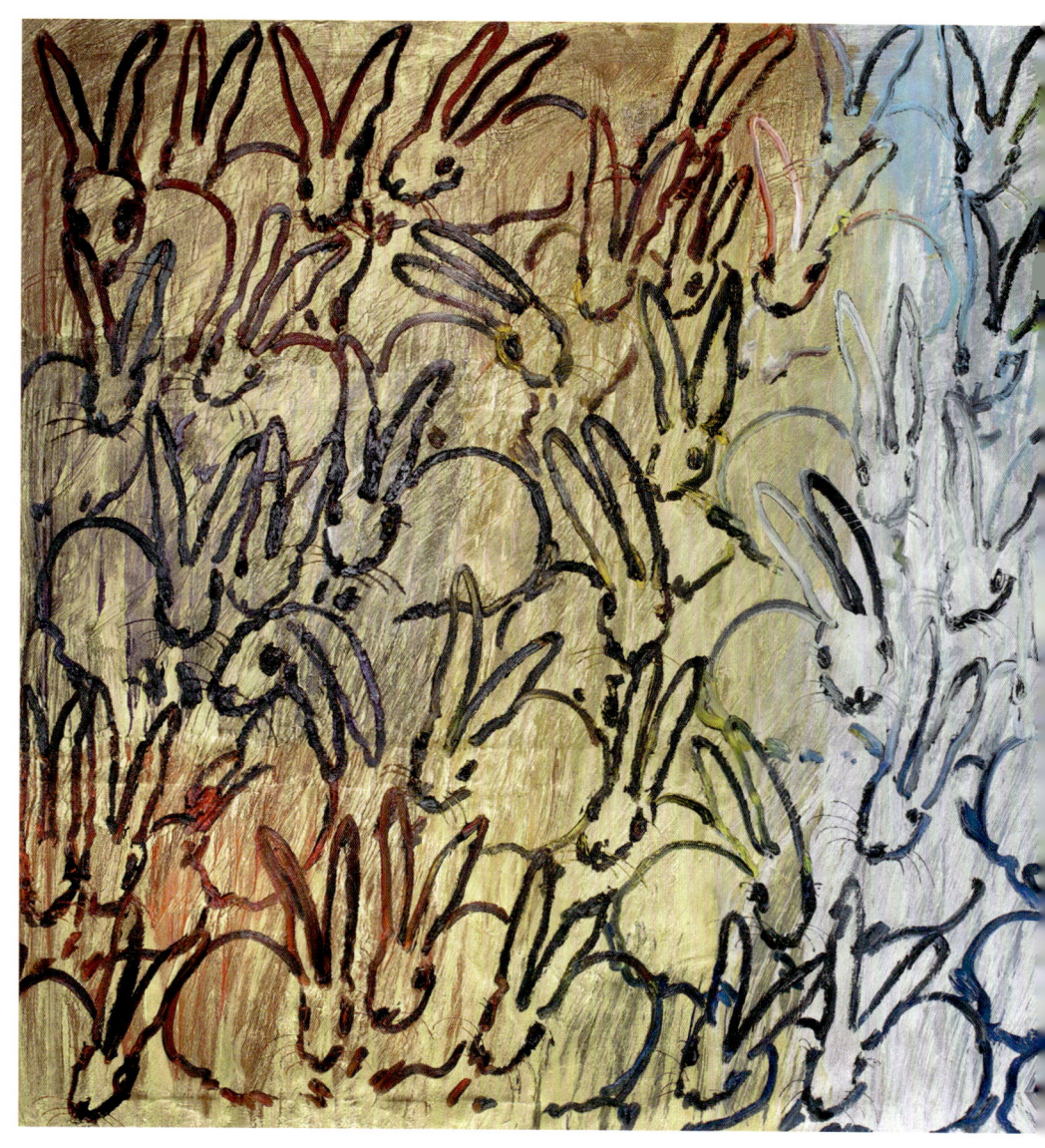

HOOPOE
2013
OIL ON CANVAS
156" X 78"

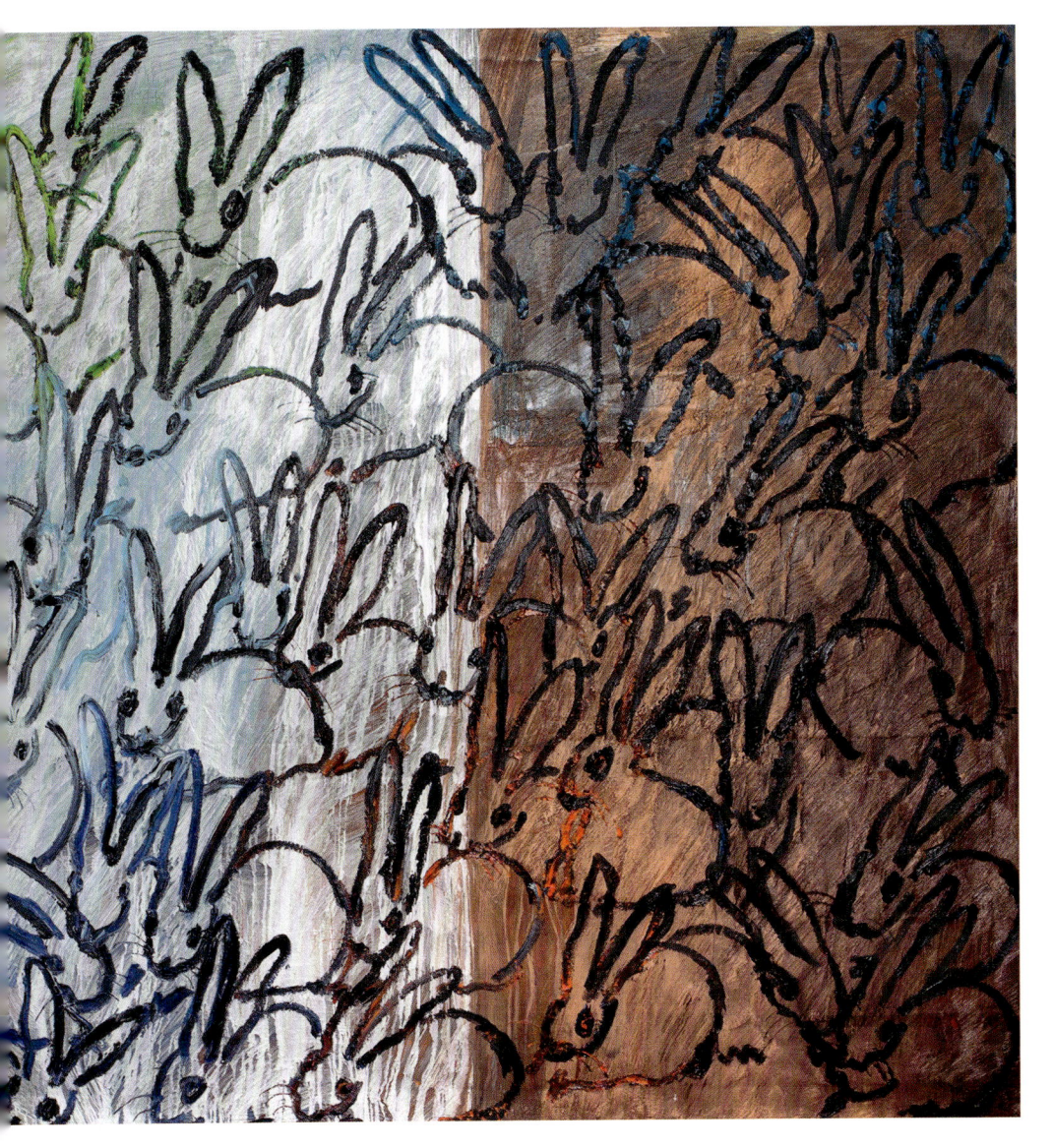

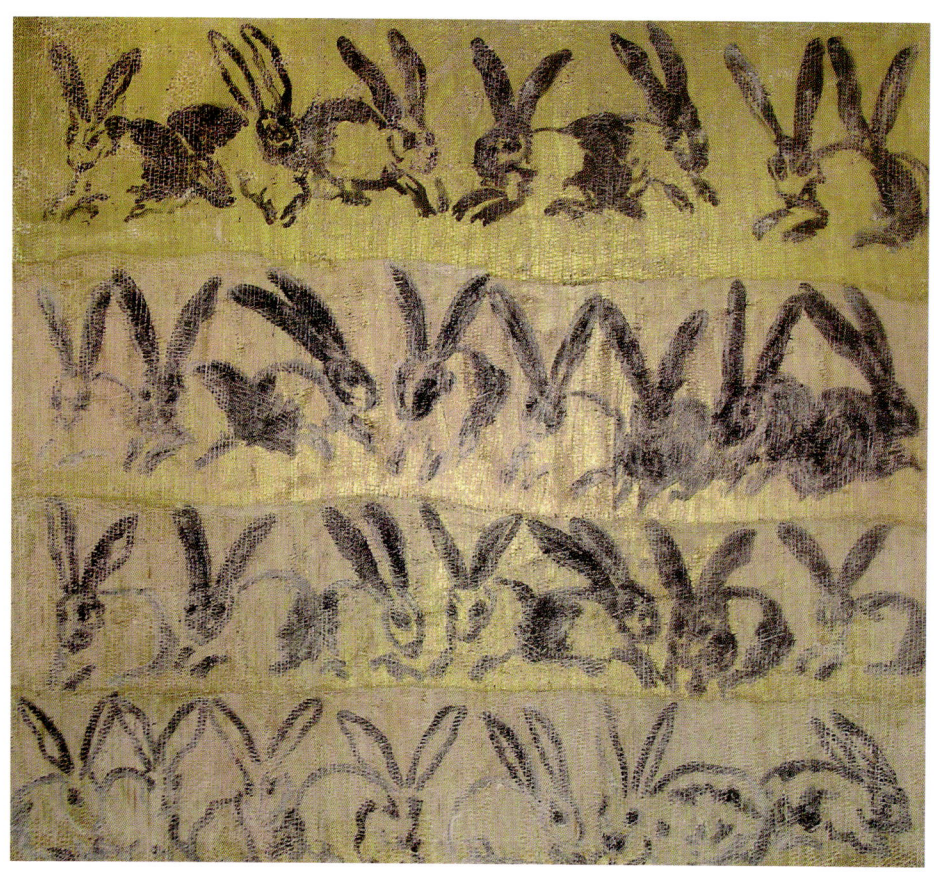

LUCKY CHARM
2005
OIL ON CANVAS
82" X 90"

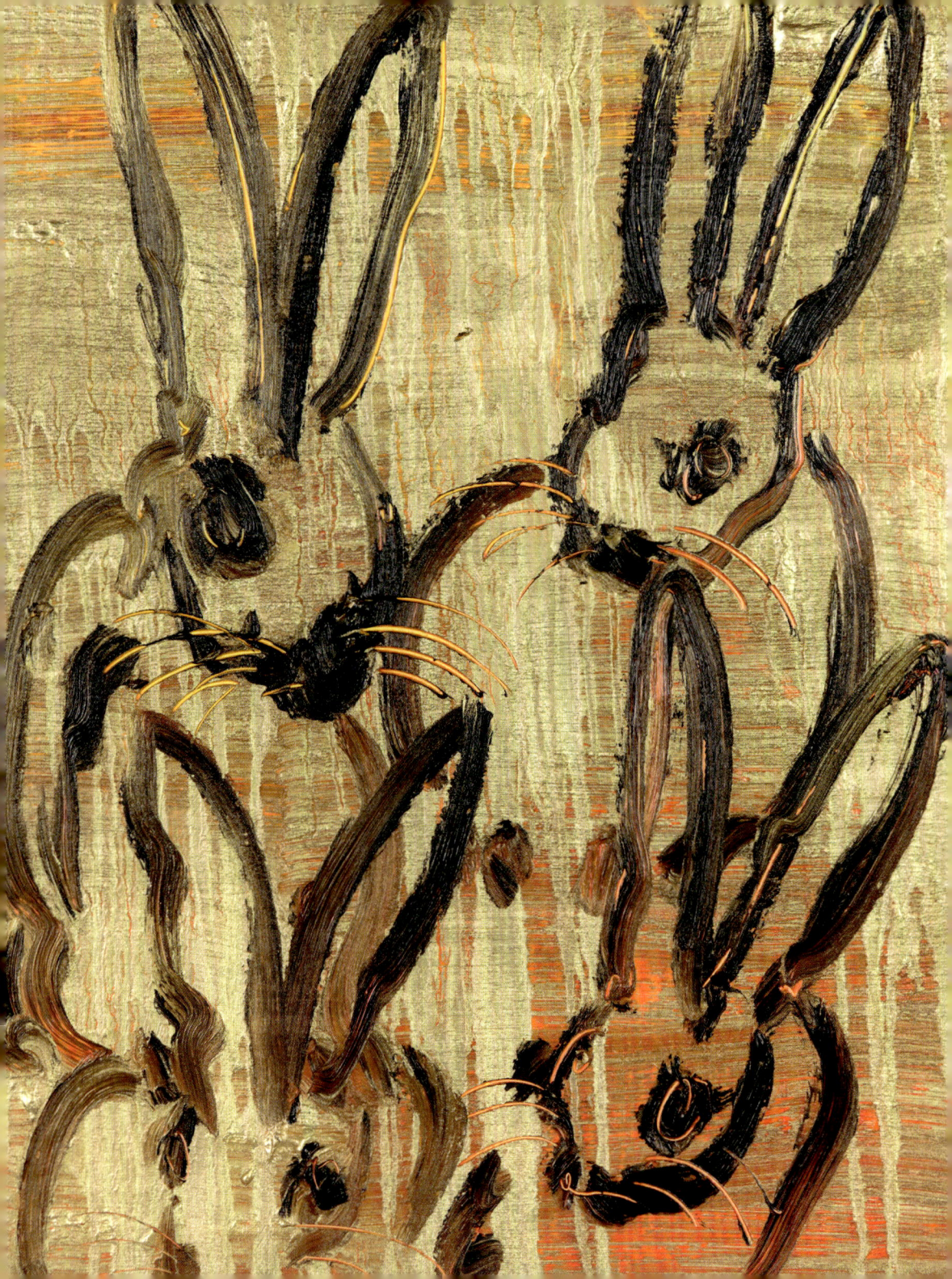

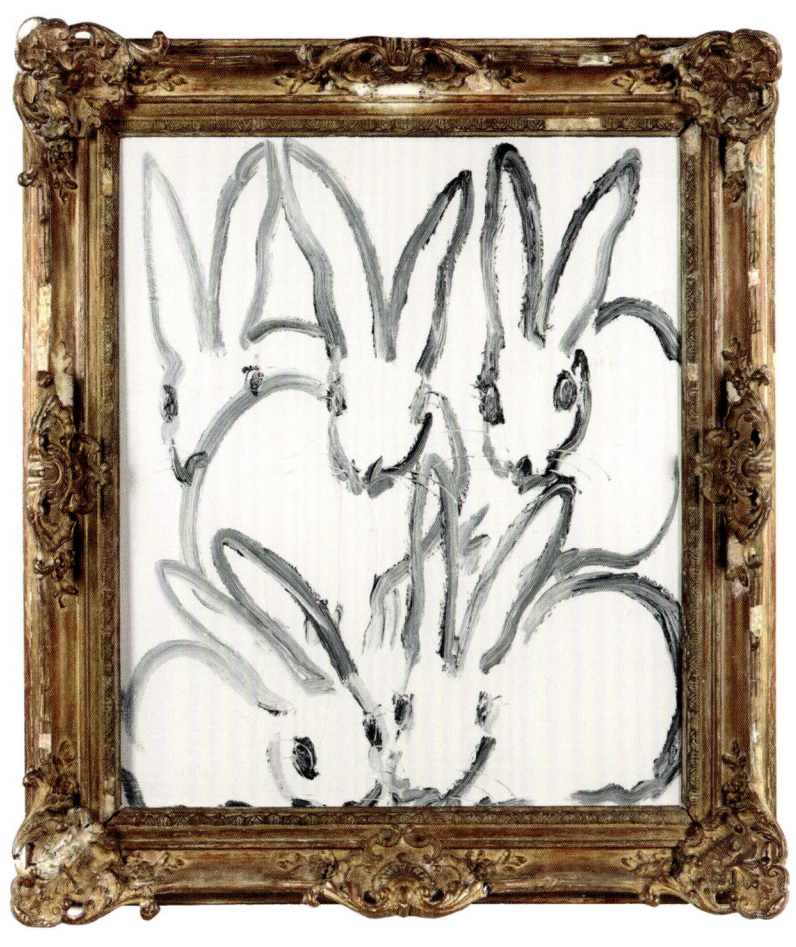

FOUR PLAY
2013
OIL ON WOOD
30" X 23"

DEBRA
2013
OIL ON WOOD
28" X 24"

GAMES
2012
OIL ON CANVAS
40" X 30"

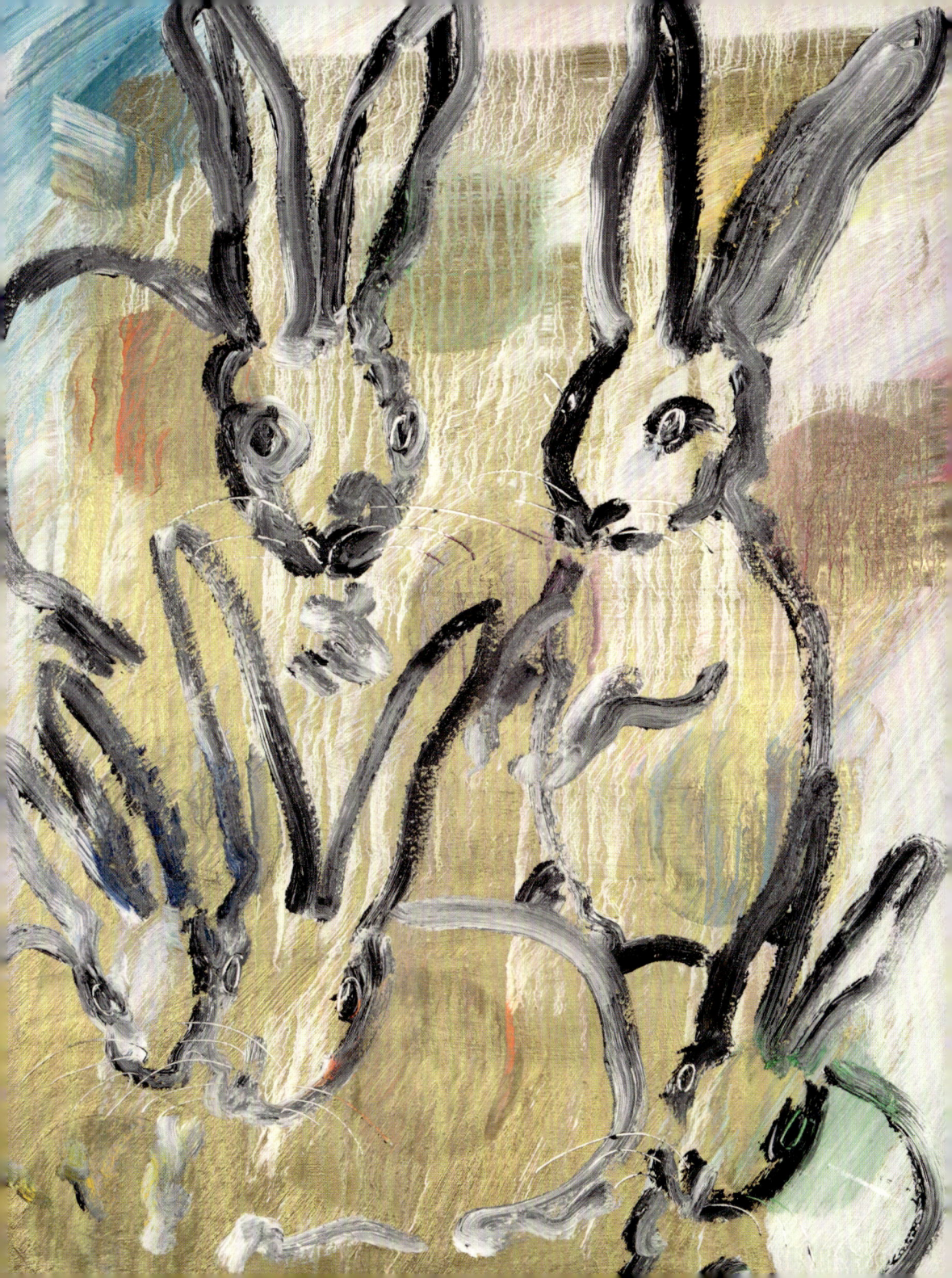

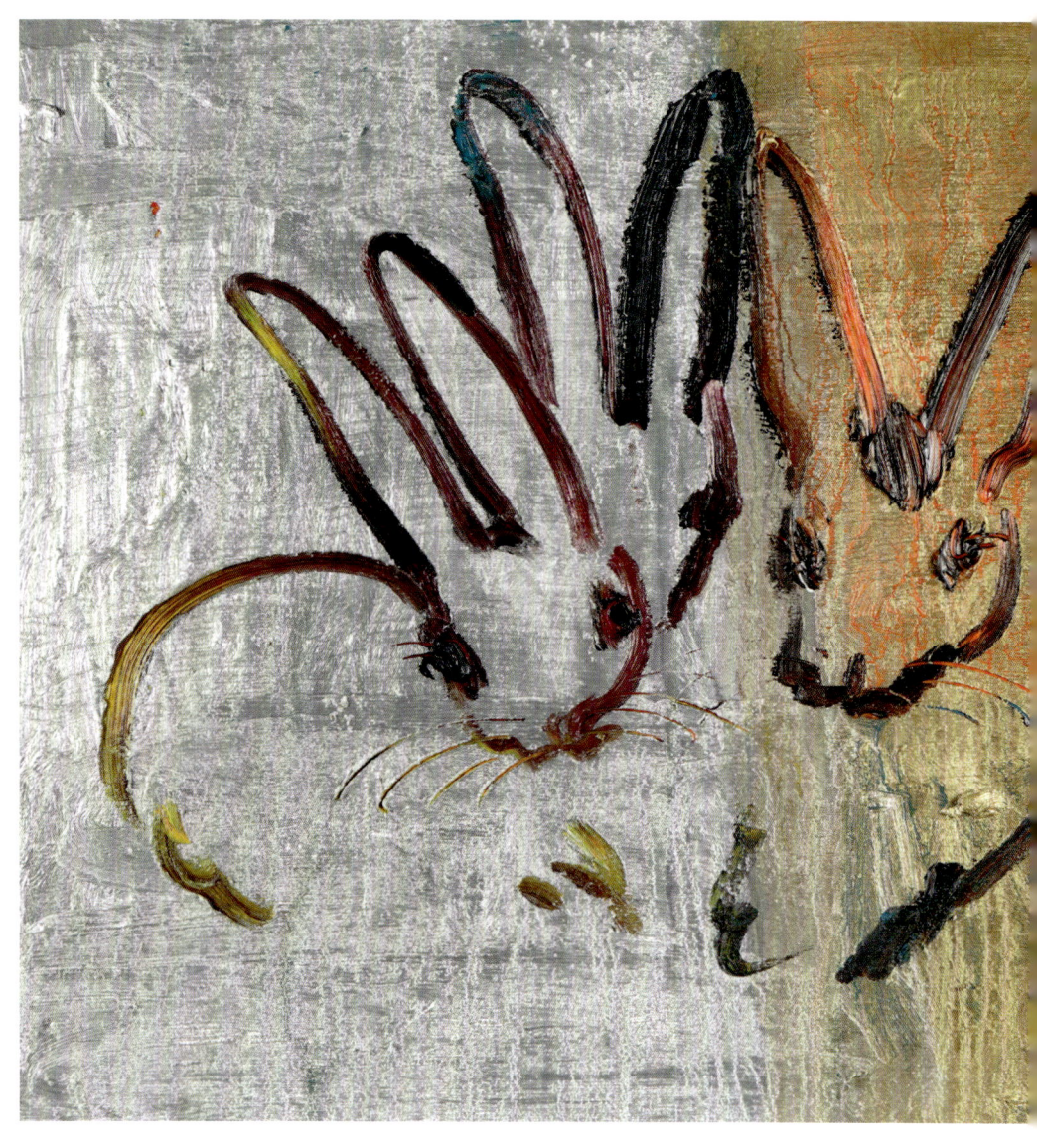

TARENTELLA
2013
OIL ON CANVAS
30" X 40"

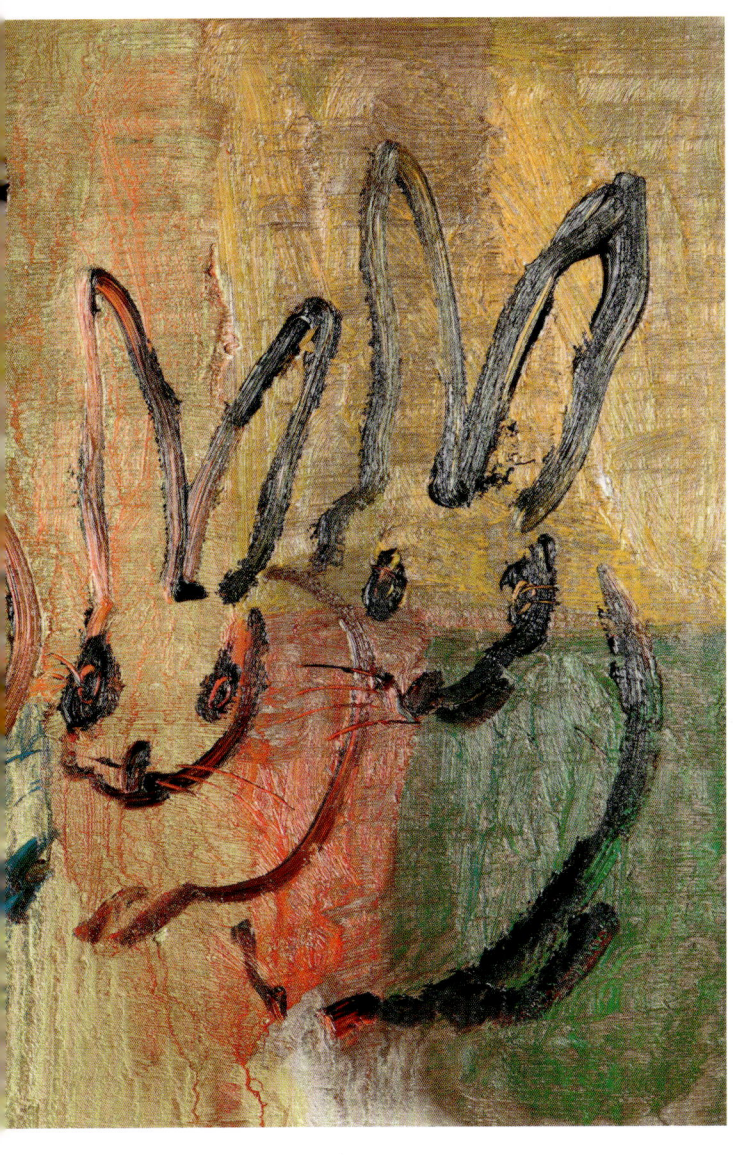

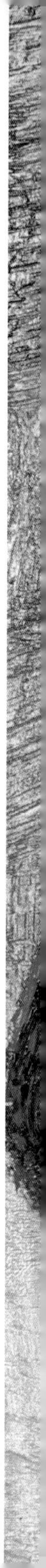

SERGE & TATIANA
2013
OIL ON WOOD
30" X 25"

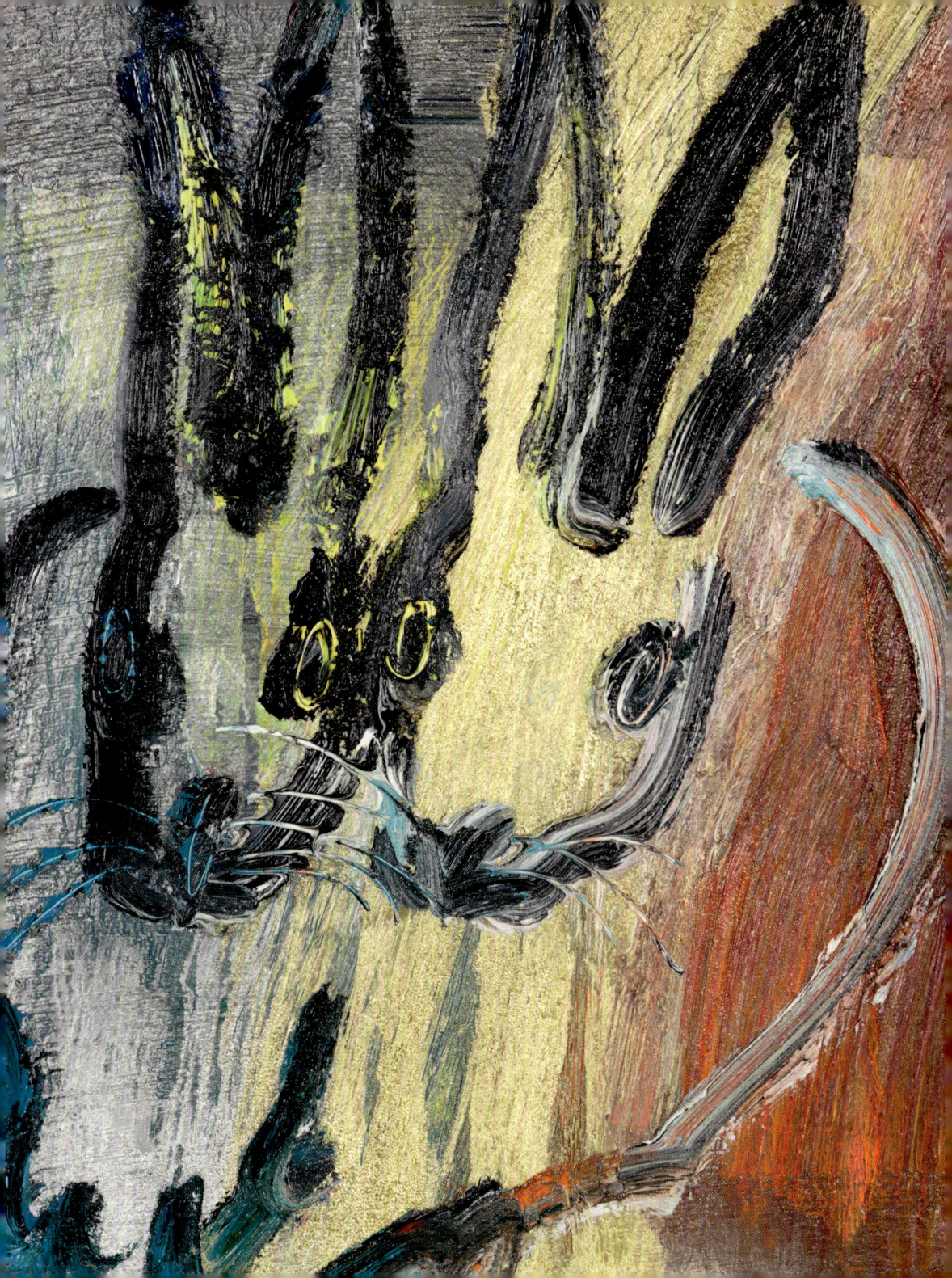

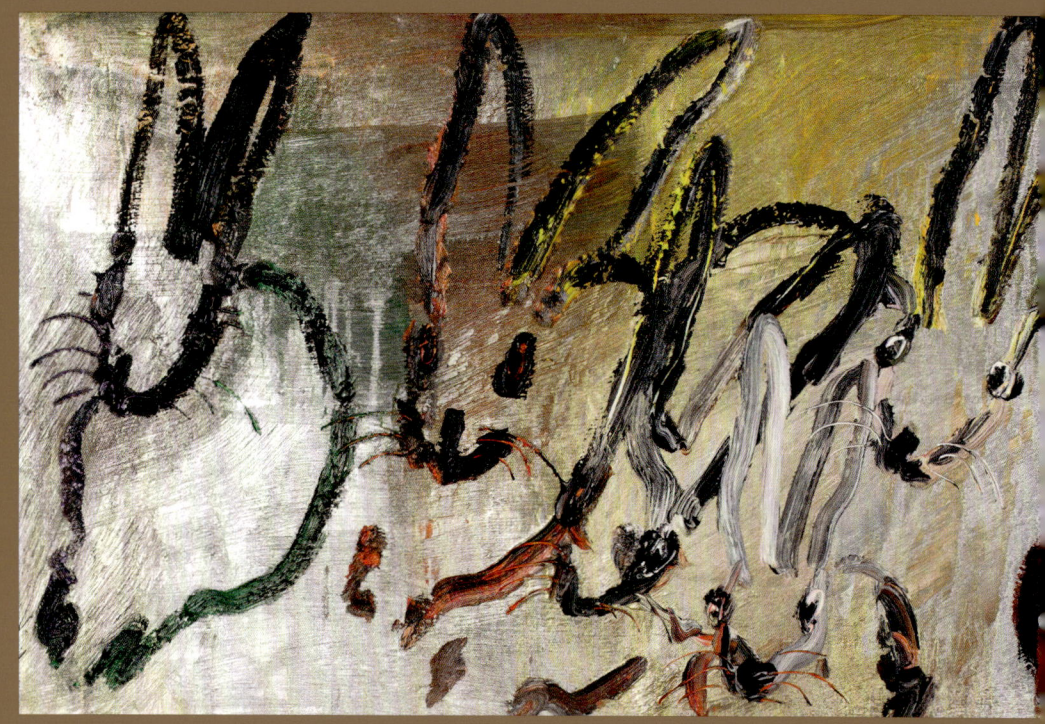

CHINENSIS #3
2013
OIL ON CANVAS
27" X 72"

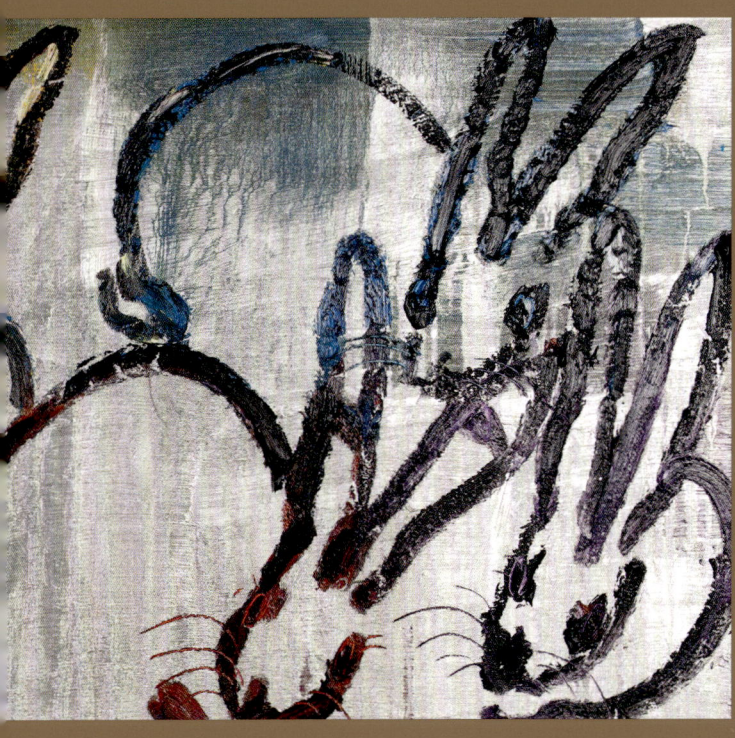

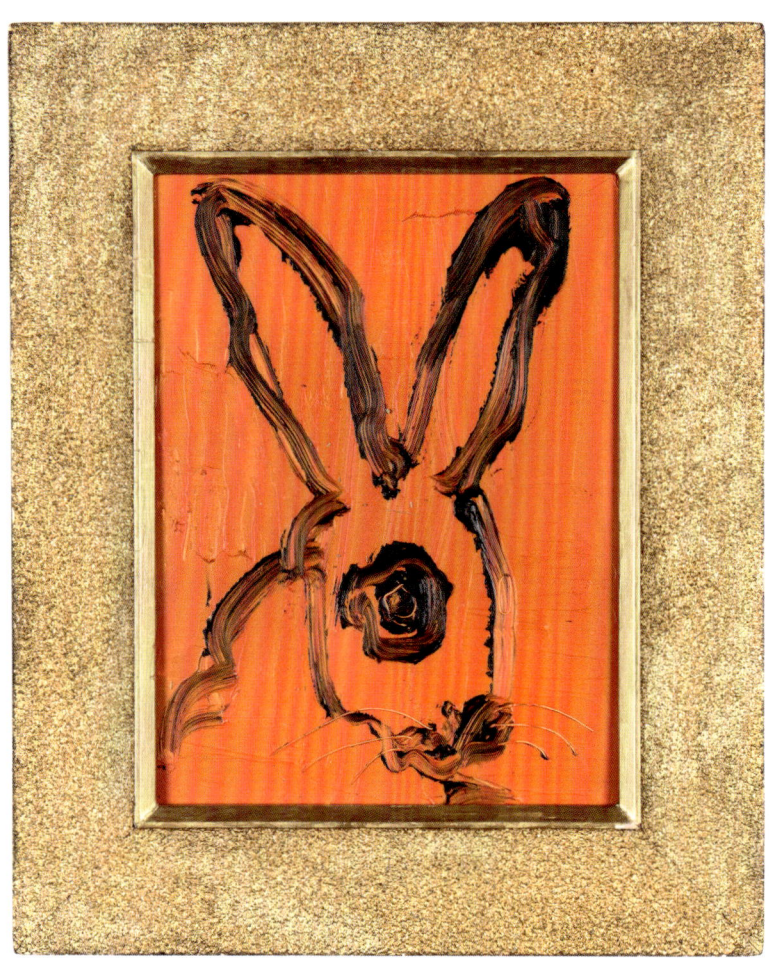

JARED
2012
OIL ON WOOD
14.5" X 11"

HARVEY
2012
OIL ON WOOD
20" X 16"

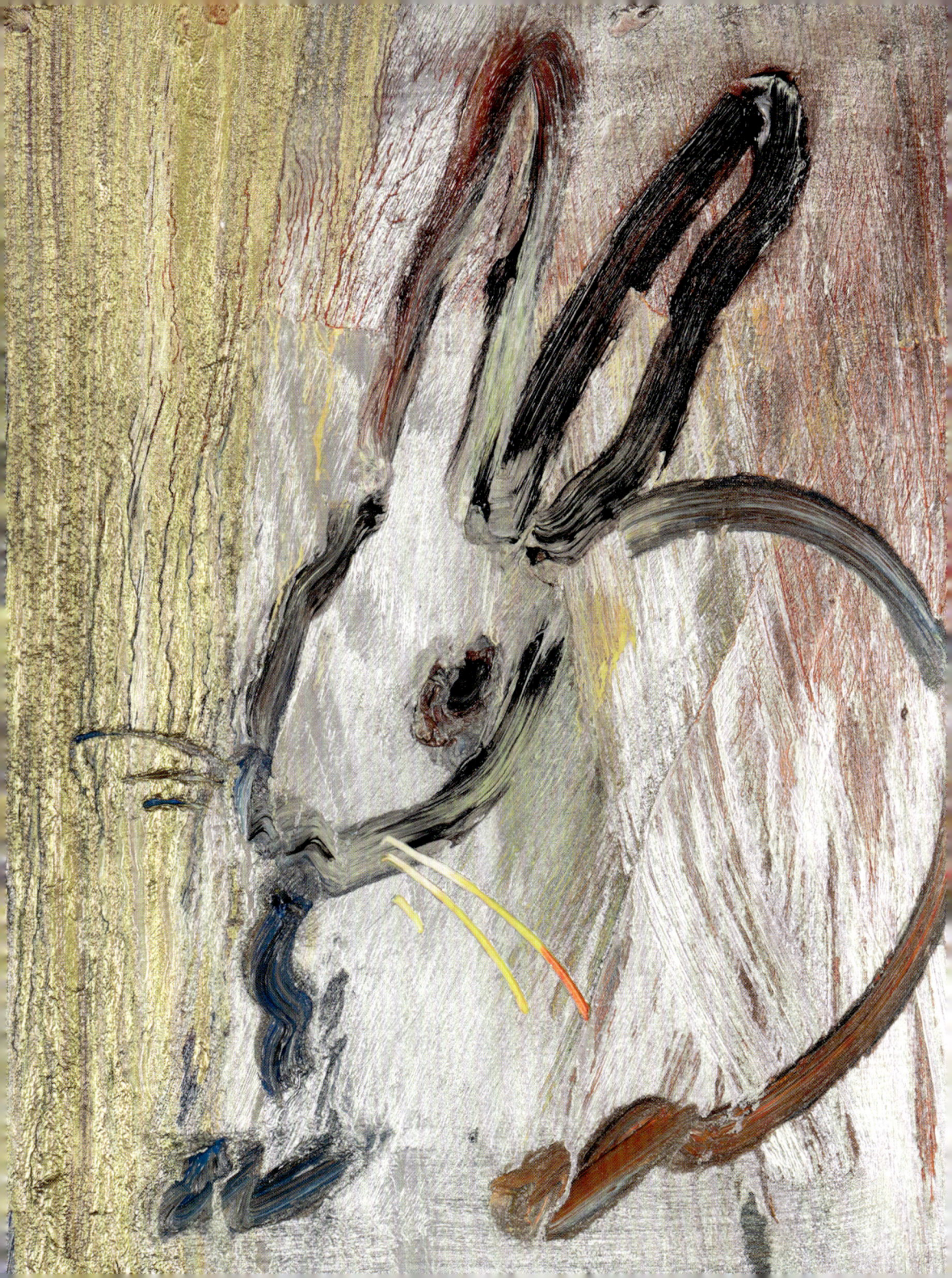

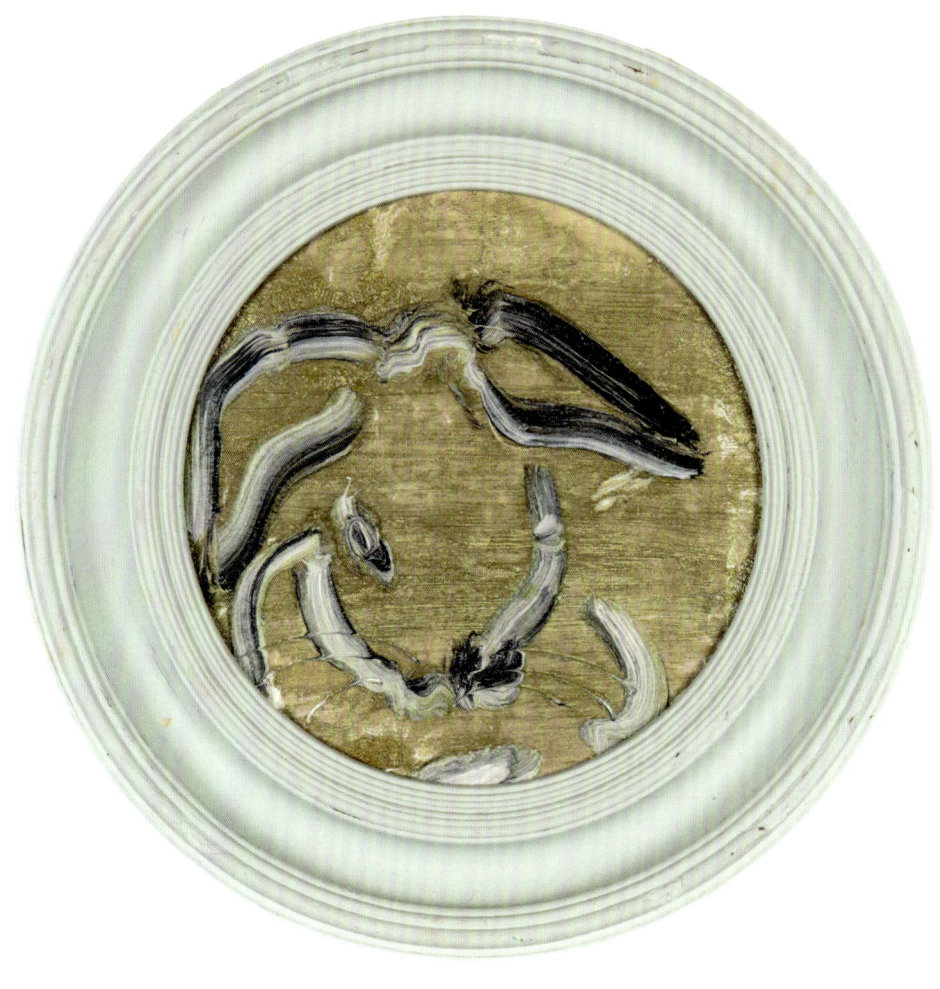

76

GOLDIE
2013
OIL ON WOOD
12" X 12"

DODGE
2013
OIL ON WOOD
32.75" X 22.5"

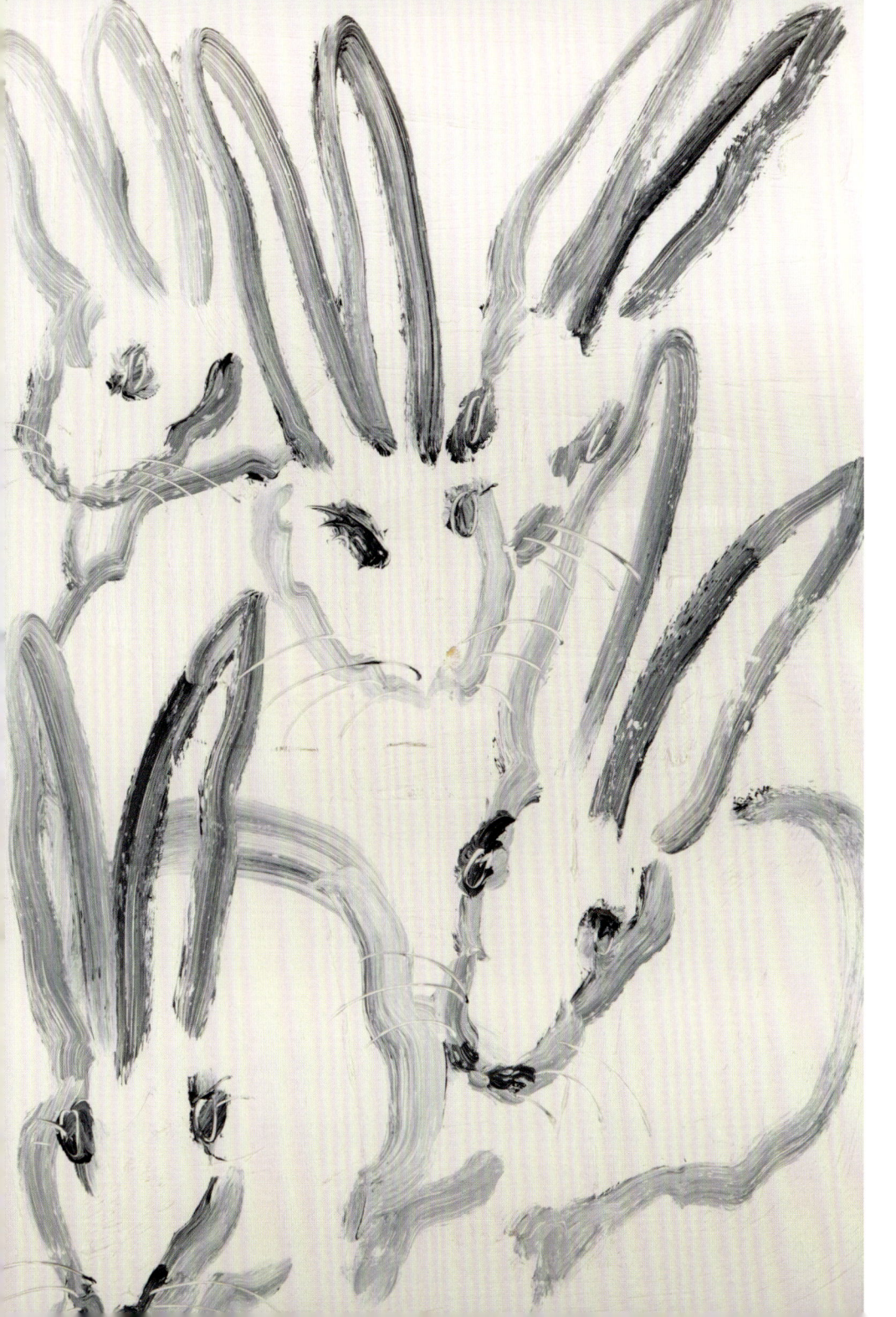

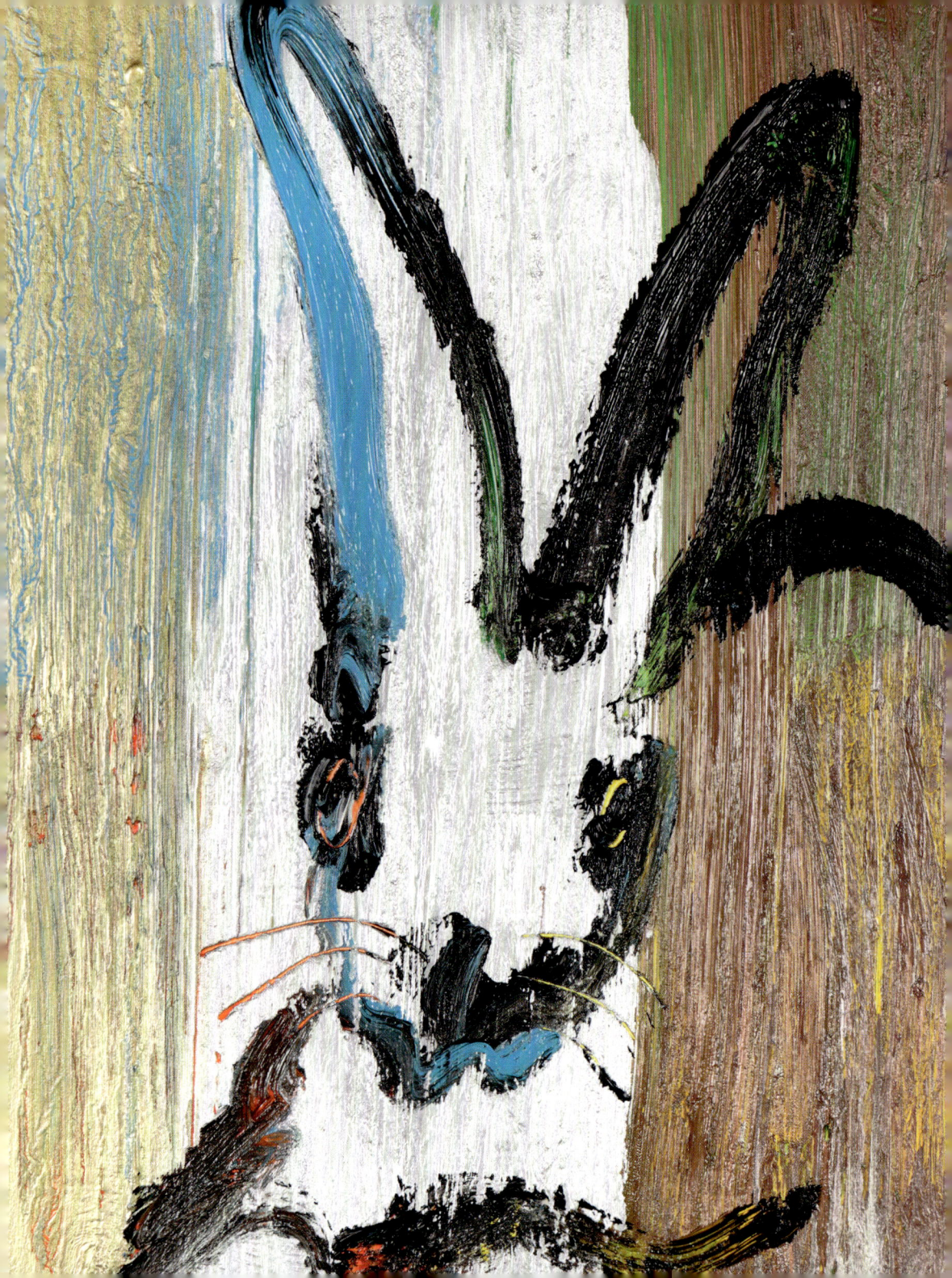

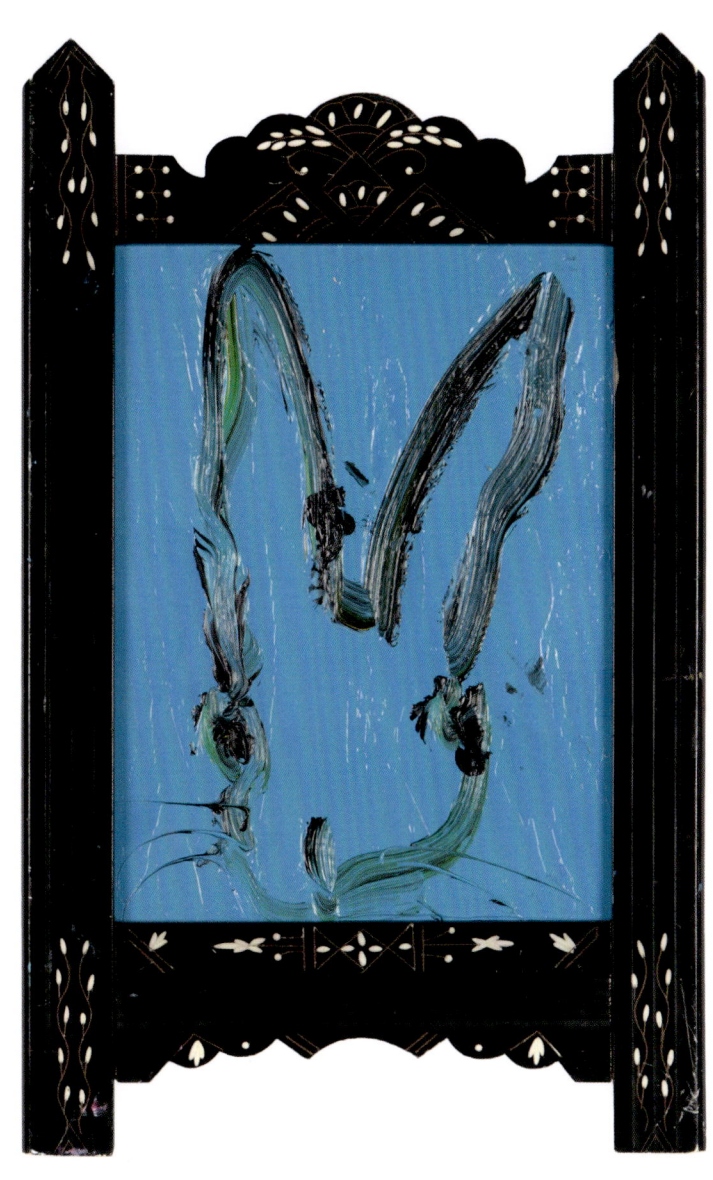

HEDDY
2013
OIL ON WOOD
10" x 8"

ARLEN
2012
OIL ON WOOD
8" x 6"

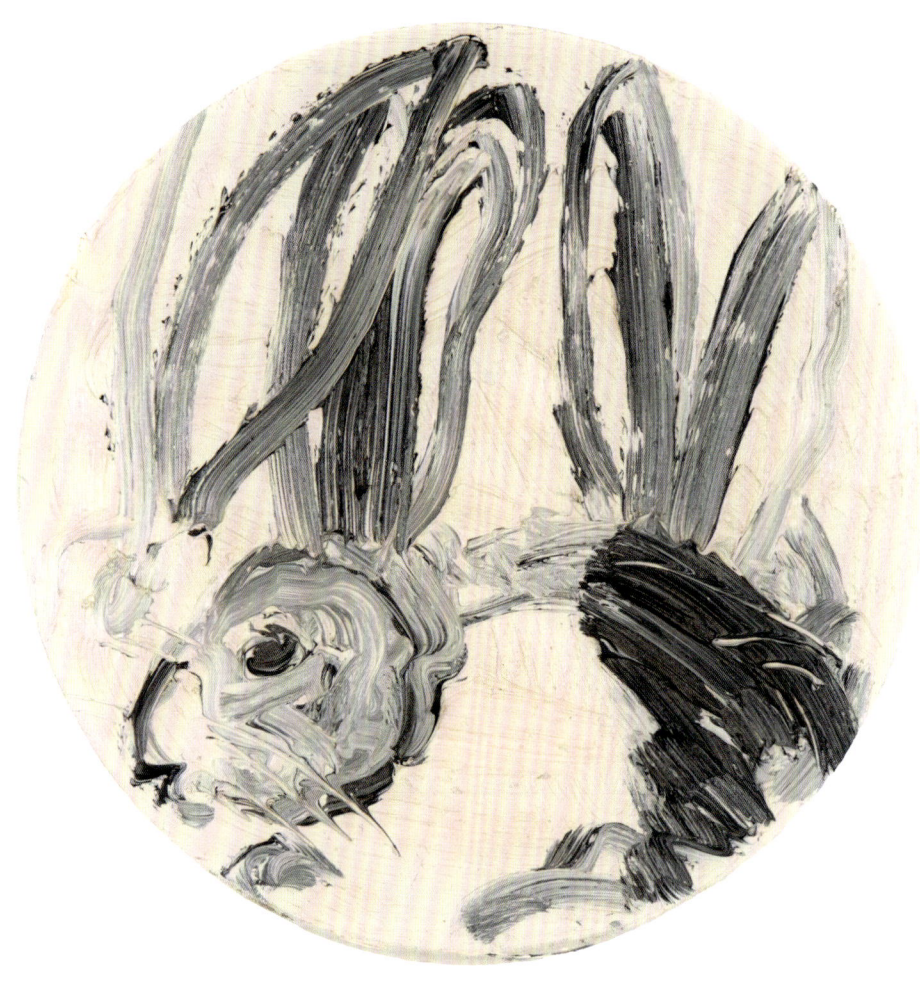

80

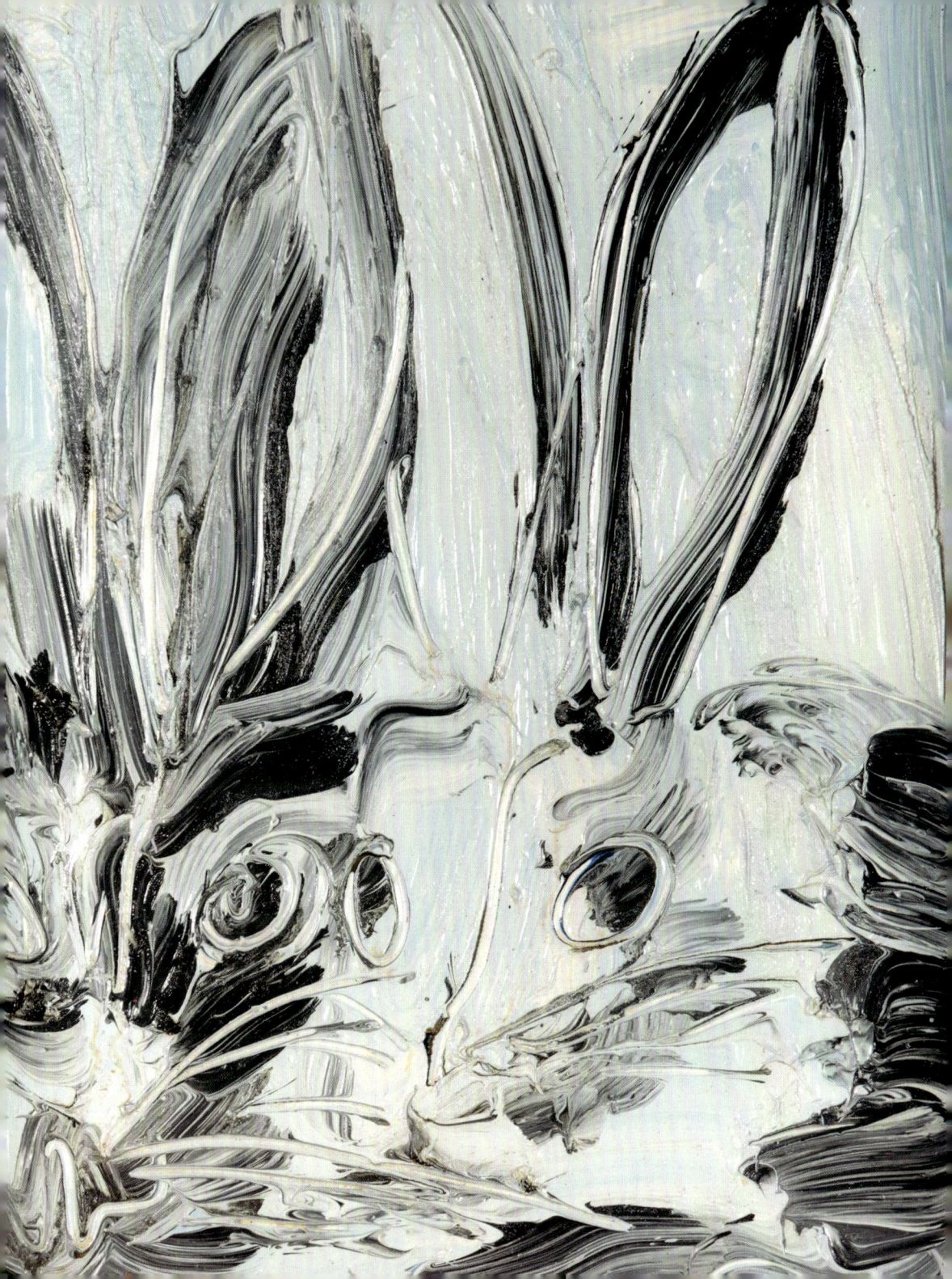

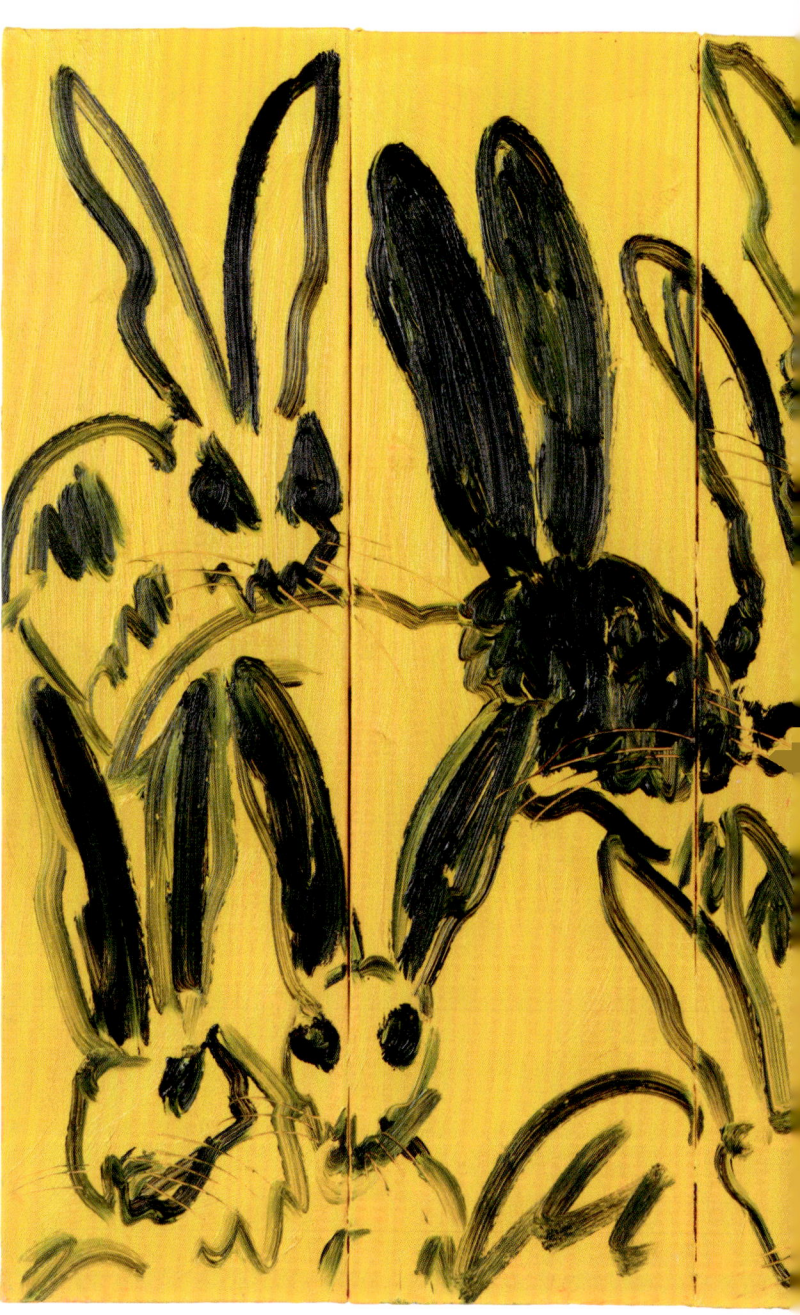

82

GENERAL ACTIVITIES
2004
OIL ON CANVAS
36" X 50"

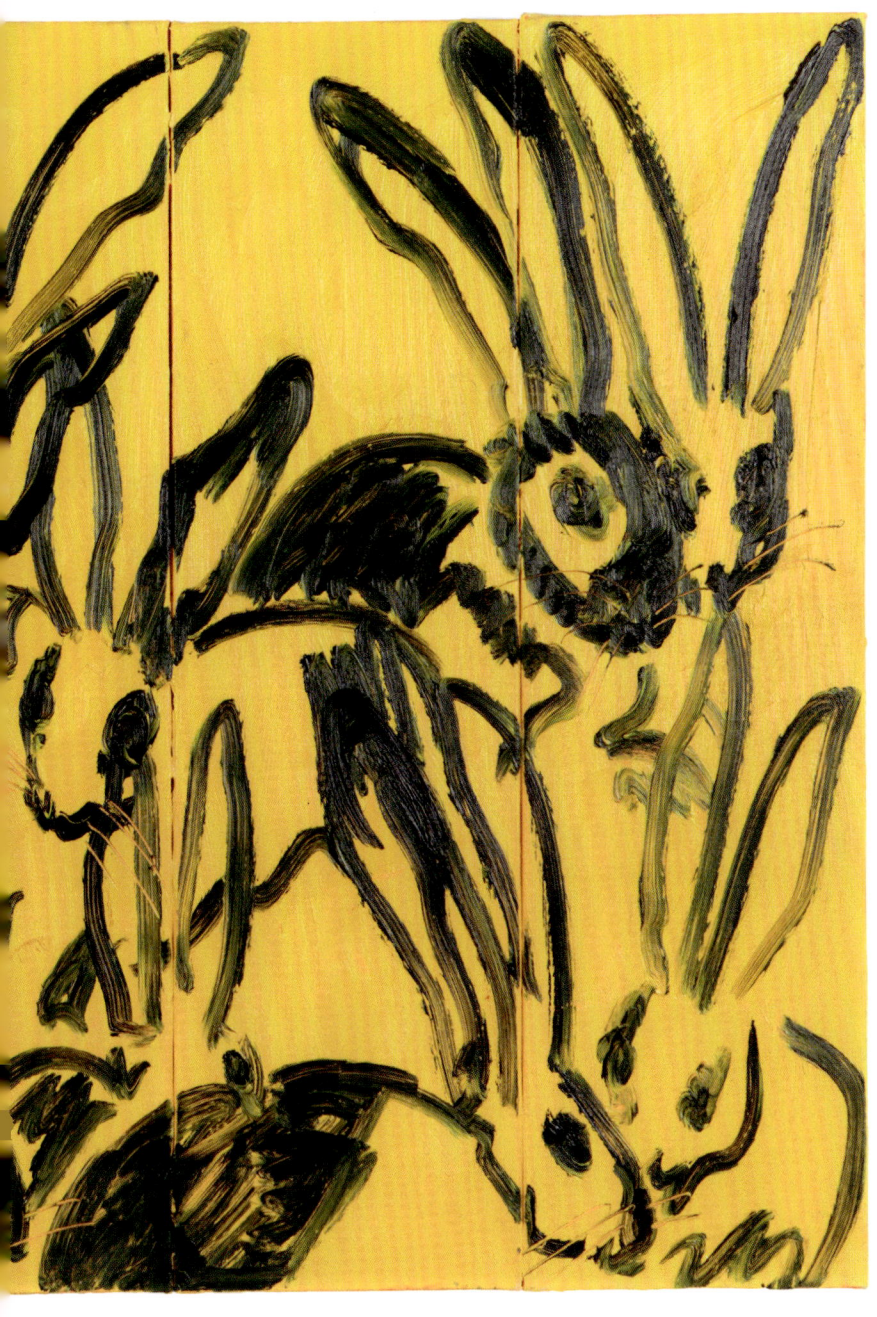

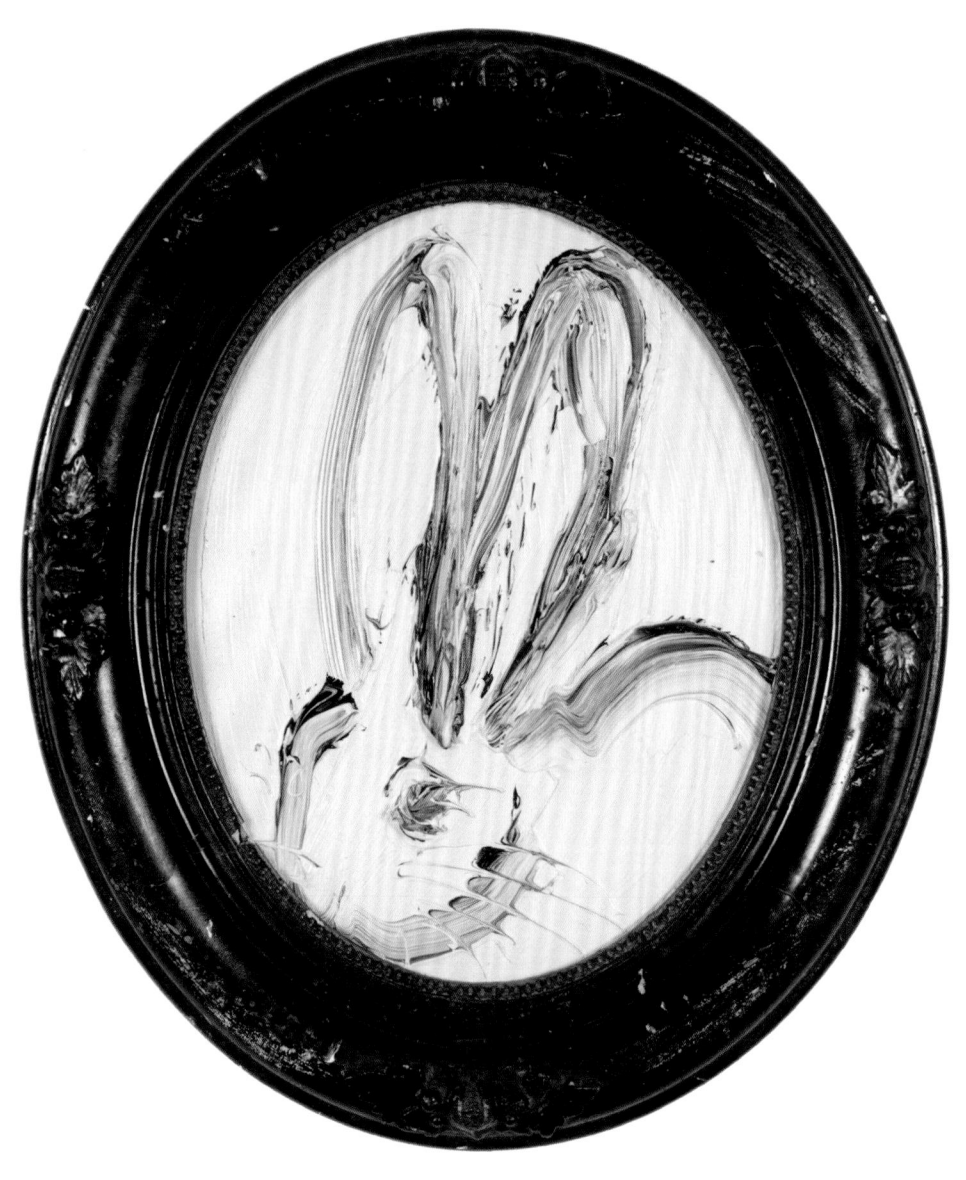

FLORENCE
2011
OIL ON WOOD
10" X 8"

FANNY
2013
OIL ON WOOD
30.5" X 24"

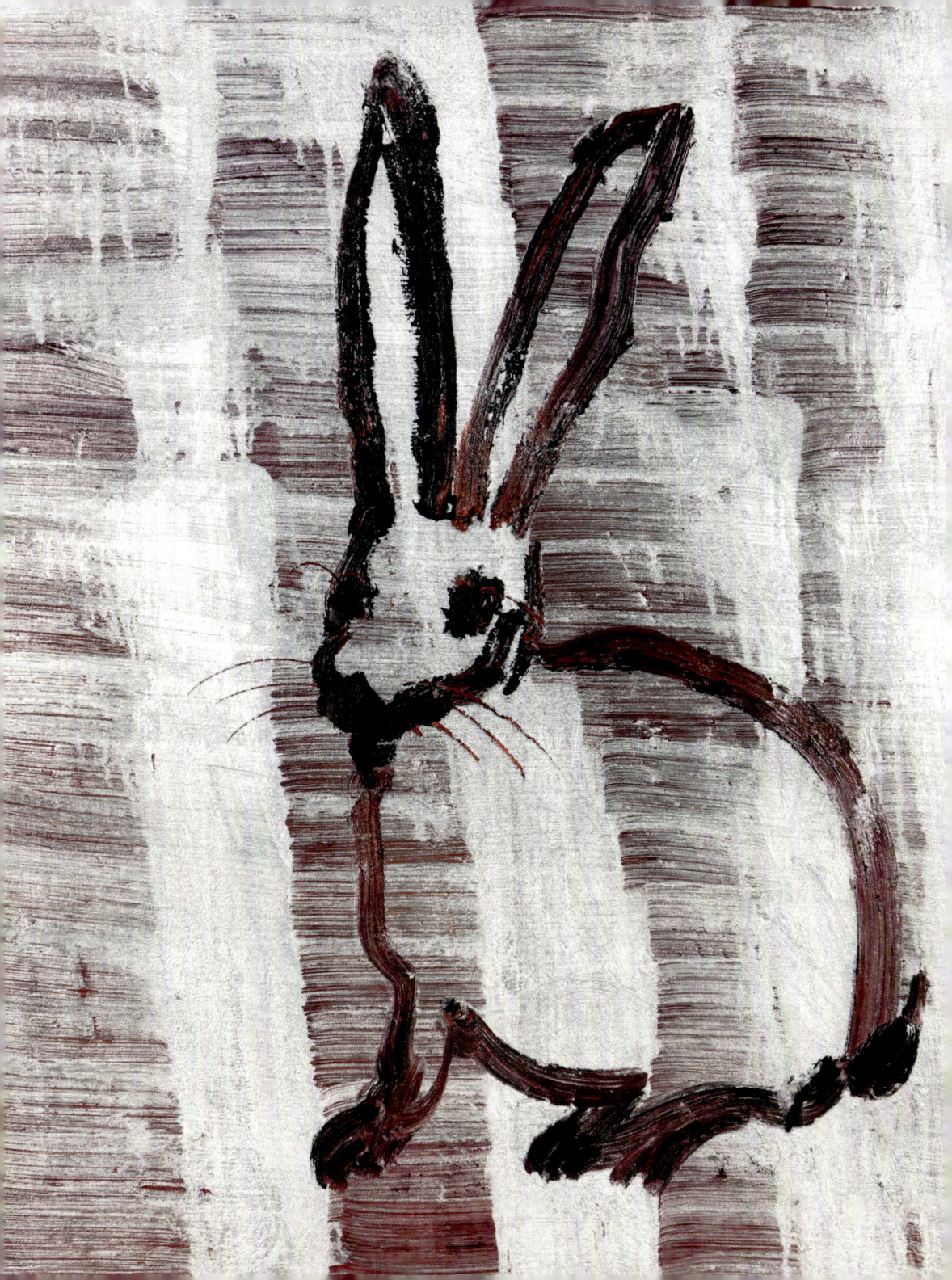

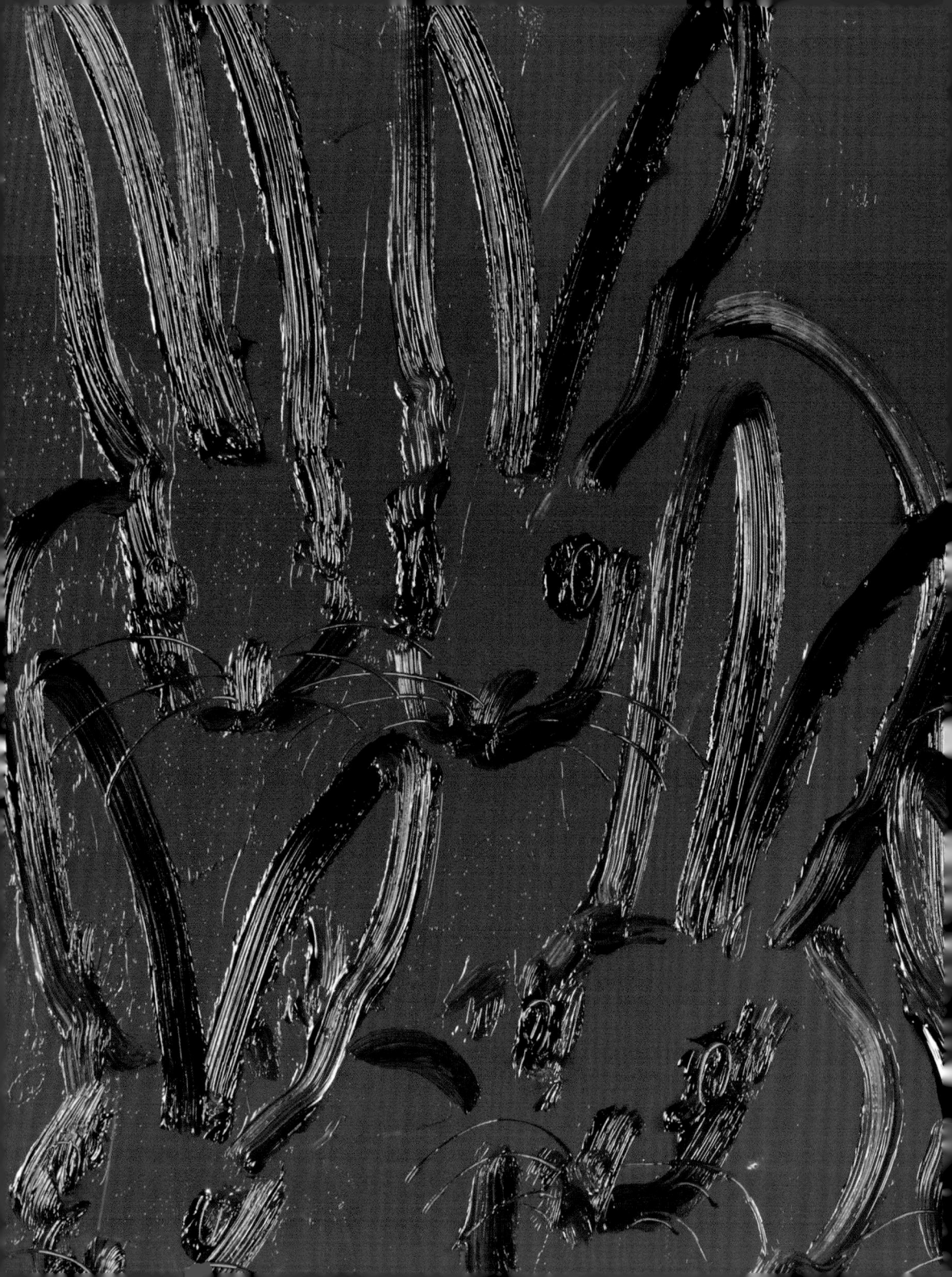

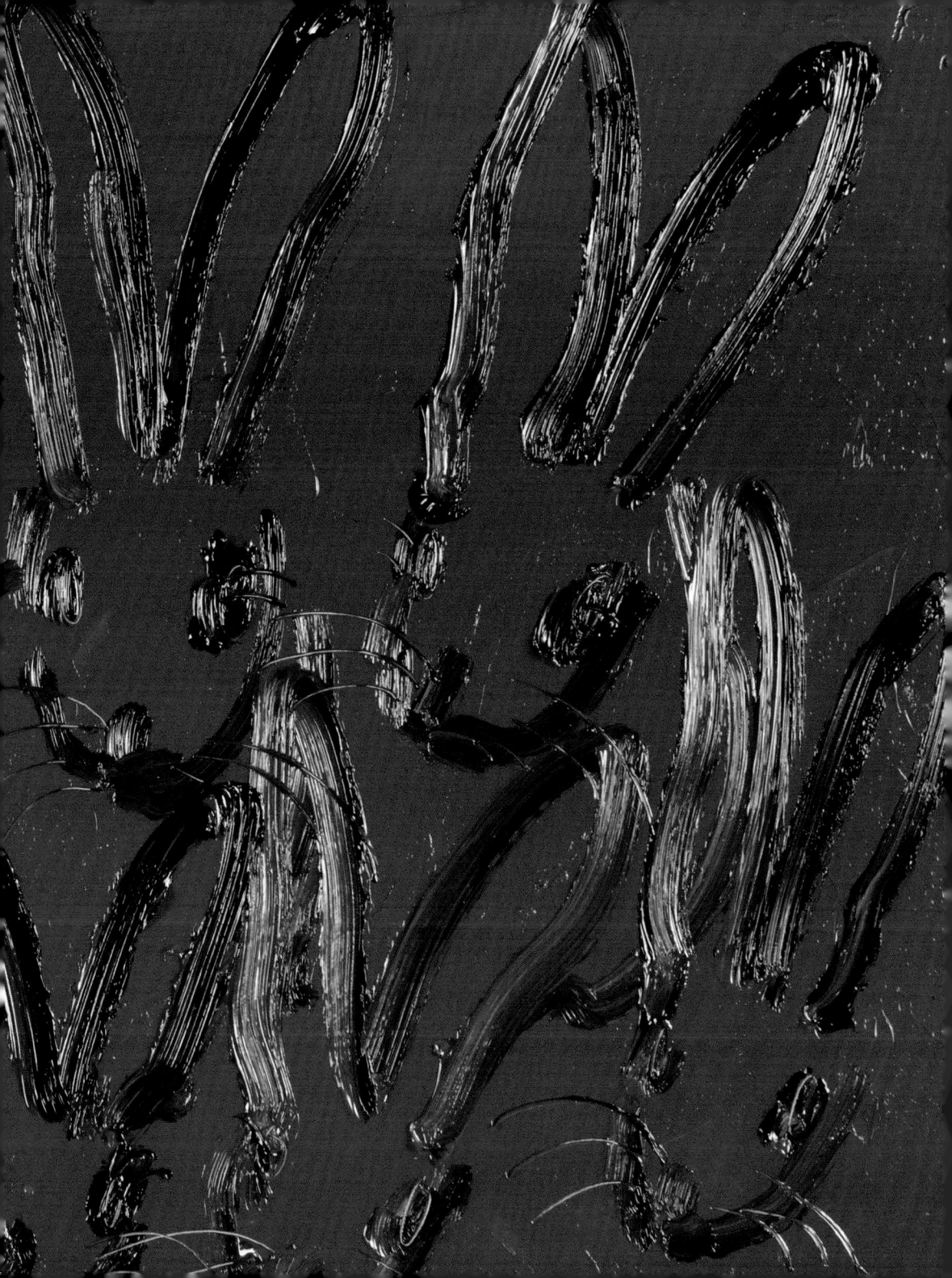

IF YOU KNOW SUZY
2013
OIL ON WOOD
24" X 20"

KINGSTON
2009
OIL ON WOOD
10" X 8"

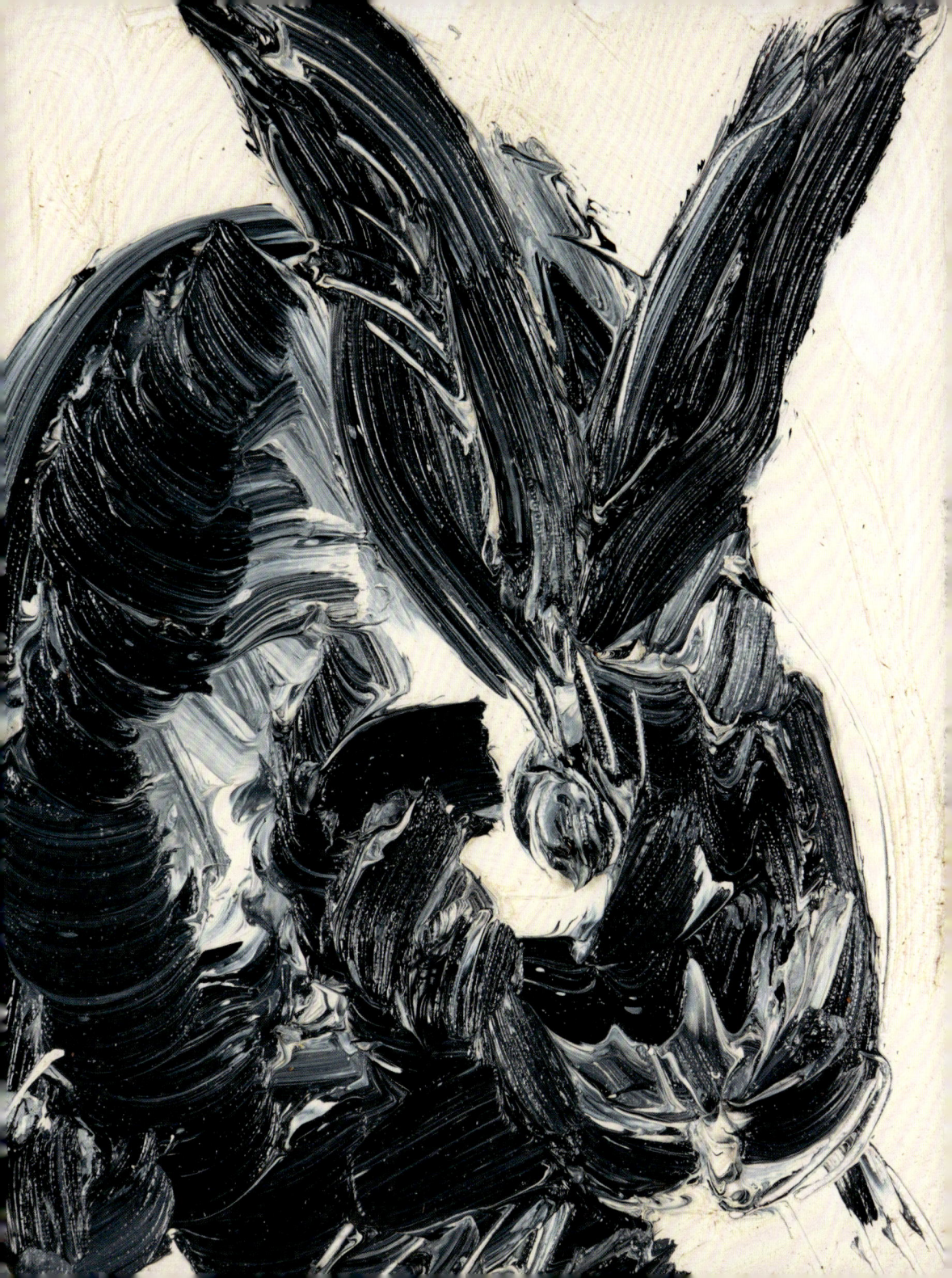

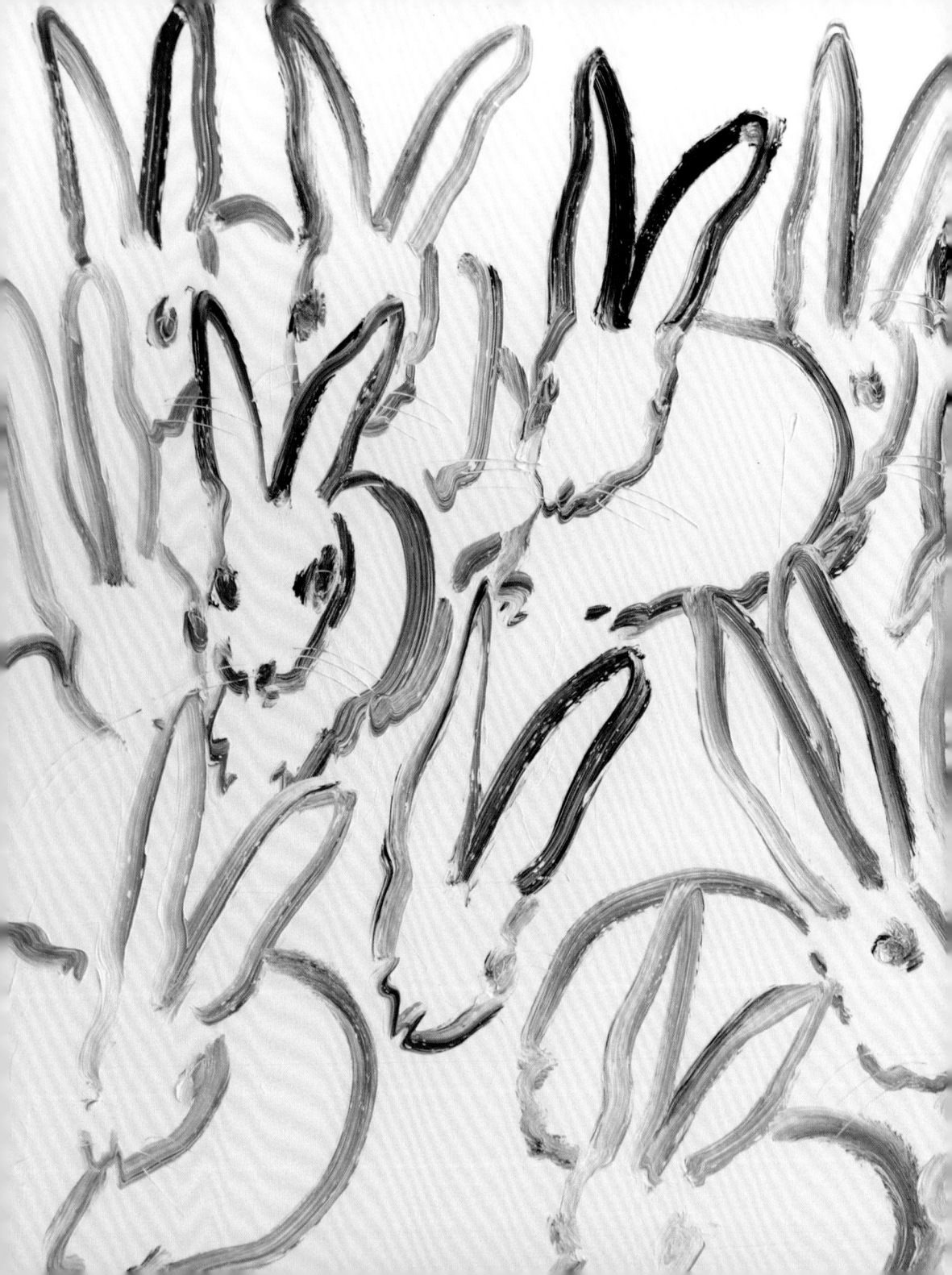

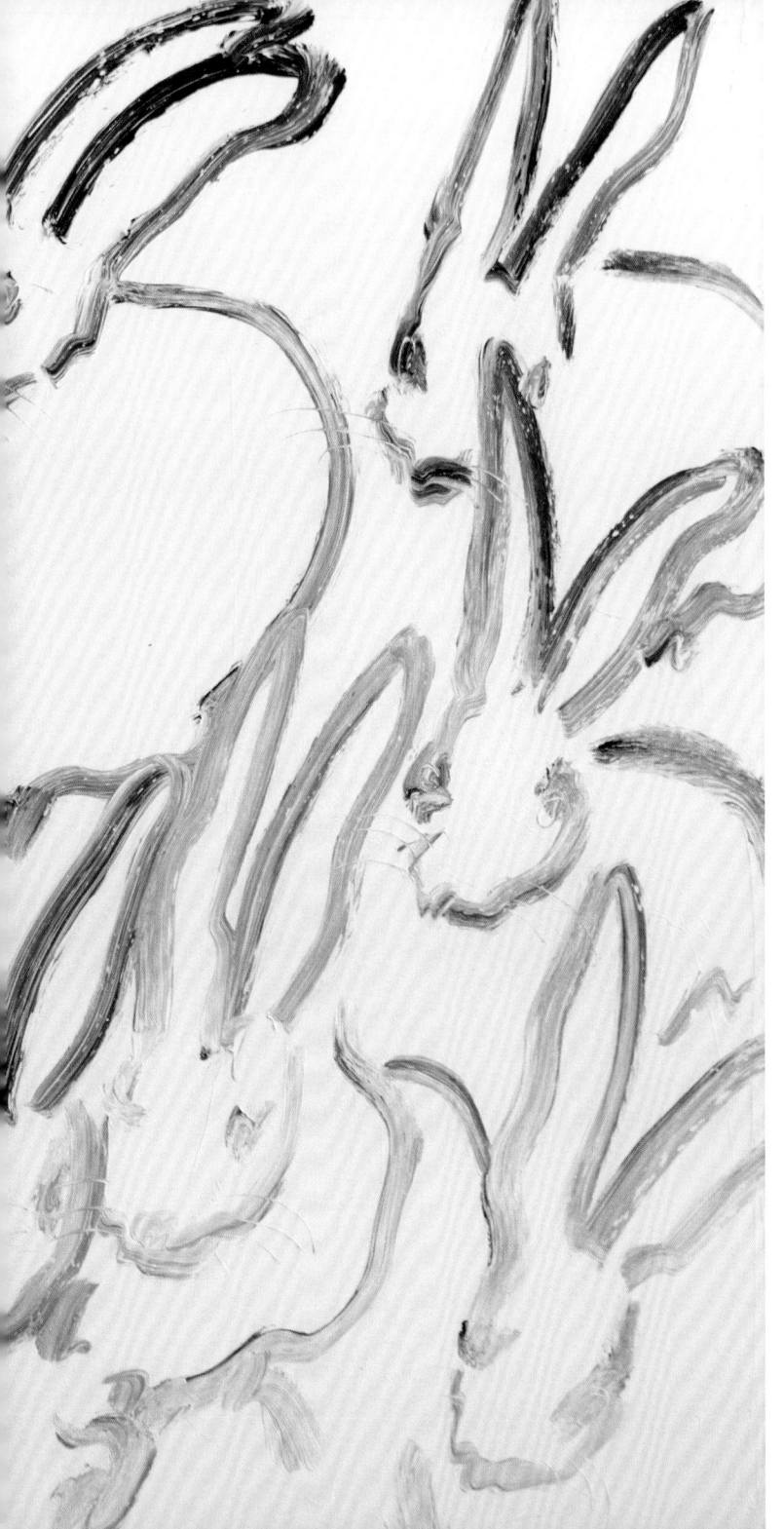

MULTIPLY
2012
OIL ON WOOD
43.5" X 60"

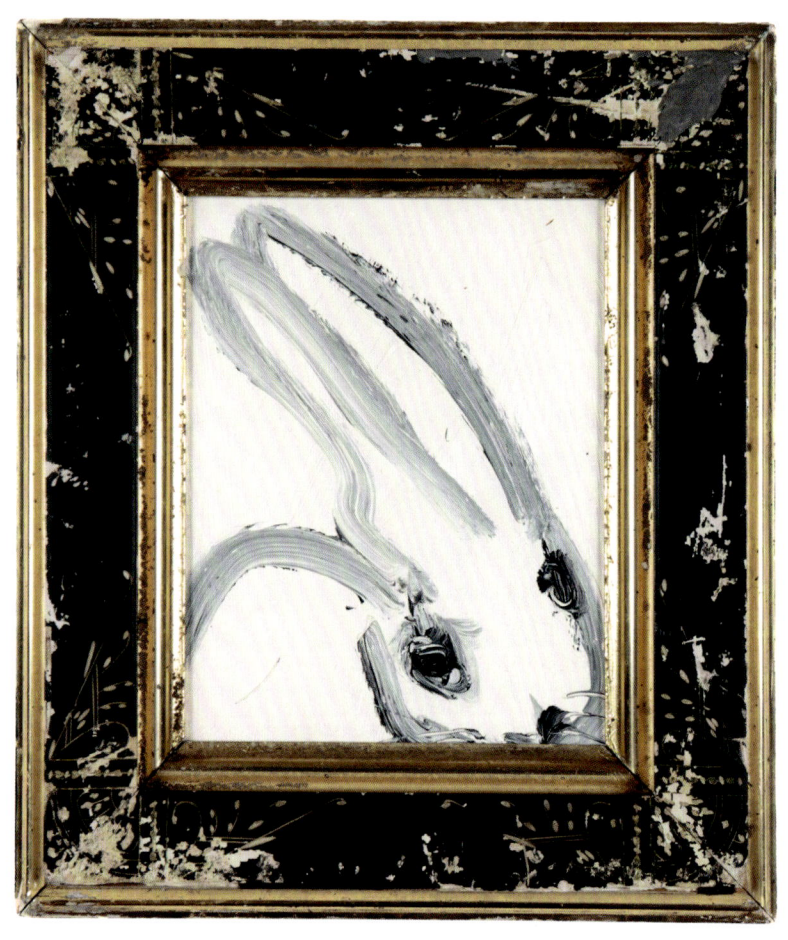

ROCKELL
2013
OIL ON WOOD
10" X 8"

RANDY
2013
OIL ON WOOD
10" X 8"

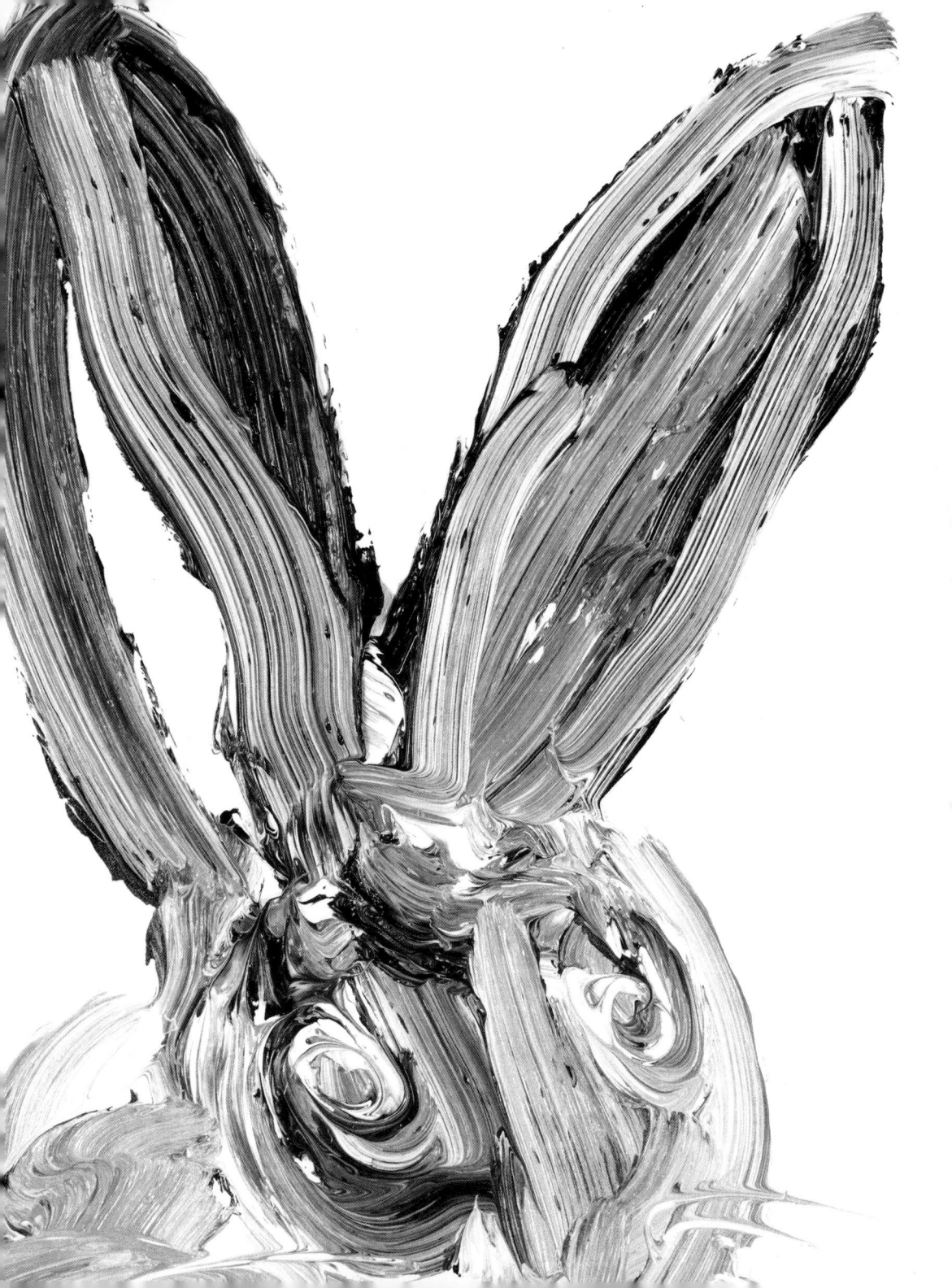

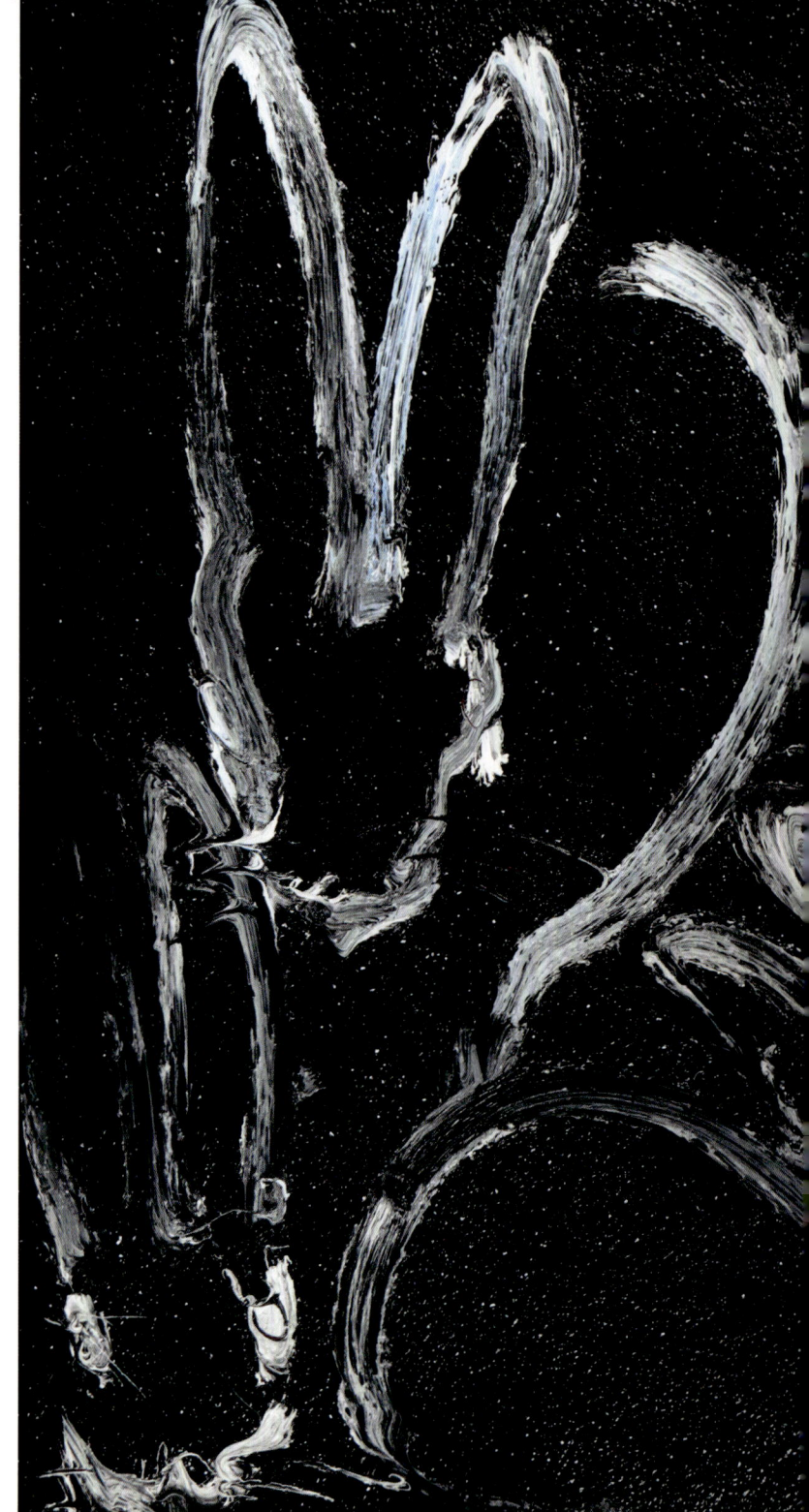

94

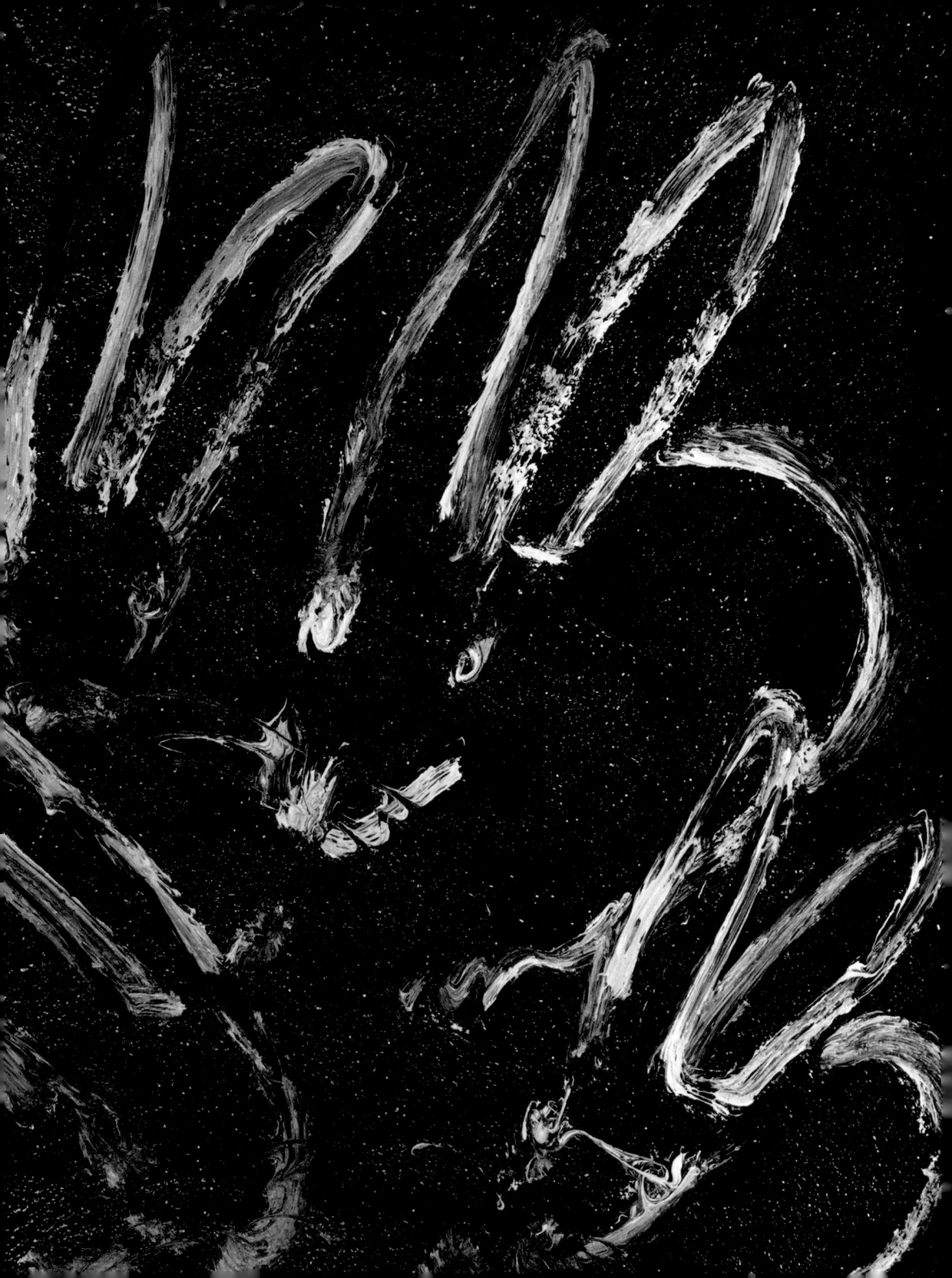

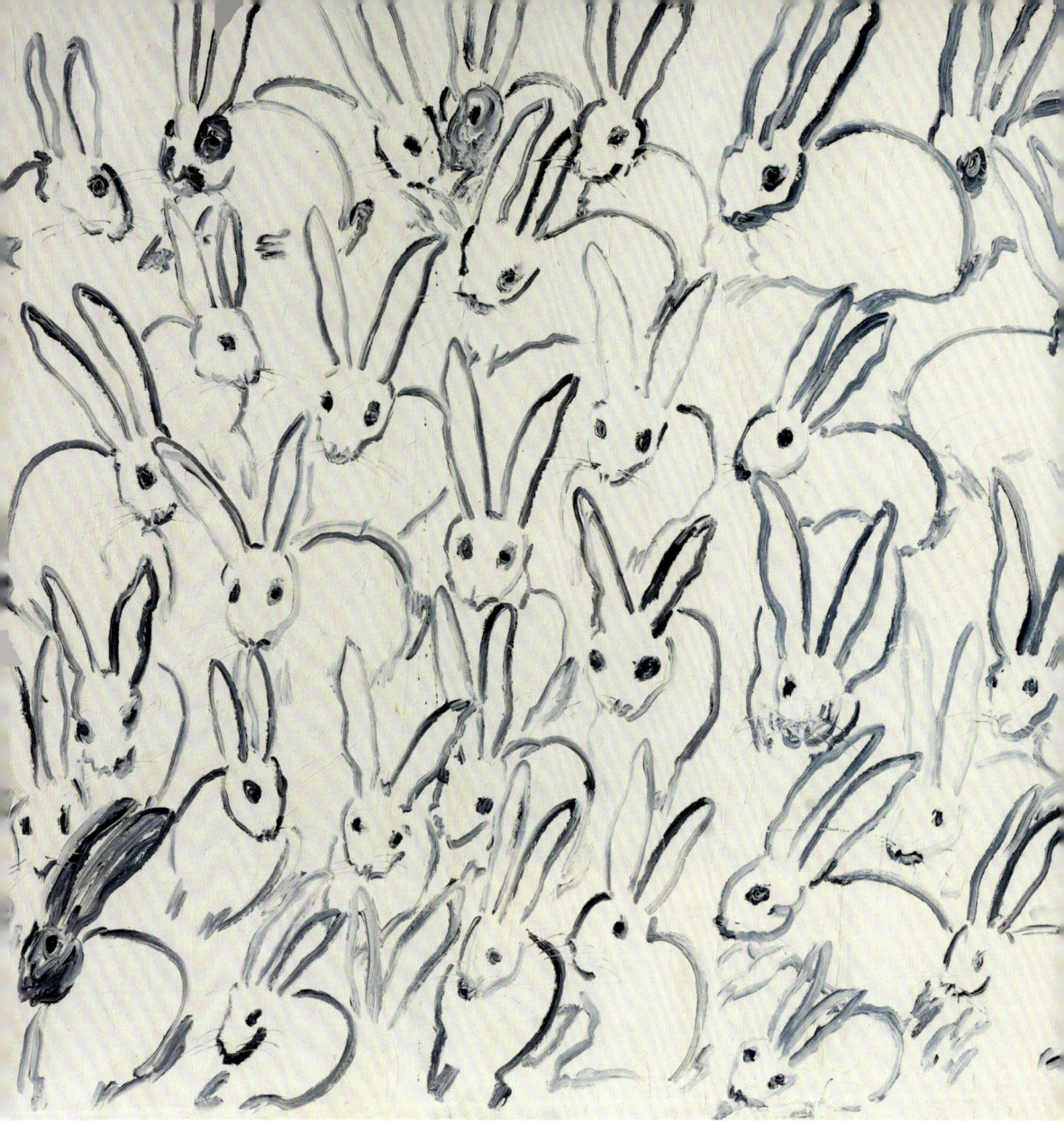

HUTCH
2009
OIL ON CANVAS
88" x 144"

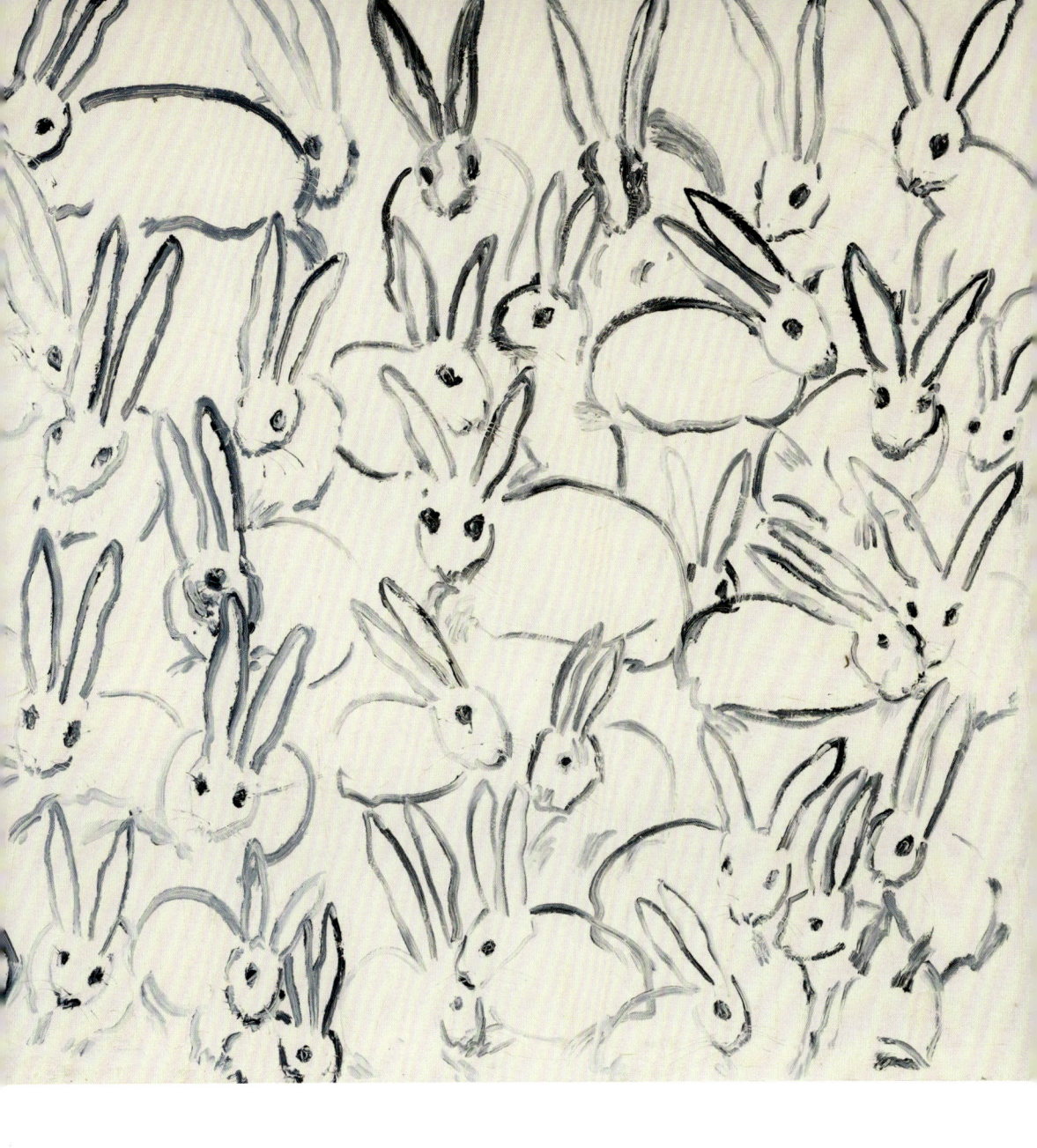

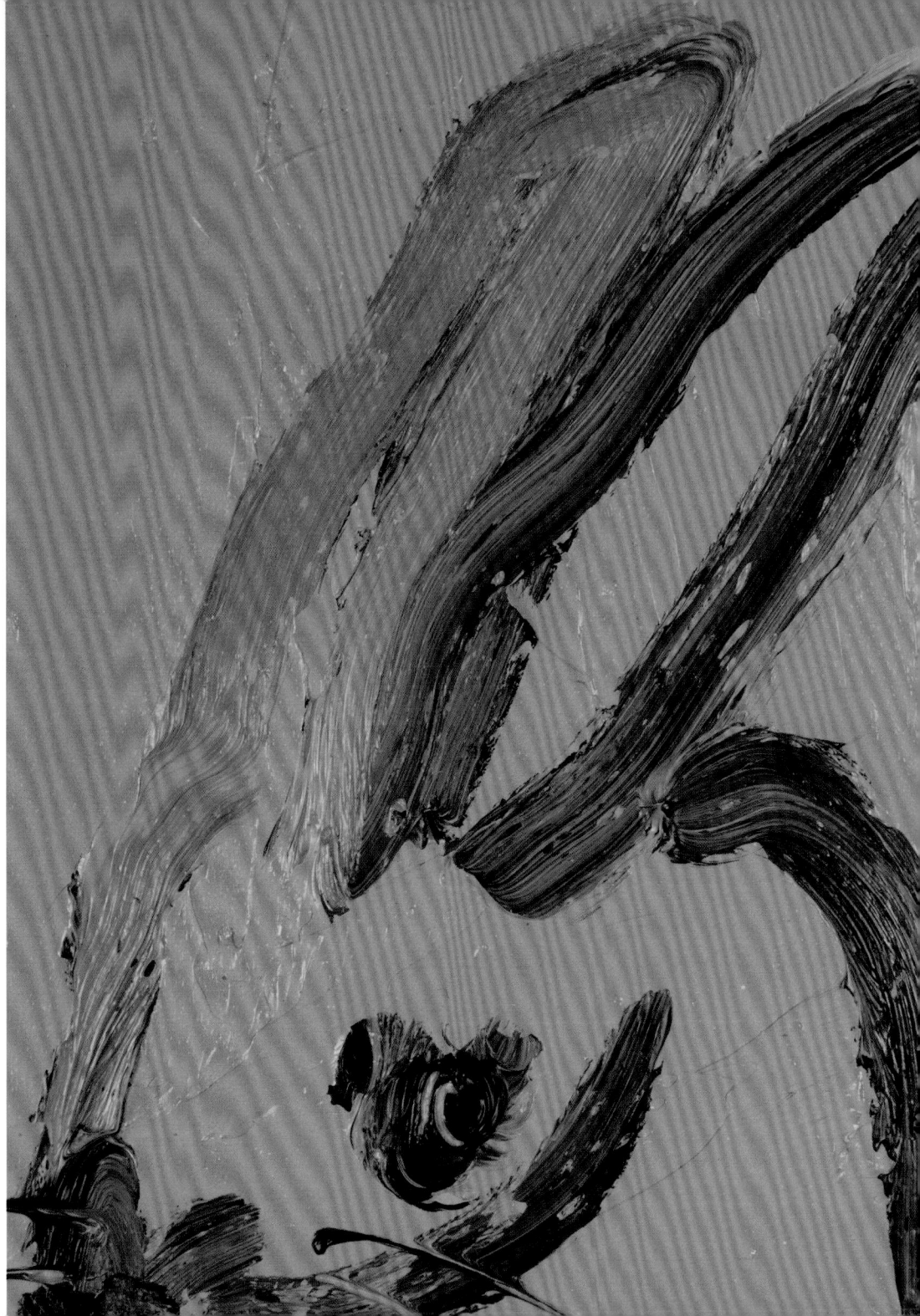

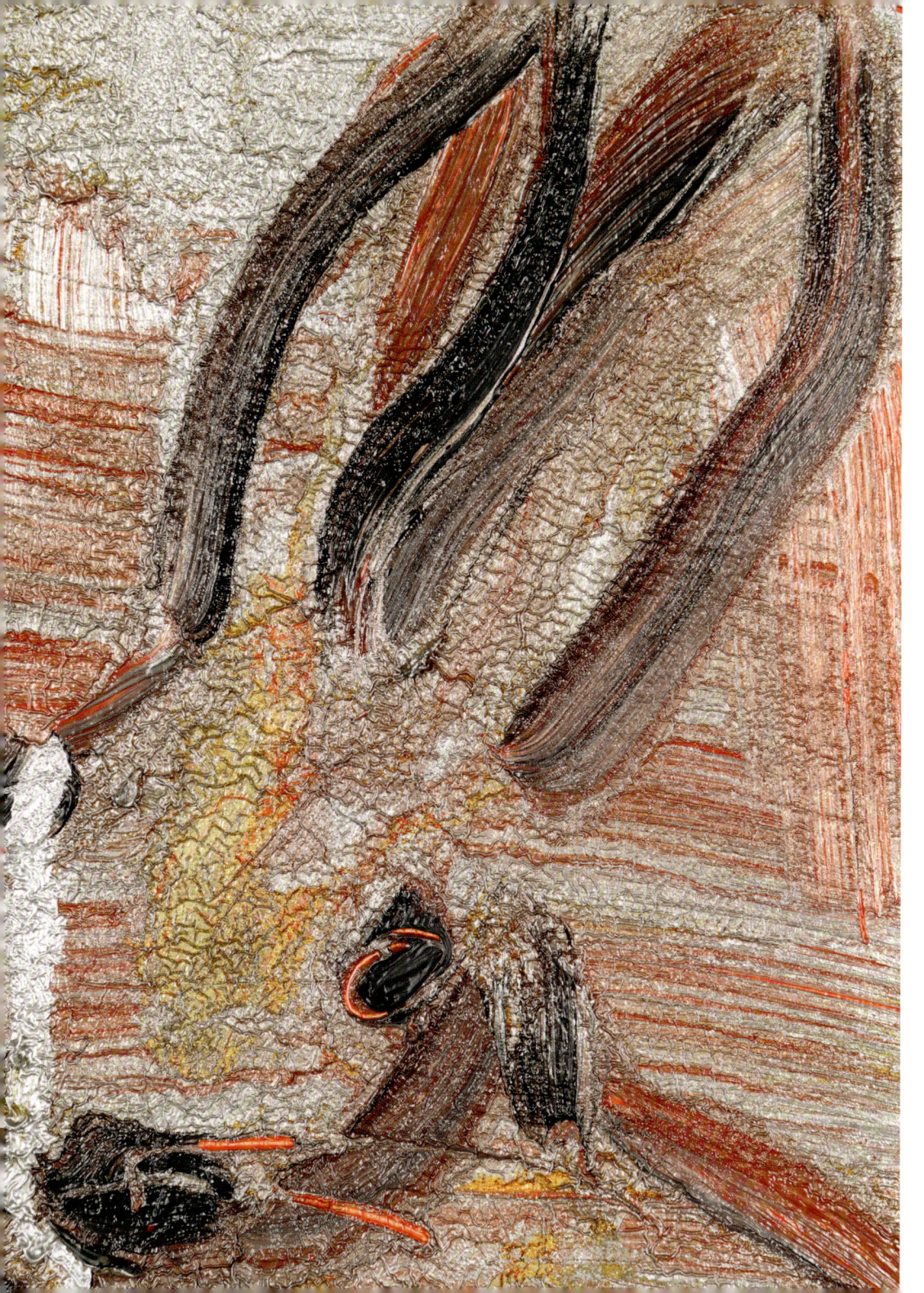

CONFEDERATE ROSE
2013
OIL ON WOOD
10" X 8"

CHUCK
2012
OIL ON WOOD
10" X 8"

100

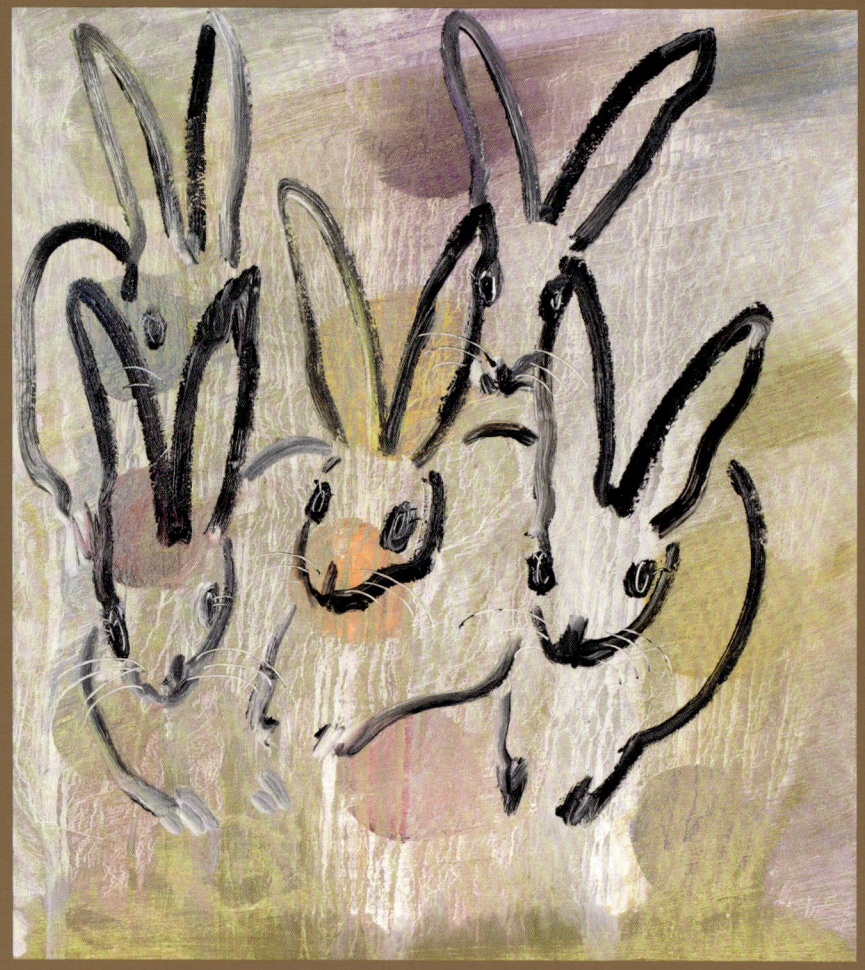

CHINENSIS
2013
OIL ON WOOD
37" X 34"

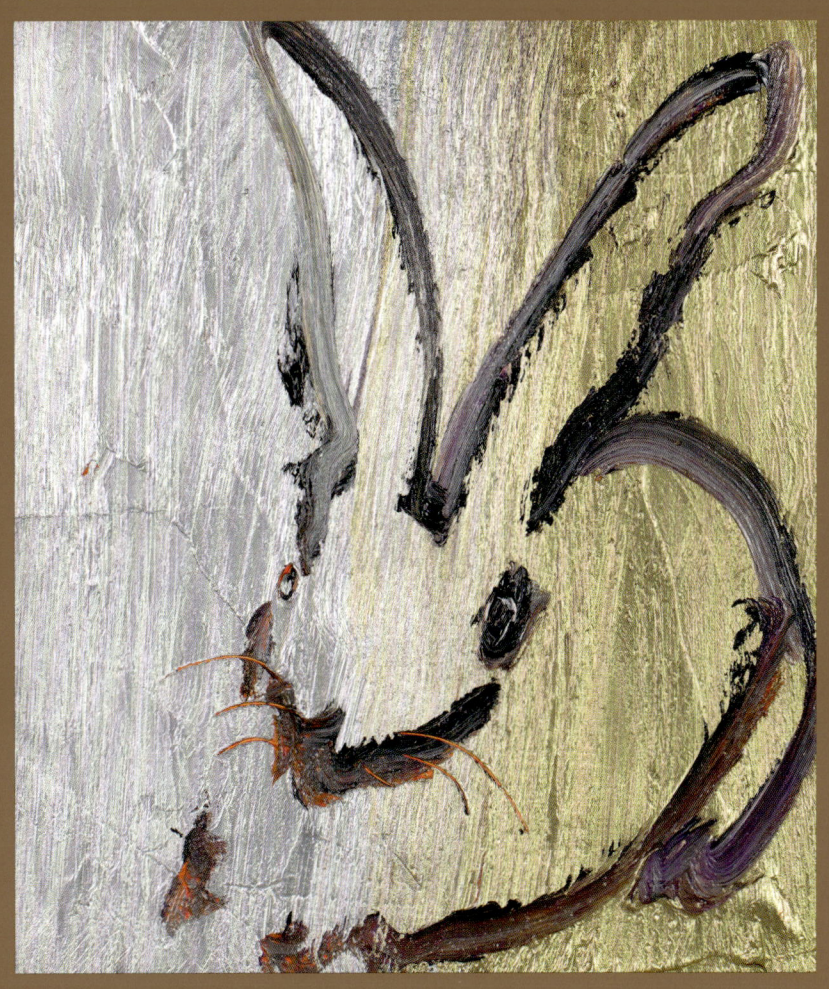

Two Metals
2013
OIL ON WOOD
18" X 14"

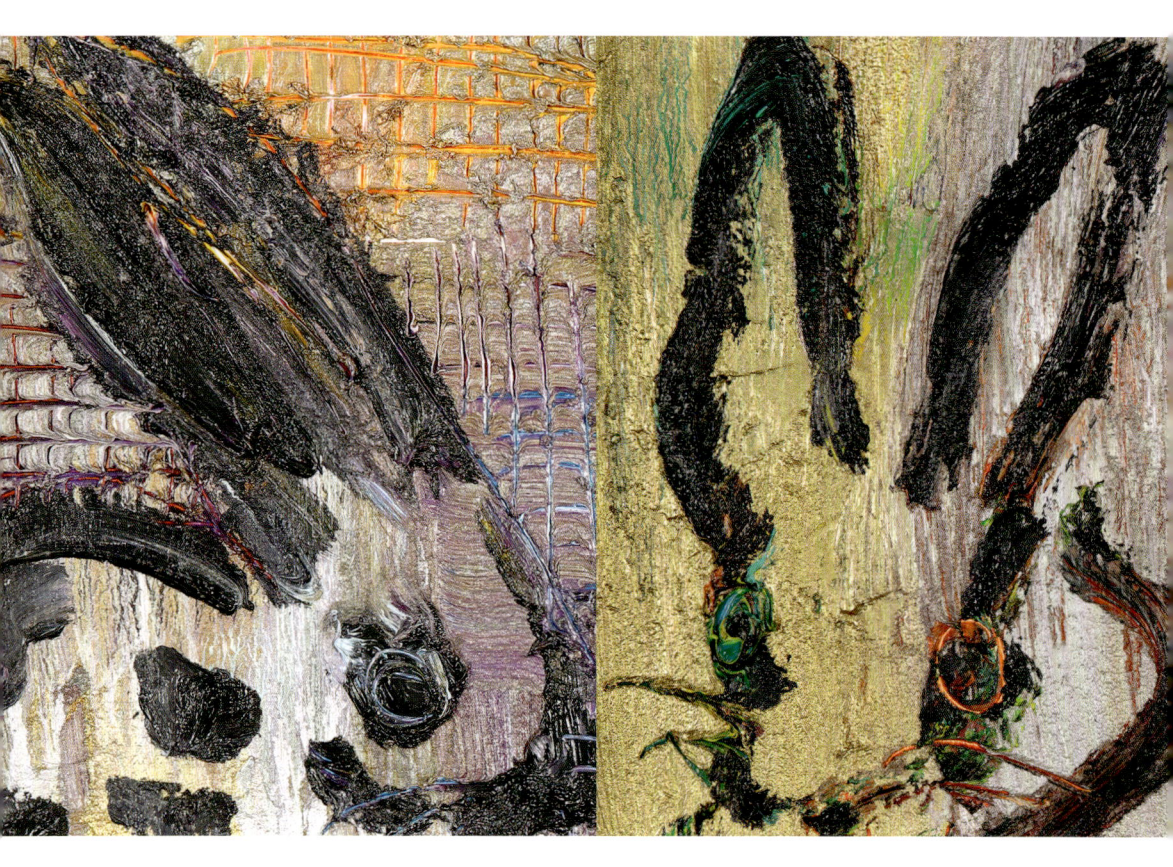

Vincent Spotted
2013
OIL ON WOOD
10" x 8"

Mark
2013
OIL ON WOOD
10" x 8"

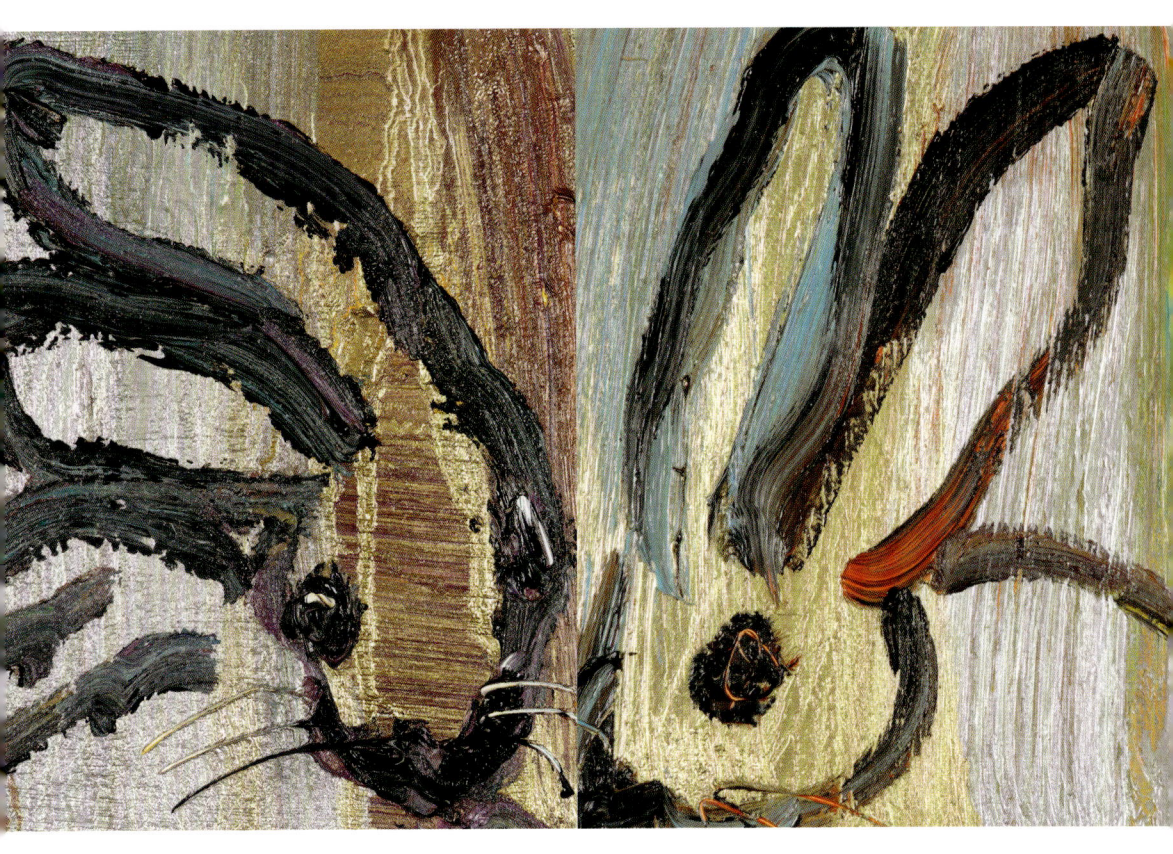

BANANA
2013
OIL ON WOOD
10" x 8"

BLUE STREAK
2013
OIL ON WOOD
12" x 10"

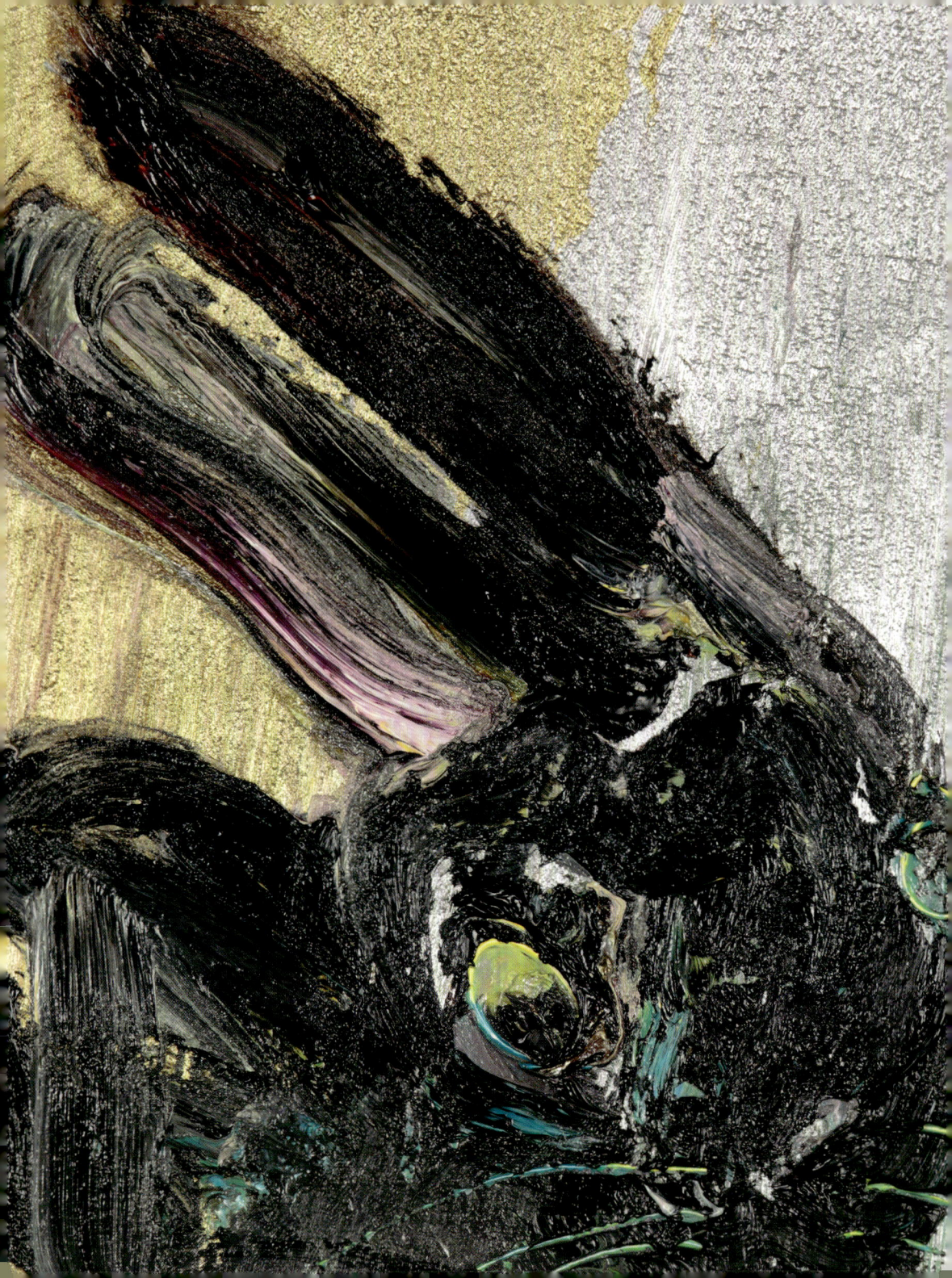

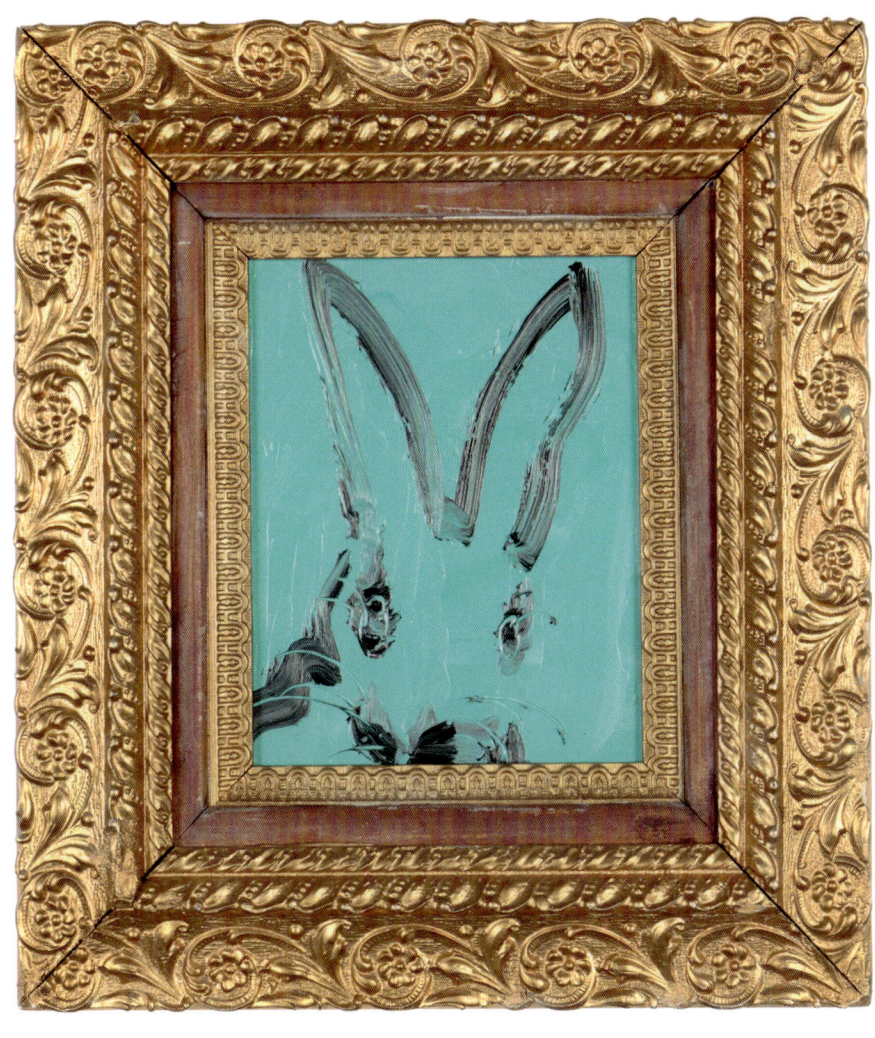

SAM
2013
OIL ON WOOD
10″ X 8″

ULRIEHT
2012
OIL ON WOOD
10″ X 8″

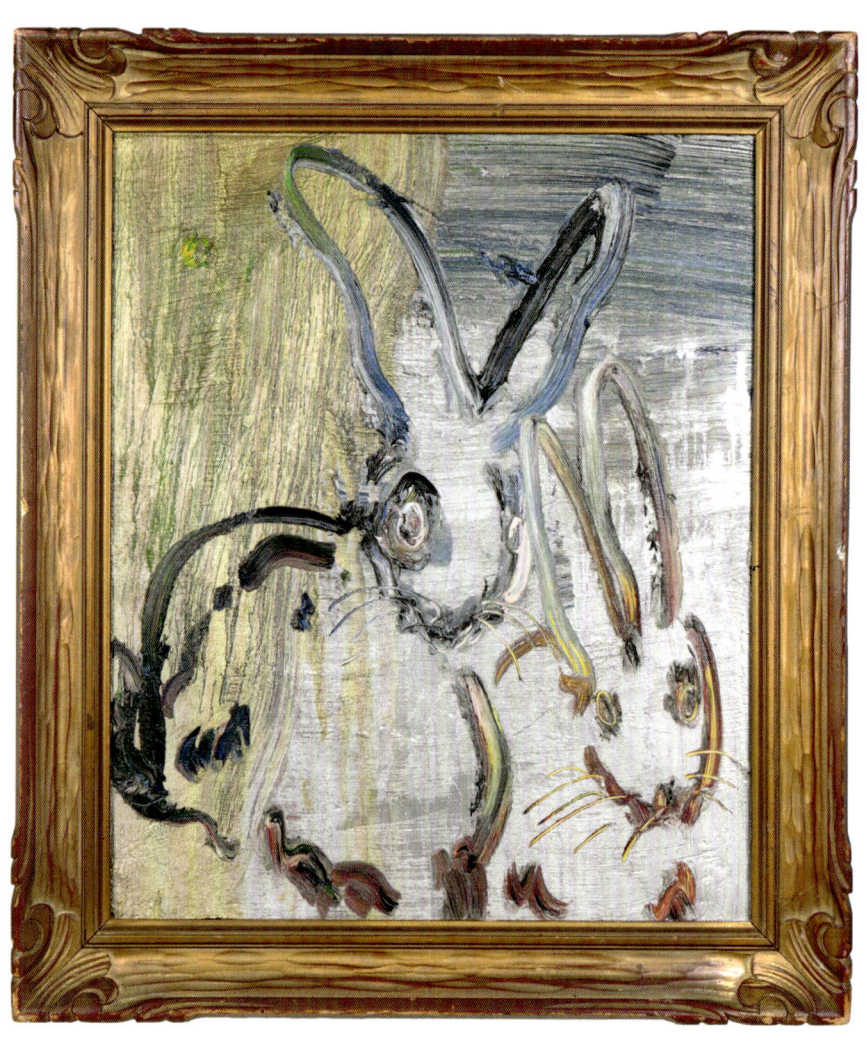

COUPLE
2013
OIL ON WOOD AND METAL
24" X 20"

SANDY
2013
OIL ON WOOD
10" X 8"

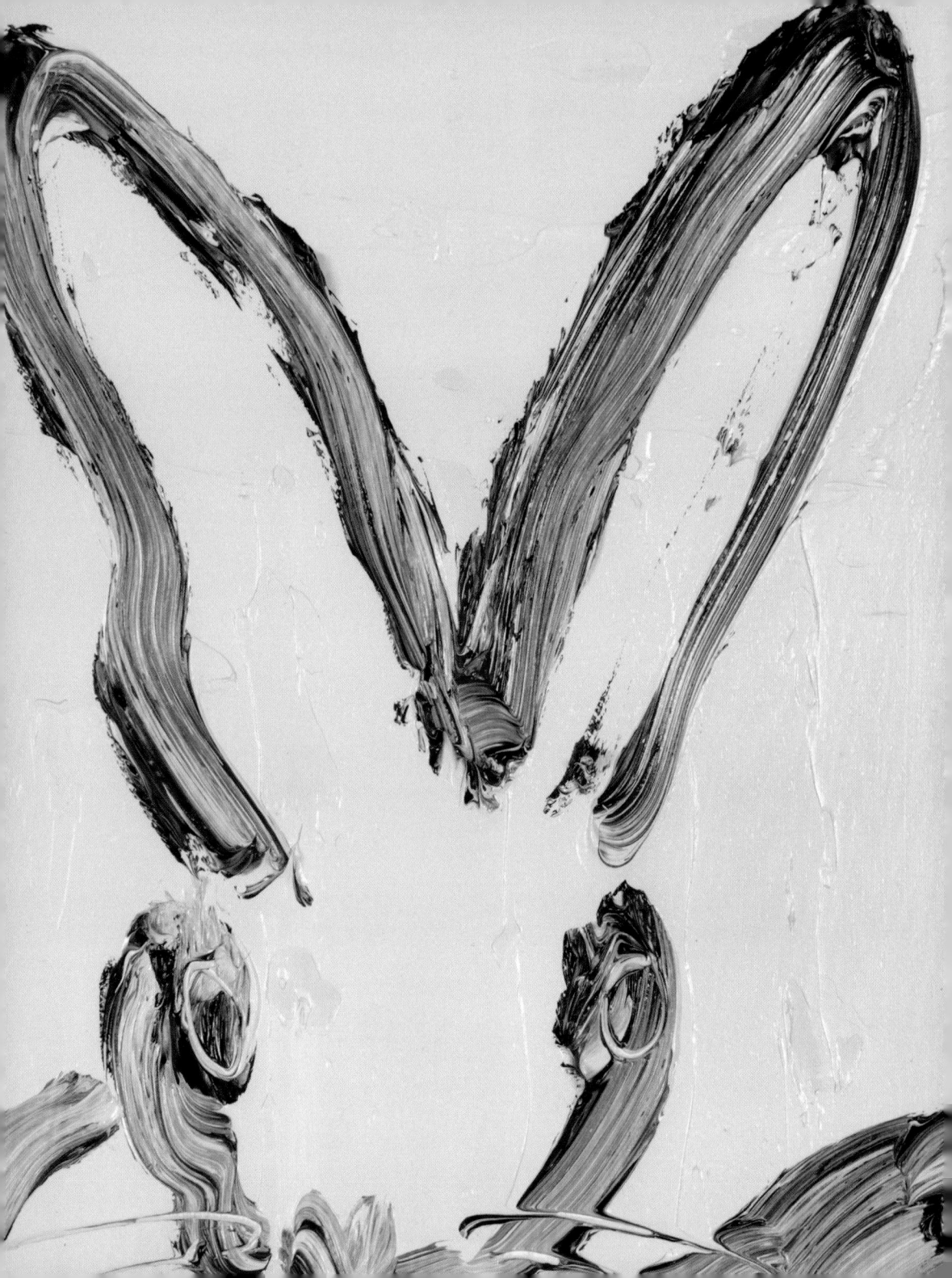

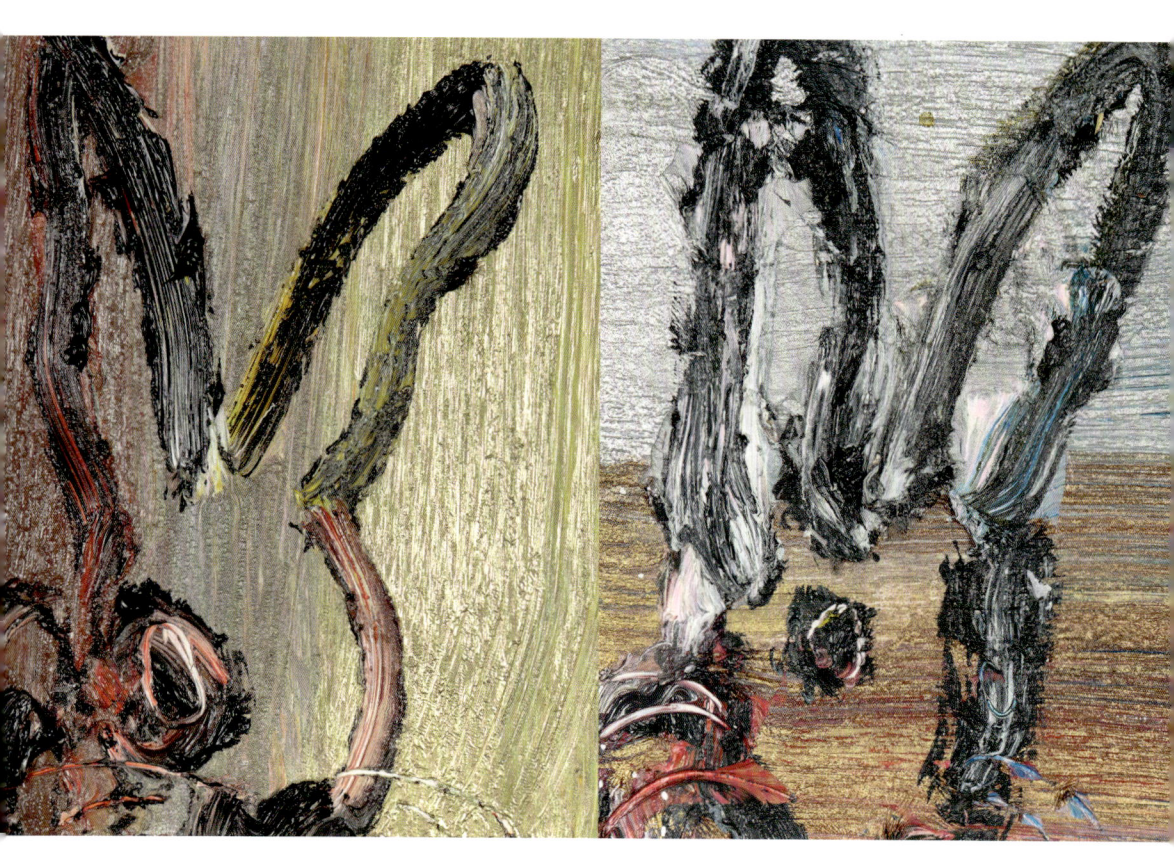

MAHOGANY
2013
OIL ON WOOD
10" X 8"

SCOTT
2012
OIL ON WOOD
10" X 8"

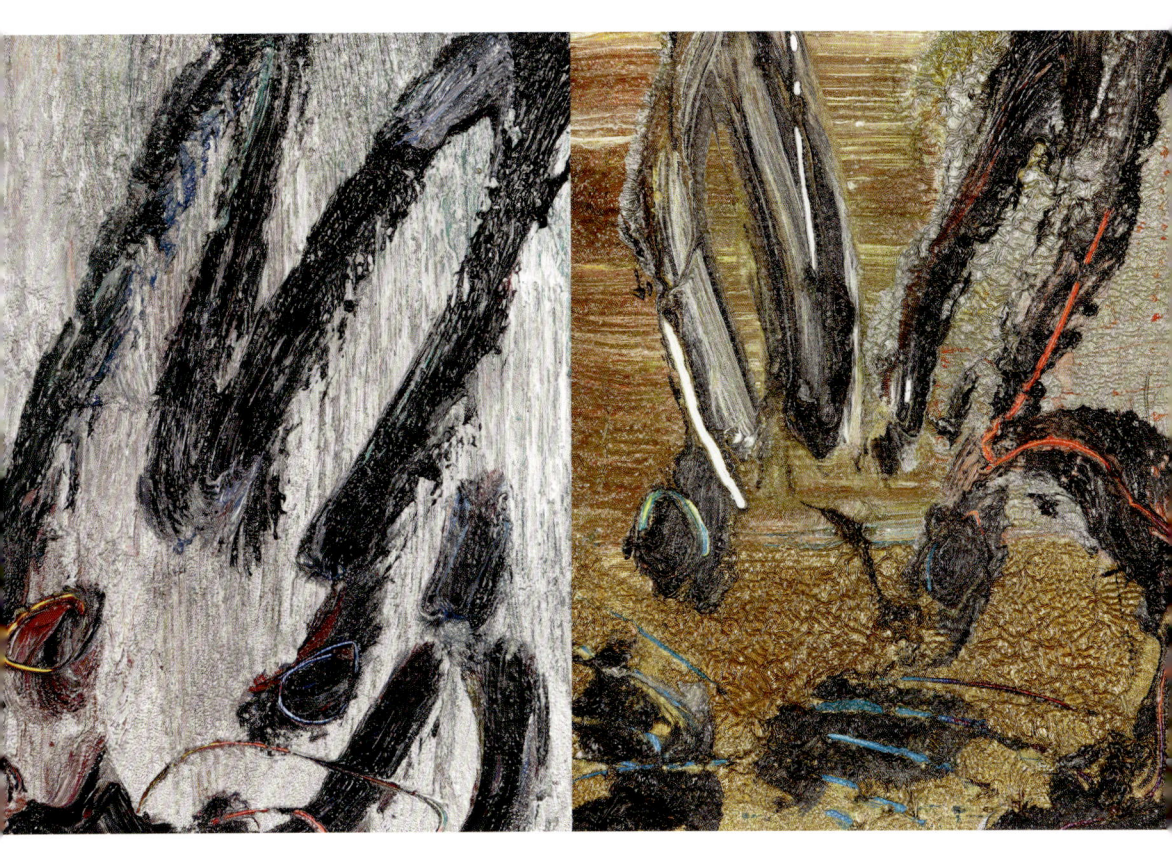

MIMI
2012
OIL ON WOOD
10" X 8"

ANGIE
2013
OIL ON WOOD
10" X 8"

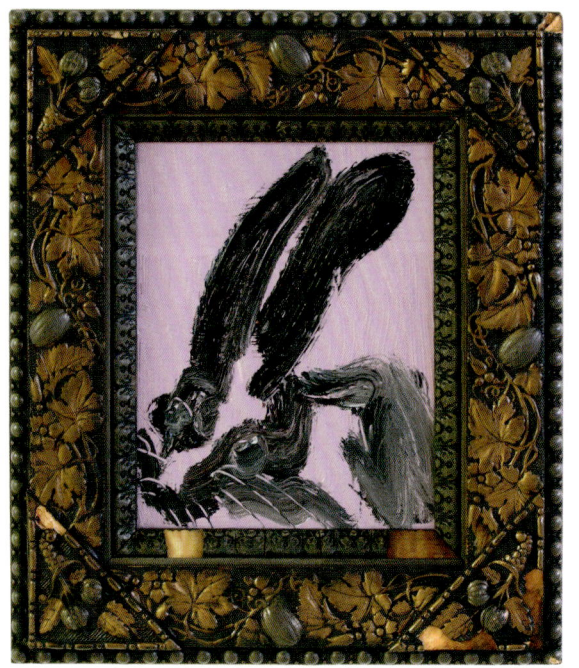

Lavendar
2009
OIL ON WOOD
10" x 8"

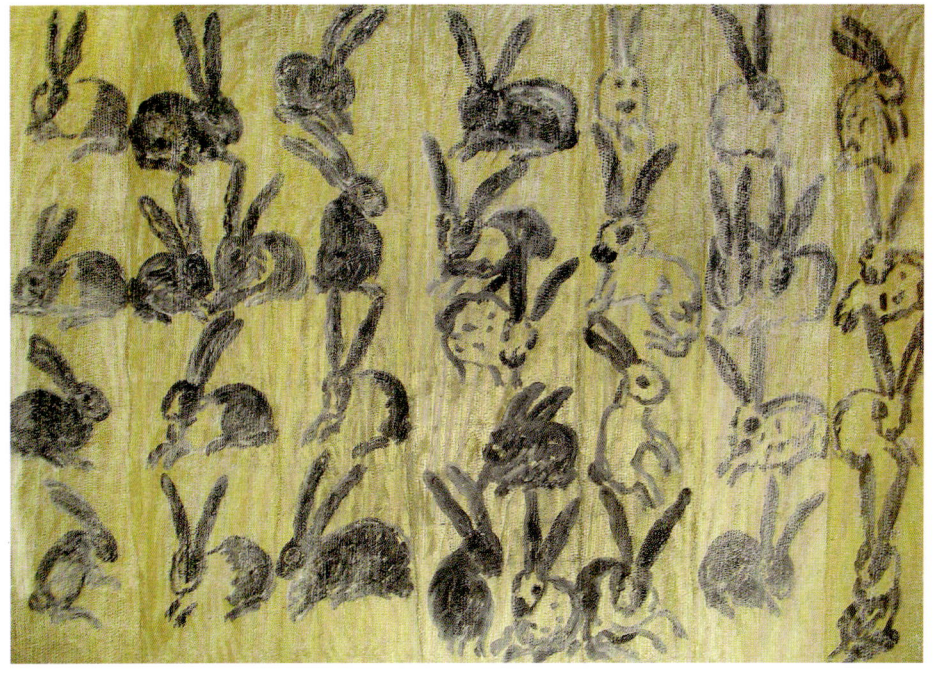

FAMILY HISTORY
2006
OIL ON CANVAS
93" X 133"

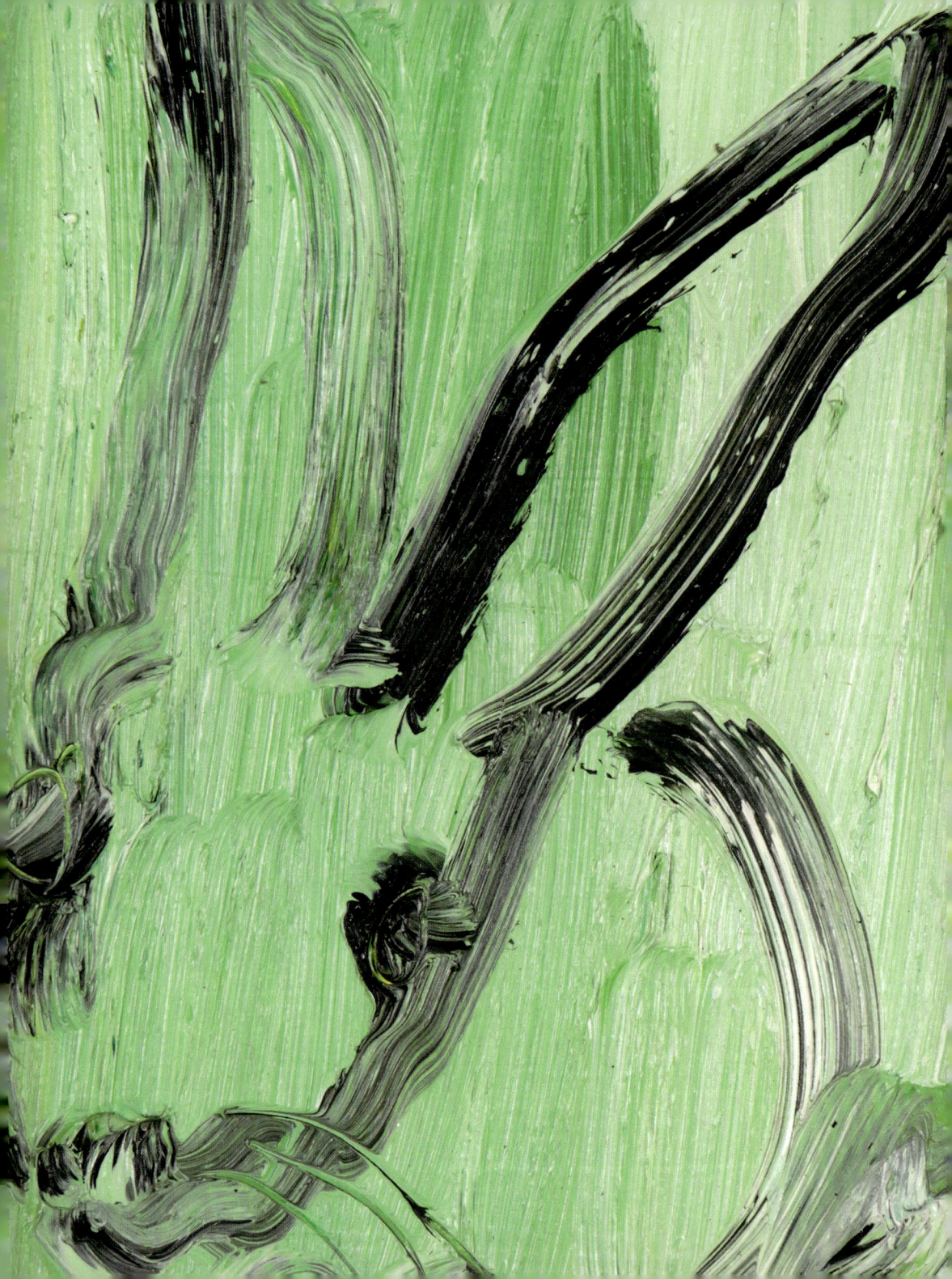

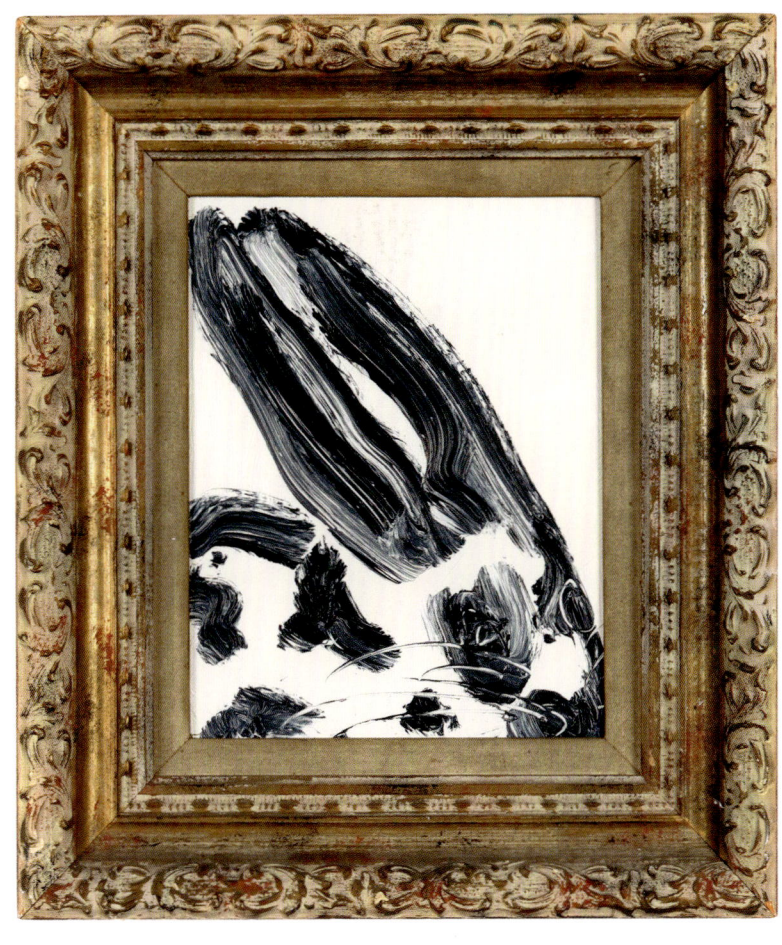

BUTCH
2013
OIL ON WOOD
10" X 8"

MICHELLE
2012
OIL ON WOOD
10" X 8"

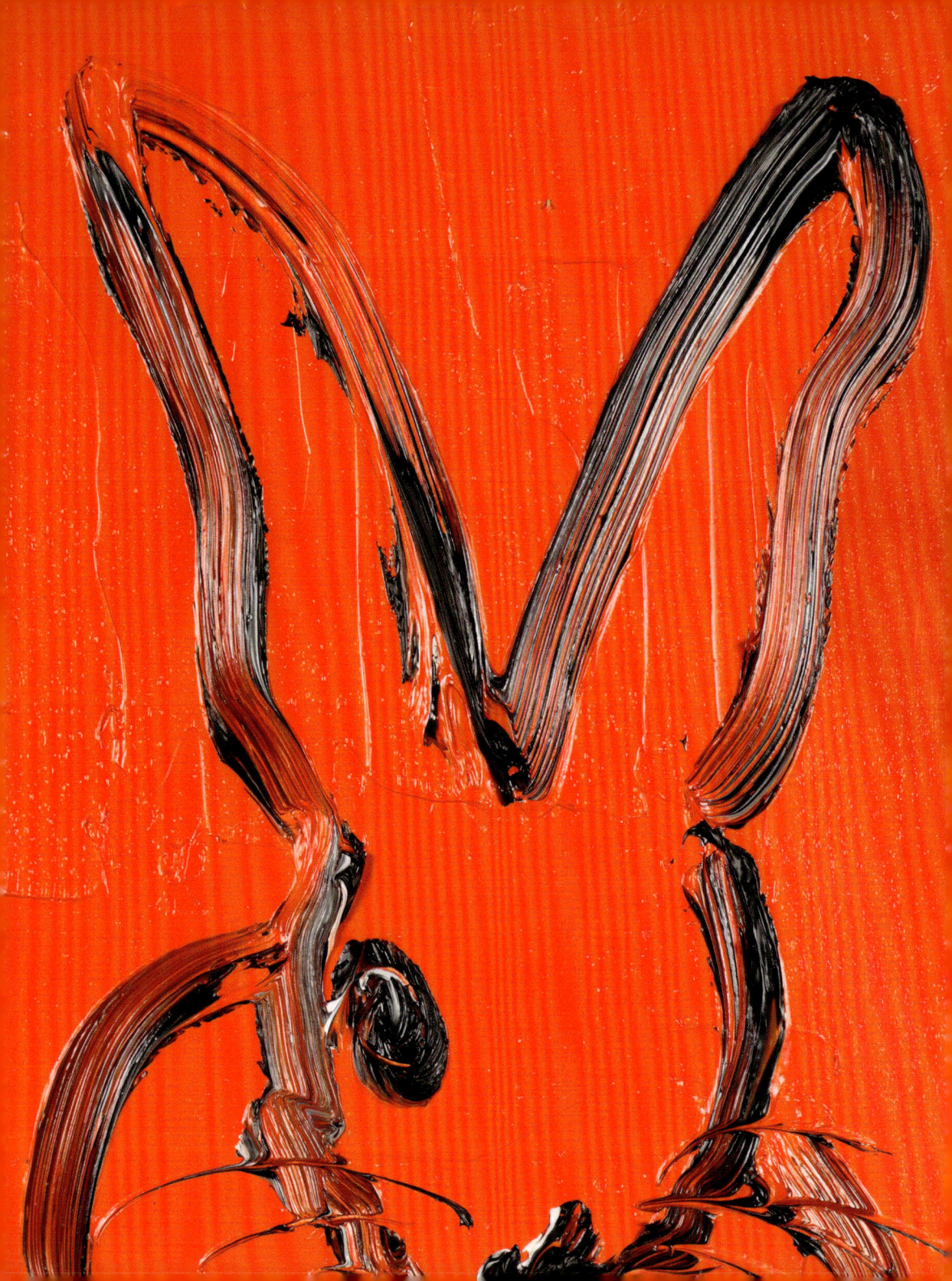

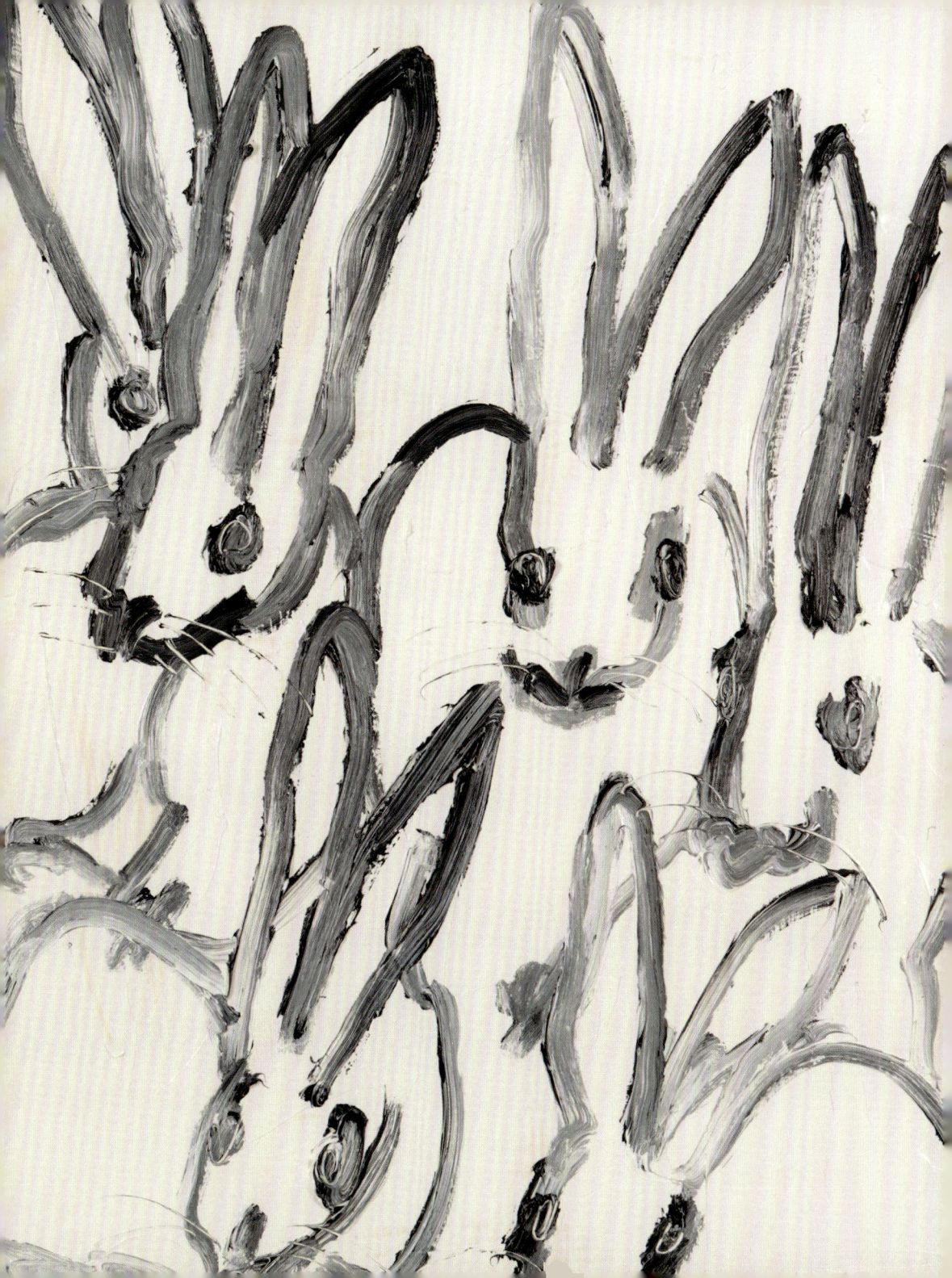

GINGER
2013
OIL ON WOOD
12" X 10"

MANASSAS
2013
OIL ON CANVAS
33" X 23"

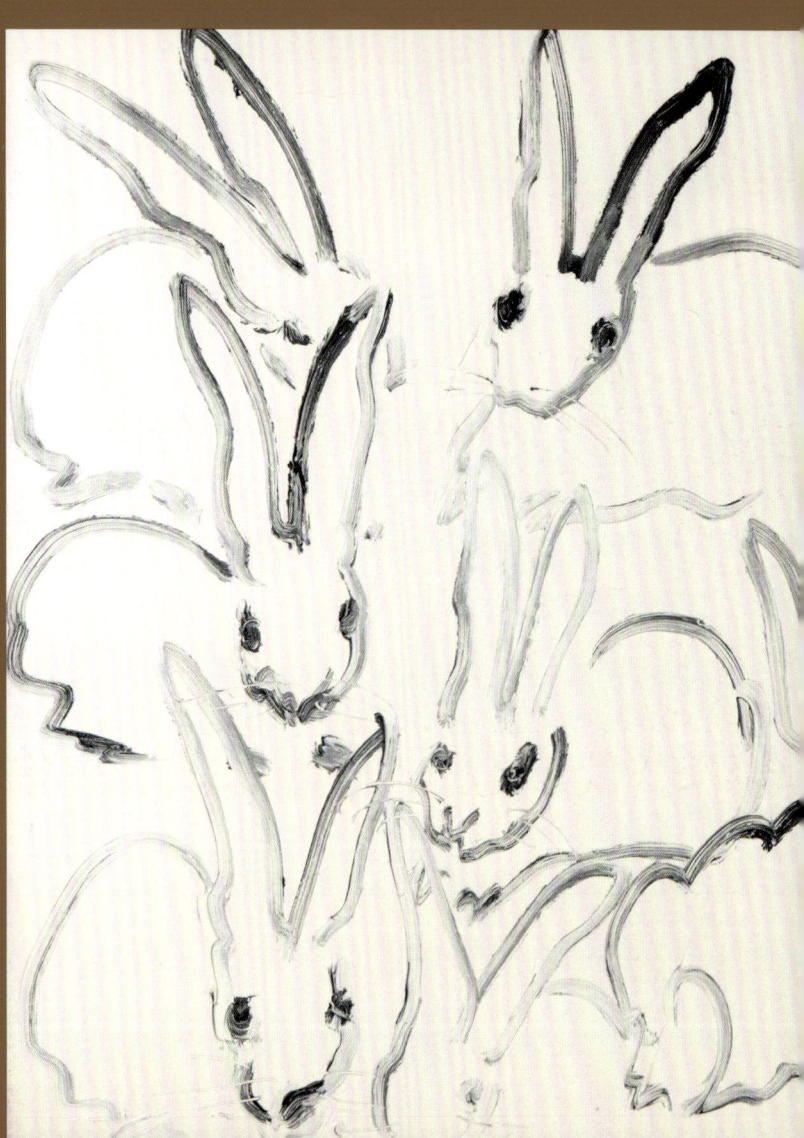

THE BEST YET
2013
OIL ON WOOD
44" X 66"

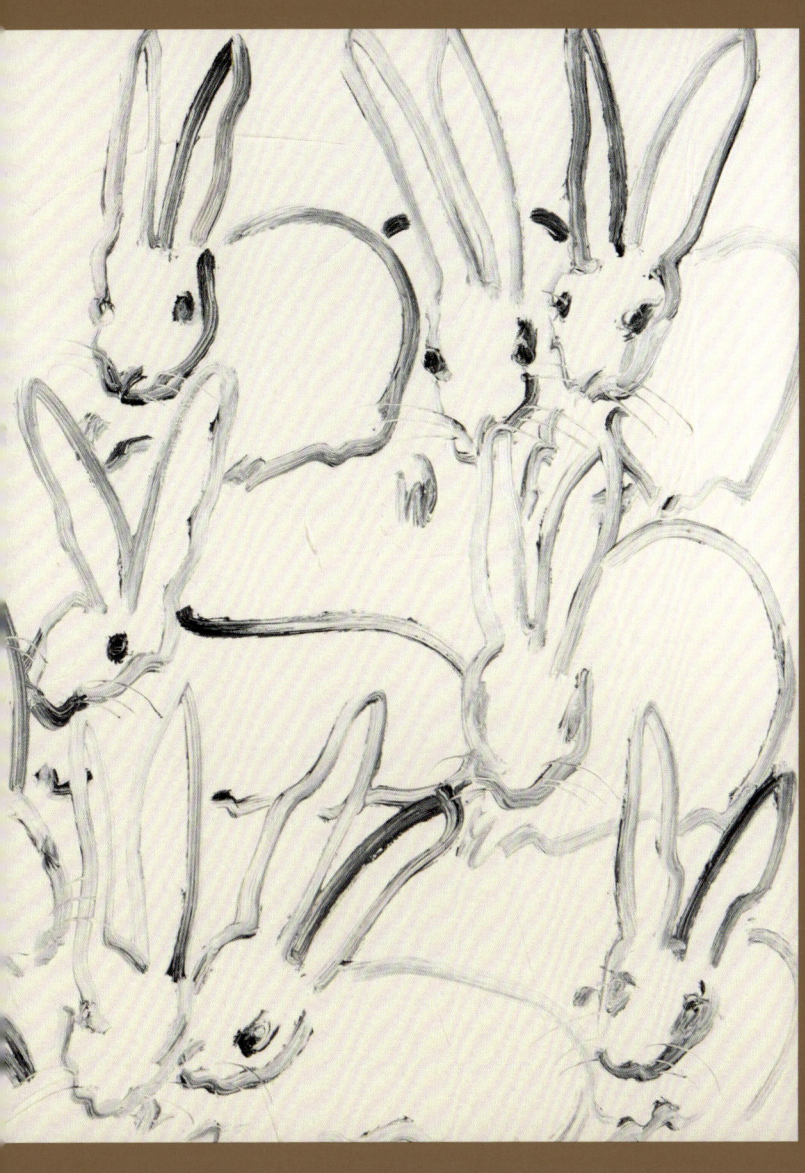

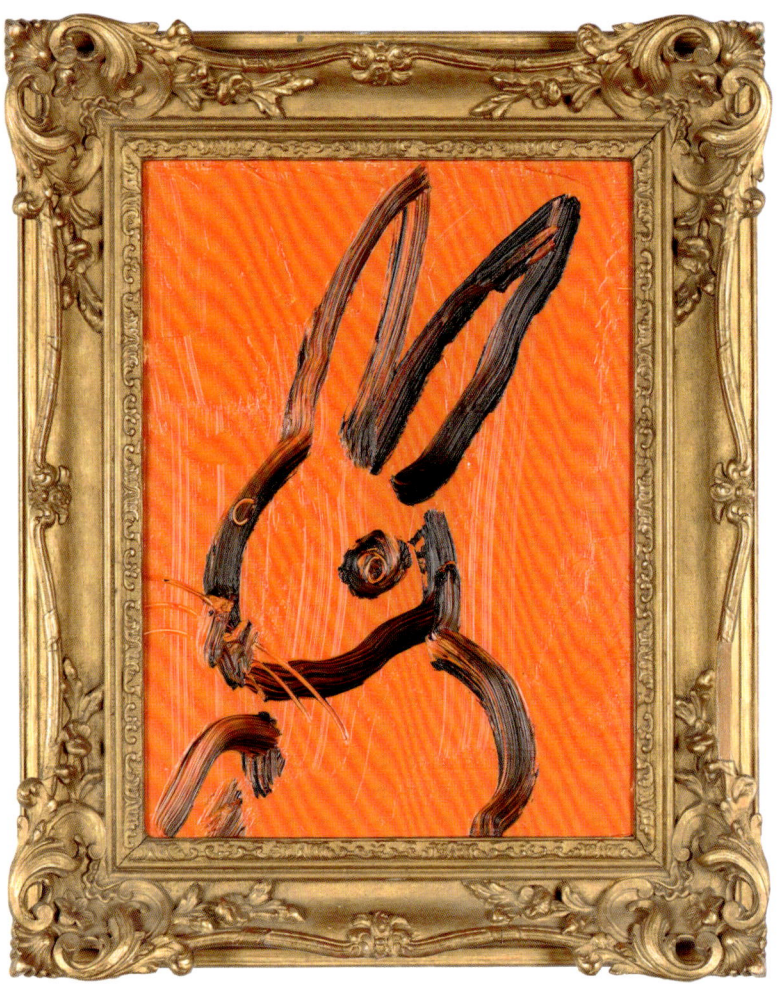

RED
2013
OIL ON WOOD
10" x 8"

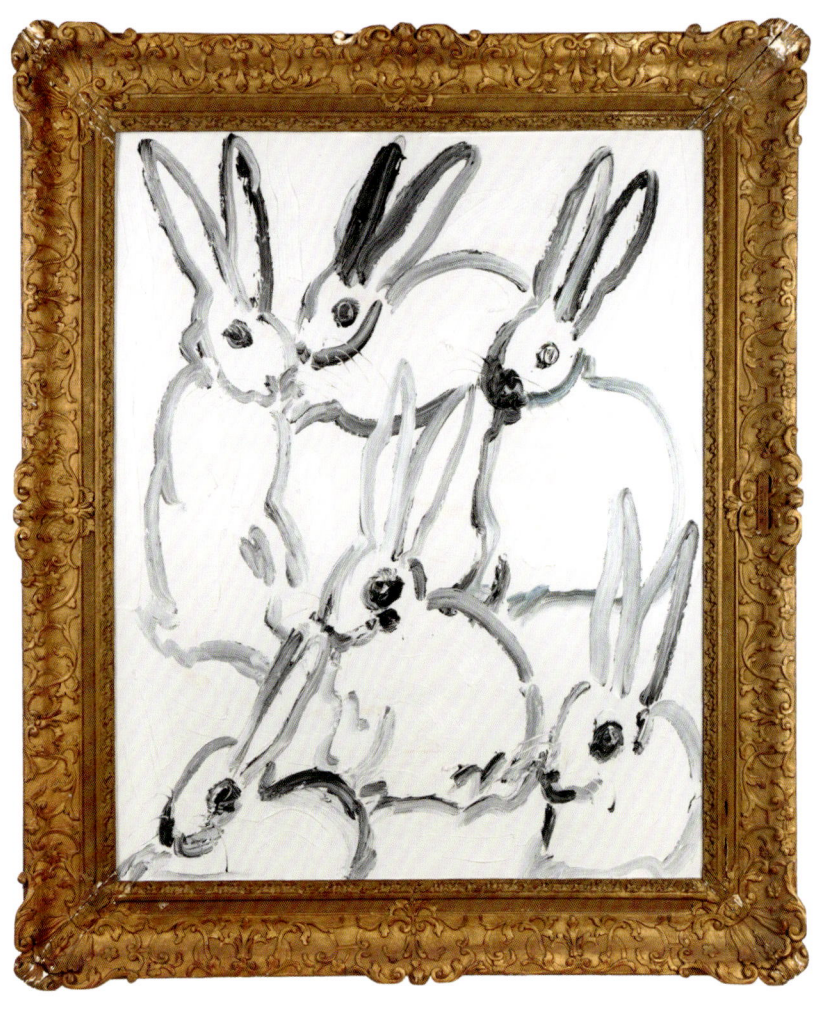

6
2012
OIL ON WOOD
42" X 32"

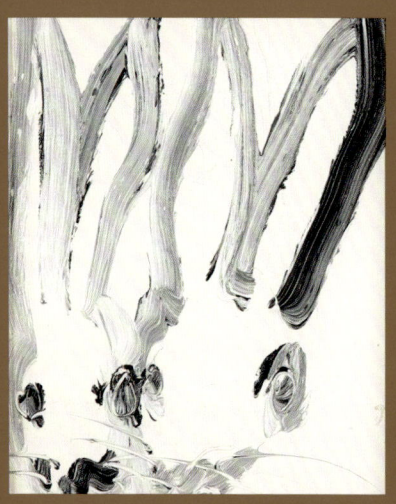
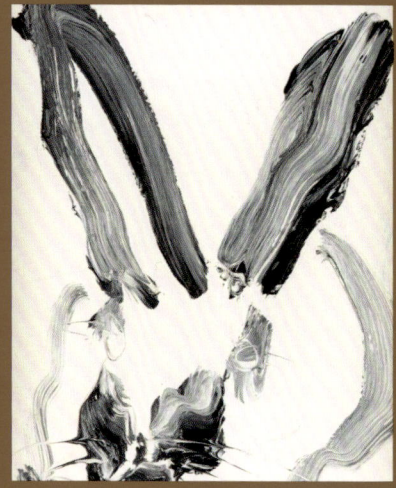
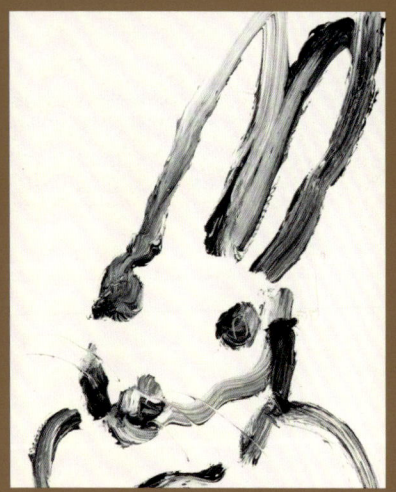
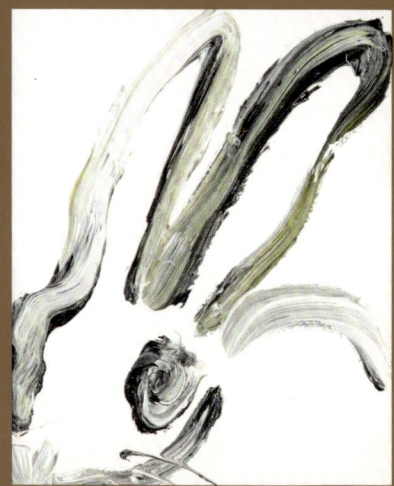

LAWRENCE BELLE
2013
OIL ON WOOD
10" X 8"
TOP, LEFT

BARBARA
2012
OIL ON WOOD
10" X 8"
BOTTOM, LEFT

JACQUELINE
2013
OIL ON WOOD
10" X 8"
TOP, RIGHT

GLORIA
2013
OIL ON WOOD
10" X 8"
BOTTOM, RIGHT

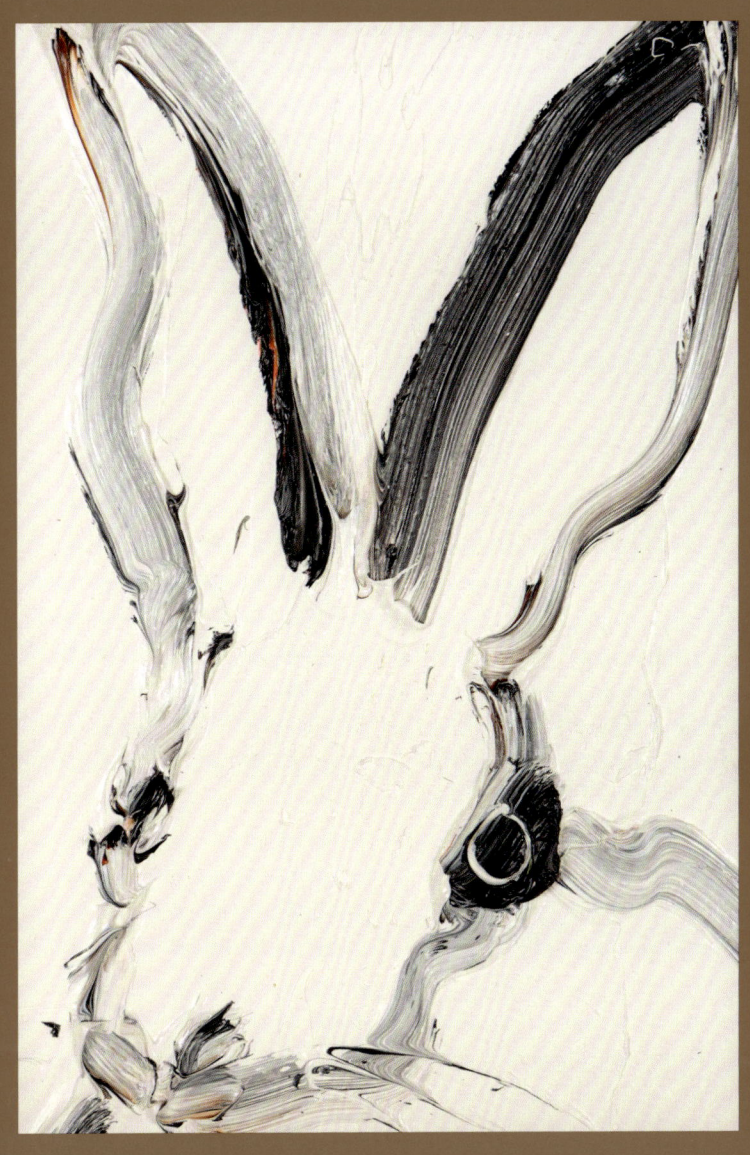

MARSHALL
2011
OIL ON WOOD
10" X 8"

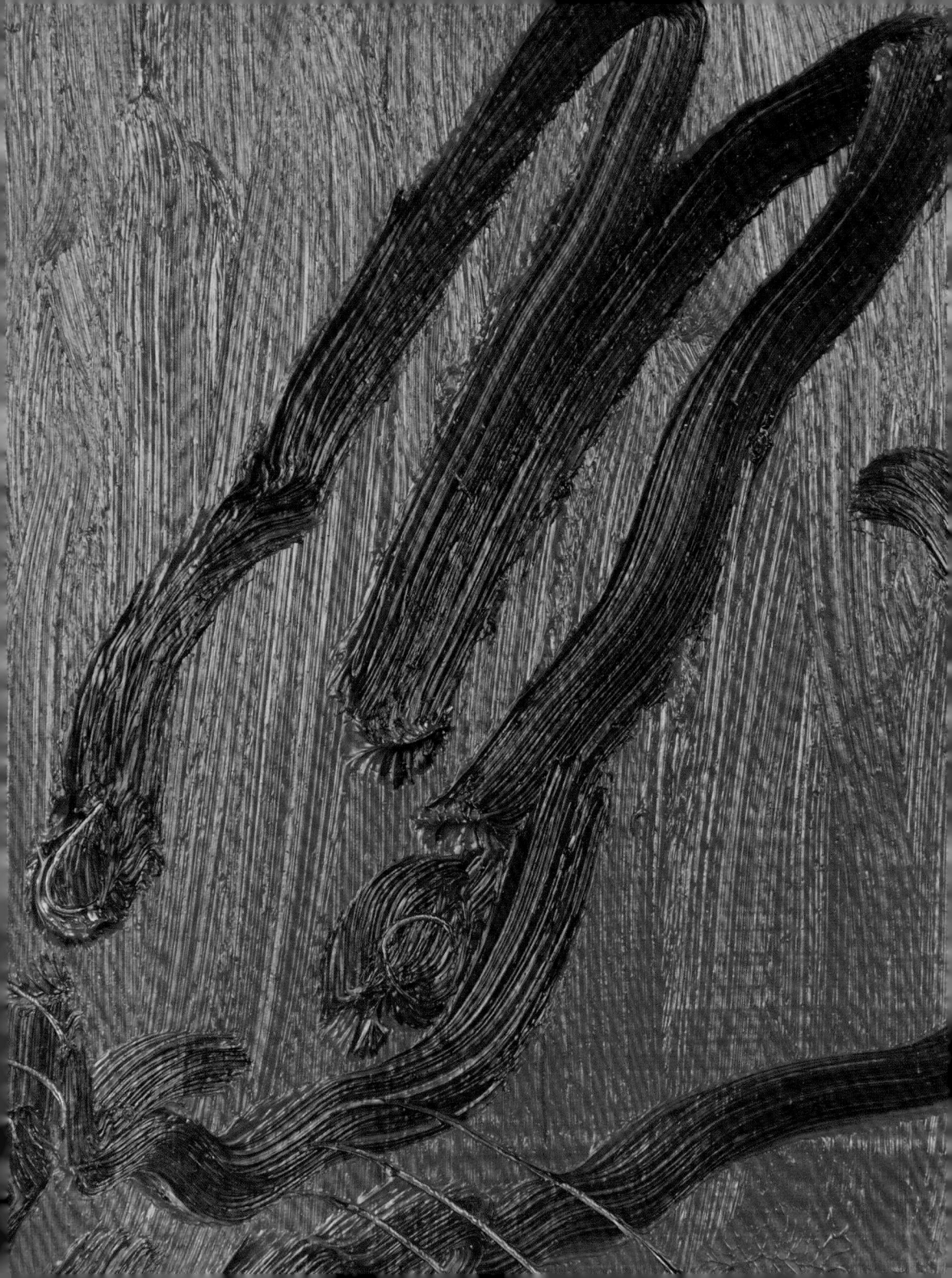

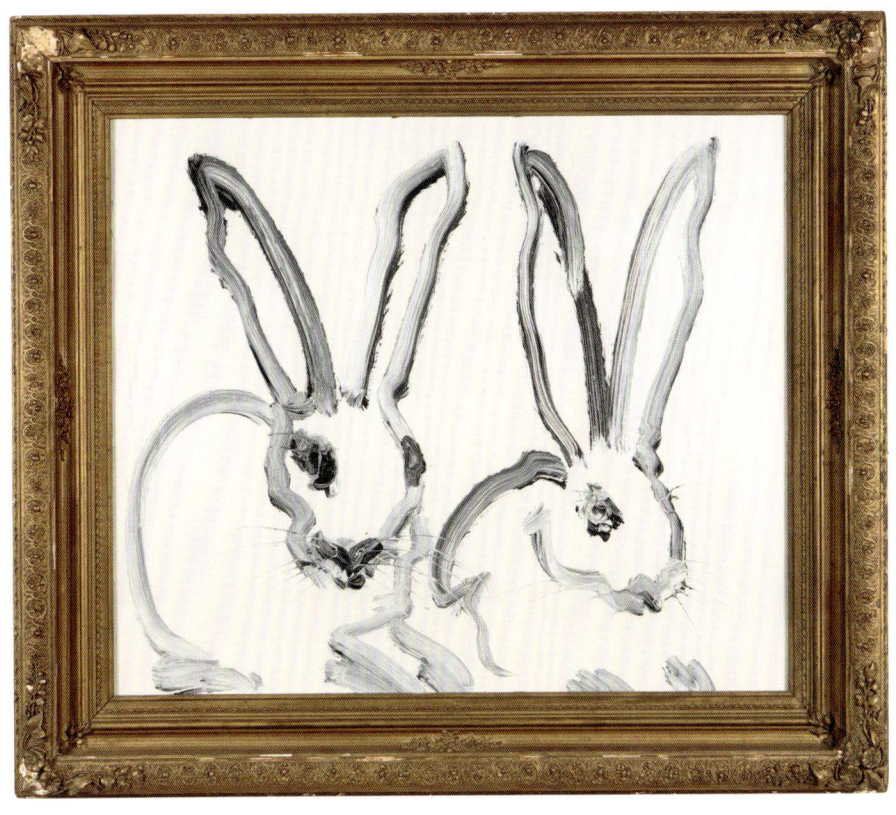

CHERRY
2010
OIL ON WOOD
10" X 8"

AMERICAN GOTHIC
2009
OIL ON WOOD
24" X 21"

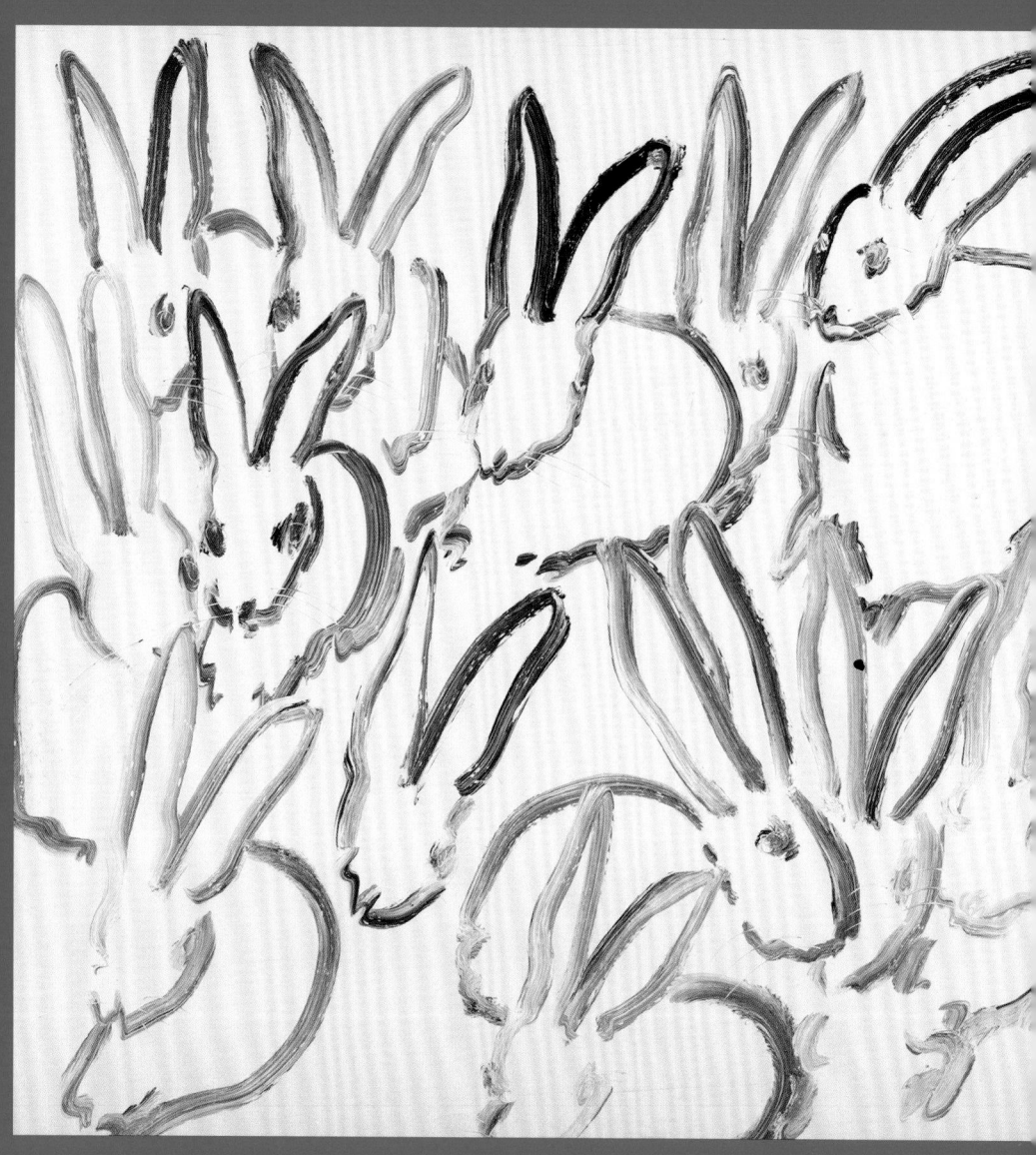

Hutch
2013
OIL ON CANVAS
45.5" x 60"

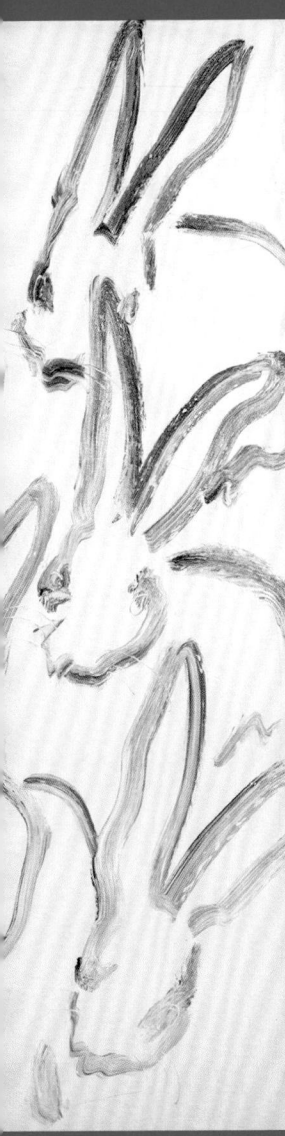

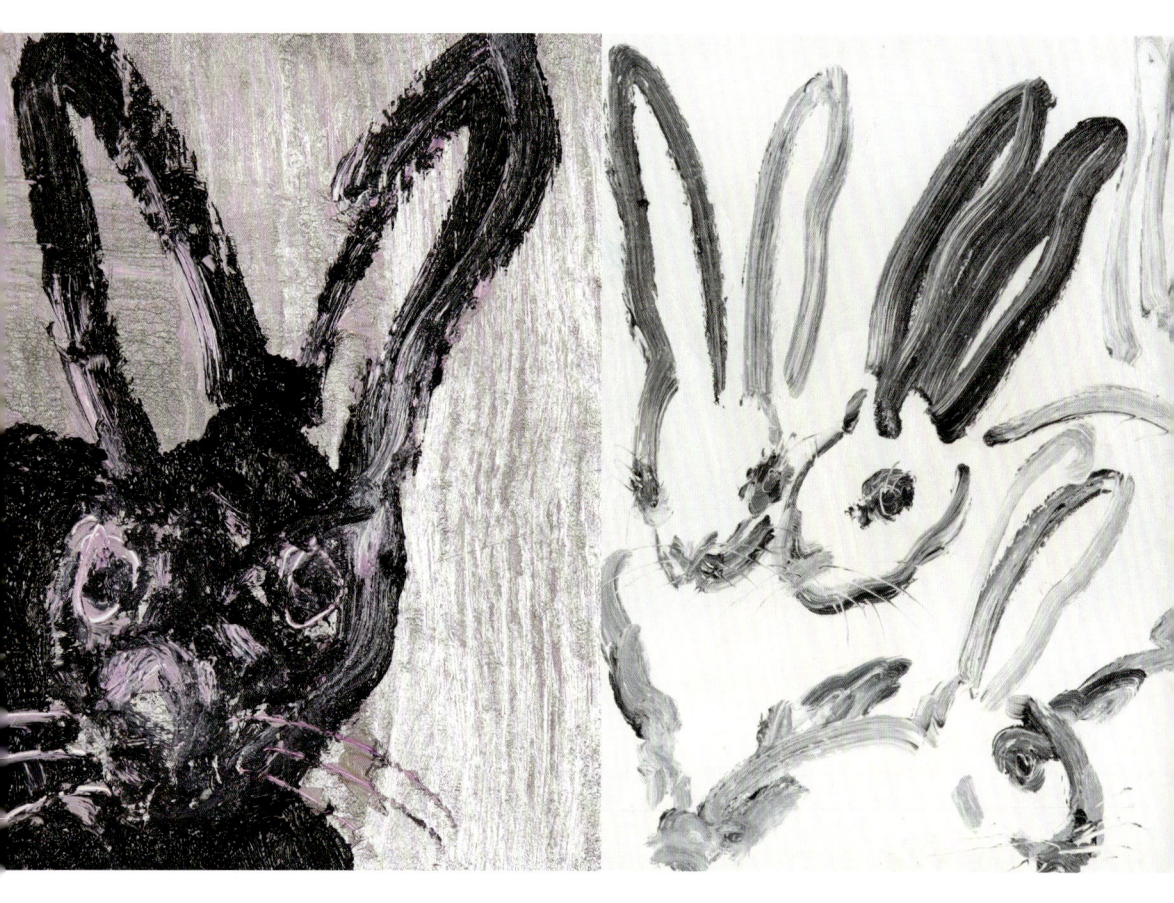

JAY
2009
OIL ON WOOD
10" X 8"

OUTING
2013
OIL ON WOOD
30.5" X 25.5"

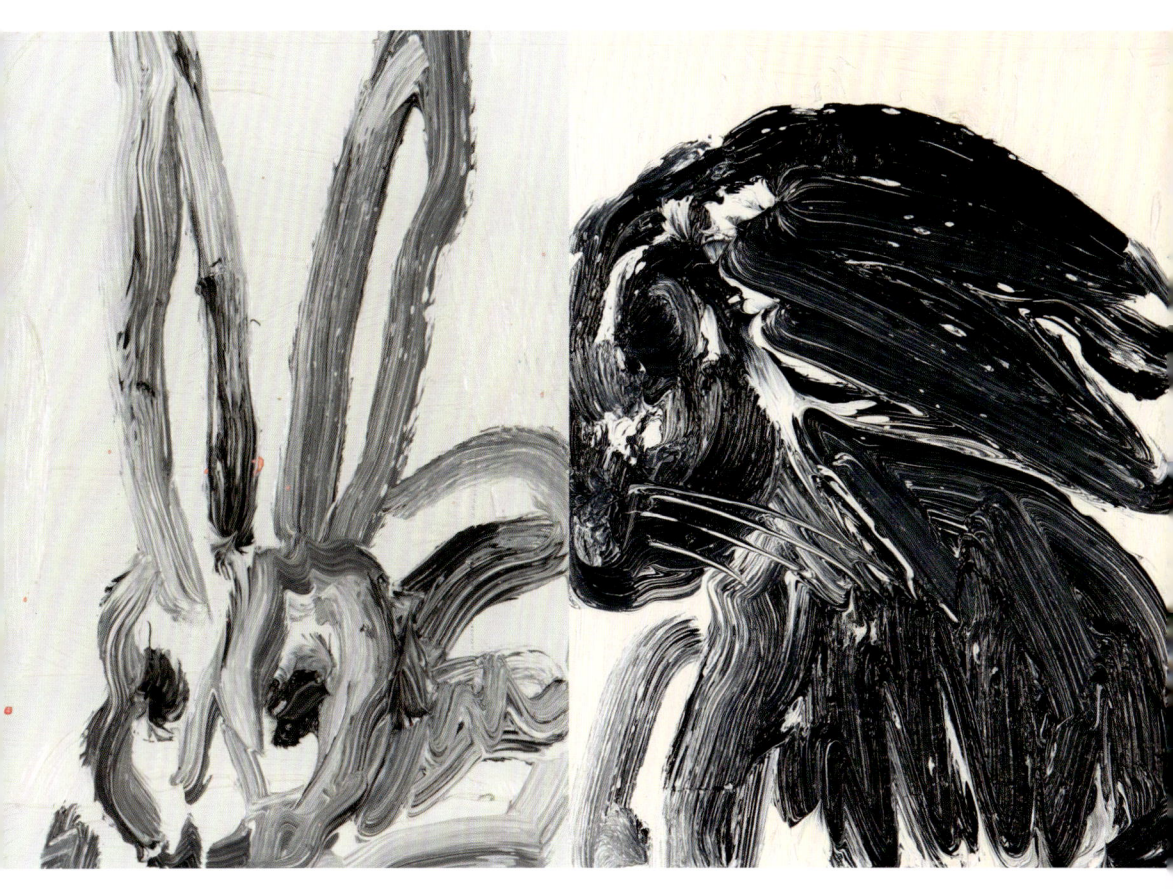

TROY
2009
OIL ON WOOD
12.5" X 9.5"

SPOOK
2011
OIL ON WOOD
10" X 8"

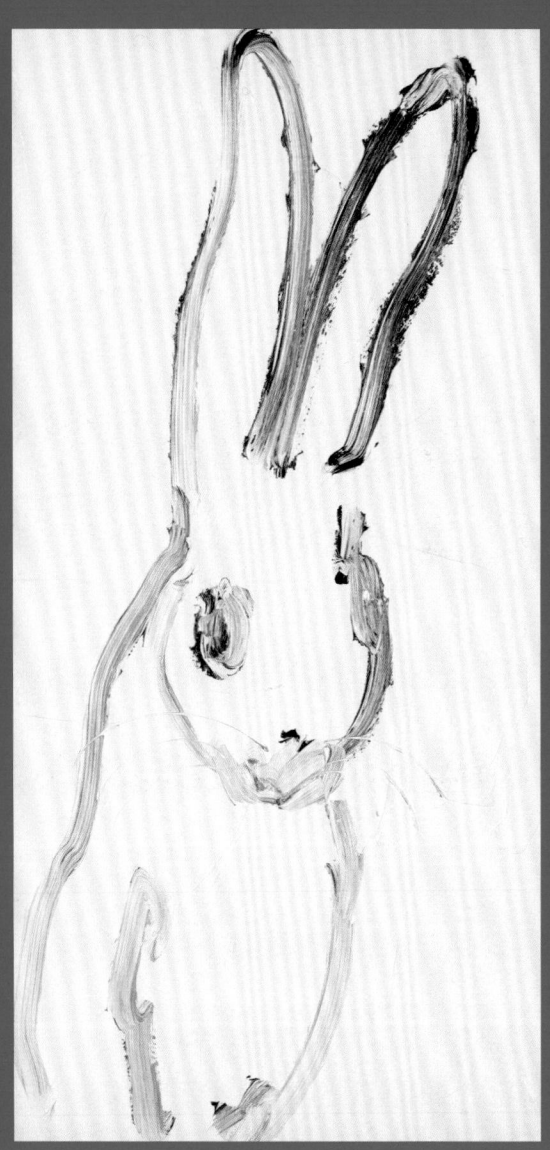

BRUCE
2013
OIL ON WOOD
25" X 12"

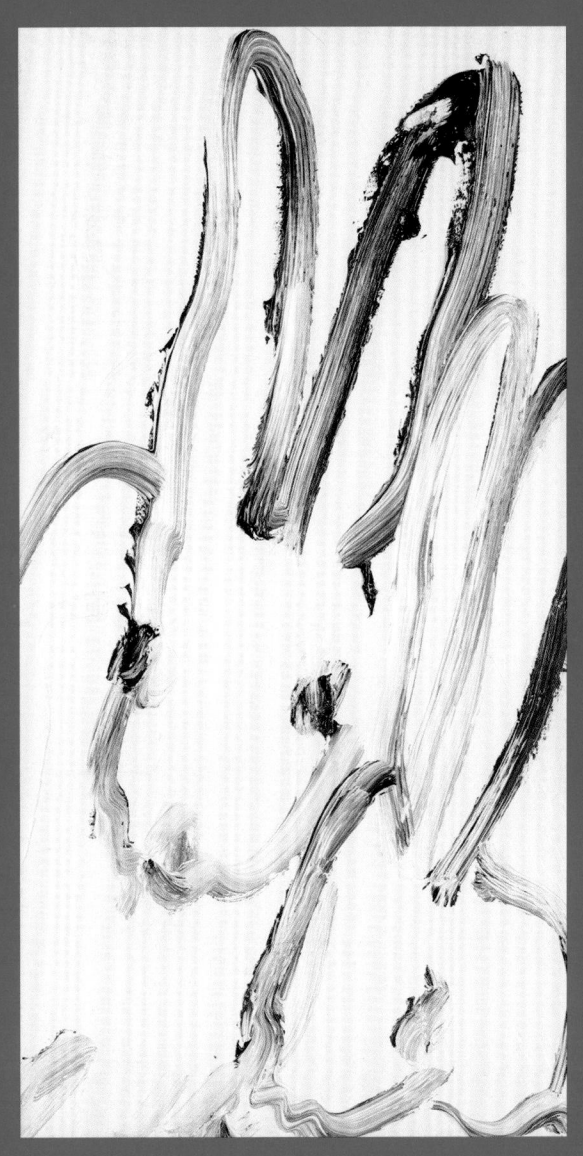

DOUBLE BUNNY #2
2013
OIL ON WOOD
18" x 8"

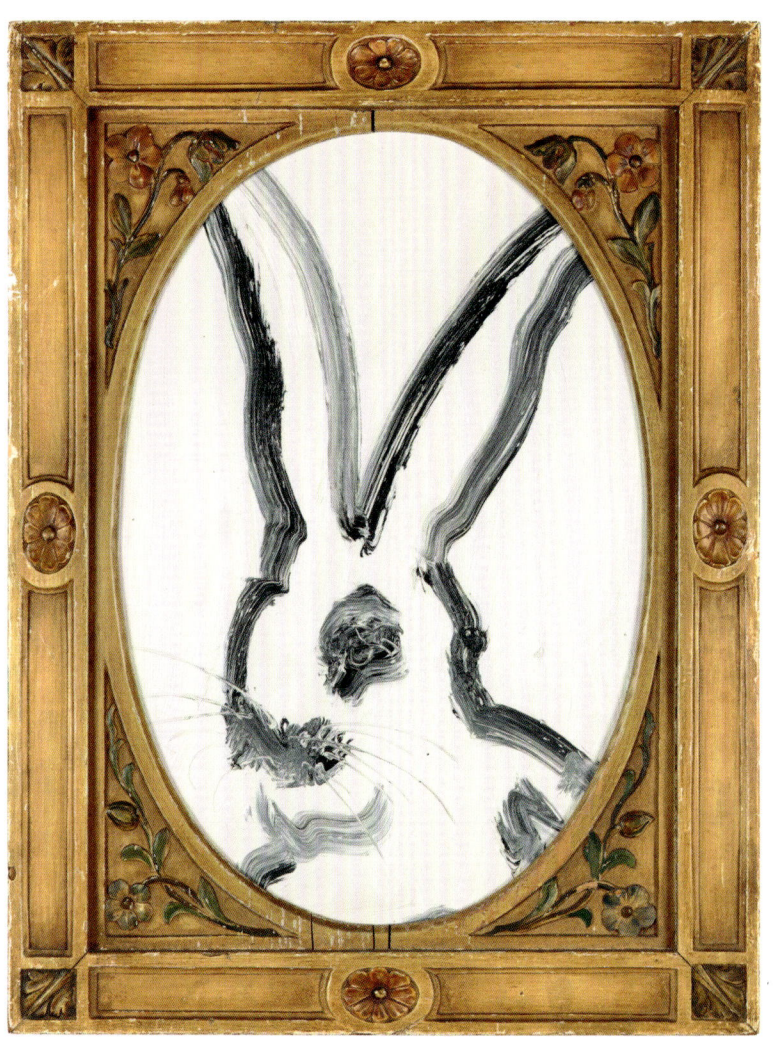

GRACE
2012
OIL ON WOOD
20.75" X 15"

HIGHLIGHT
2013
OIL ON WOOD
10" X 8"

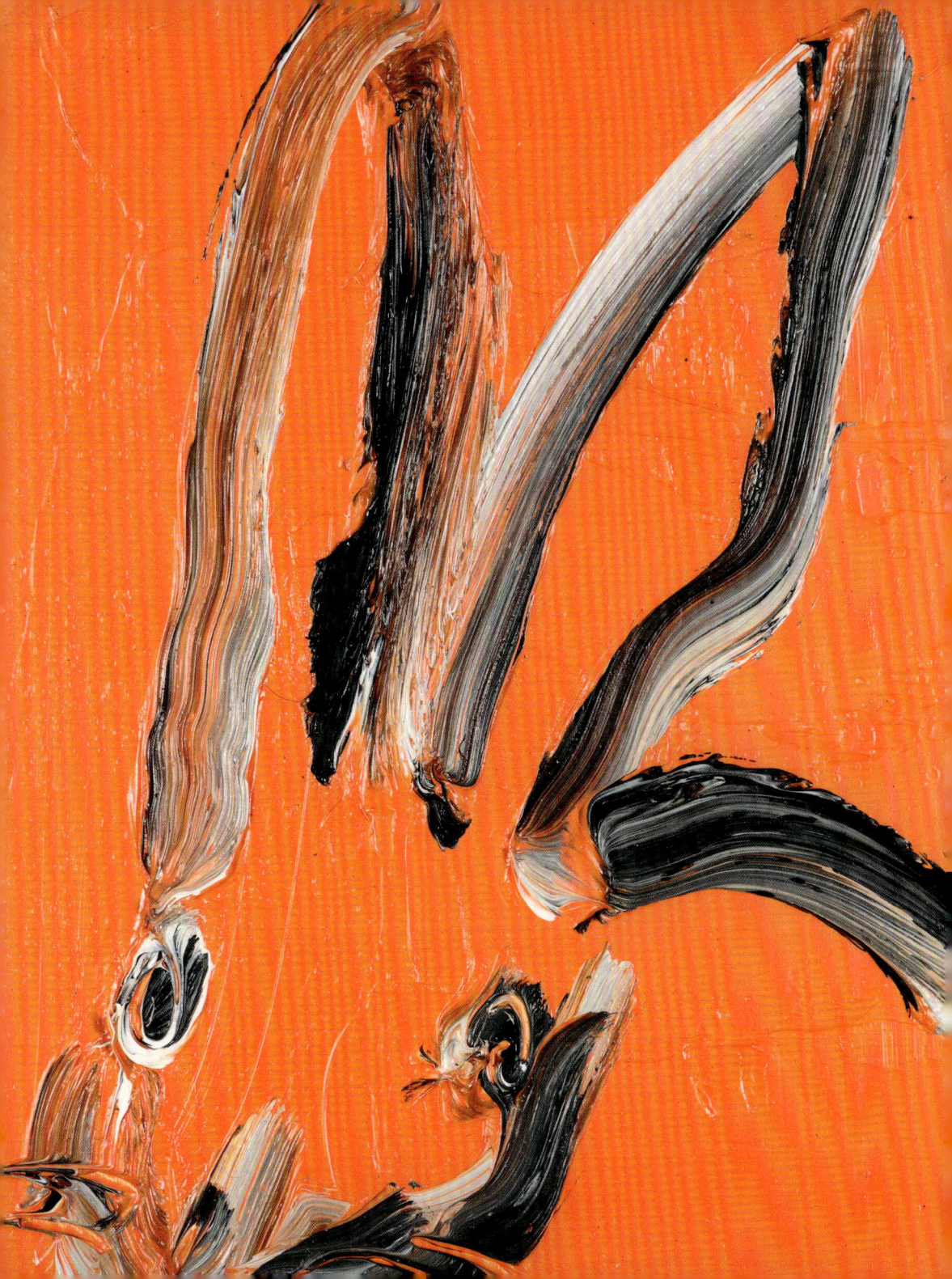

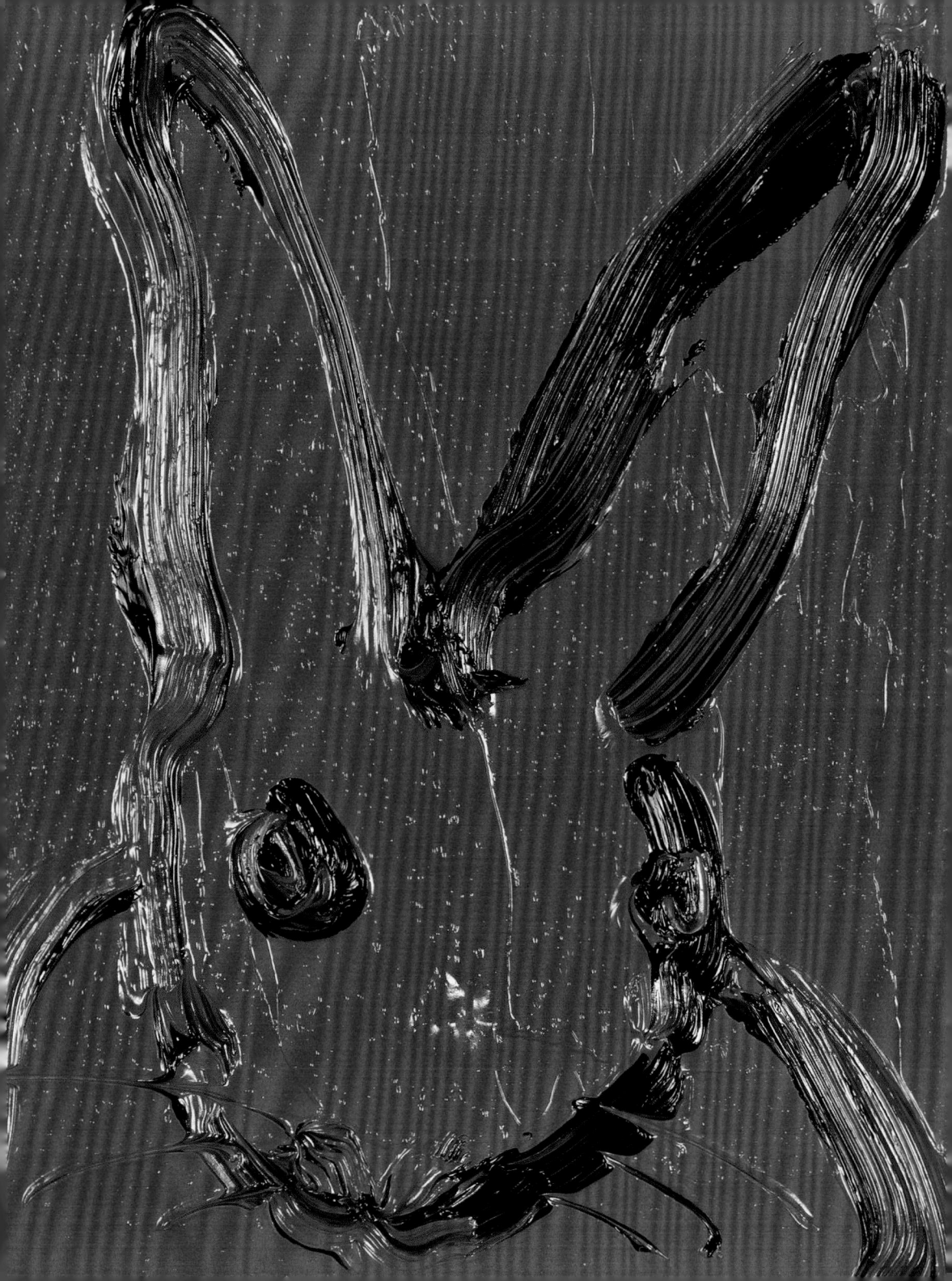

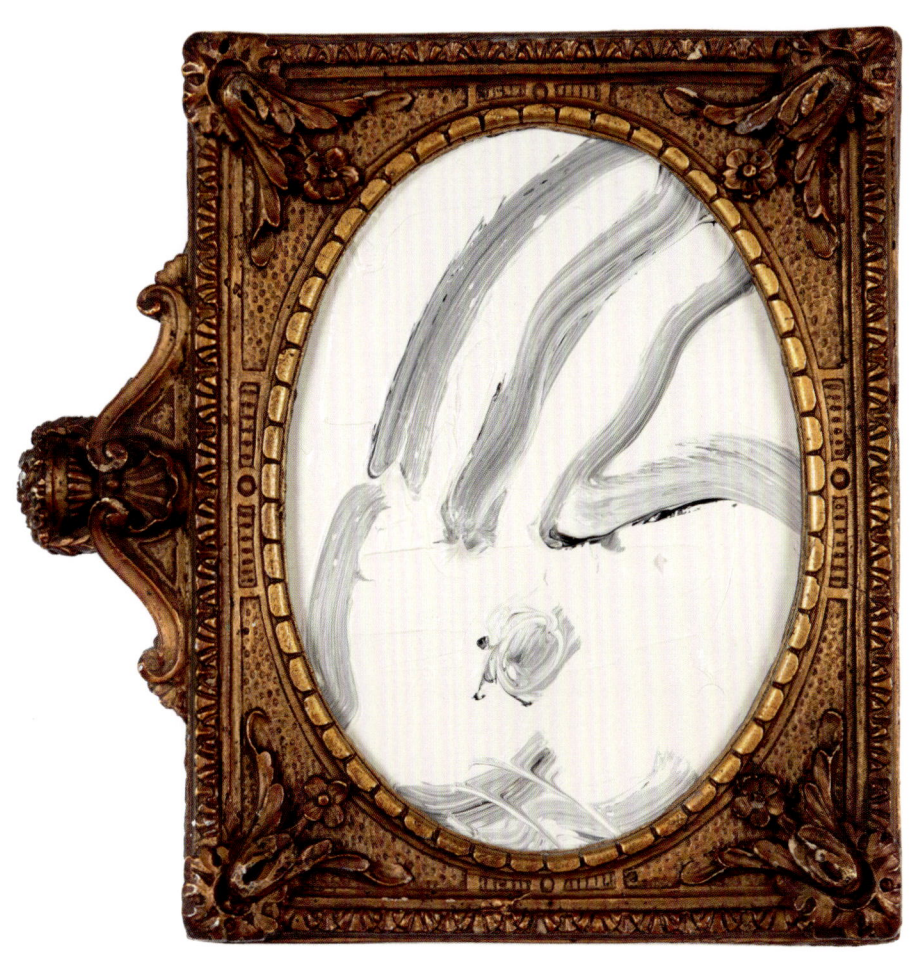

MARTHA
2013
OIL ON WOOD
12" X 9"

NATASHA
2013
OIL ON WOOD
8" X 6"

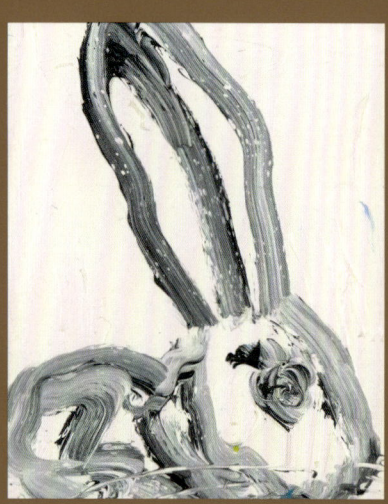
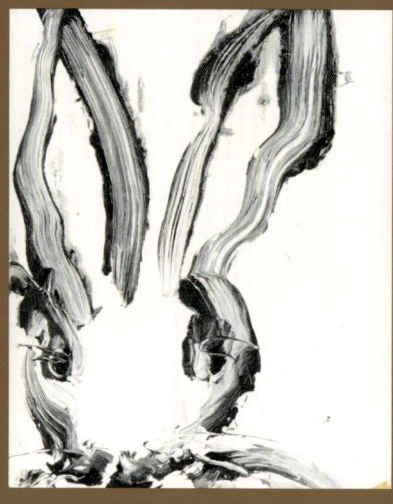

134

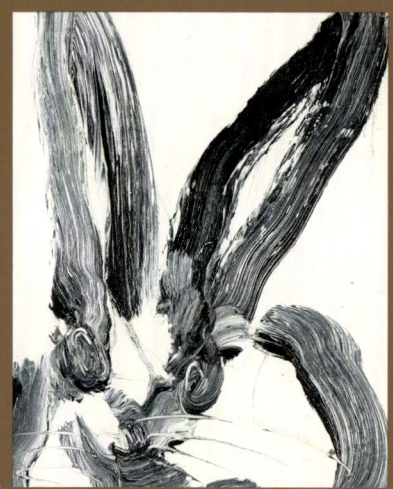
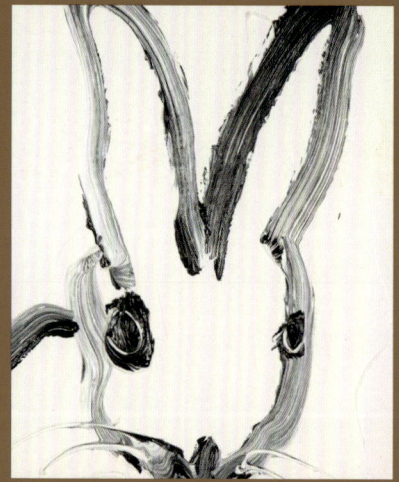

Angelica
2013
OIL ON WOOD
10" x 8"
TOP, LEFT

Bryan
2013
OIL ON WOOD
10" x 8"
BOTTOM, LEFT

Wilson
2012
OIL ON WOOD
10" x 8"
TOP, RIGHT

St. Francis-Ville
2013
OIL ON WOOD
10" x 8"
BOTTOM, RIGHT

Bill
2012
OIL ON WOOD
10" x 8"

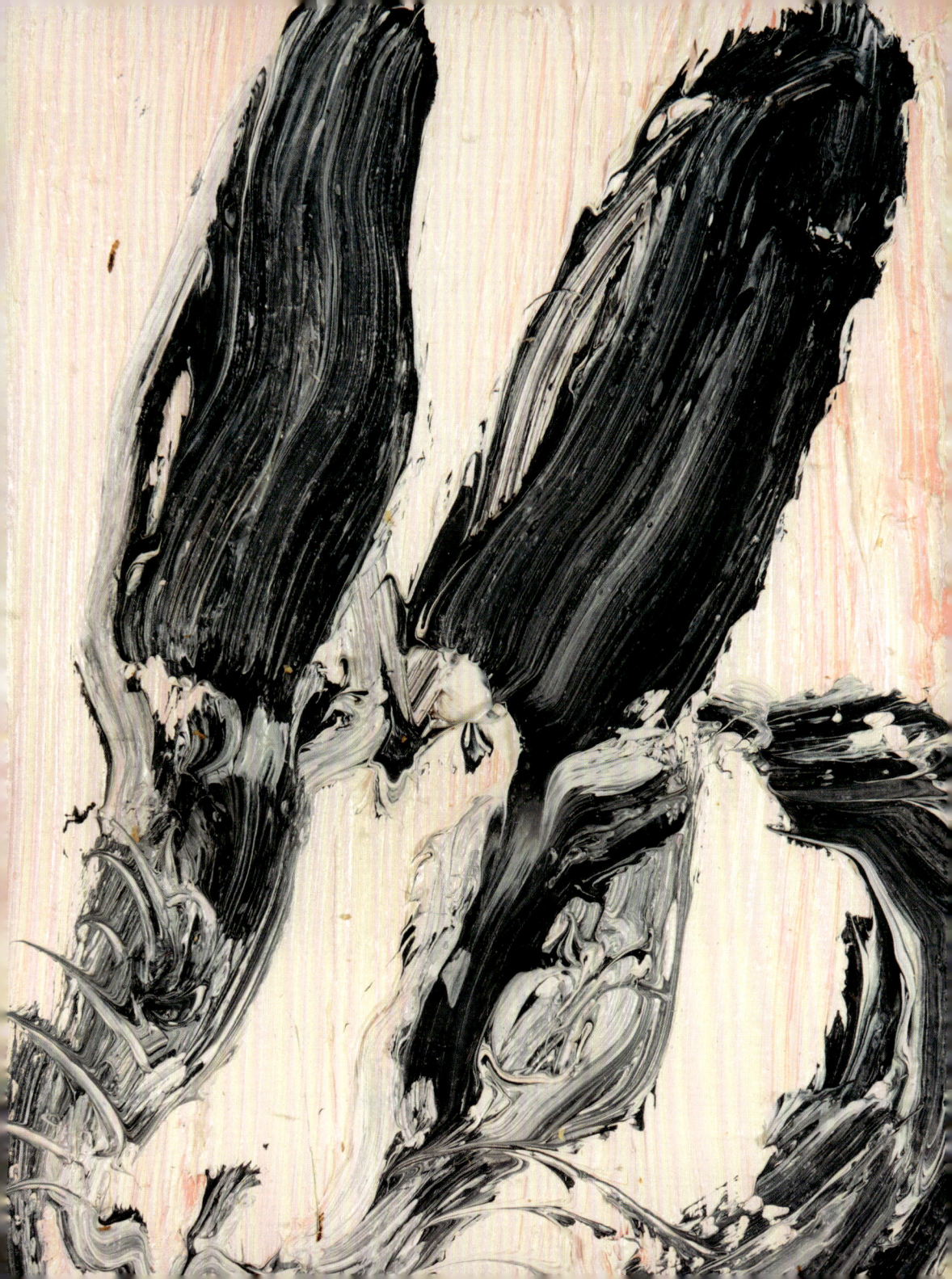

Flopsy
2013
OIL ON WOOD
10" X 8"

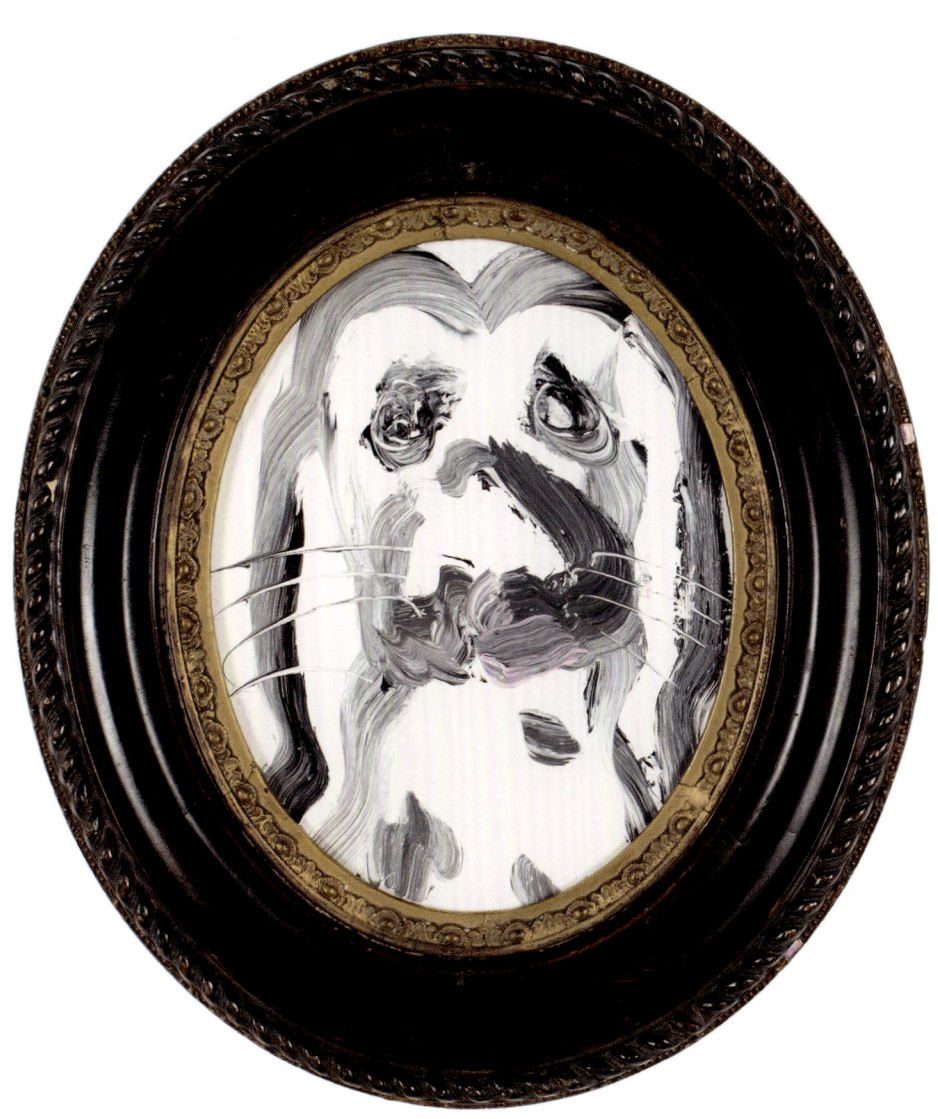

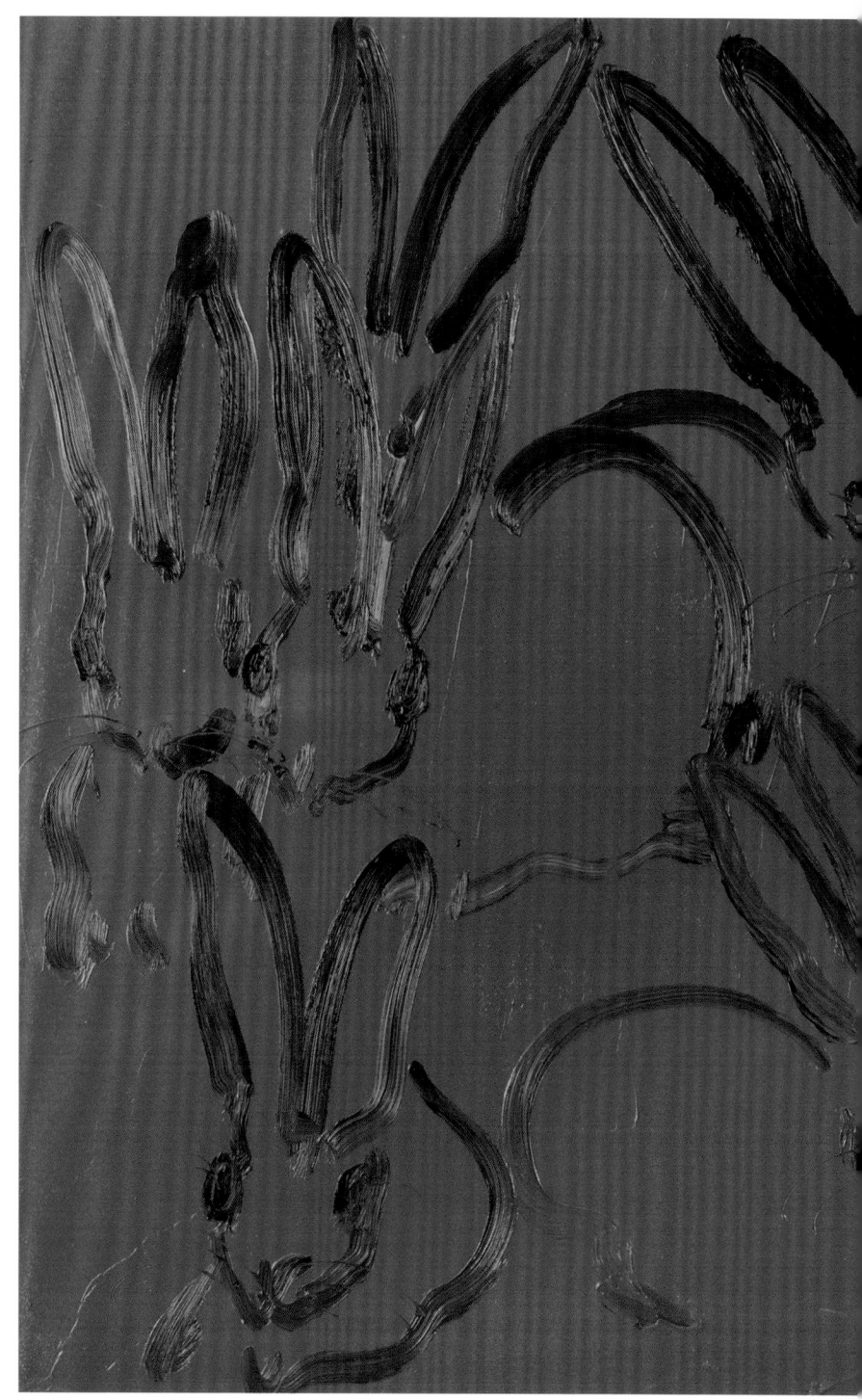

BAYOU TECHE
2012
OIL ON CANVAS
36" X 48"

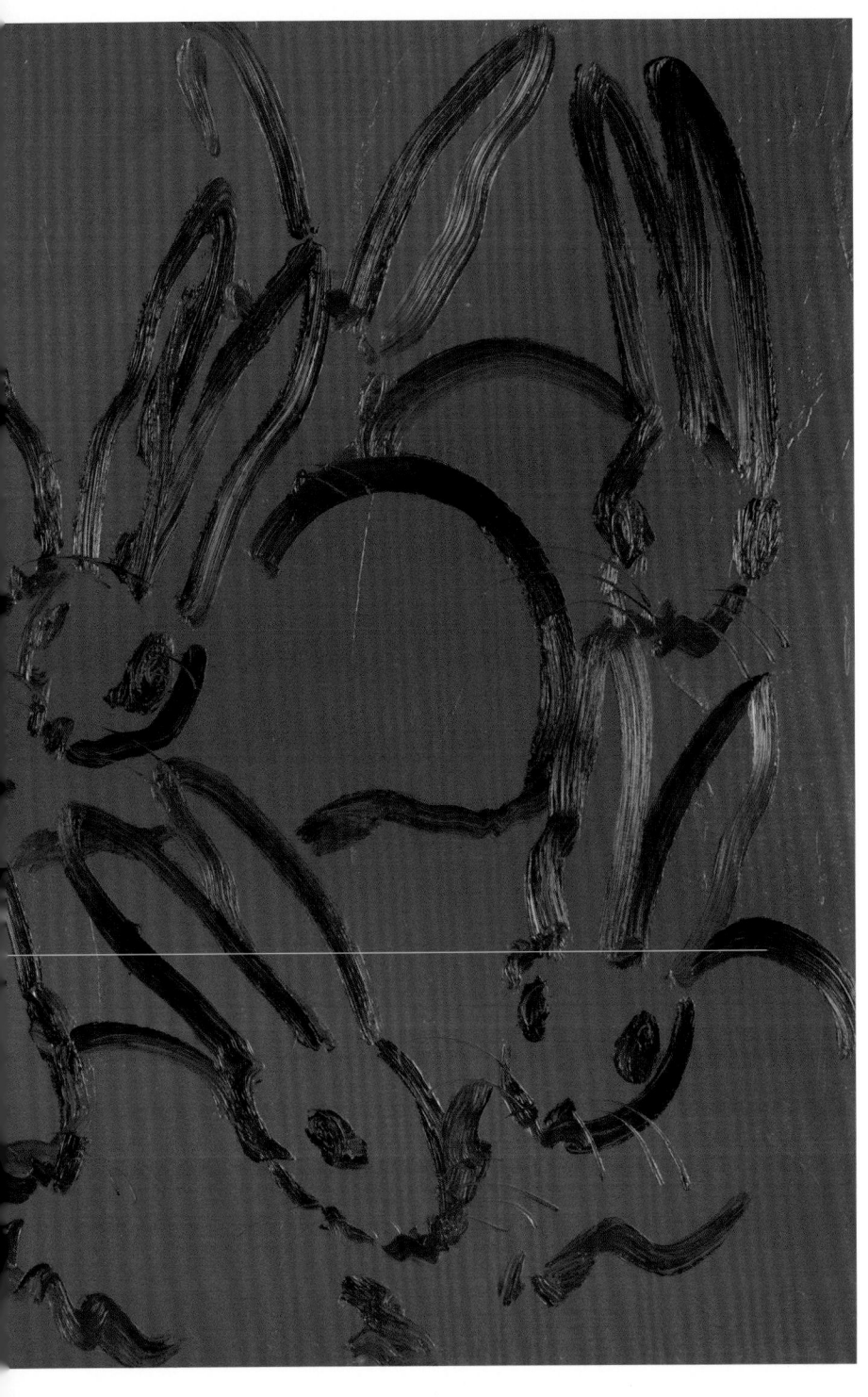

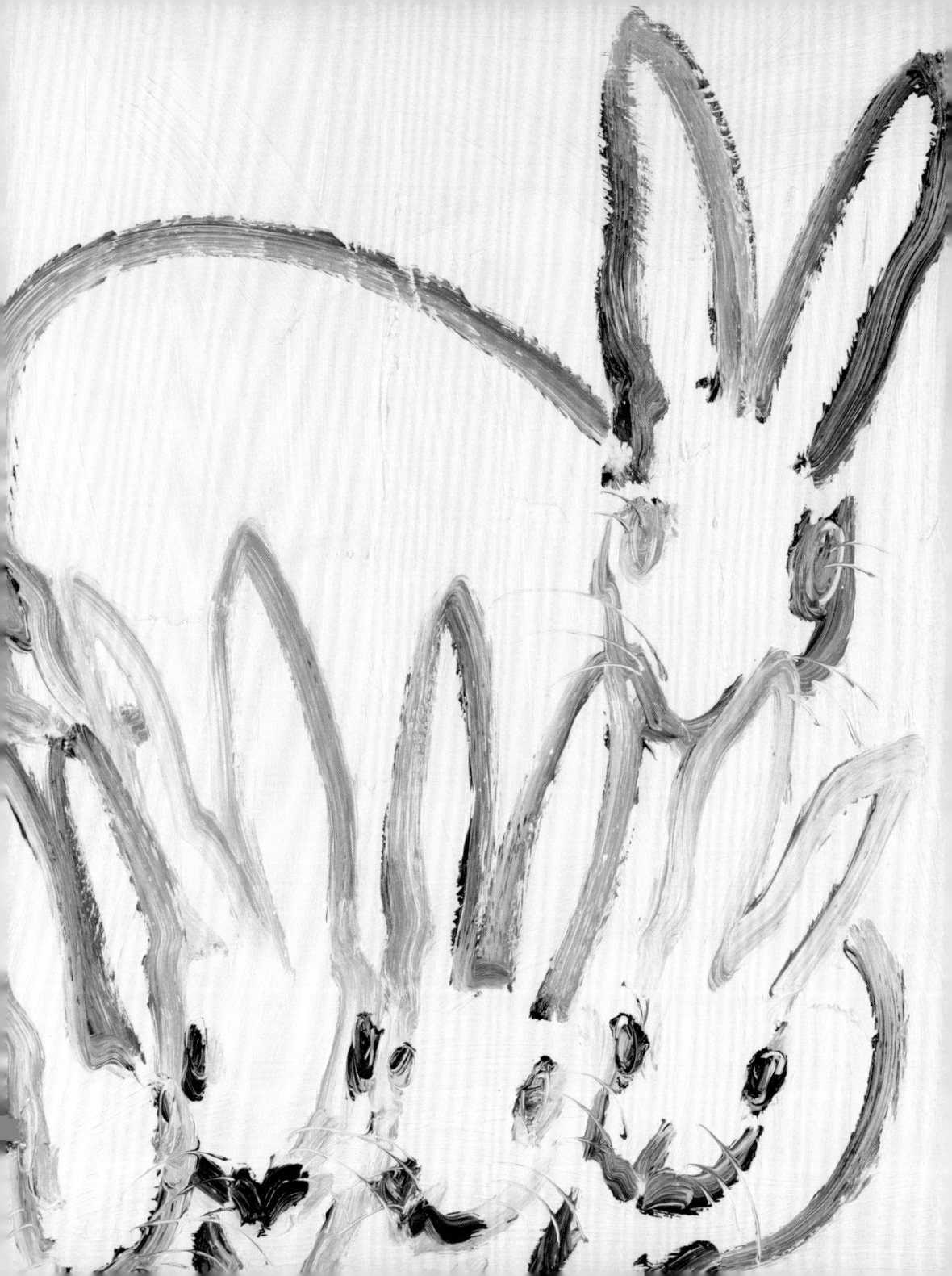

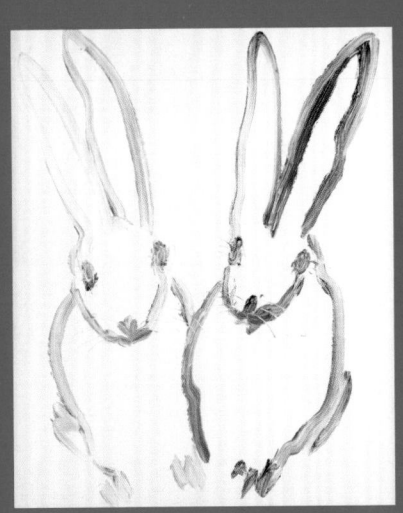

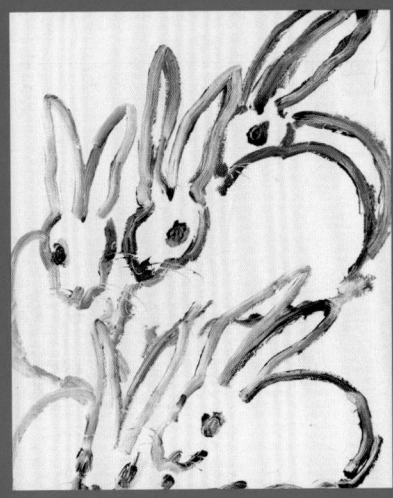

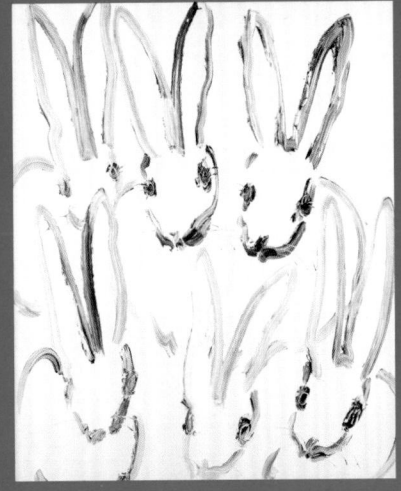

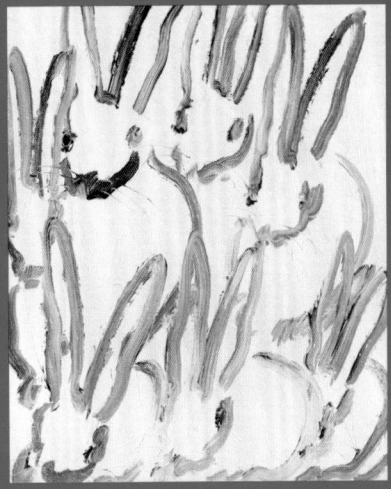

DELIVERY
2013
OIL ON WOOD
24" X 20"

SALVADOR & LULA
2013
OIL ON WOOD
24" X 20"
TOP, LEFT

OFFSPRING 2
2013
OIL ON WOOD
30" X 24"
BOTTOM, LEFT

QUADRILL
2013
OIL ON WOOD
33" X 26"
TOP, RIGHT

PORTRAIT STILL LIFE
2012
OIL ON WOOD
36" X 24"
BOTTOM, RIGHT

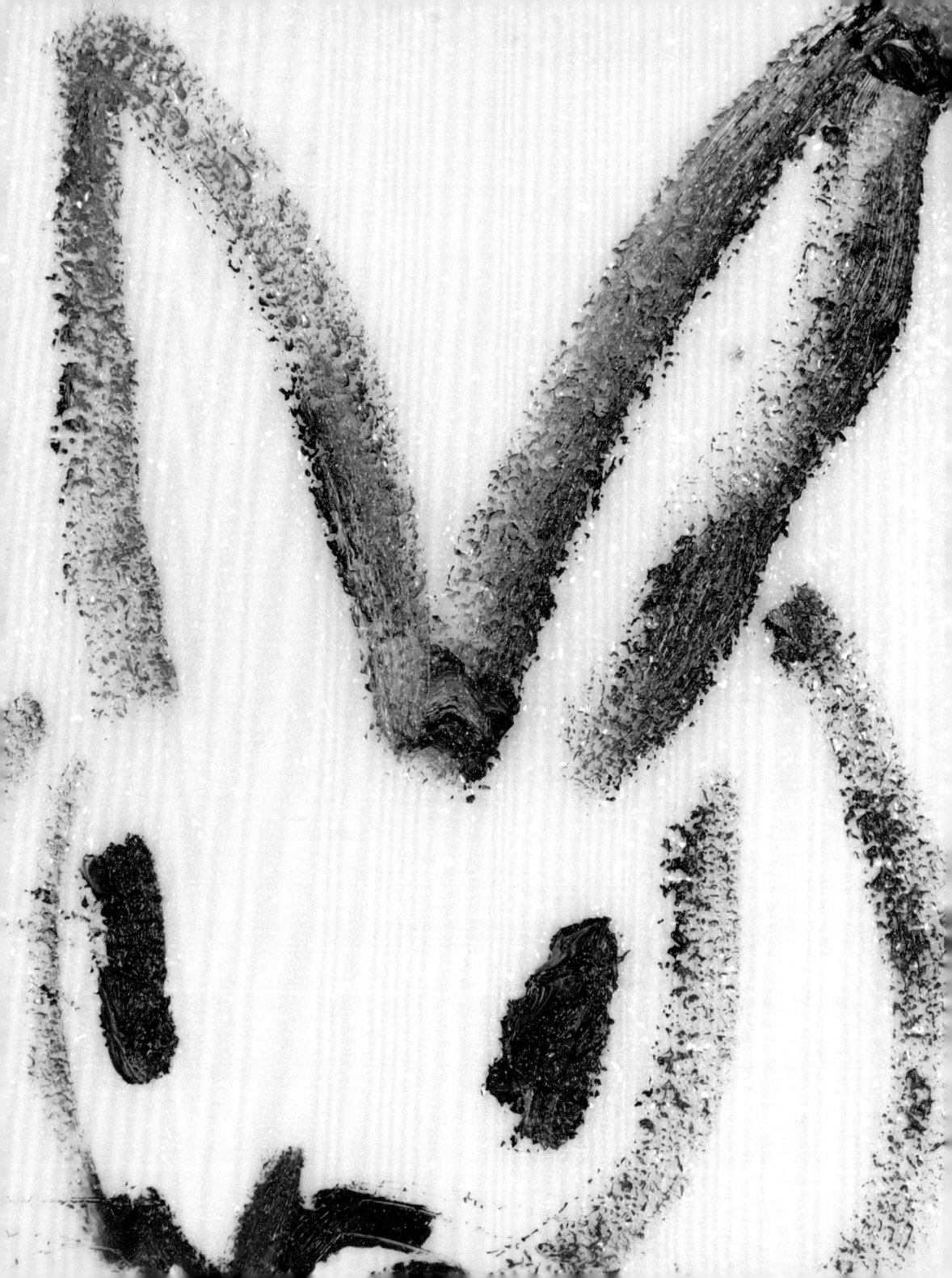

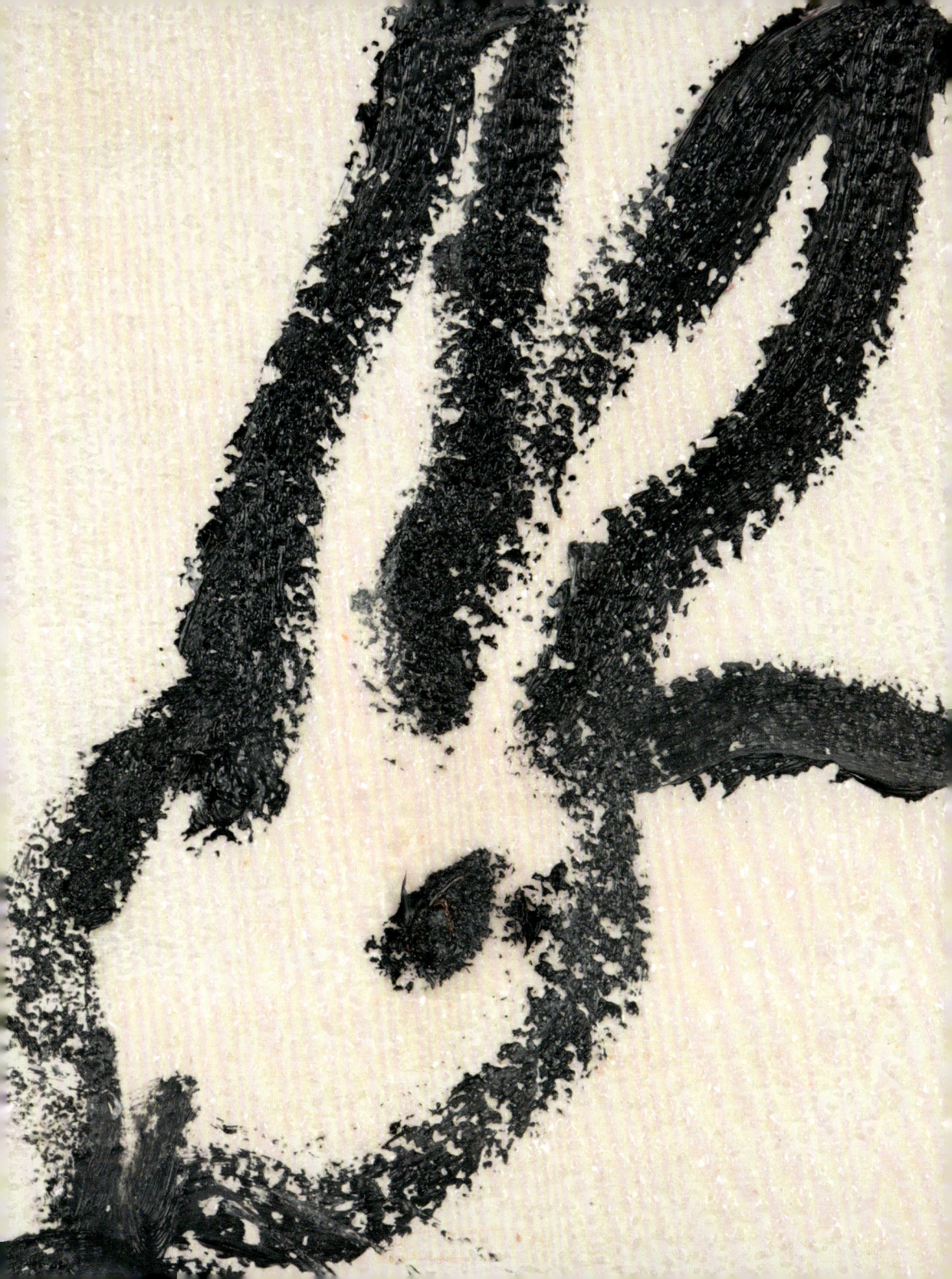

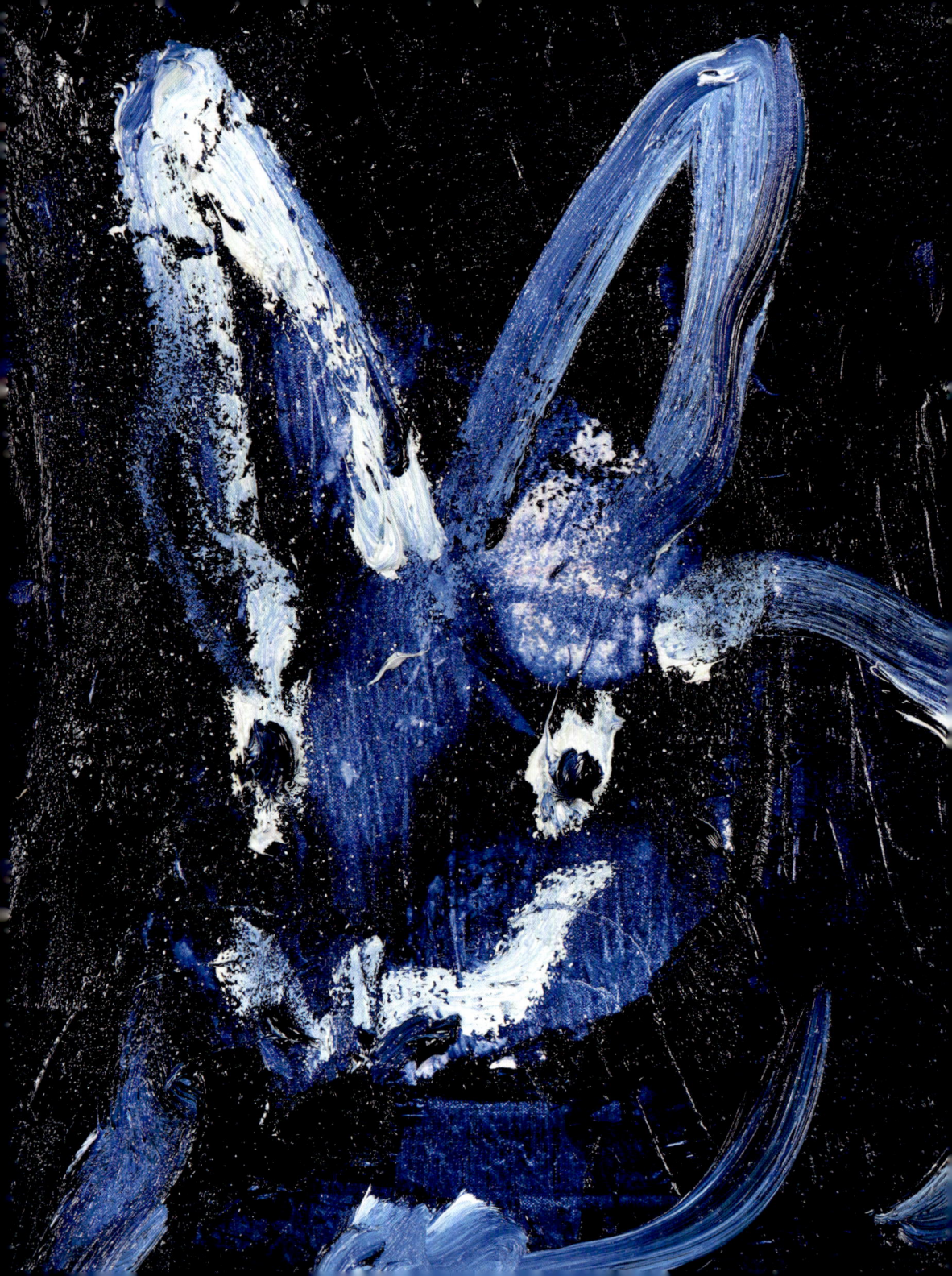

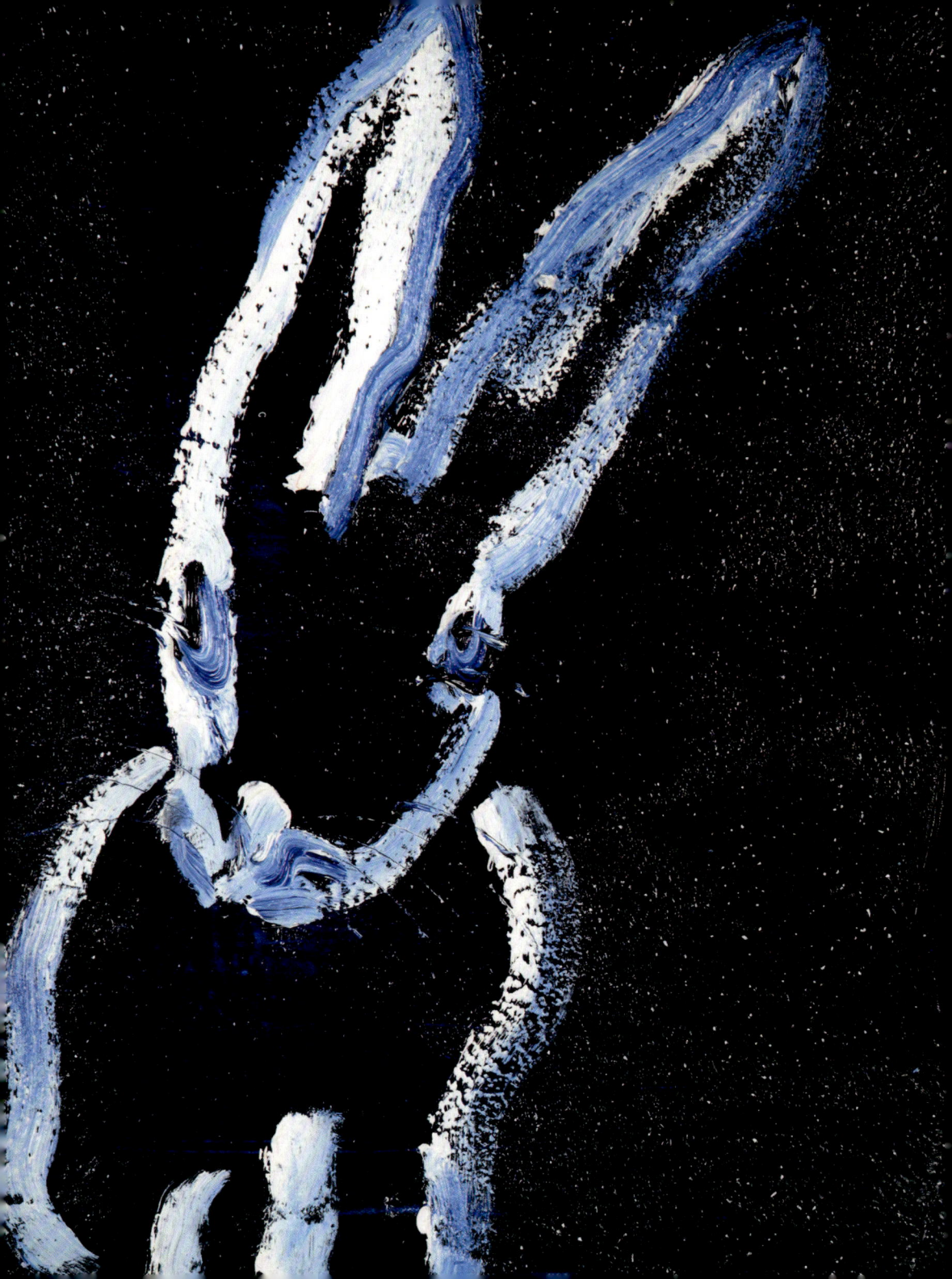

JANE
2013
OIL ON WOOD WITH
DIAMOND DUST
10" X 8"
PAGE 142

JOE
2013
OIL ON WOOD
10" X 8"
PAGE 143

LILIANA
2012
OIL ON CANVAS WITH
DIAMOND DUST
20" X 16"
PAGE 144

HEIDI
2013
OIL ON CANVAS WITH
DIAMOND DUST
20" X 16"
PAGE 145

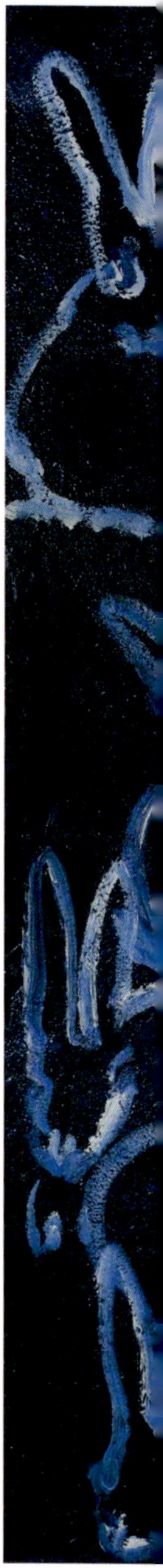

MIDNIGHT IN THE GARDEN OF GOOD & EVIL
2013
OIL ON CANVAS
72" X 72"

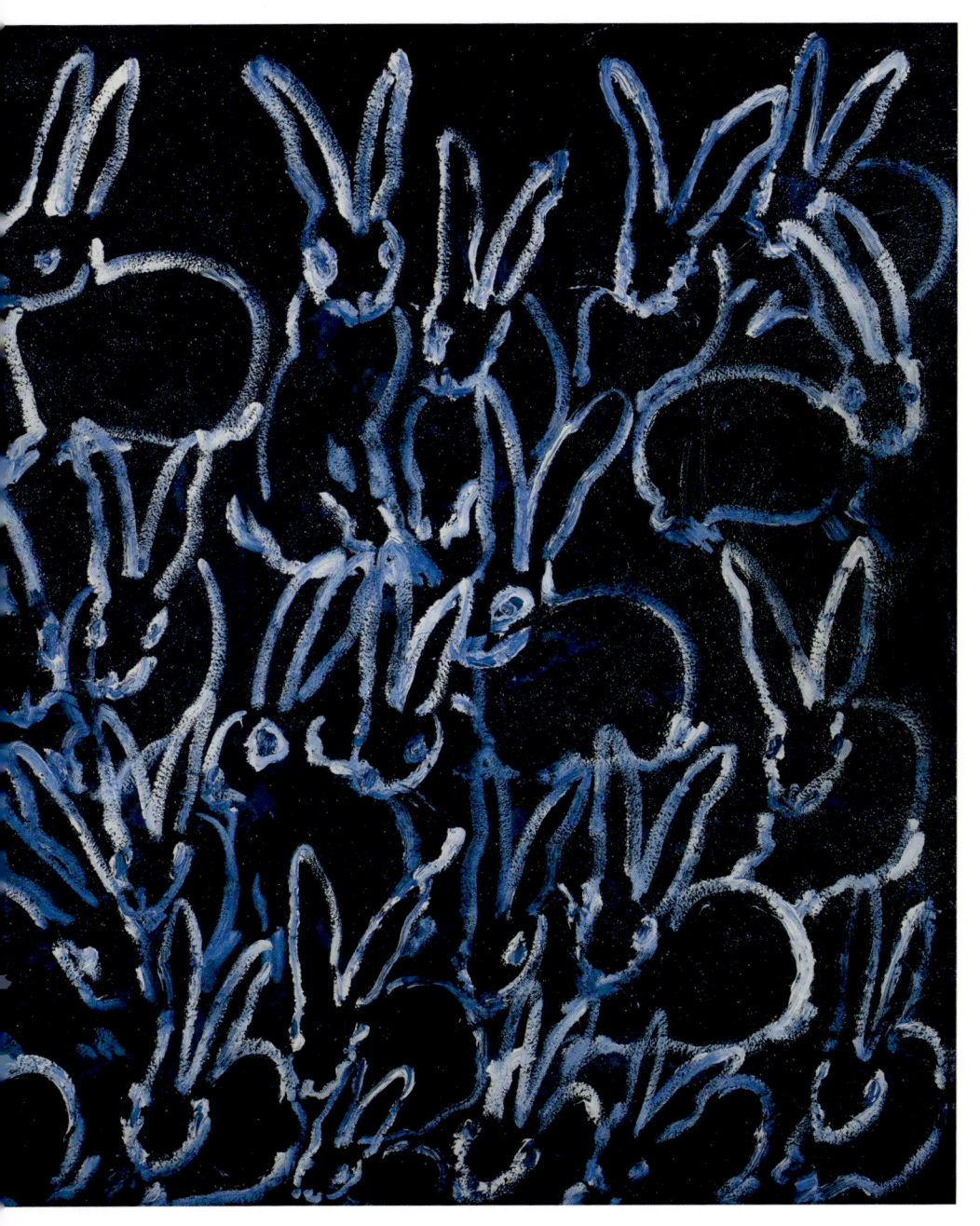

Pierre
2013
OIL ON CANVAS AND DIAMOND DUST
20" x 16"

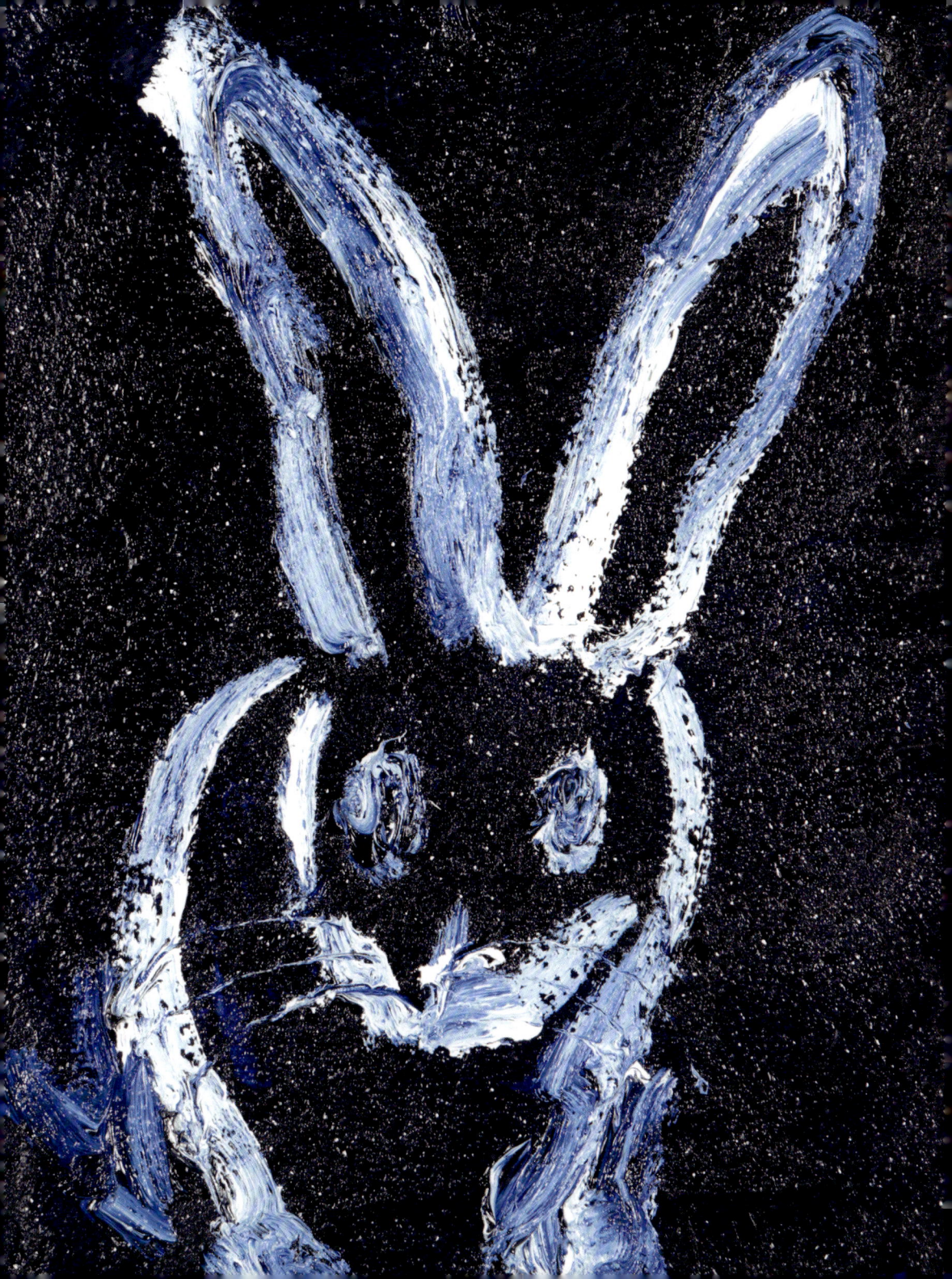

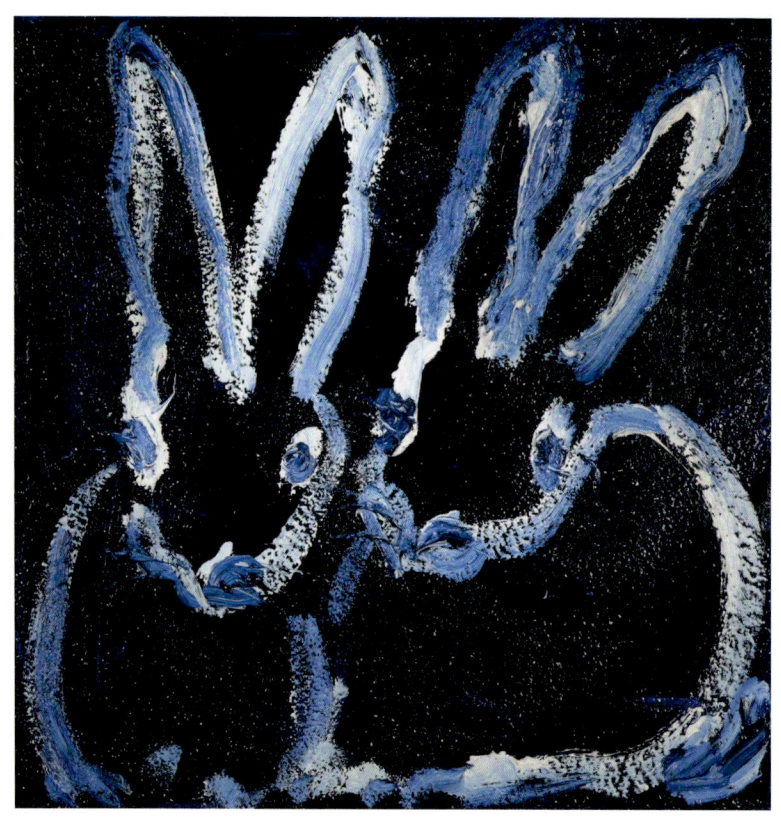

A Girl's Best Friend
2013
OIL ON CANVAS WITH DIAMOND DUST
37" x 37"

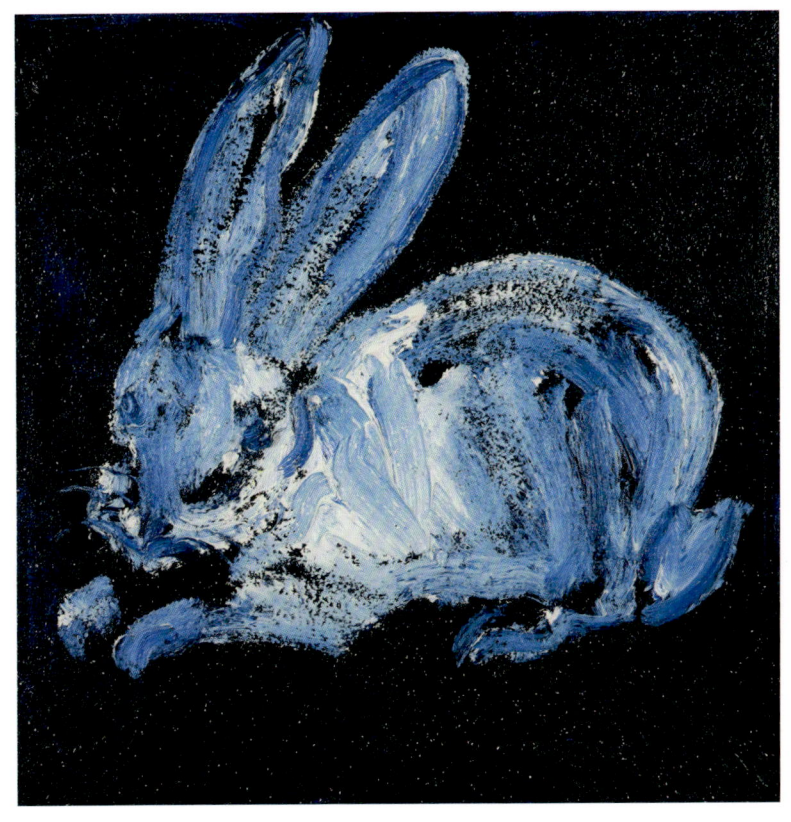

PIXIE
2013
OIL ON CANVAS WITH DIAMOND DUST
37" X 37"

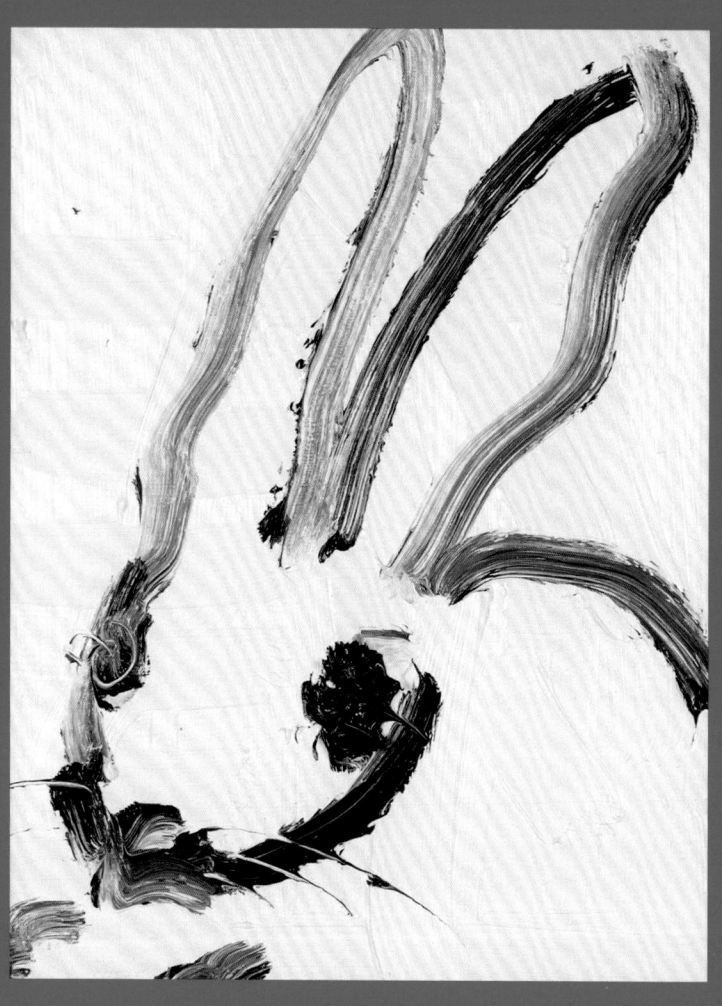

152

SYLVIA
2013
OIL ON WOOD
10" X 8"

ROBBIN & SHELLY
2013
OIL ON CANVAS
28" X 22"

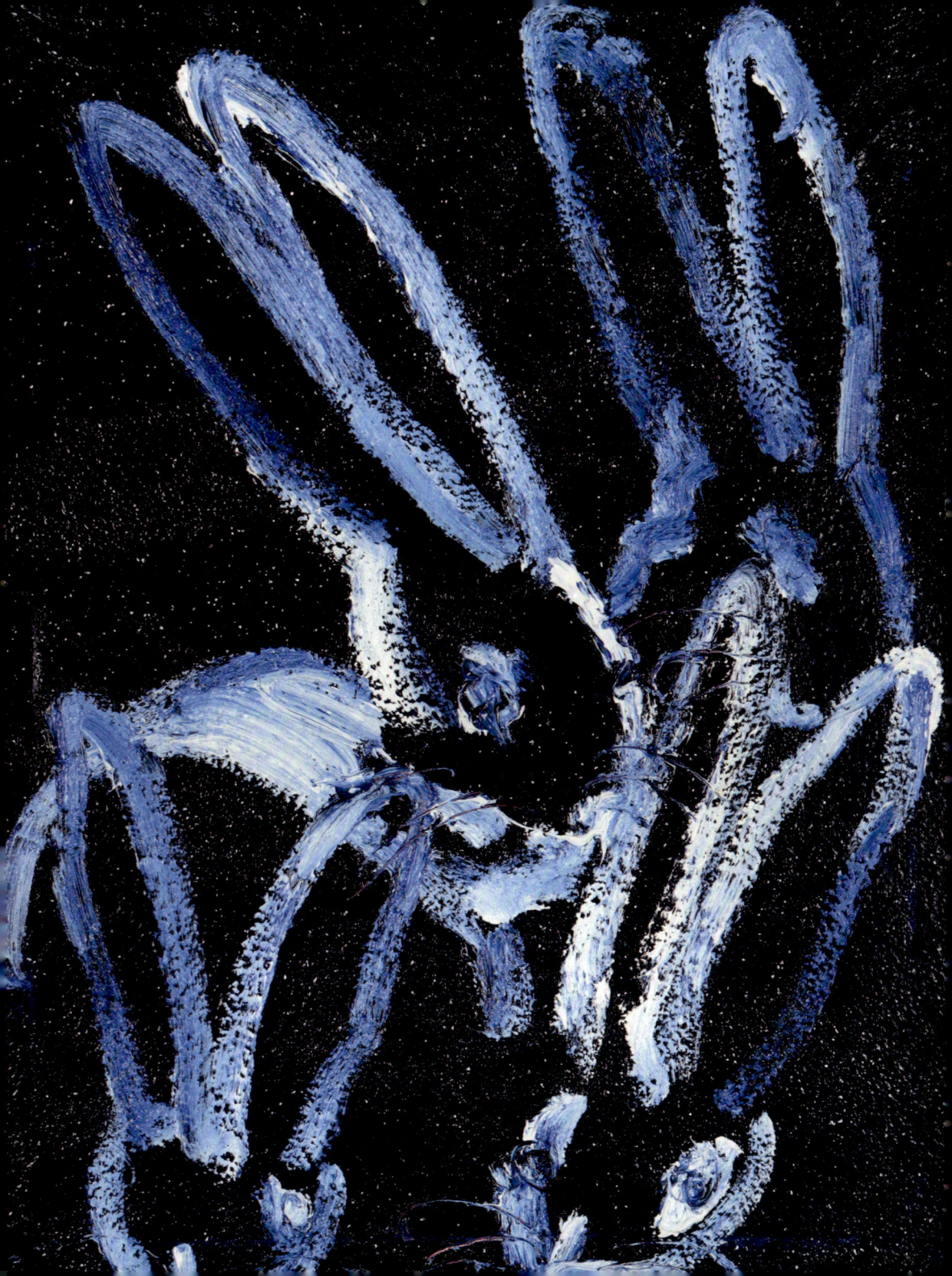

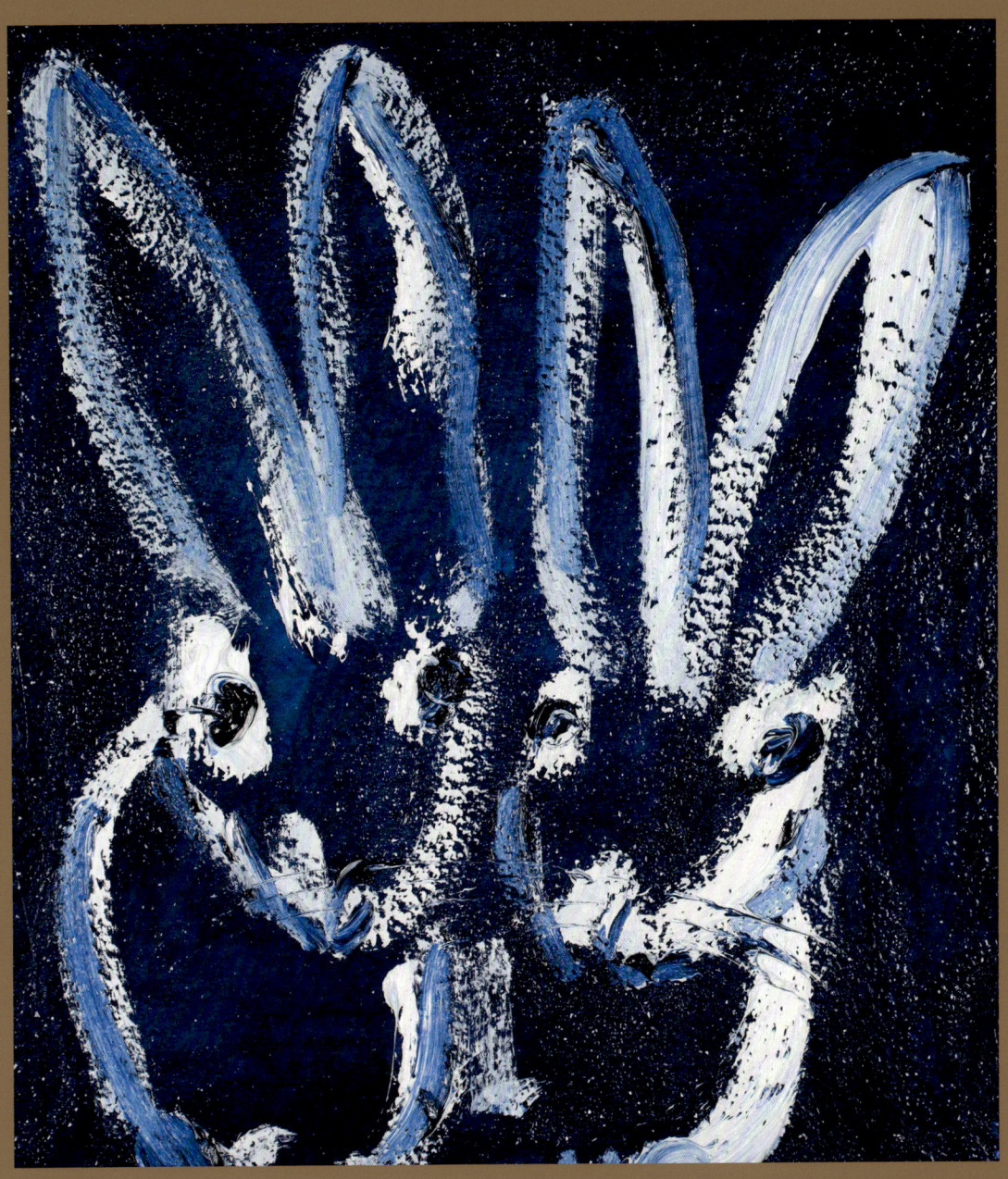

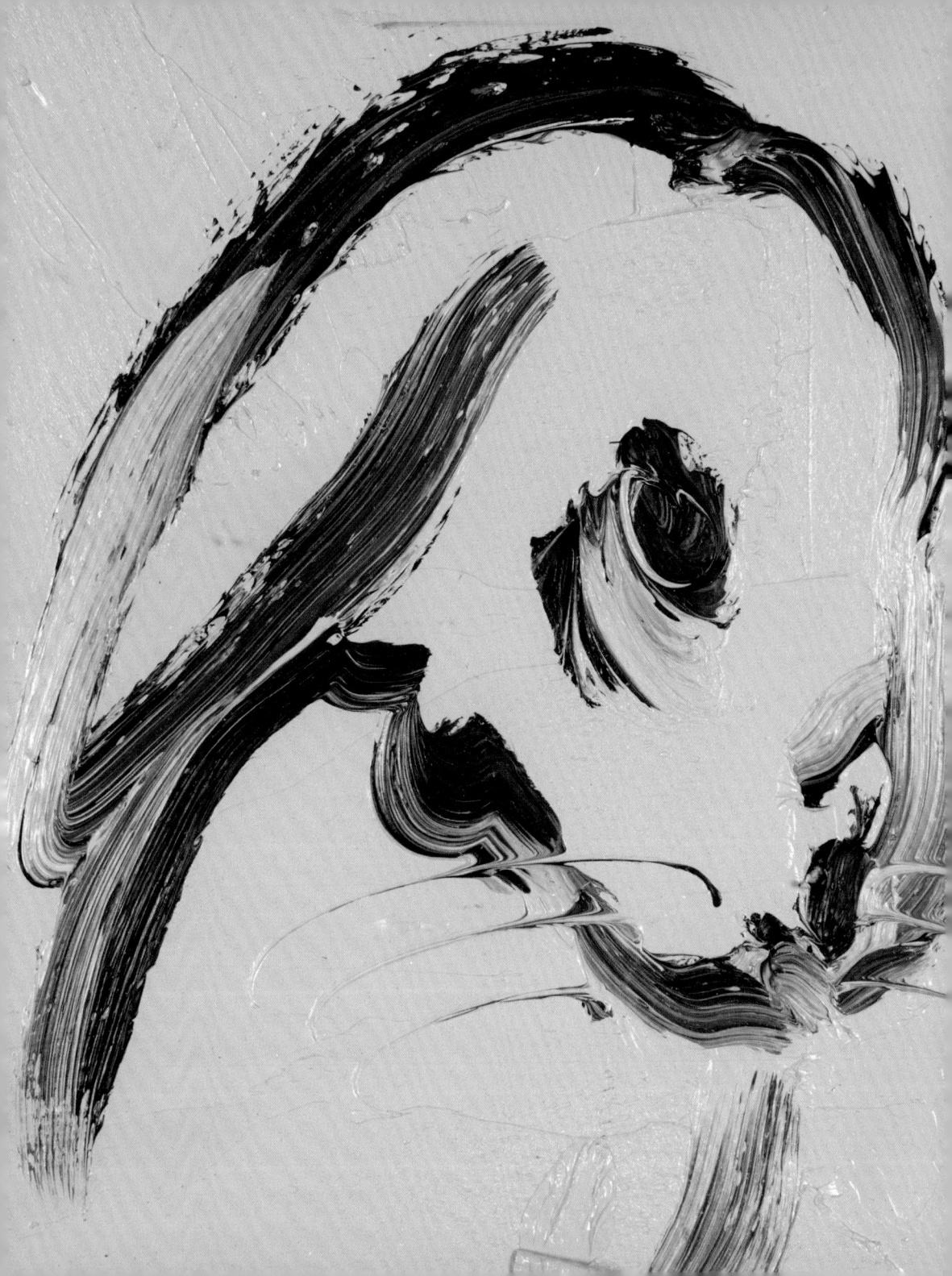

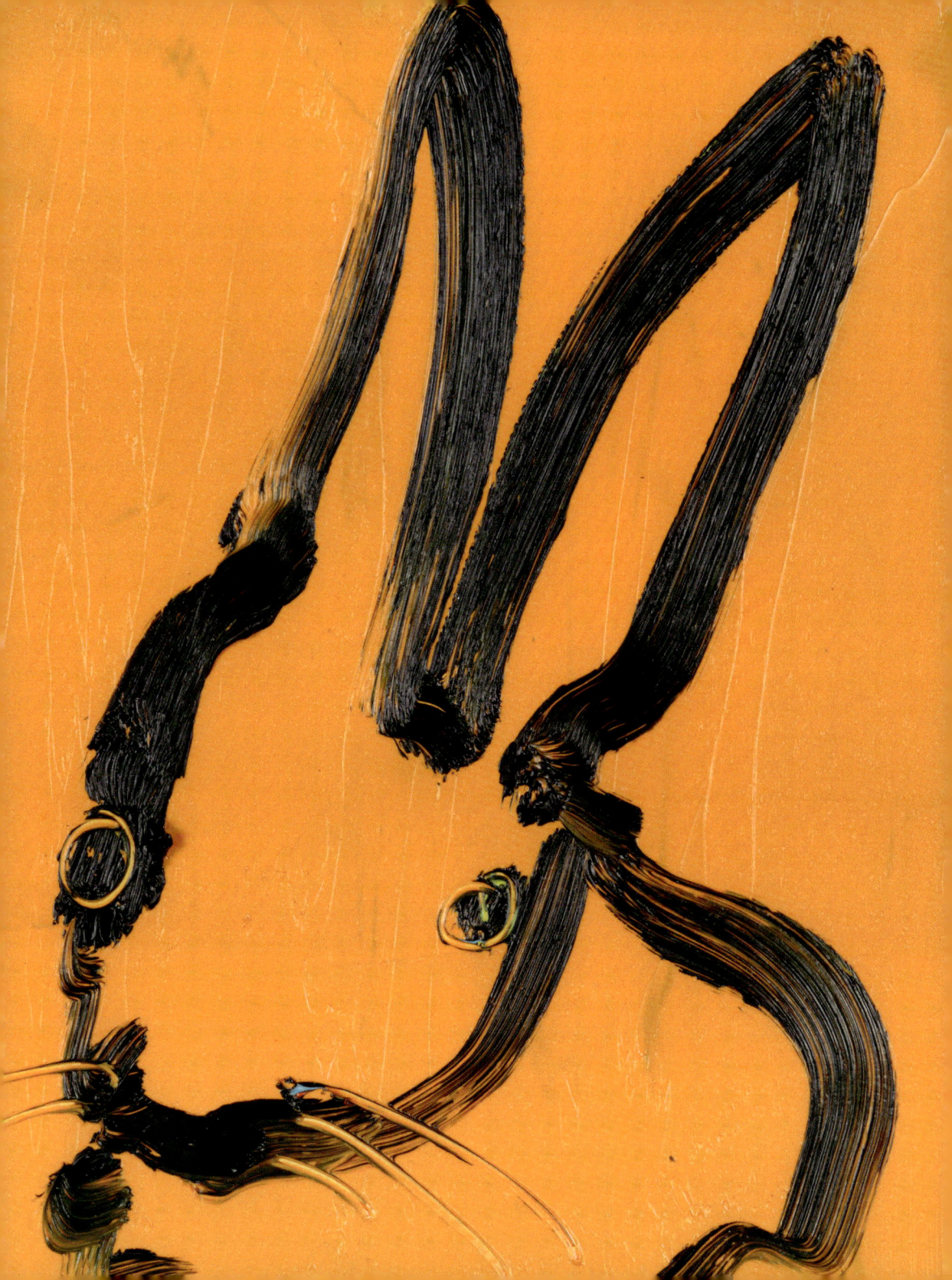

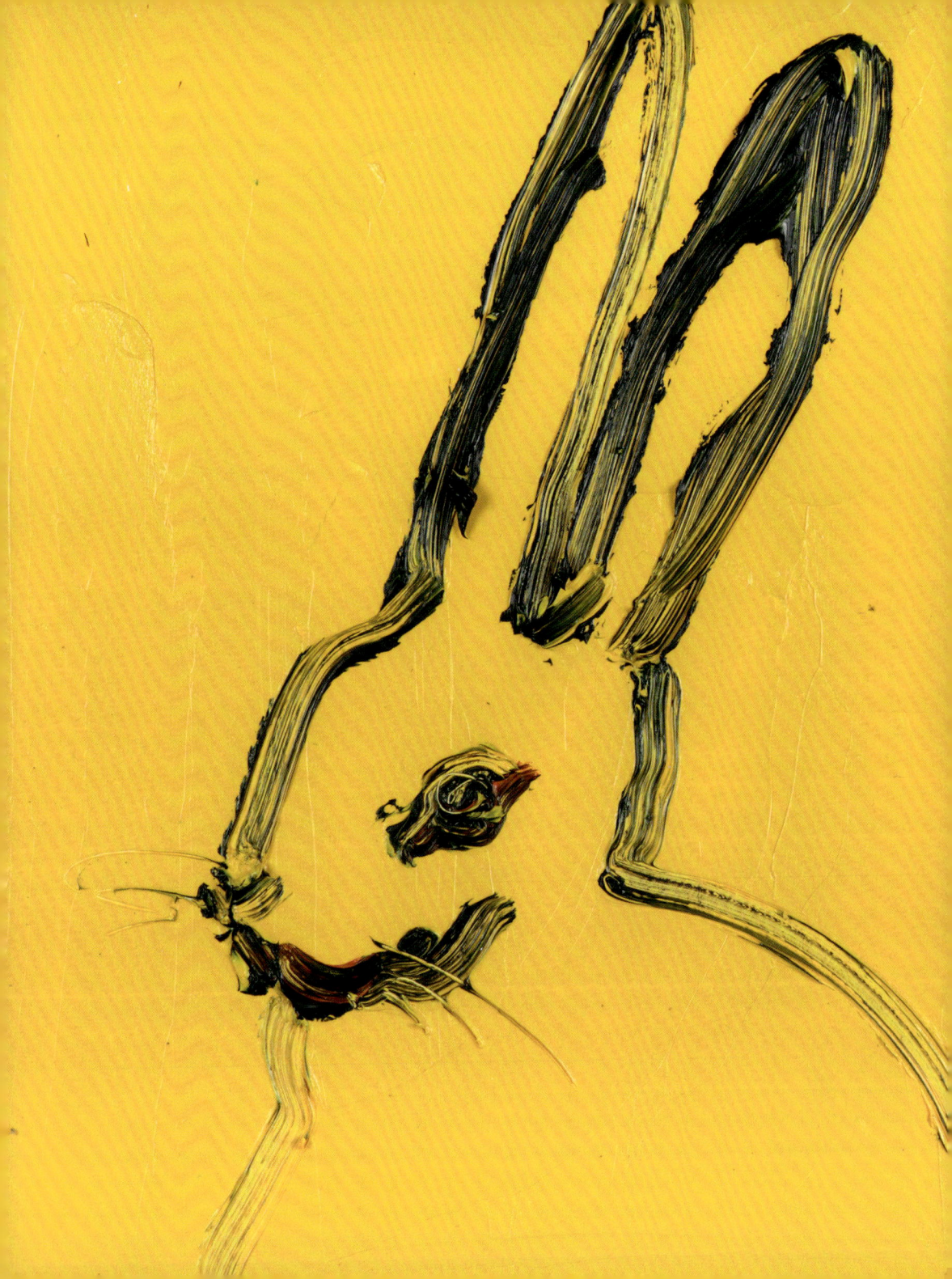

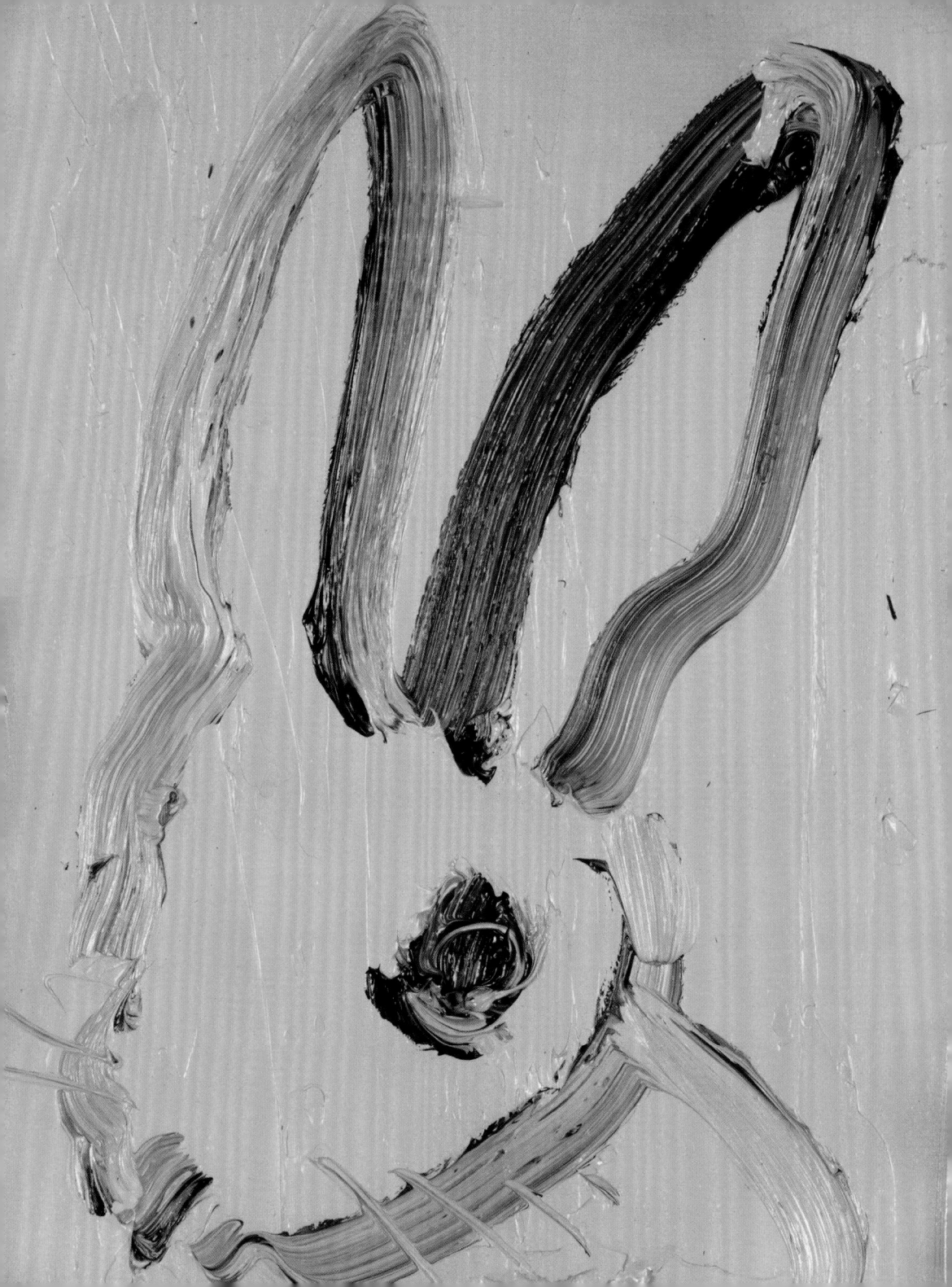

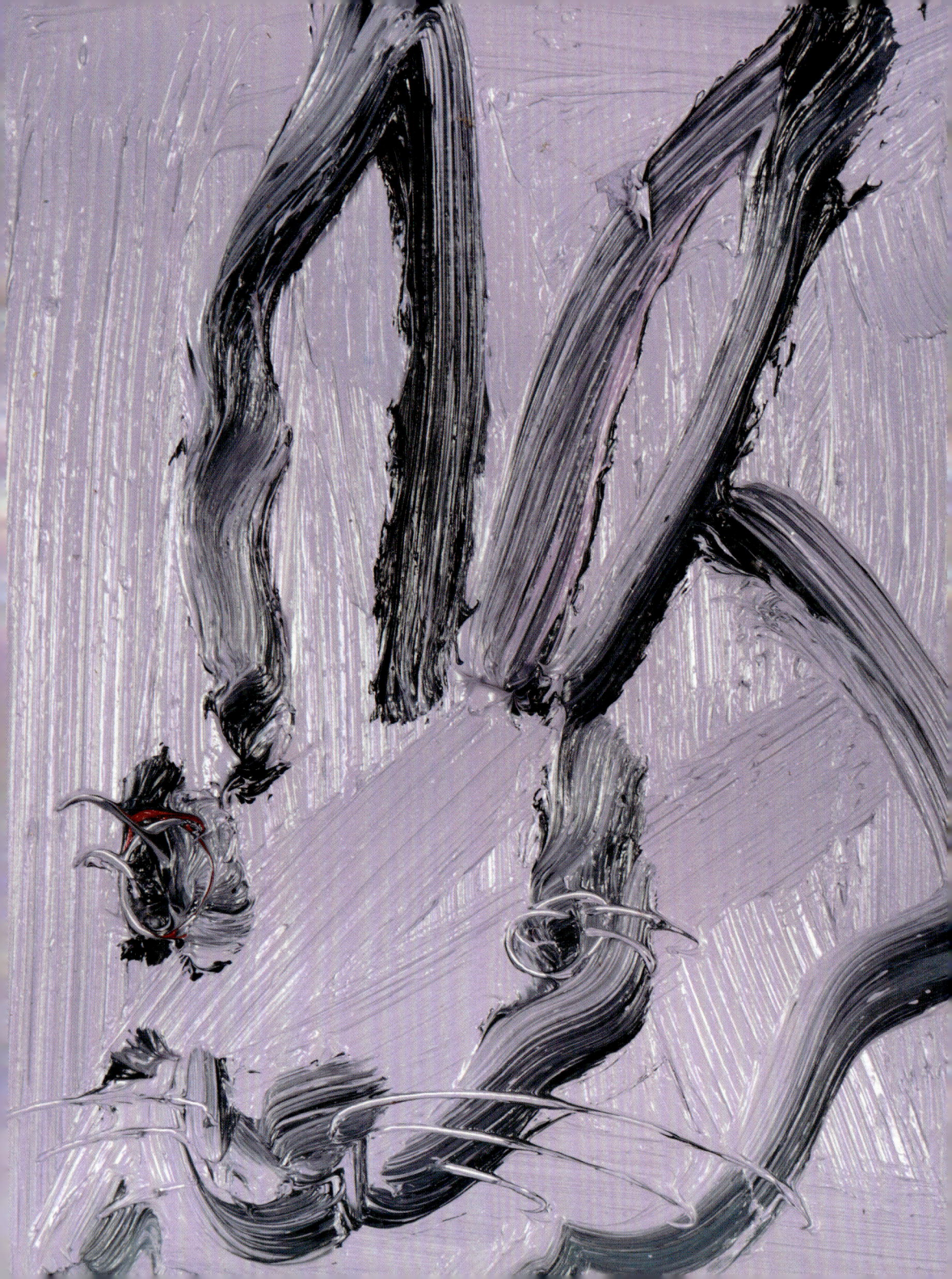

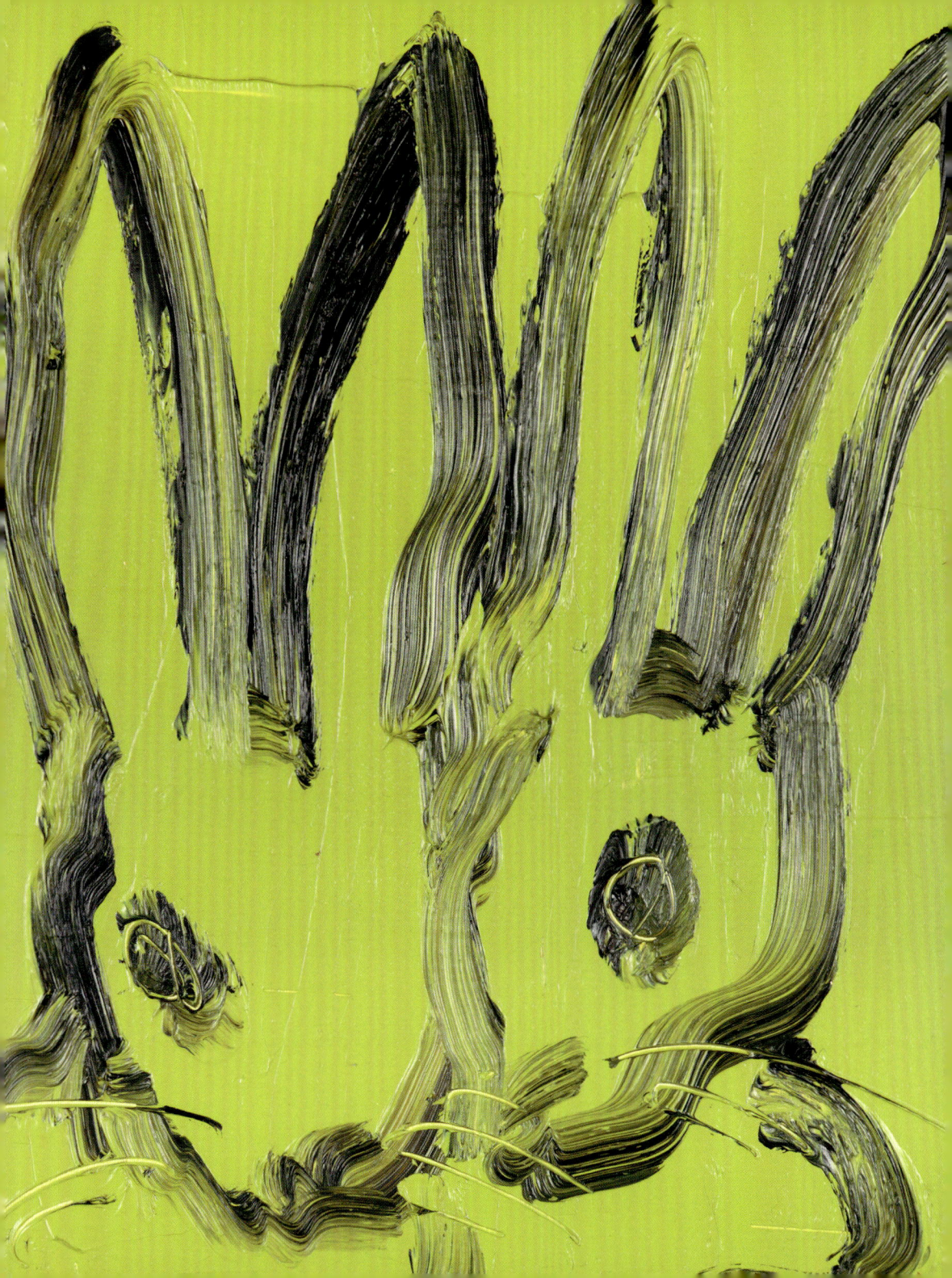

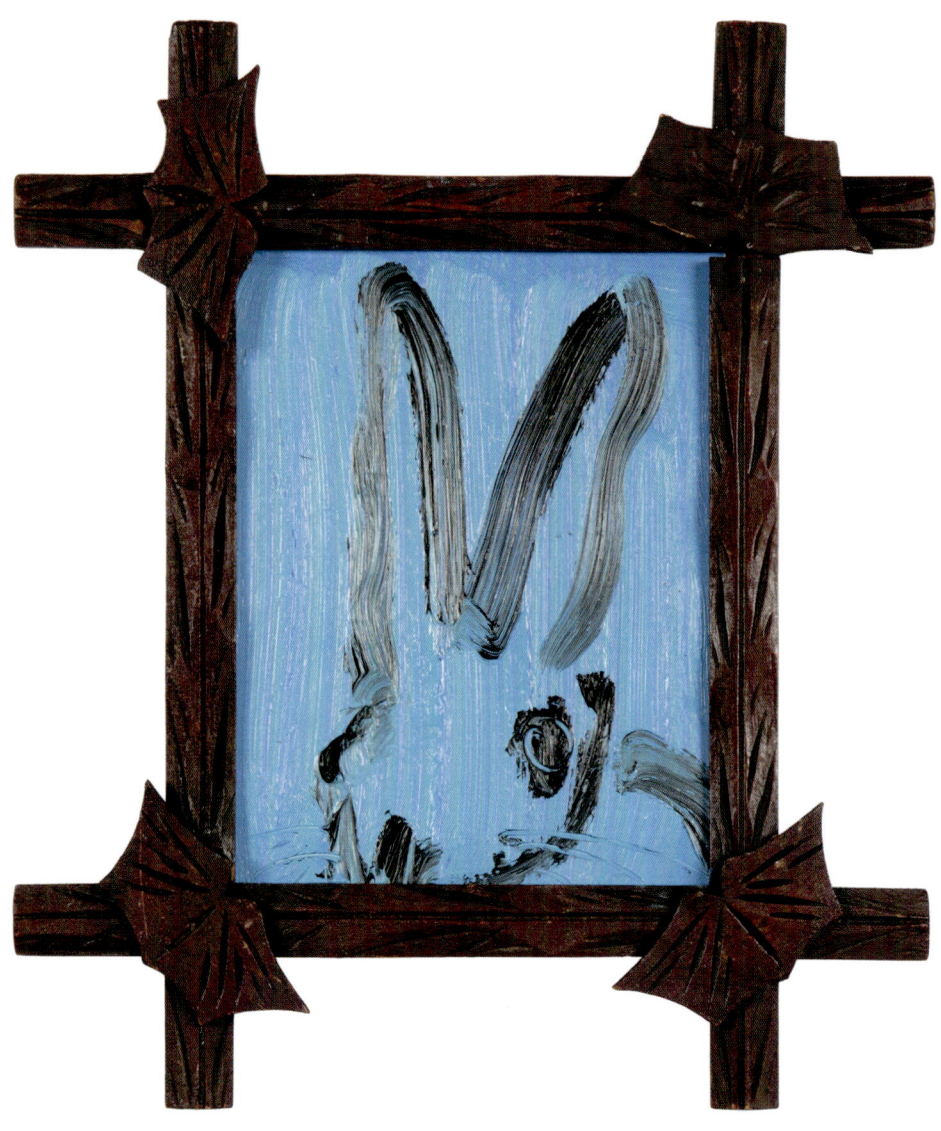

162

Jimmy
2012
OIL ON WOOD
10" x 8"

Lazy Susan
2013
OIL ON WOOD
10" x 8"

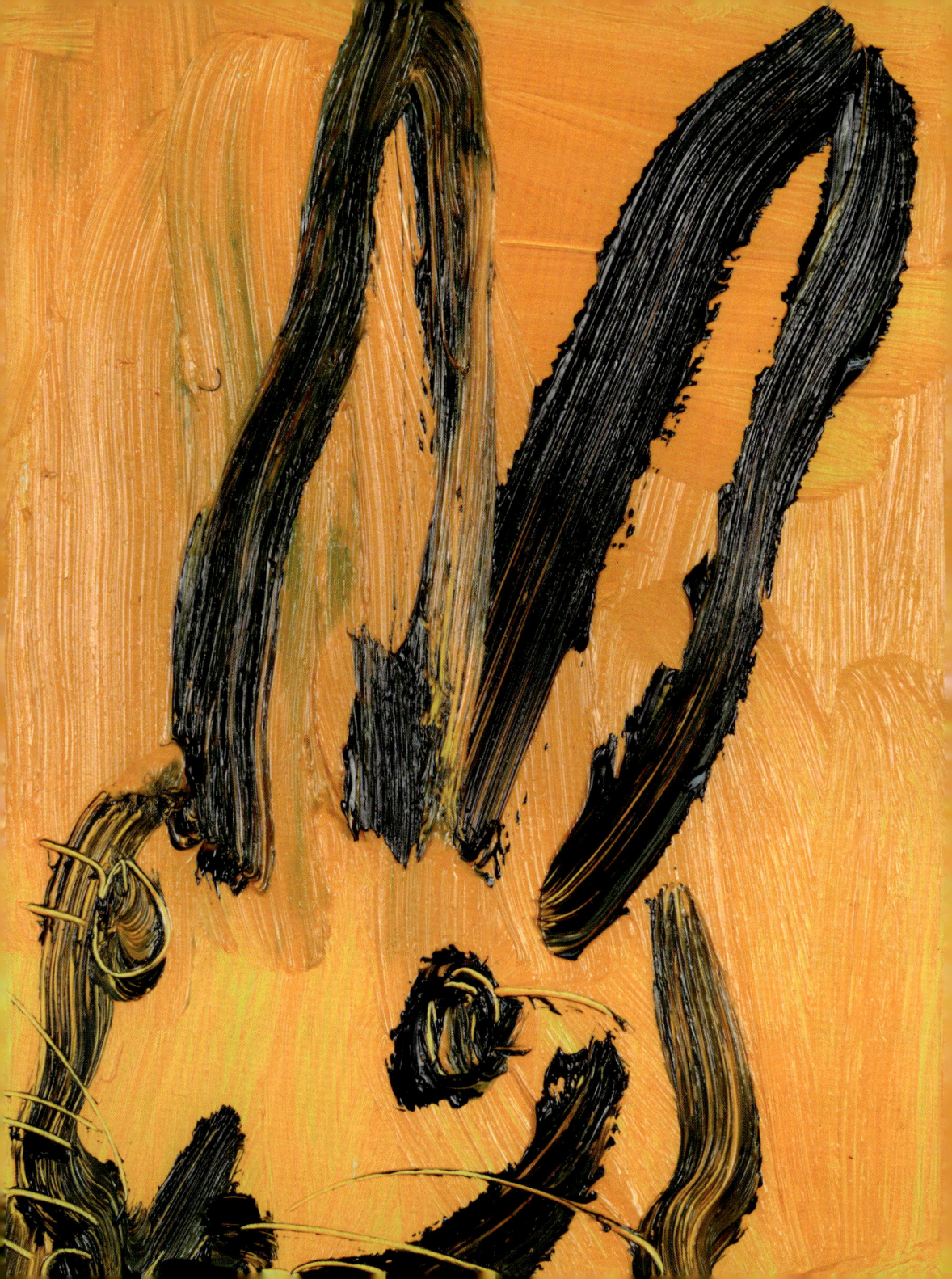

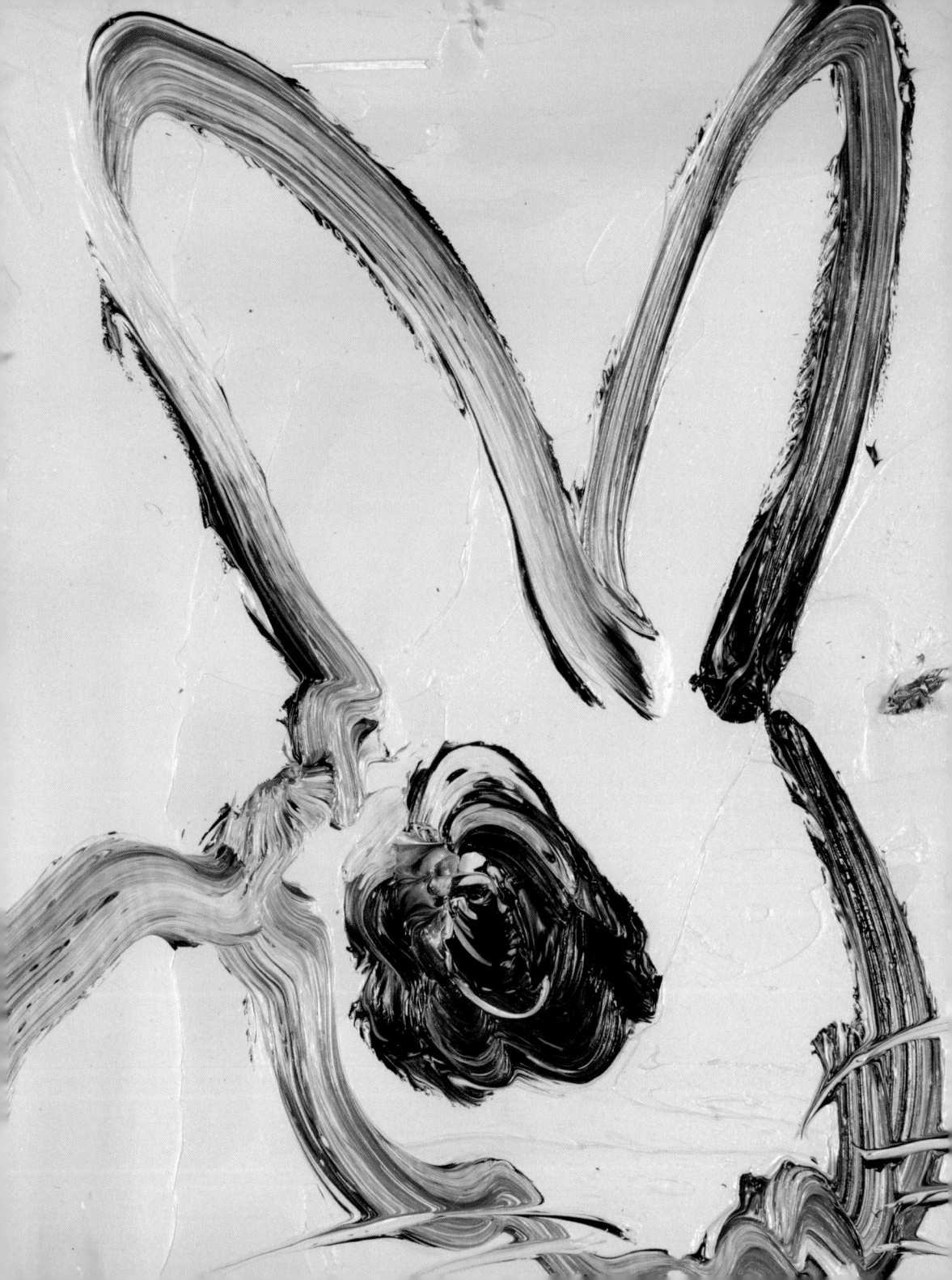

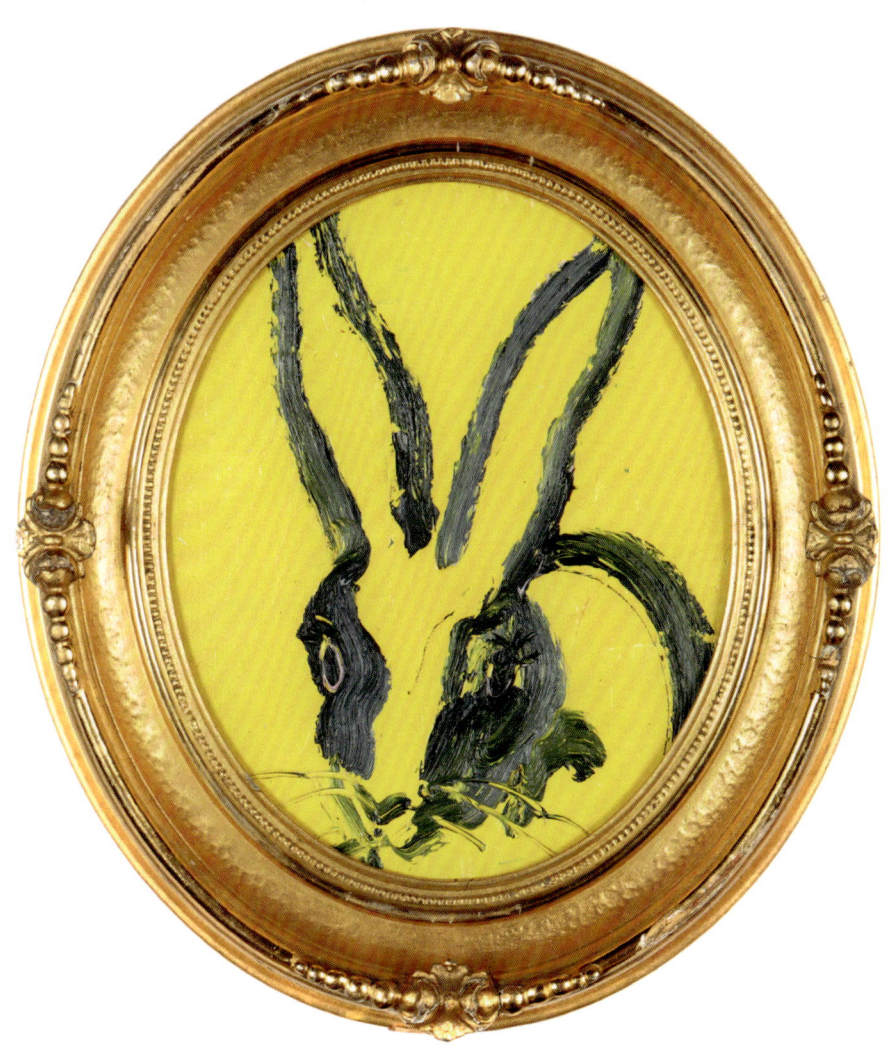

JEREMY
2013
OIL ON WOOD
10" X 8"

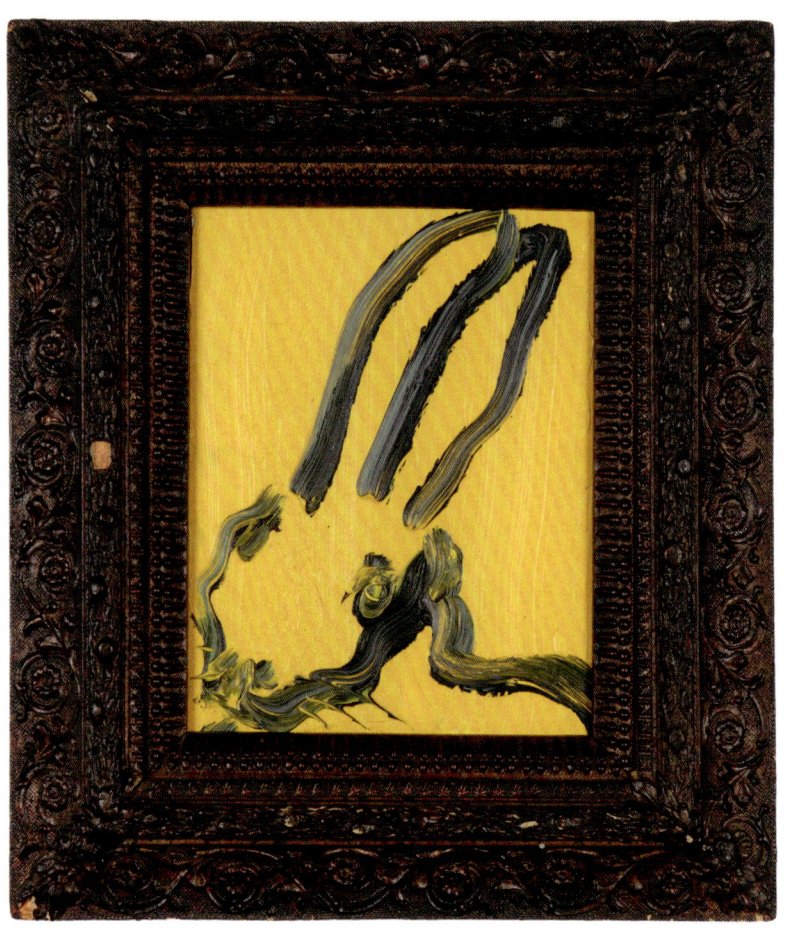

166

CARMEN
2013
OIL ON WOOD
10" X 8"

ROSETTA
2011
OIL ON WOOD
10" X 8"

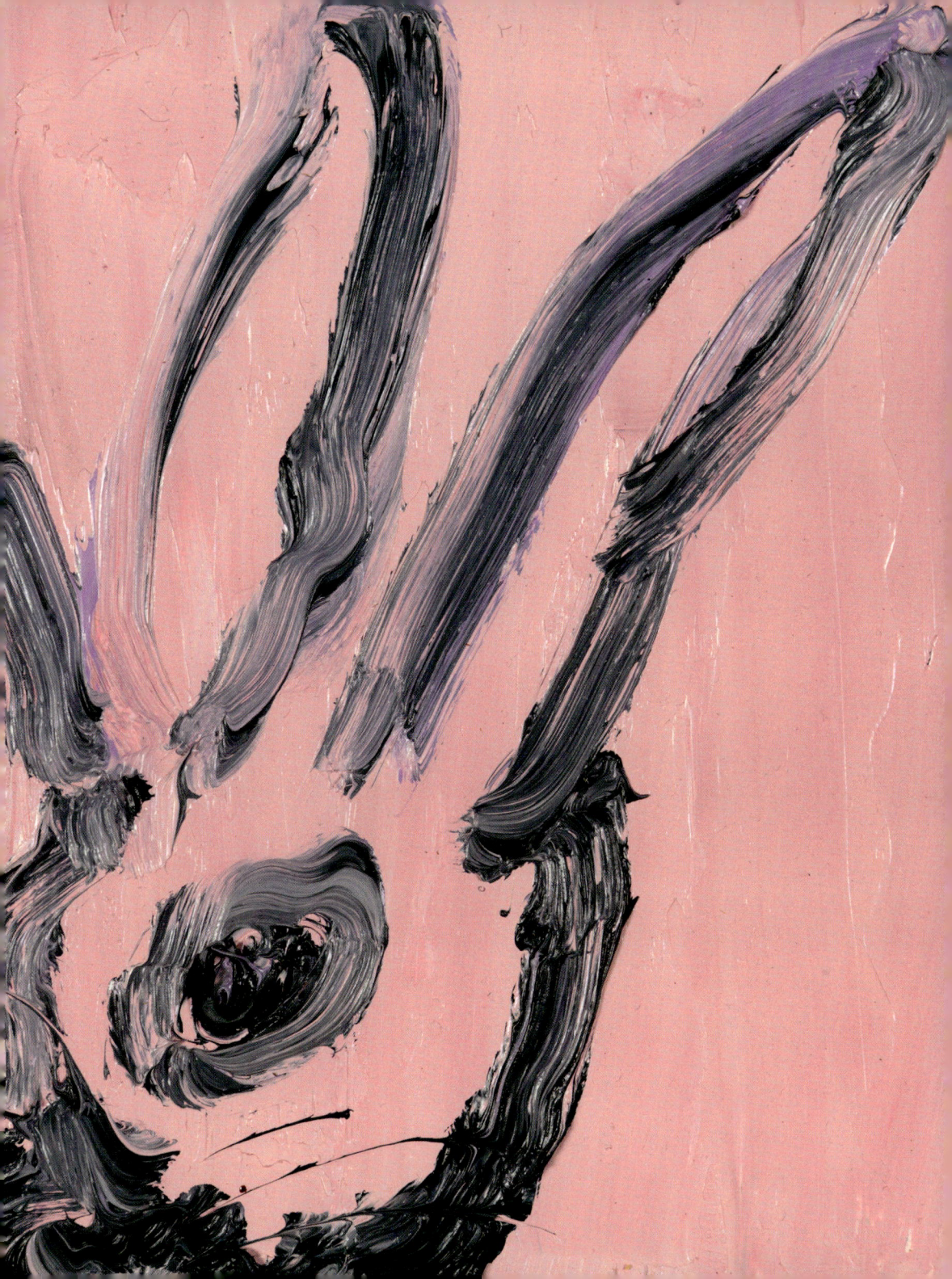

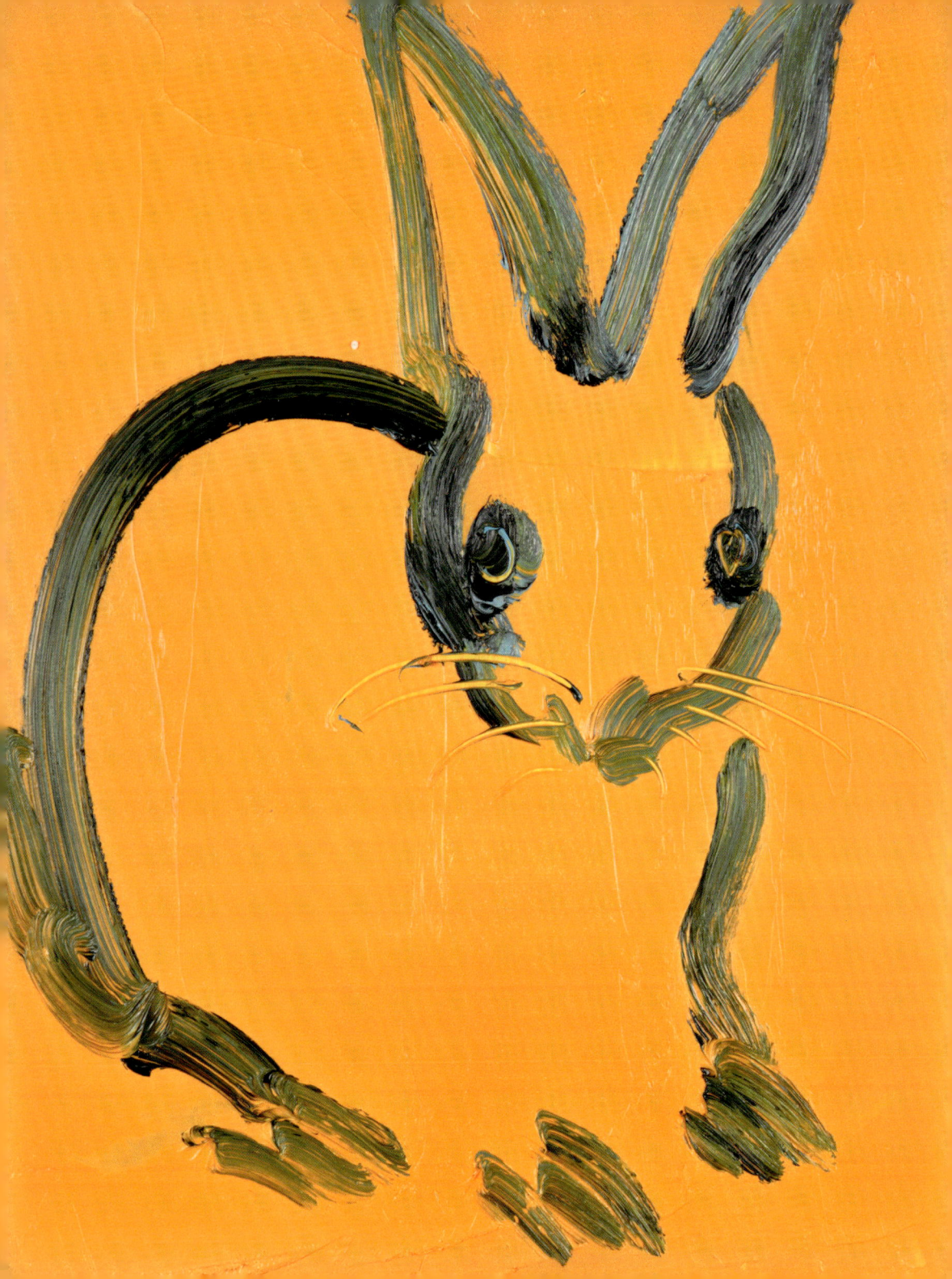

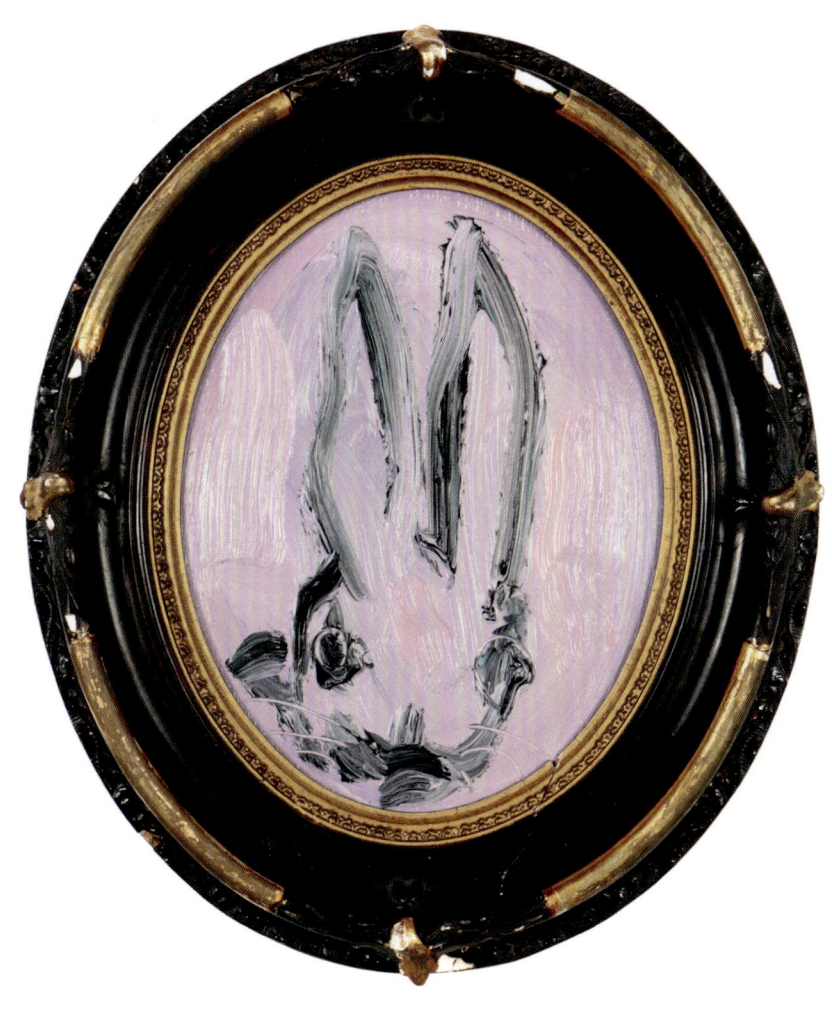

MATILDA
2013
OIL ON WOOD
10" X 8"

MONIQUE II
2012
OIL ON WOOD
10" X 8"

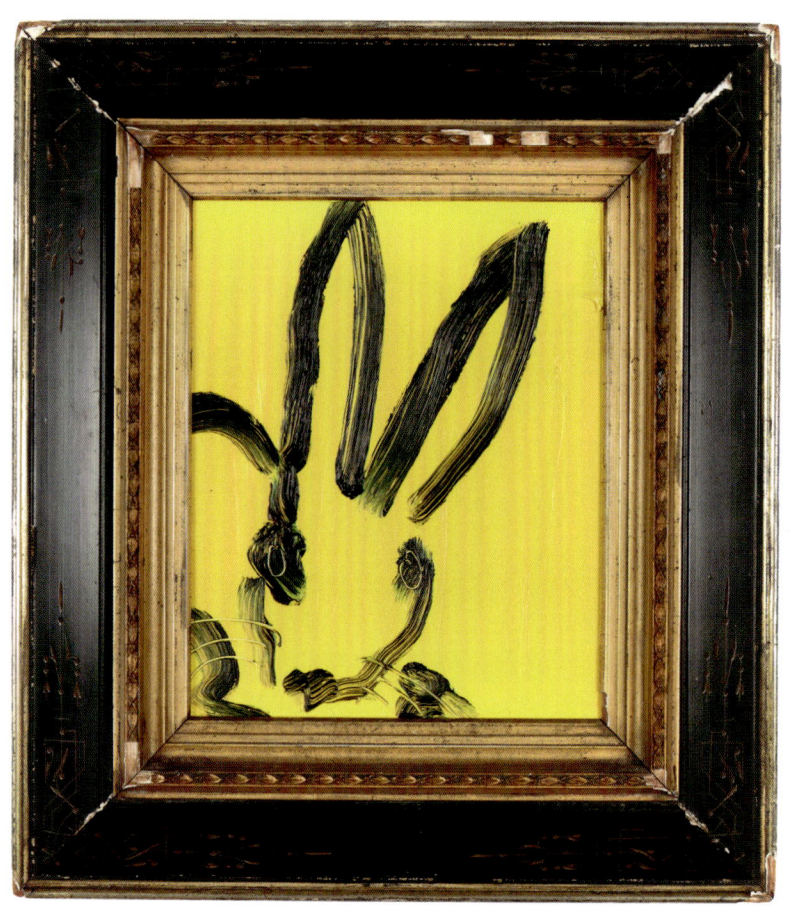

LUCIA
2013
OIL ON WOOD
12" X 10"

FRANK
2013
OIL ON WOOD
10" X 8"

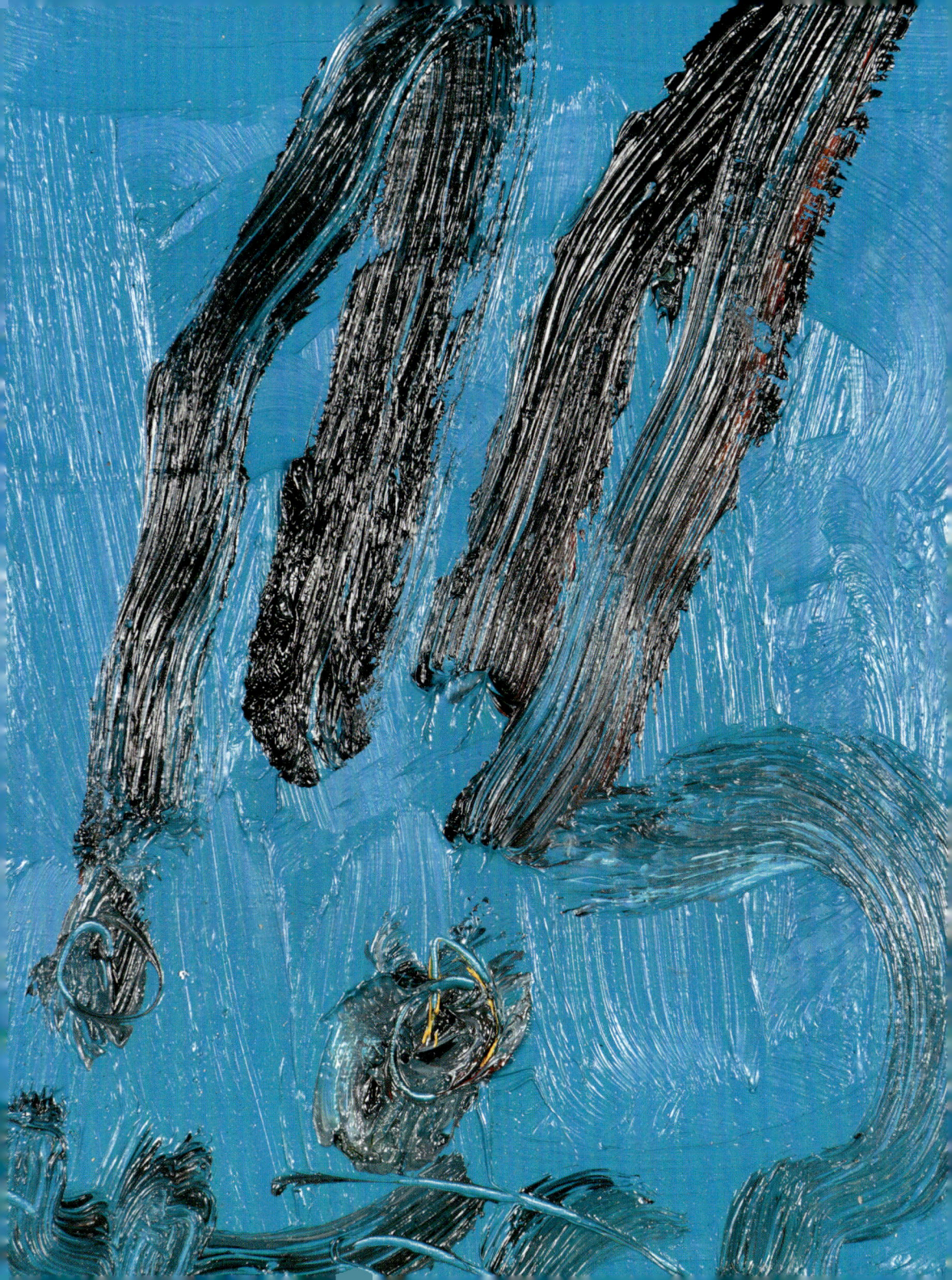

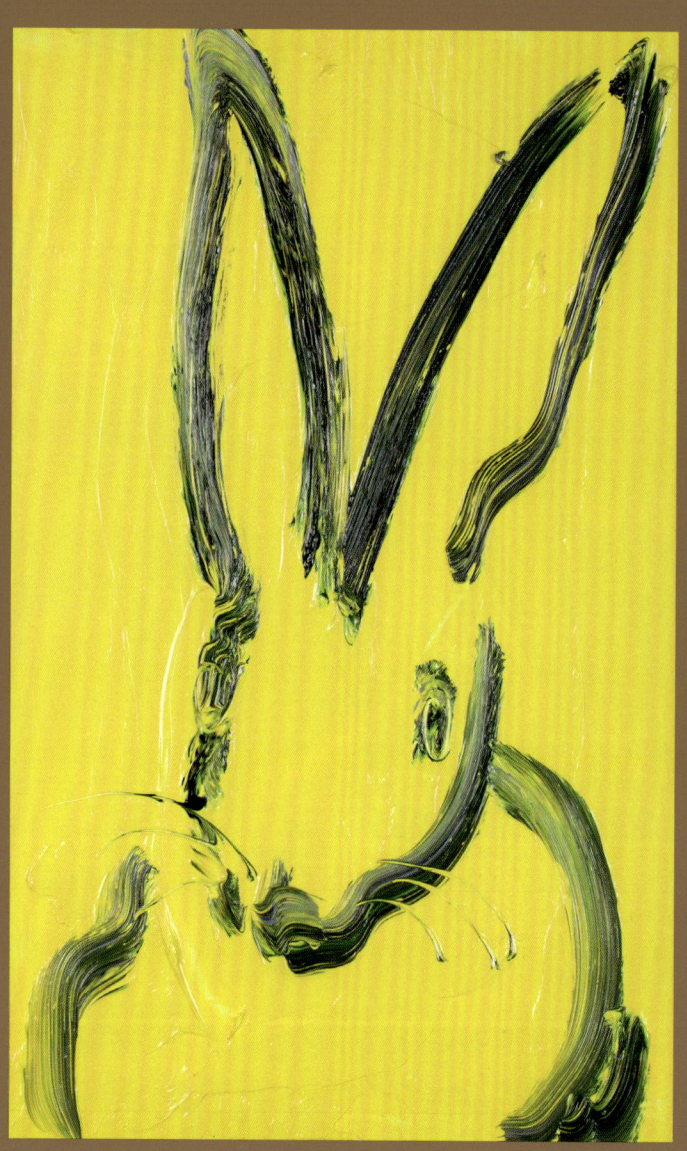

Daffodil
2013
OIL ON WOOD
15.5" X 11"

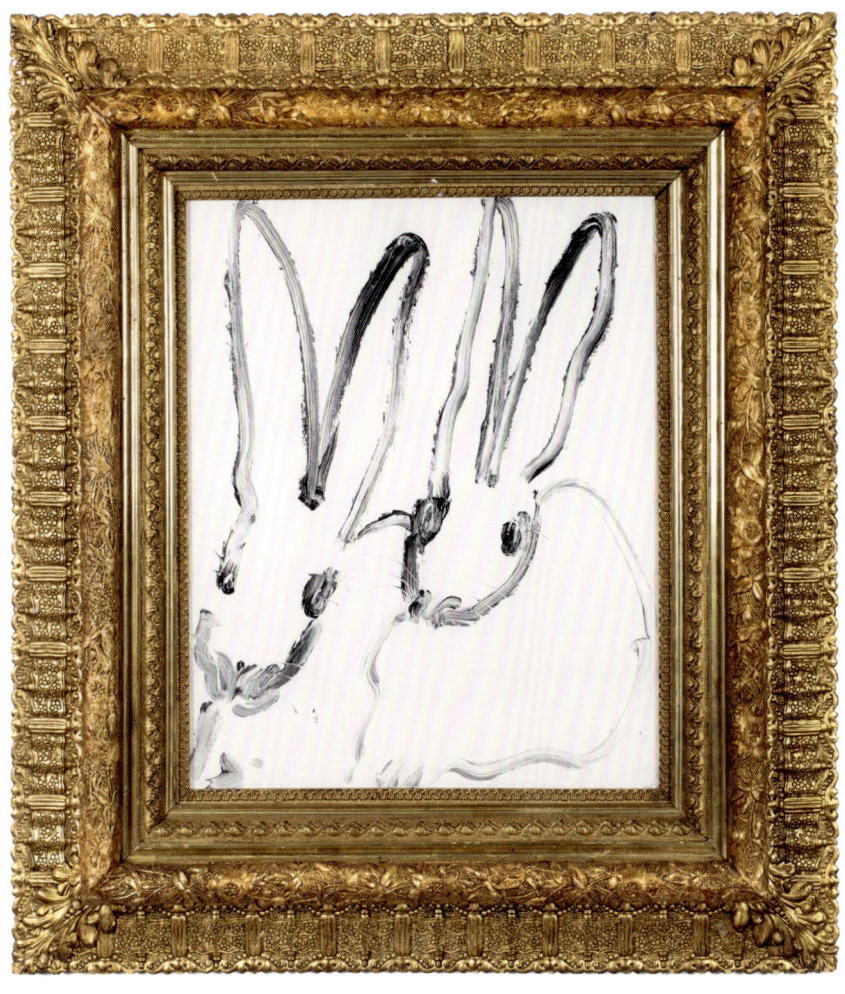

Double Bunny
2013
OIL ON WOOD
22" X 18"

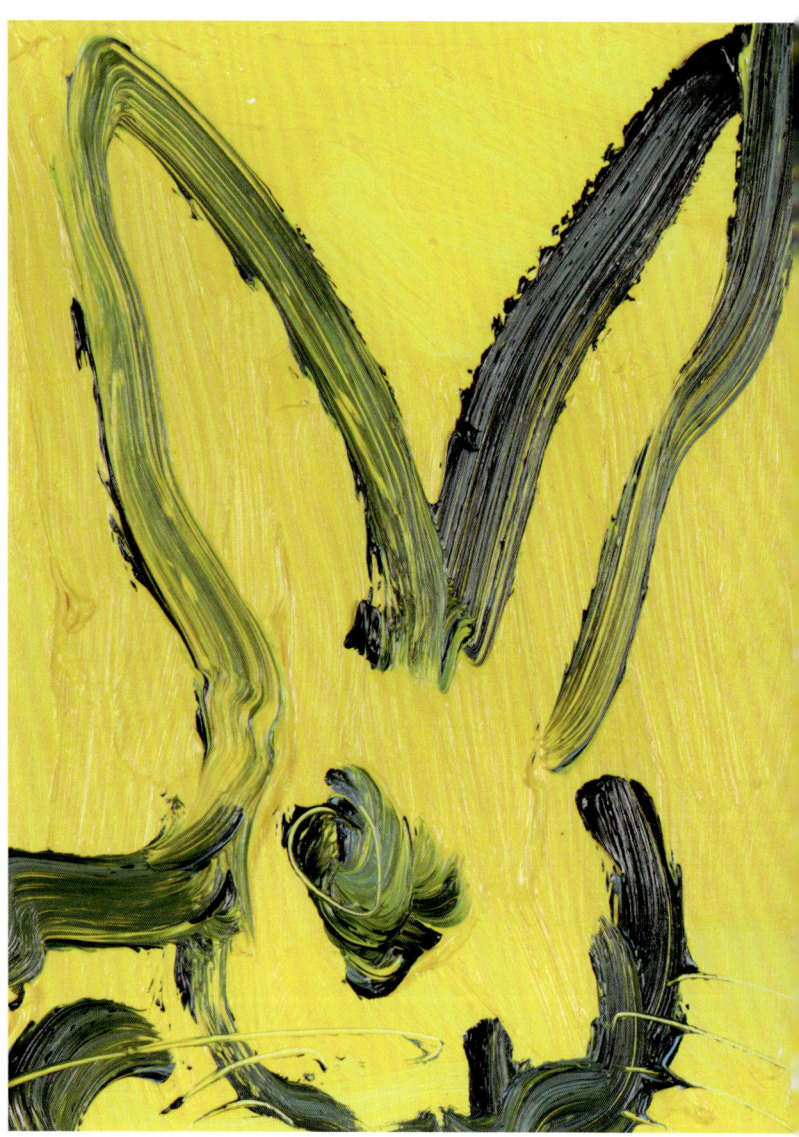

THE BEST
2013
OIL ON WOOD
10" X 8"

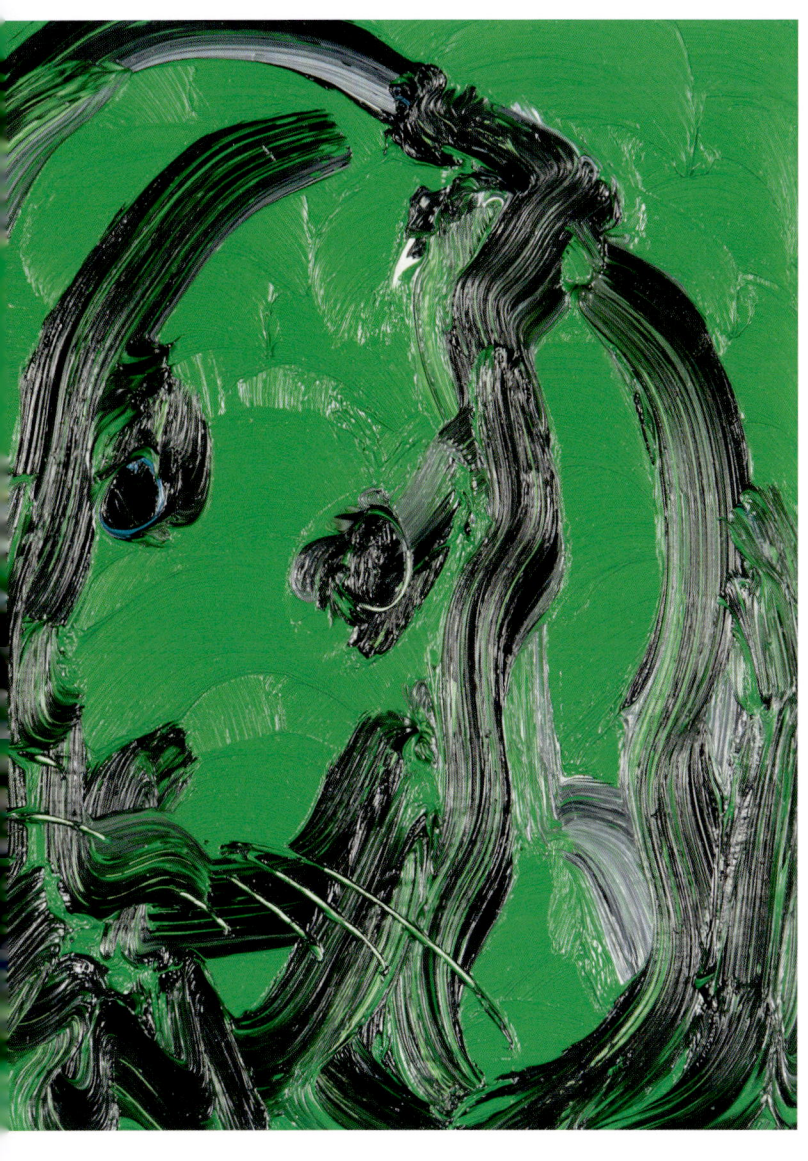

DON
2013
OIL ON WOOD
10" x 8"

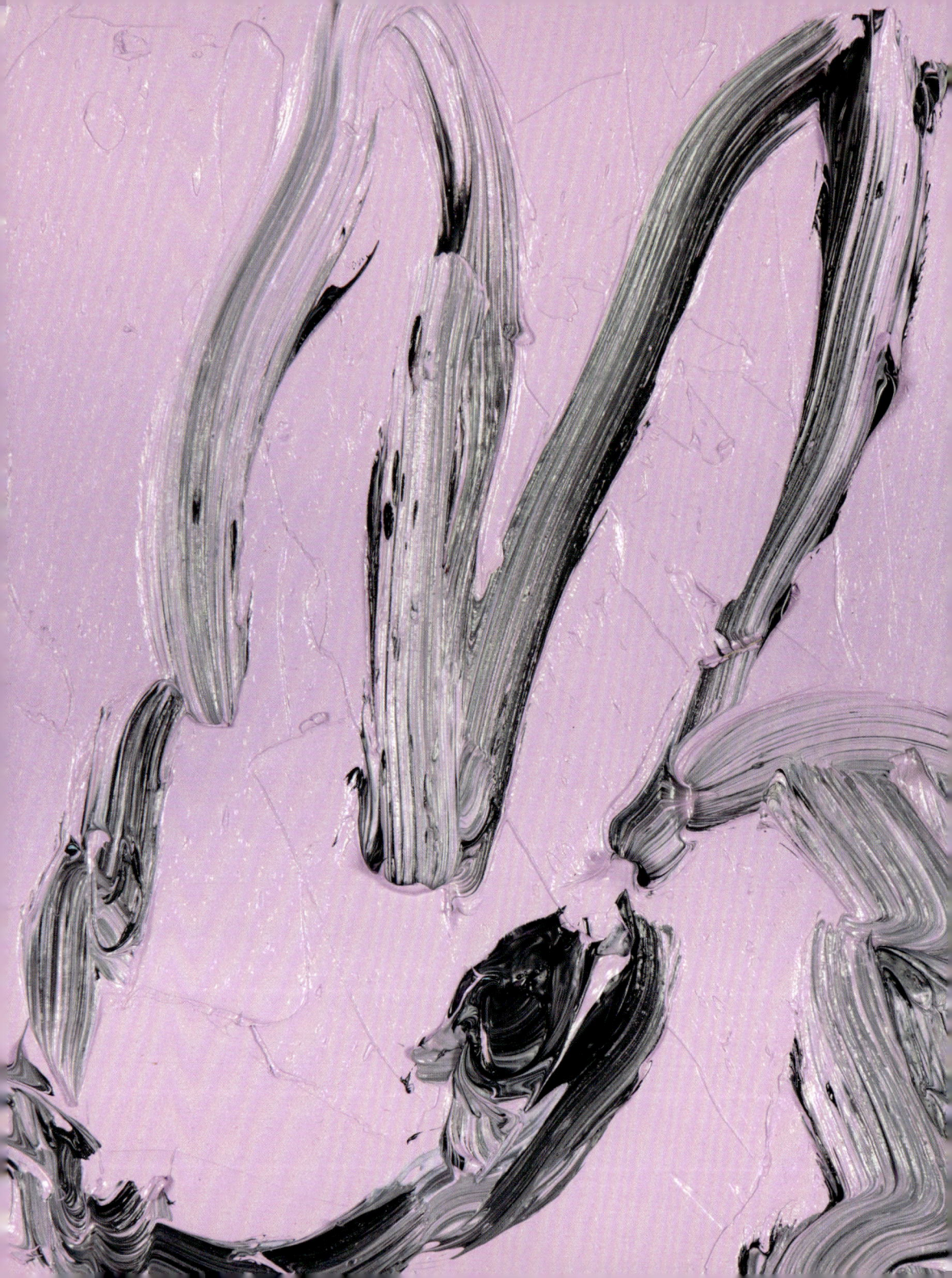

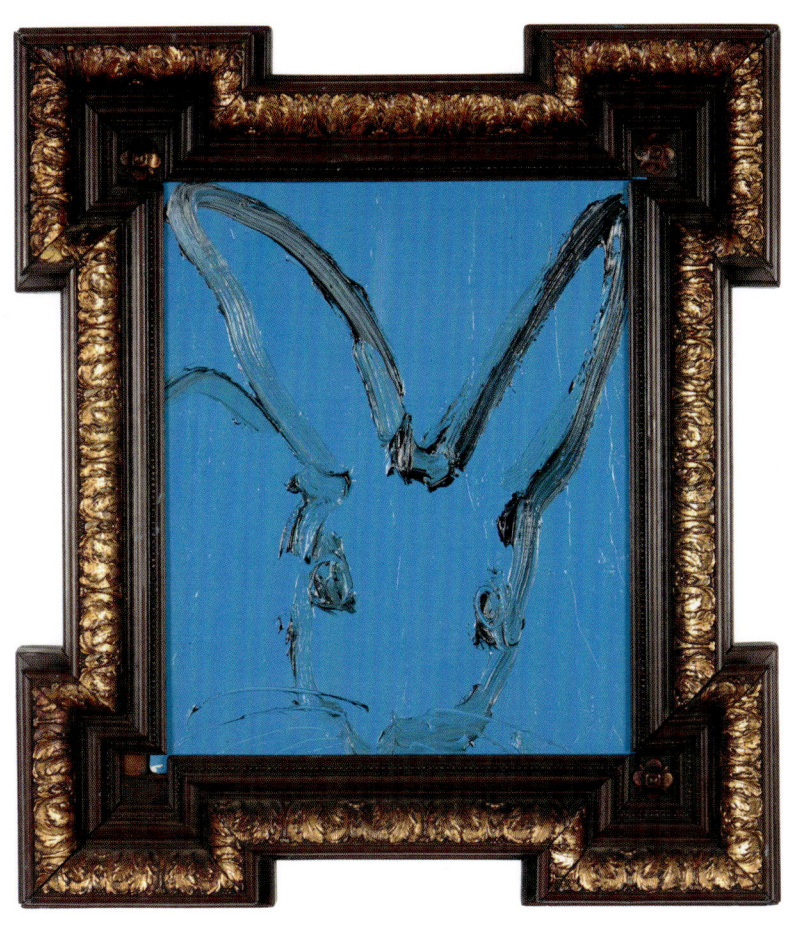

EPETHA
2013
OIL ON WOOD
10" X 8"

MARLYNE
2012
OIL ON WOOD
10" X 8"

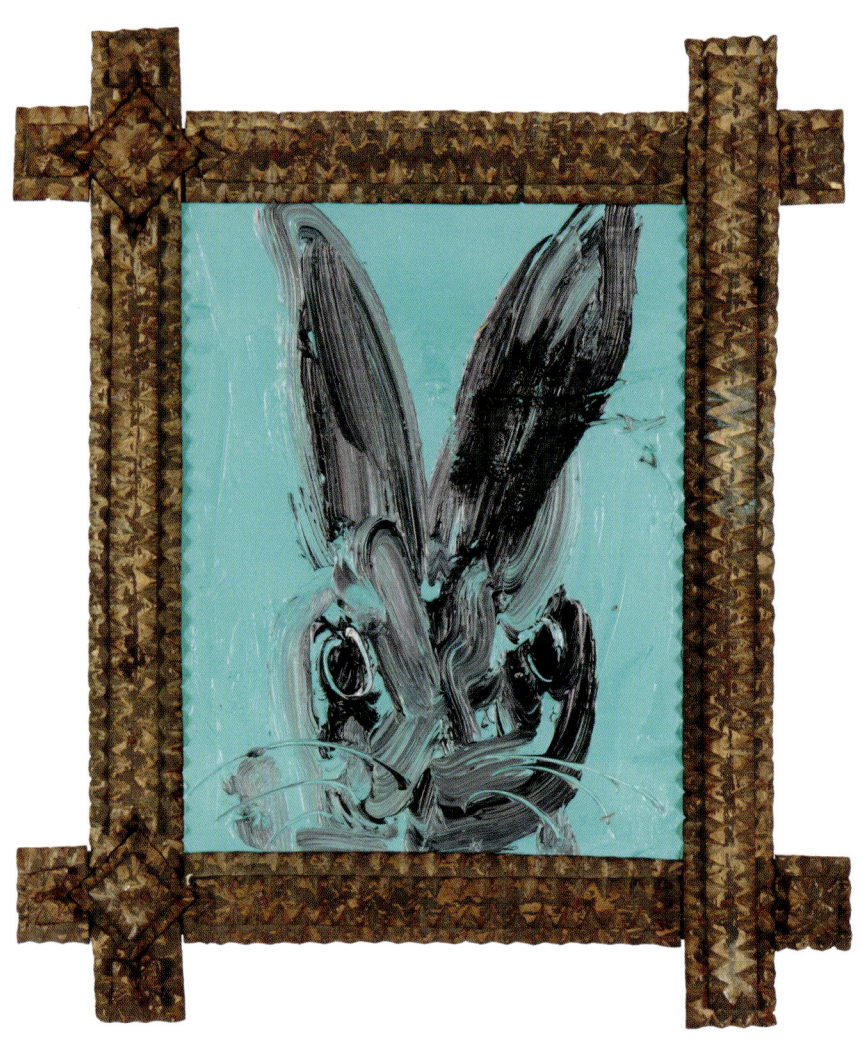

178

Oz
2012
OIL ON WOOD
10" X 8"

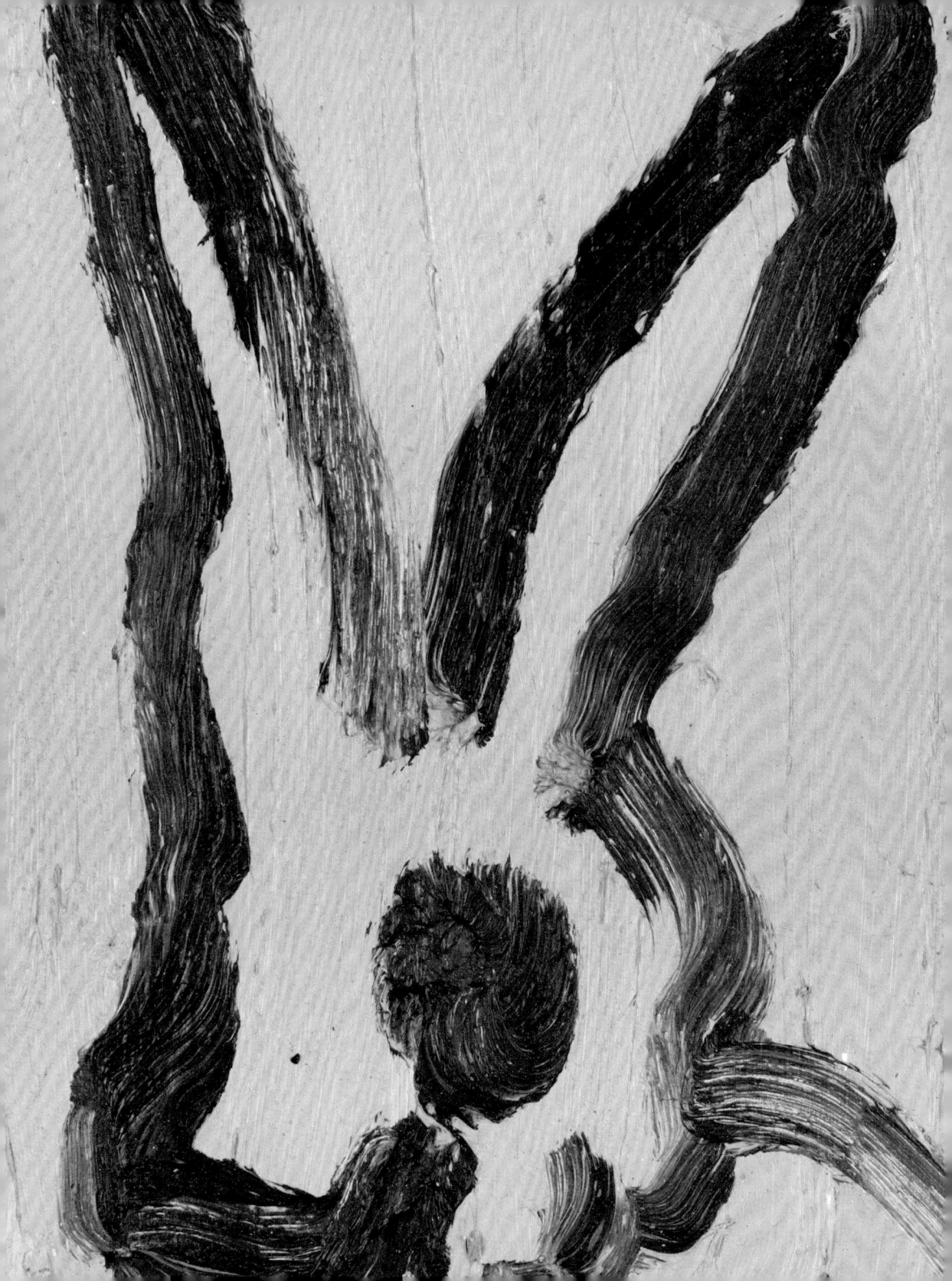

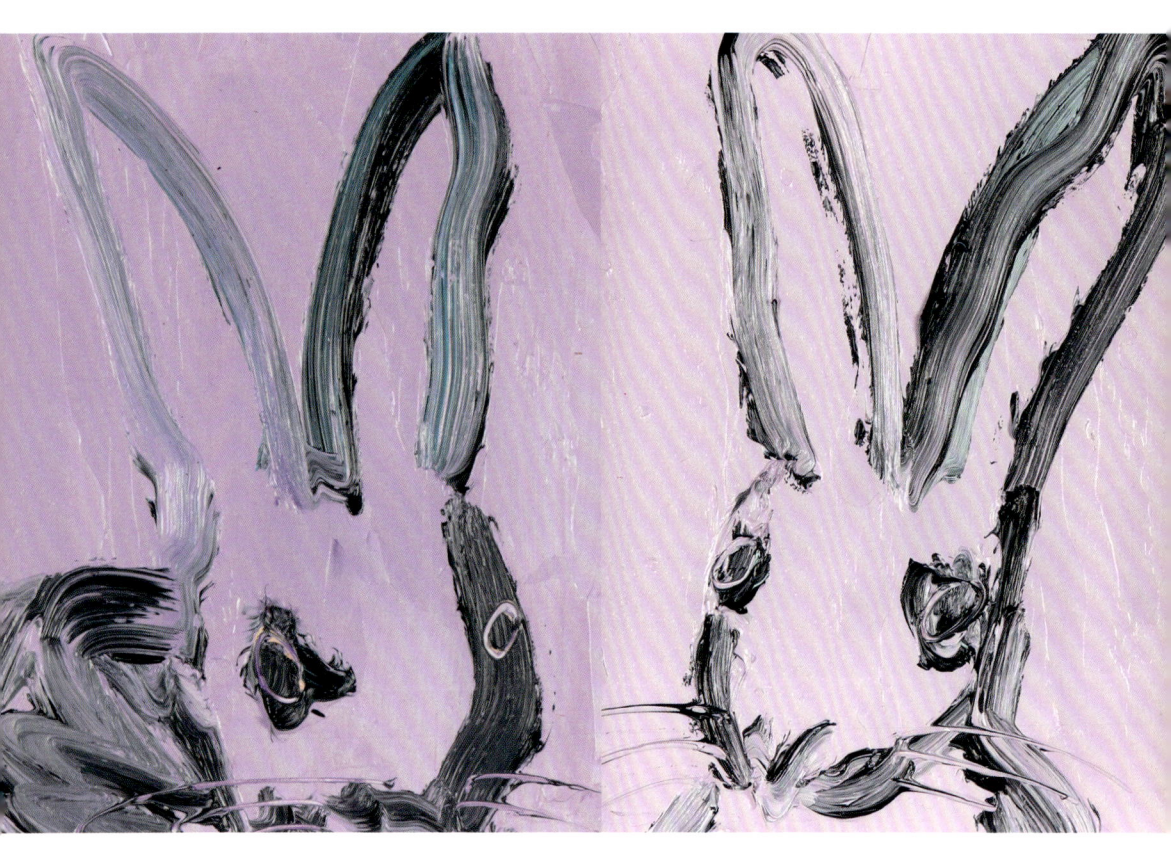

LAVENDER
2012
OIL ON CANVAS
10" X 8"

MARCUS
2013
OIL ON WOOD
10" X 8"

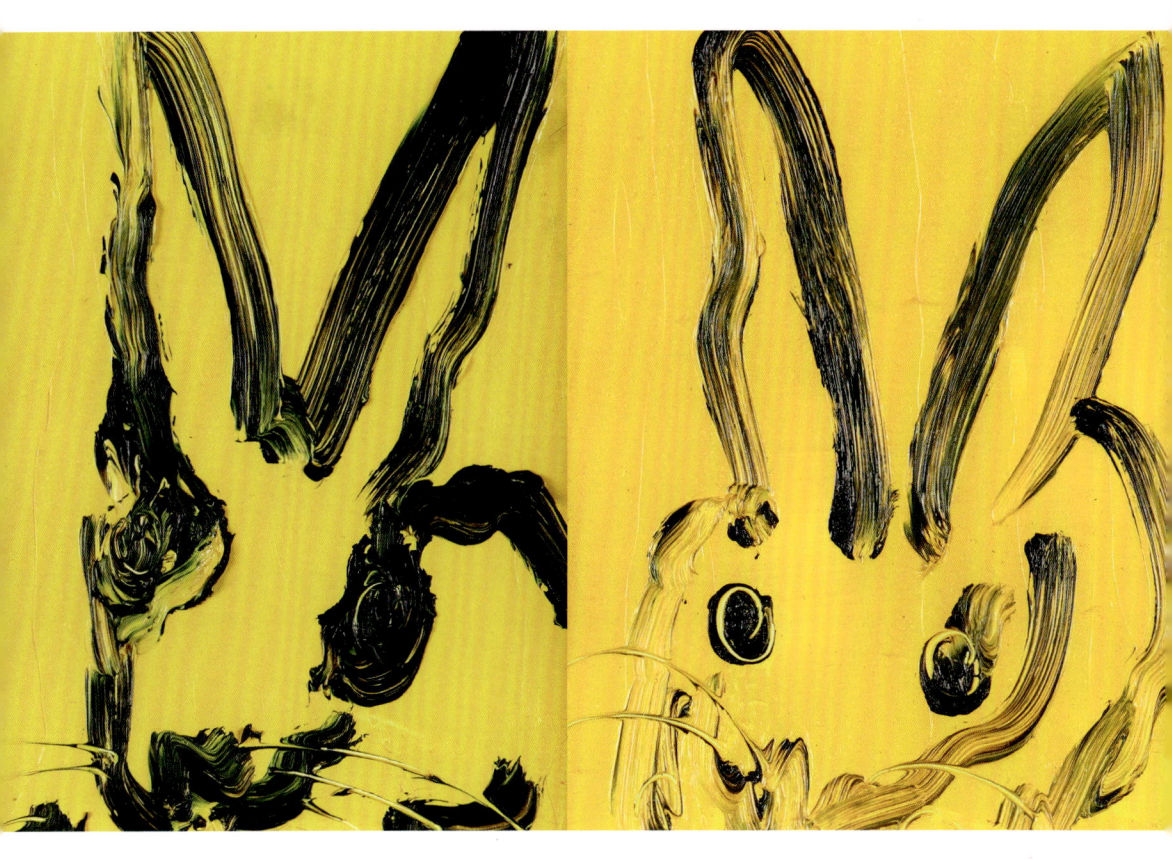

BRANDON
2012
OIL ON WOOD
10" X 8"

FRANCINCE
2012
OIL ON WOOD
10" X 8"

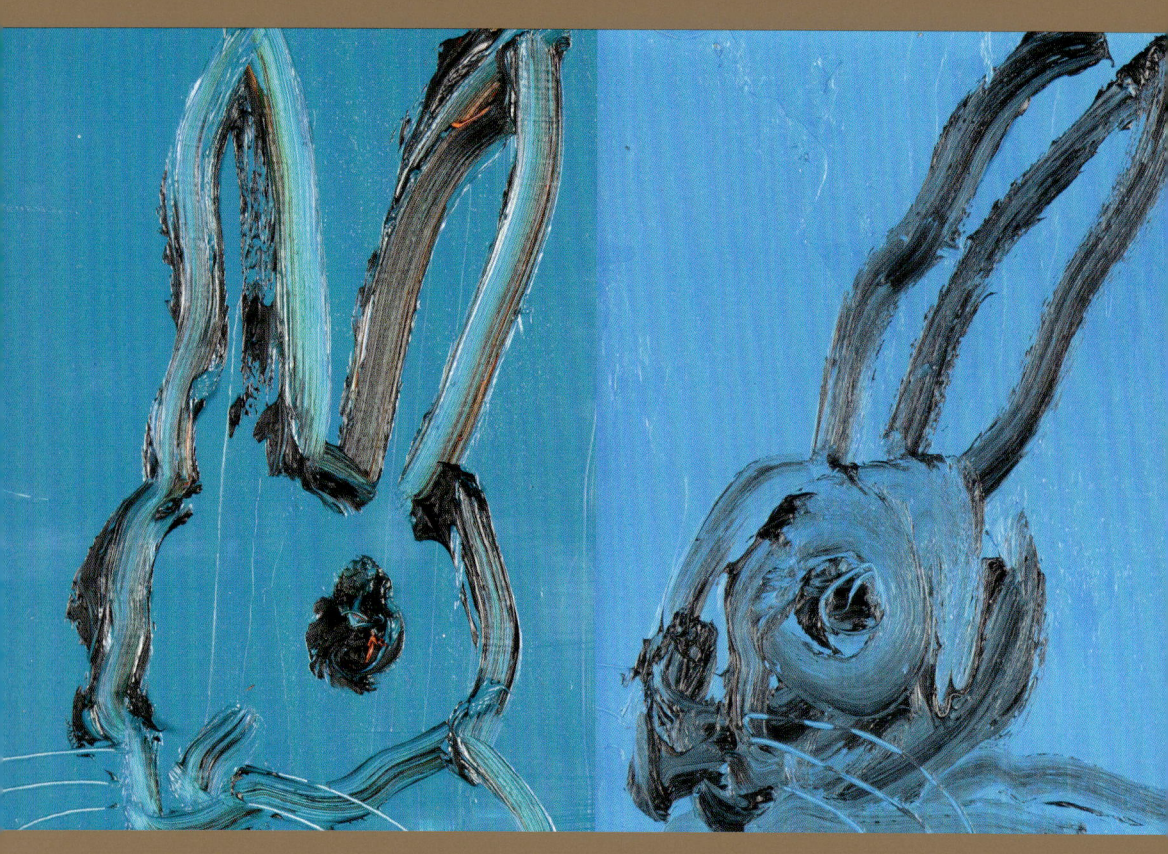

GREGORY
2012
OIL ON WOOD
10" X 8"

ERIC
2013
OIL ON WOOD
10" X 8"

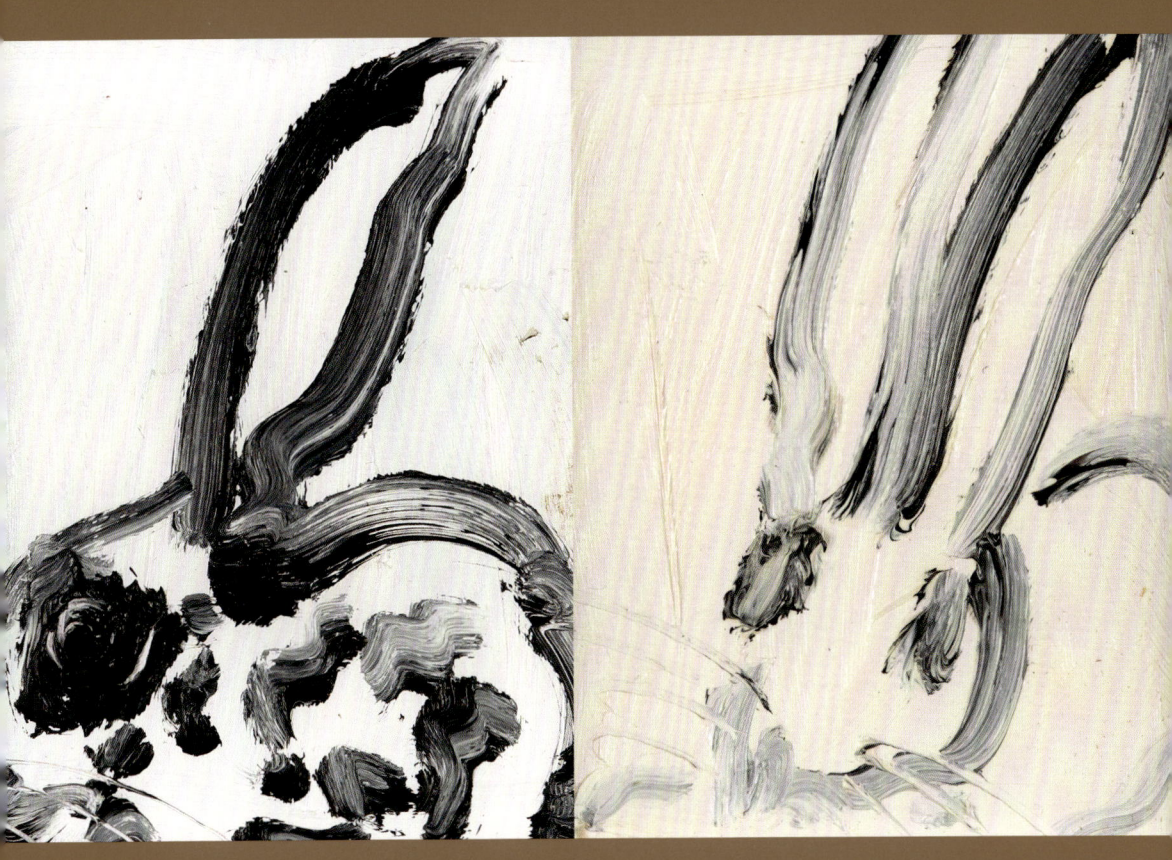

THE NEIGHBOR
2013
OIL ON WOOD
10" X 8"

BUTLER
2012
OIL ON WOOD
10" X 8"

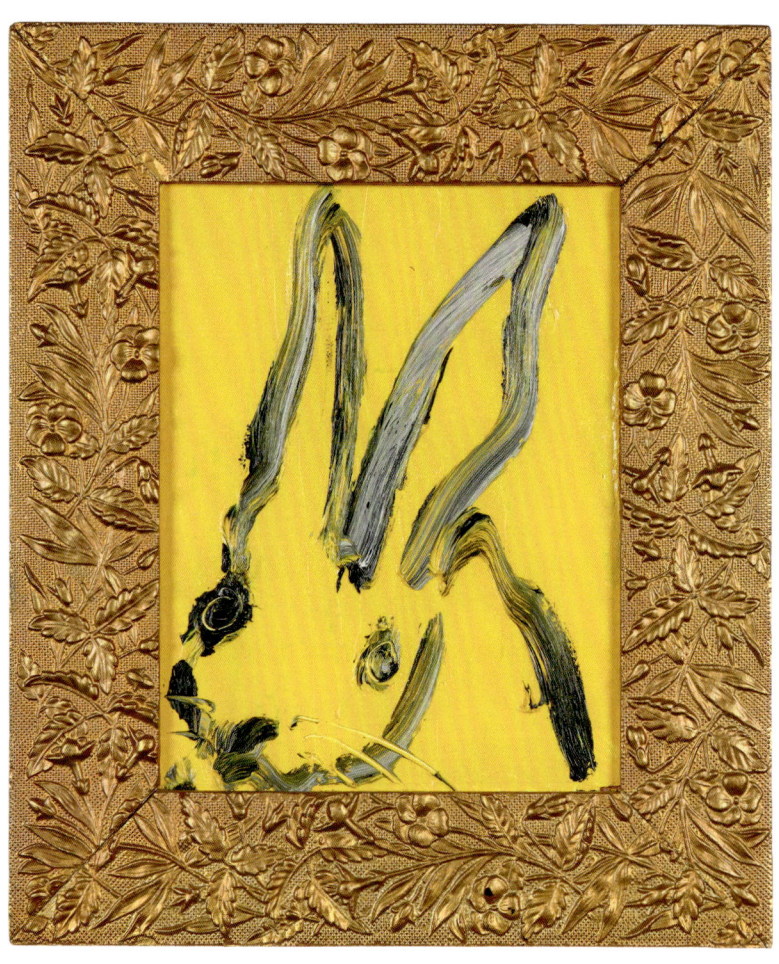

Woodsy
2012
OIL ON WOOD
10" x 8"

Blue Eyes
2011
OIL ON WOOD
10" x 8"

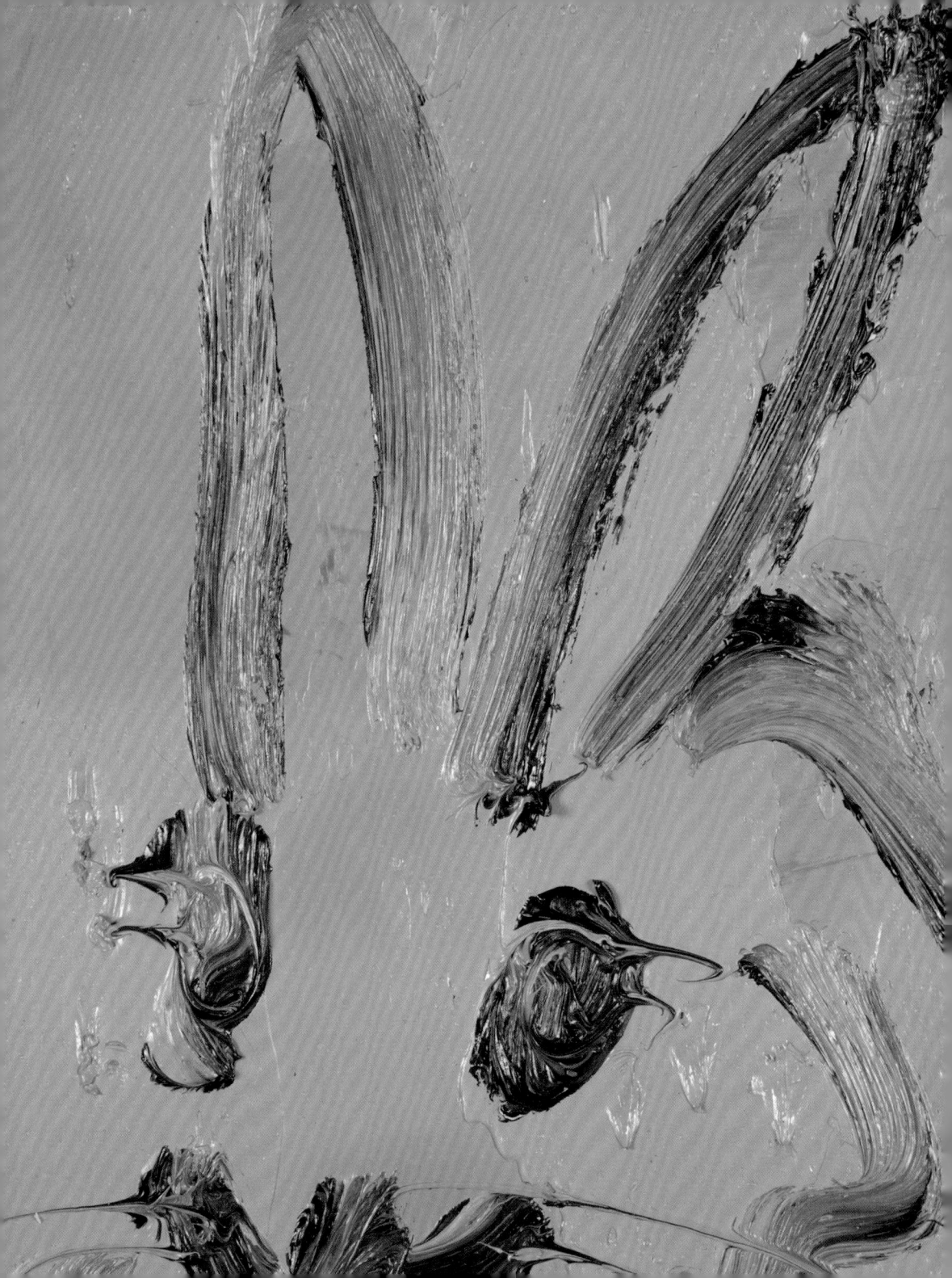

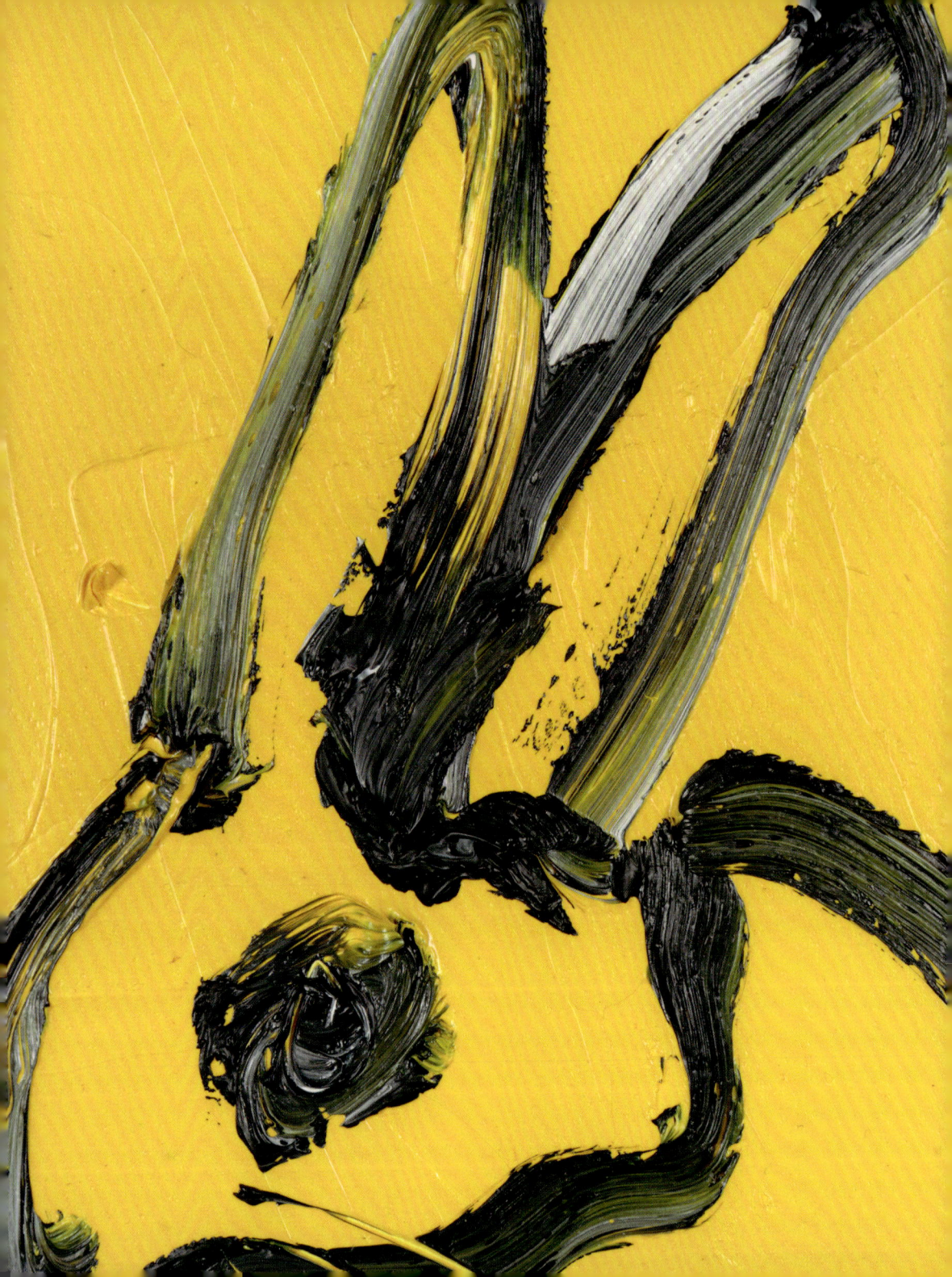

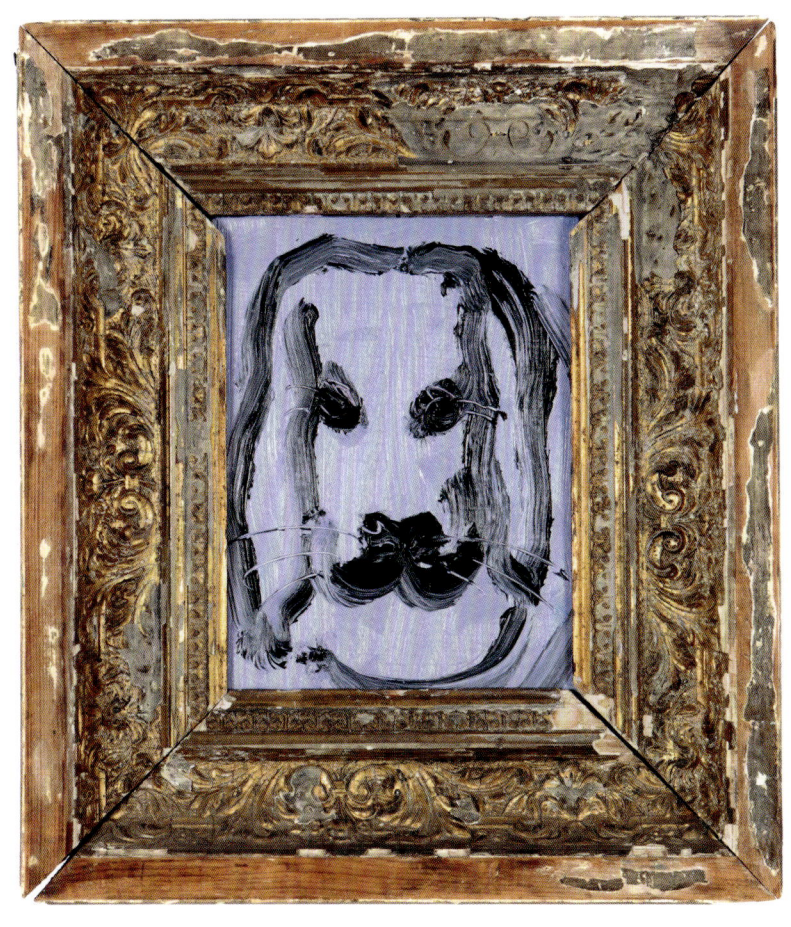

EAST LAKE
2012
OIL ON WOOD
10" X 8"

DONNA
2013
OIL ON WOOD
10" X 8"

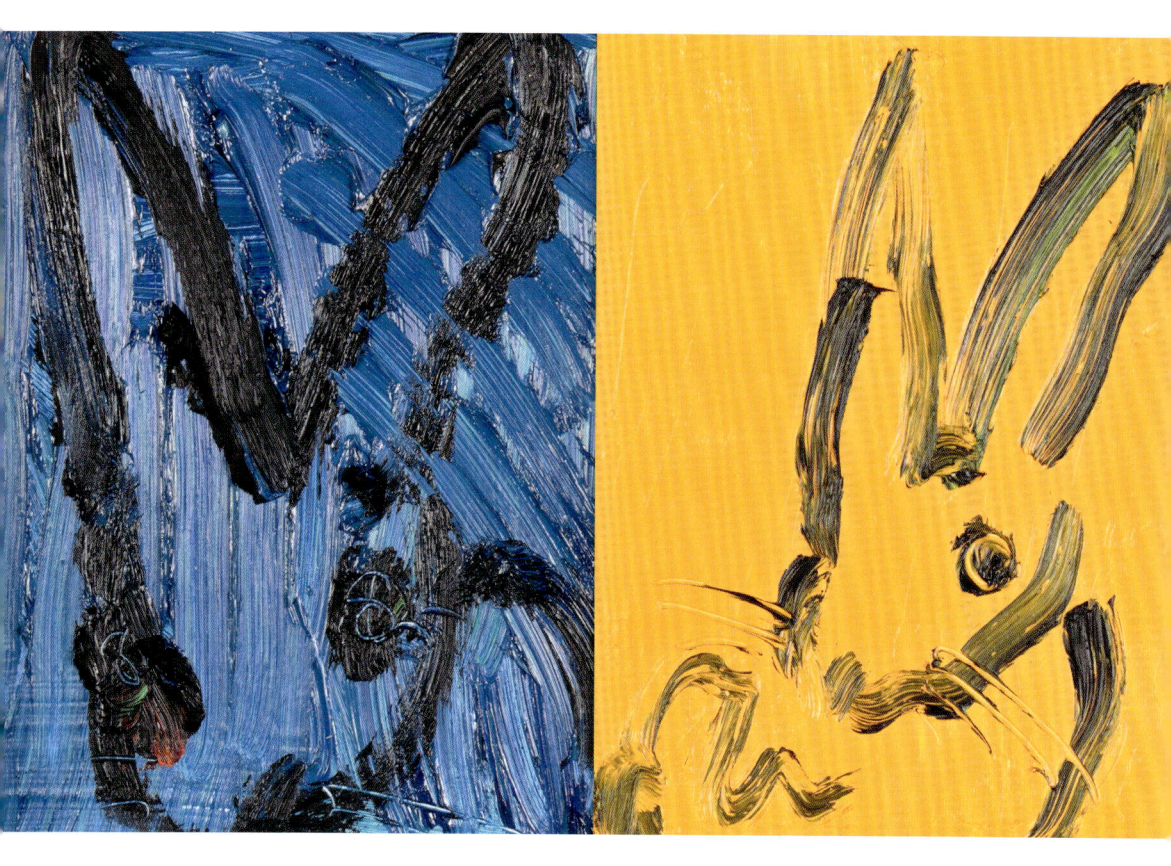

JOEL
2013
OIL ON WOOD
10" x 8"

MARCIA
2013
OIL ON WOOD
10" x 8"

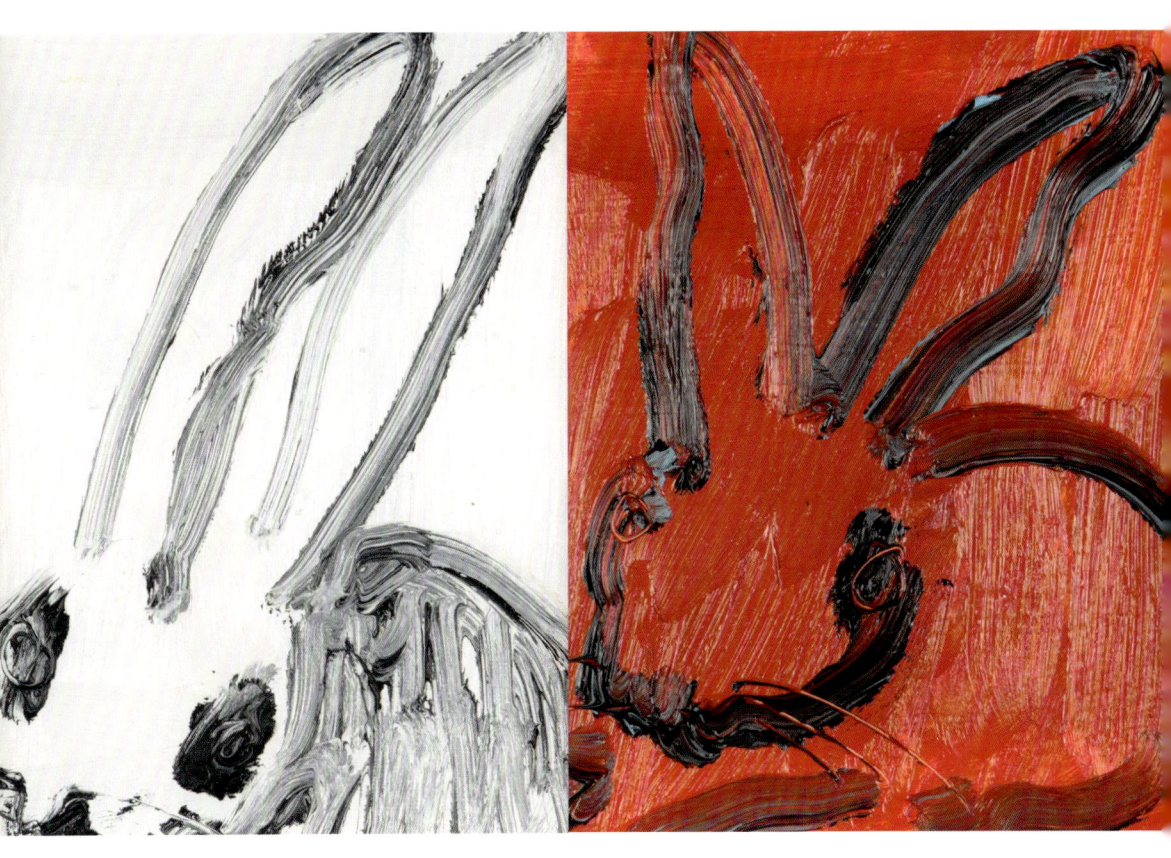

AESTHETIC
MOVEMENT
2013
OIL ON WOOD
10" X 8"

ROSE DORE
2013
OIL ON WOOD
10 " X 8"

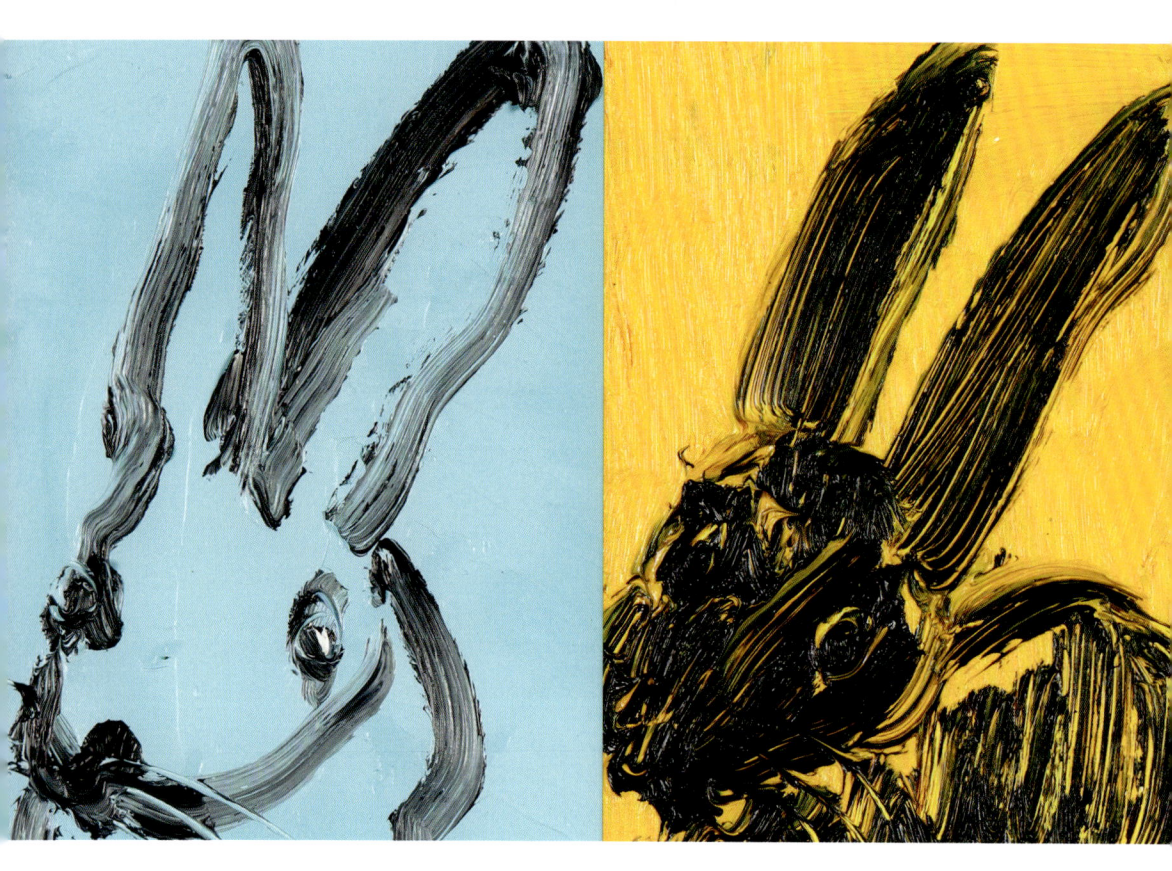

GARY
2013
OIL ON WOOD
10" X 8"

TWIN OAKS
2013
OIL ON WOOD
10" X 8"

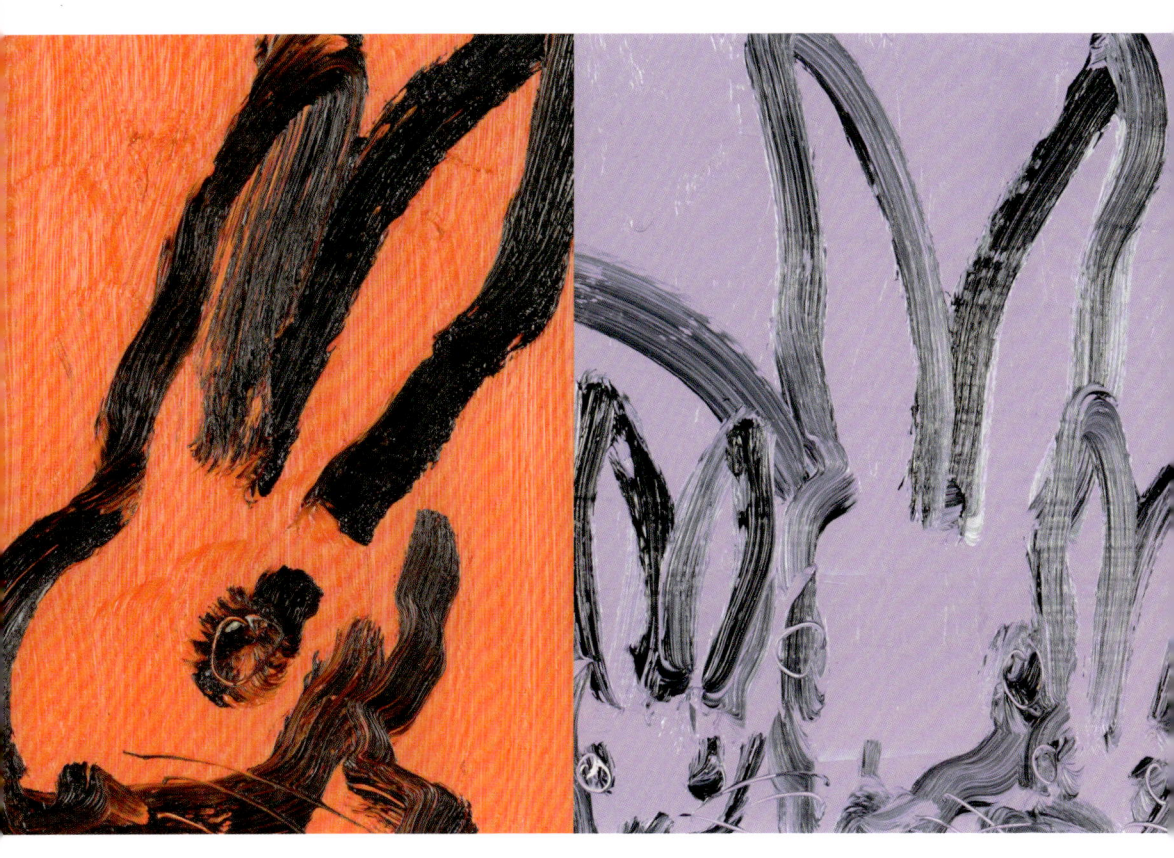

RED II
2013
OIL ON WOOD
10" X 8"

ZENAP
2013
OIL ON WOOD
12" X 10"

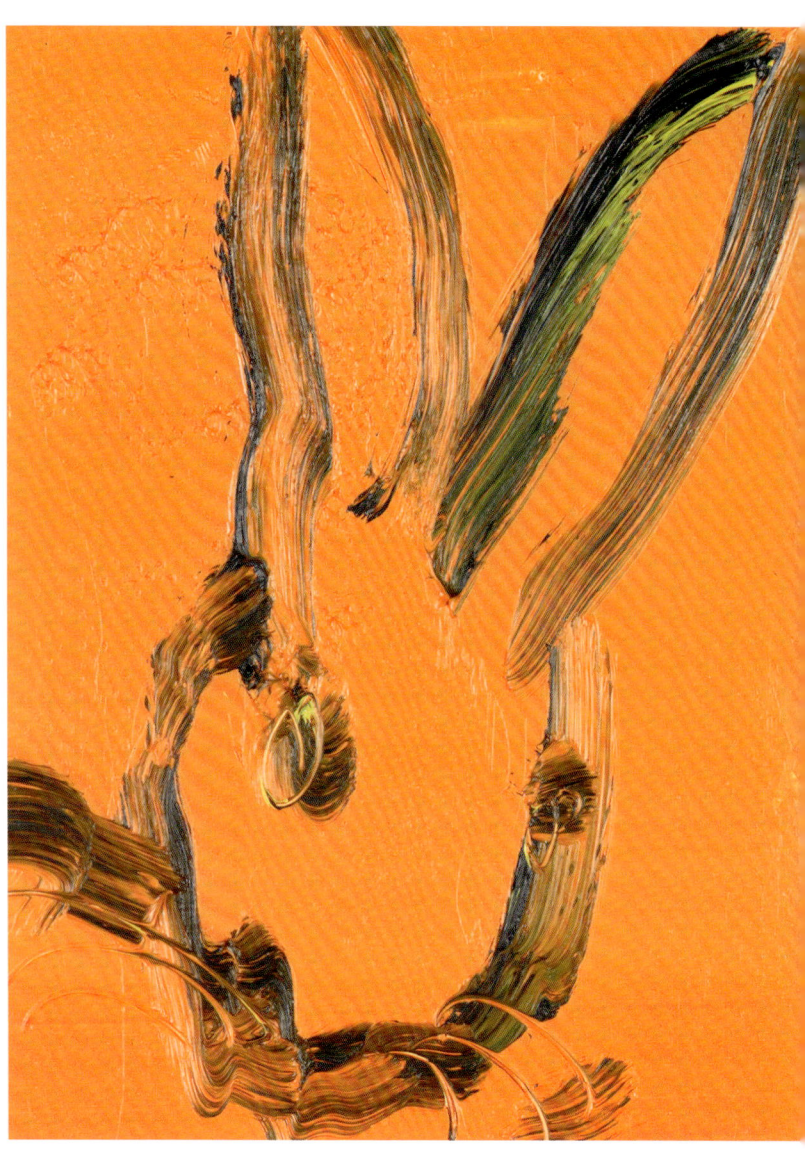

RICK
2012
OIL ON WOOD
10" X 8"

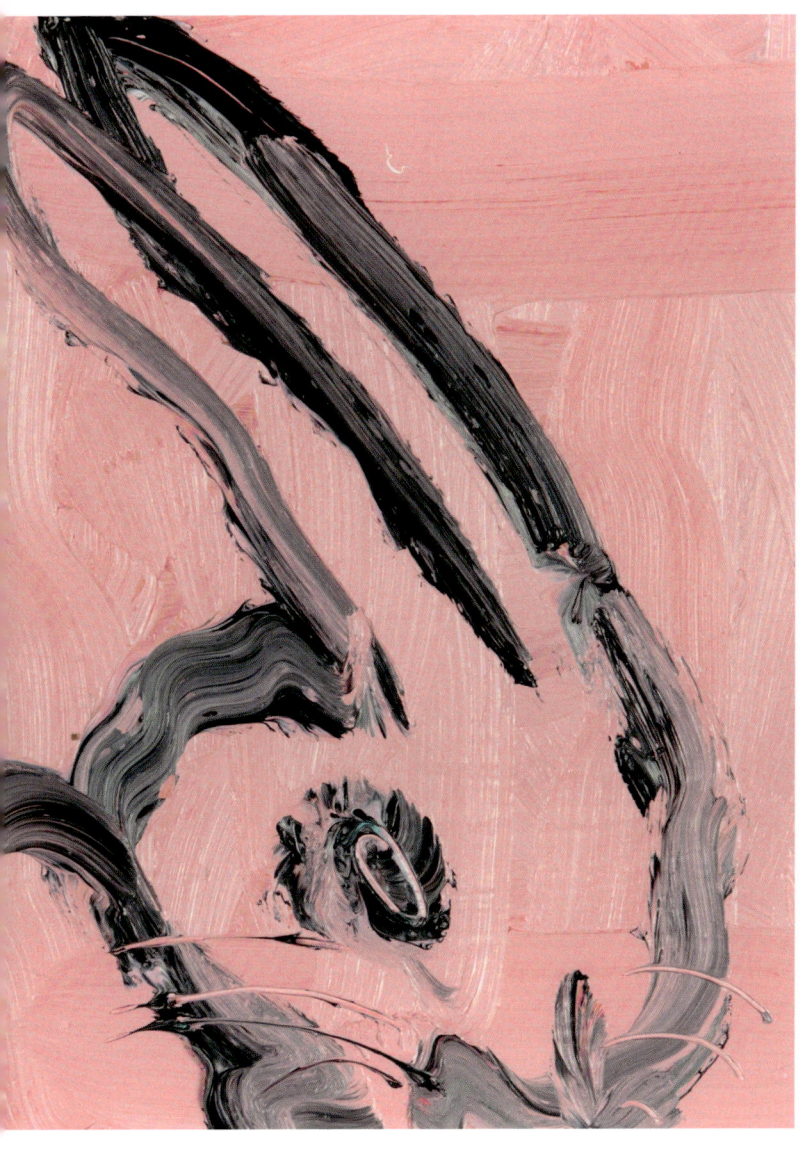

EMILY
2012
OIL ON WOOD
10" X 8"

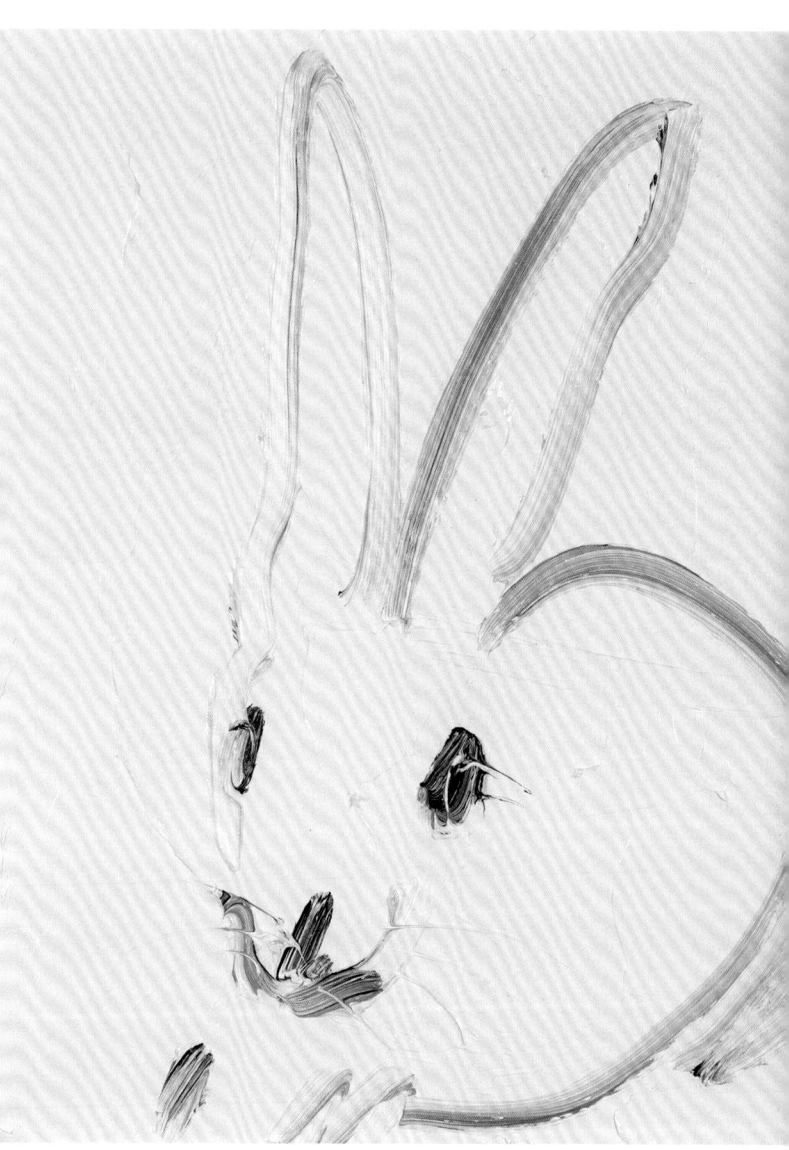

JORDANA
2013
OIL ON WOOD
18" X 15"

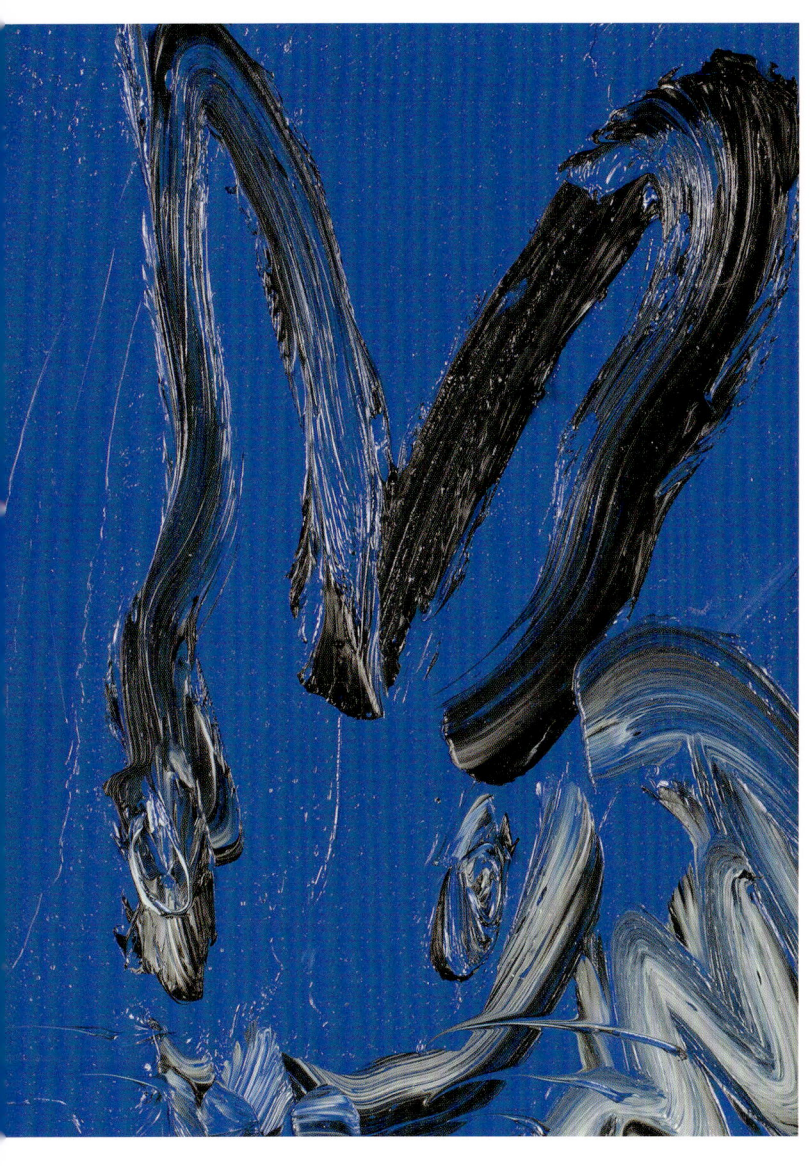

JEFFREY
2013
OIL ON WOOD
10" X 8"

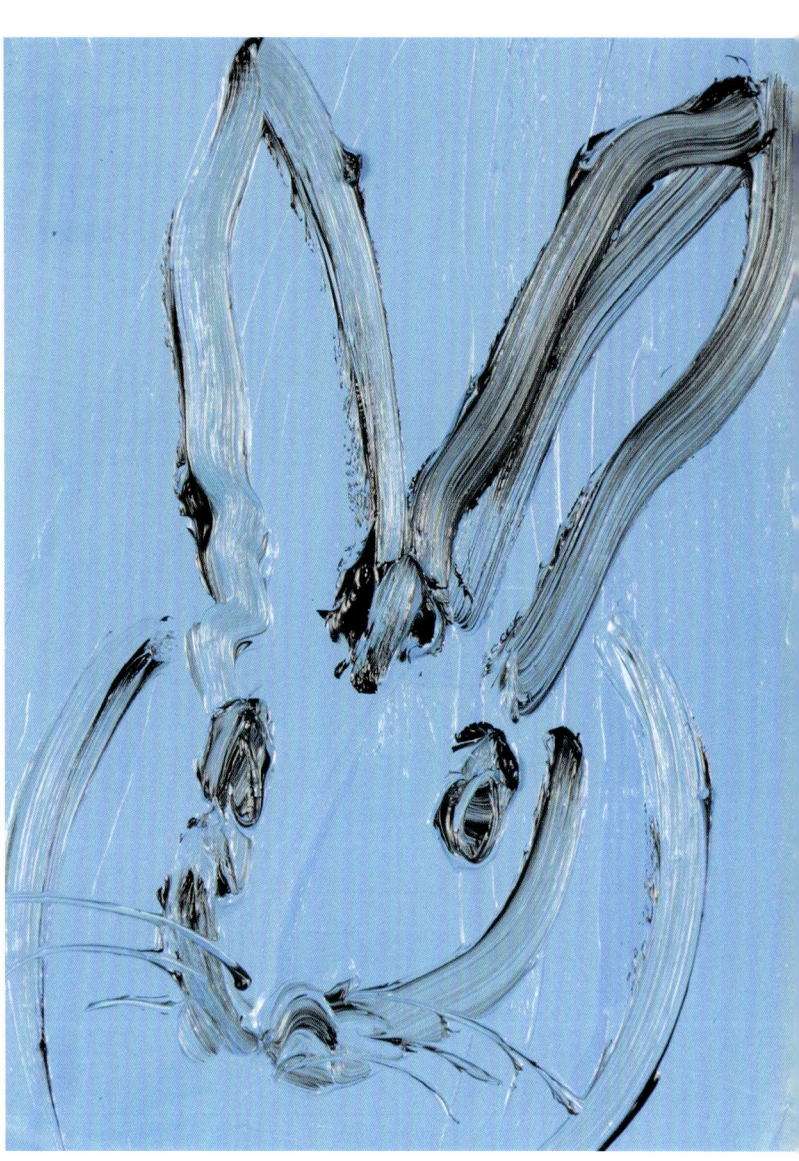

Margo
2012
OIL ON WOOD
10" X 8"

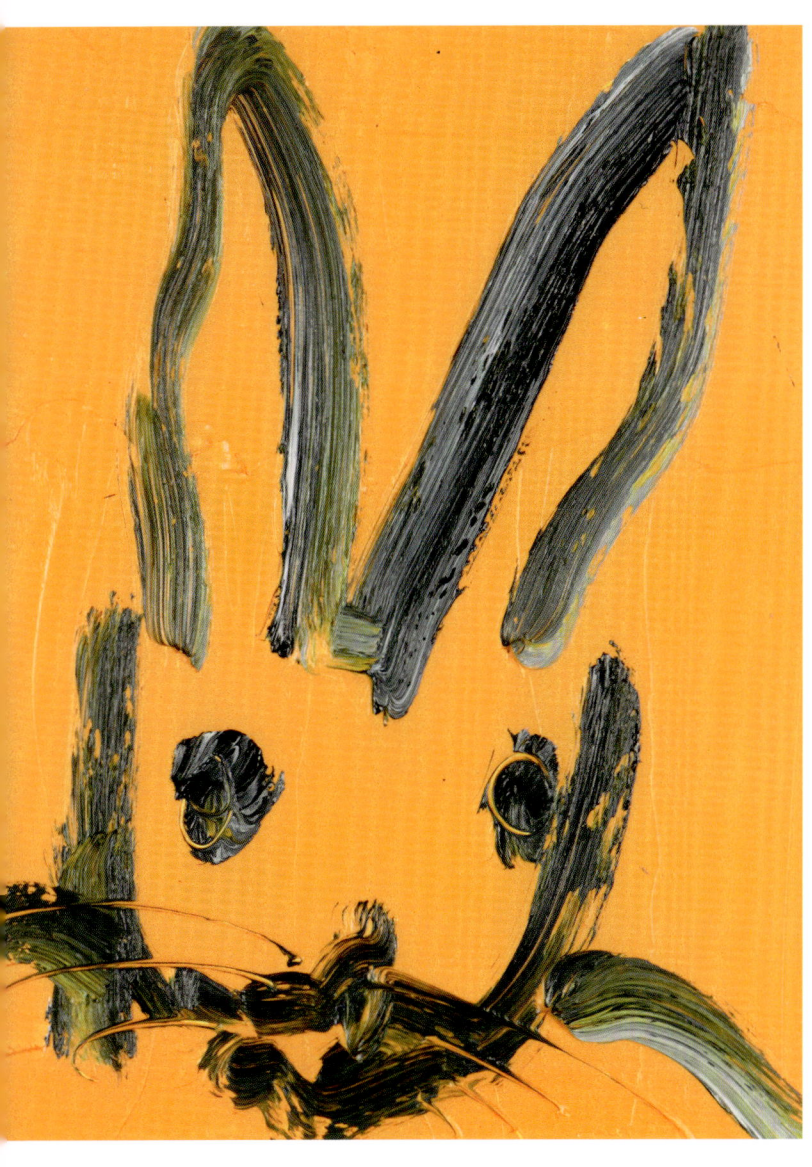

OLD YELLOW
2013
OIL ON WOOD
10" X 8"

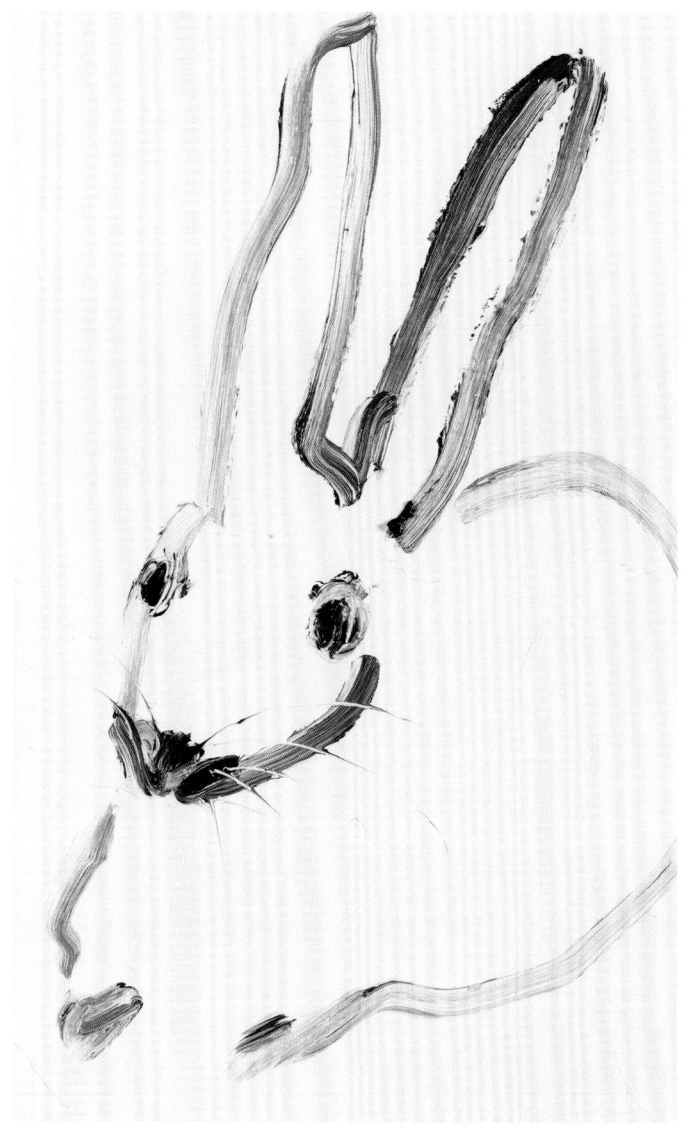

PHILLIP
2013
OIL ON WOOD
21″ X 12″

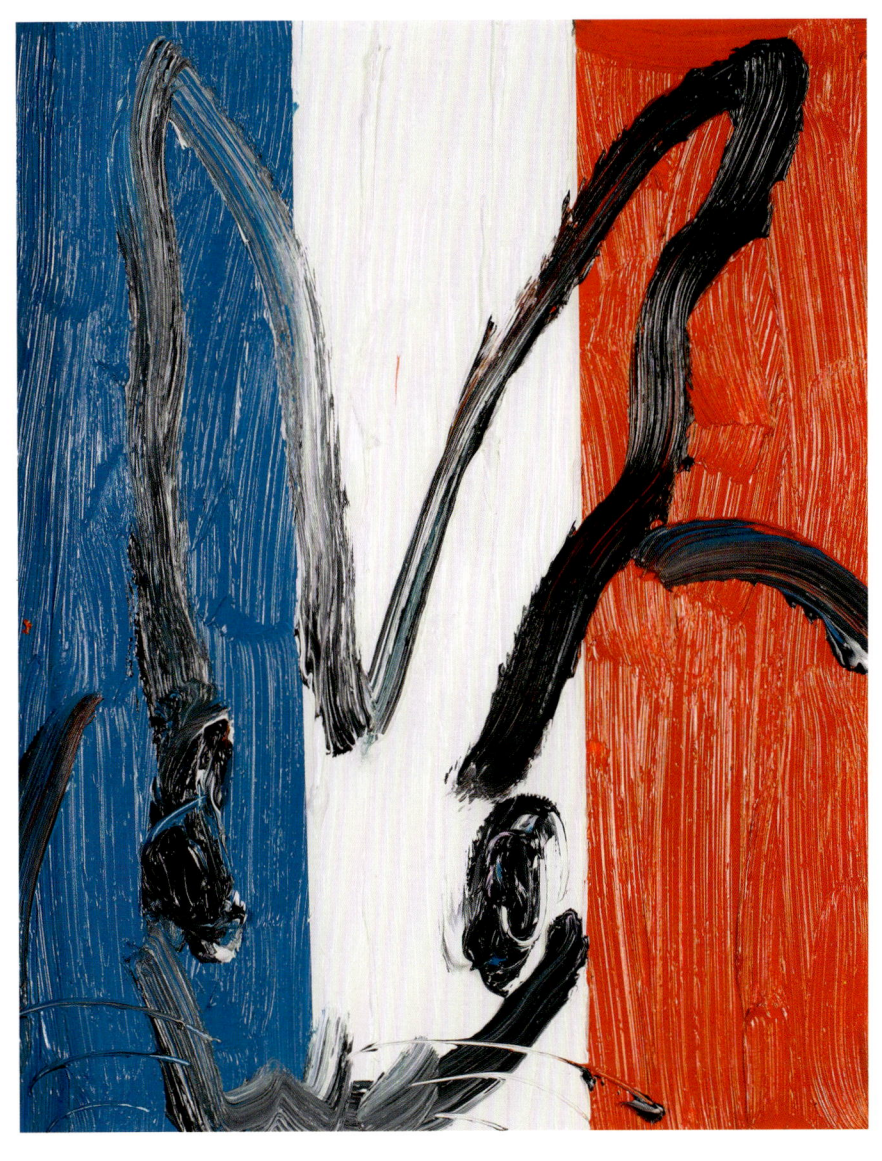

4TH OF JULY
2012
OIL ON WOOD
10" X 8"

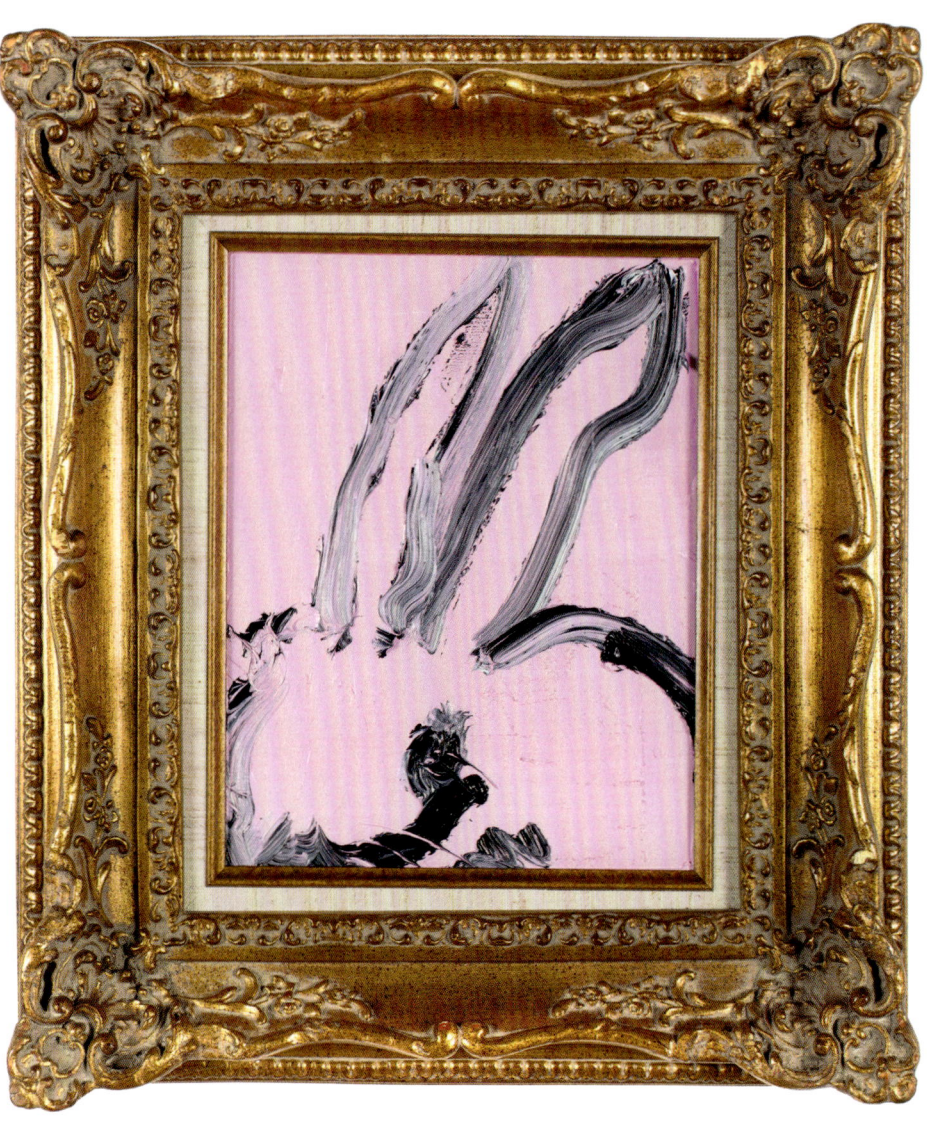

FIONA
2013
OIL ON WOOD
10" X 8"

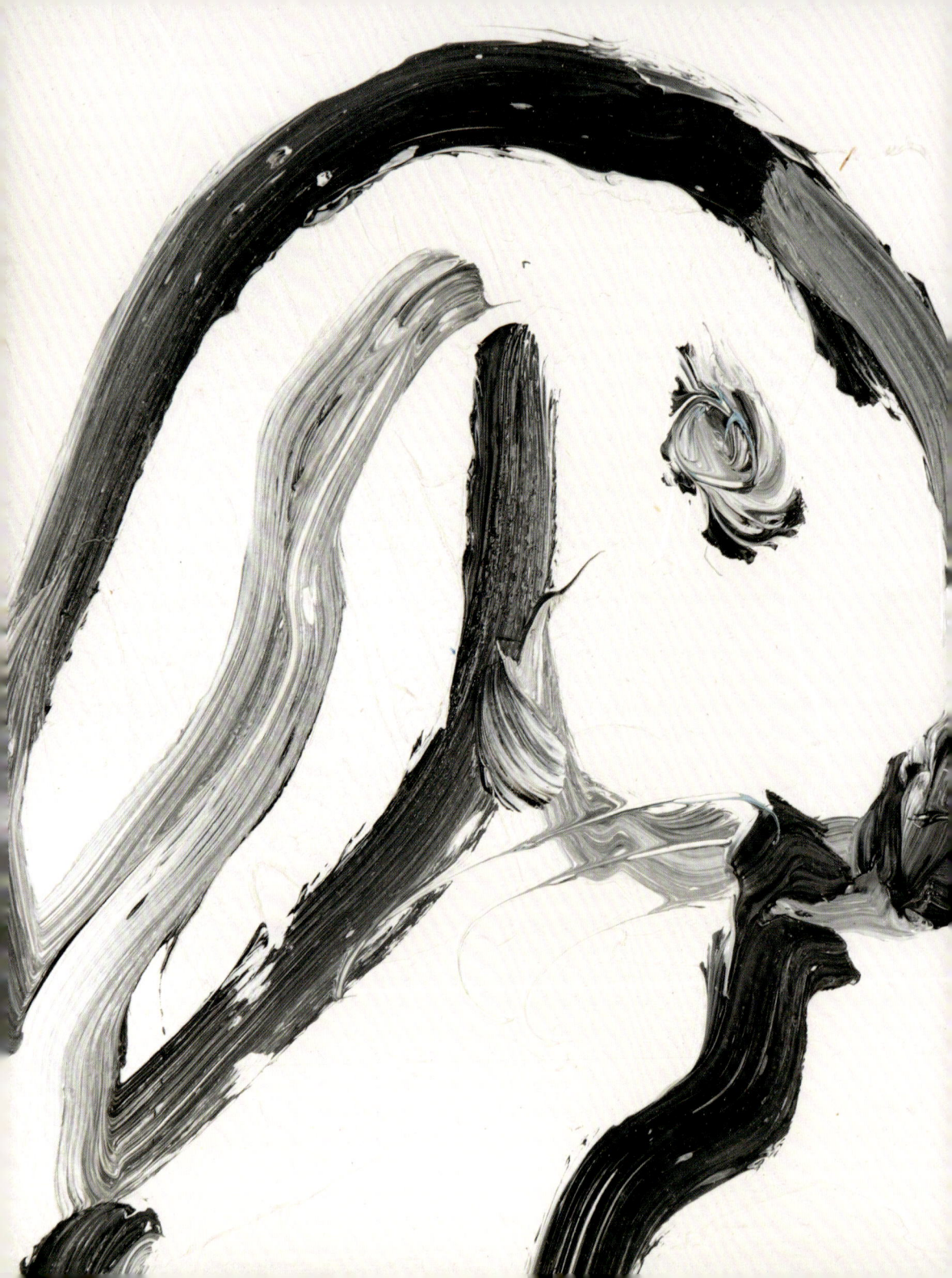

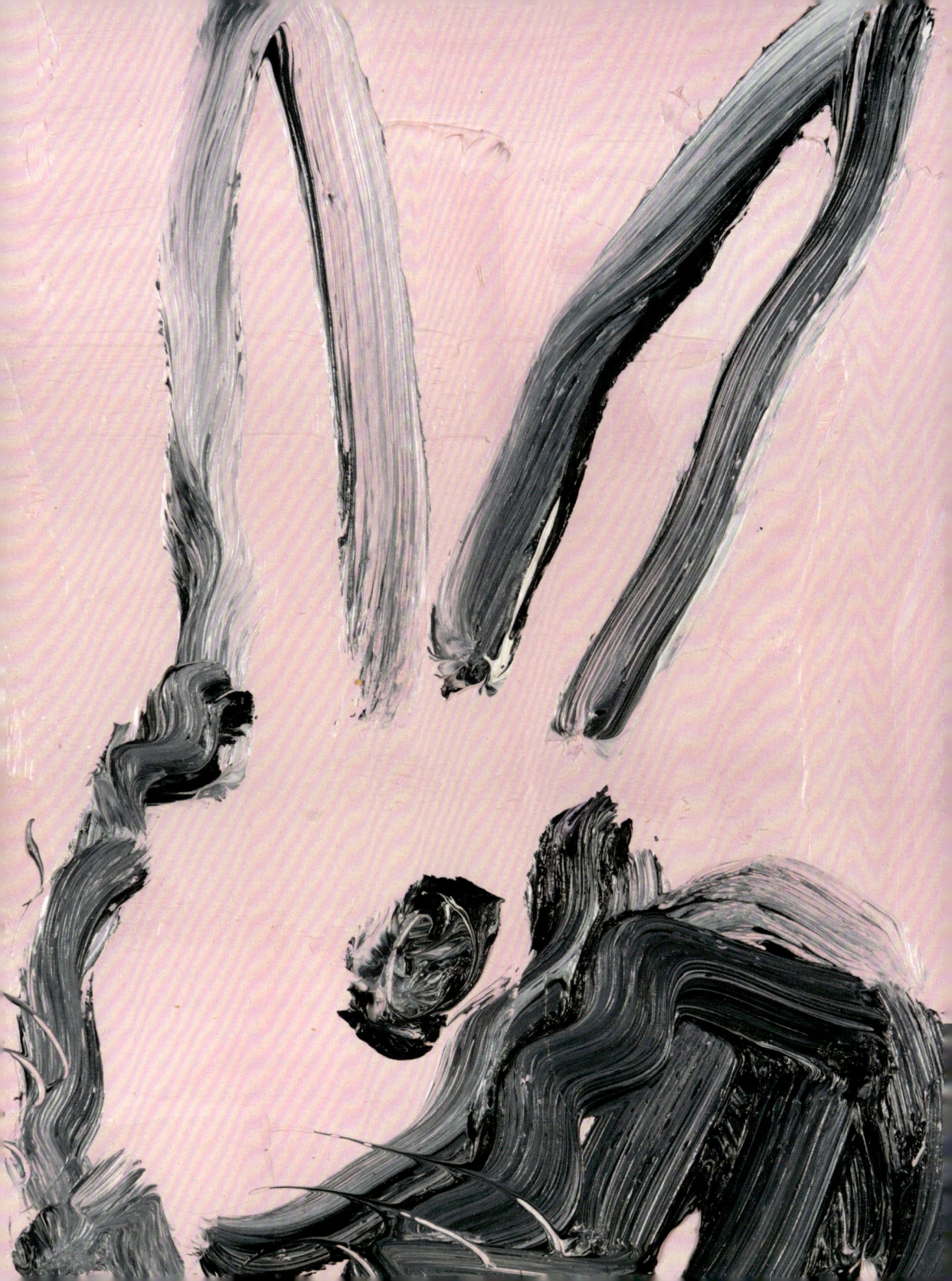

THE OTHER WAY 1
2013
OIL ON WOOD
10" X 8"

AMY
2013
OIL ON WOOD
10" X 8"

204

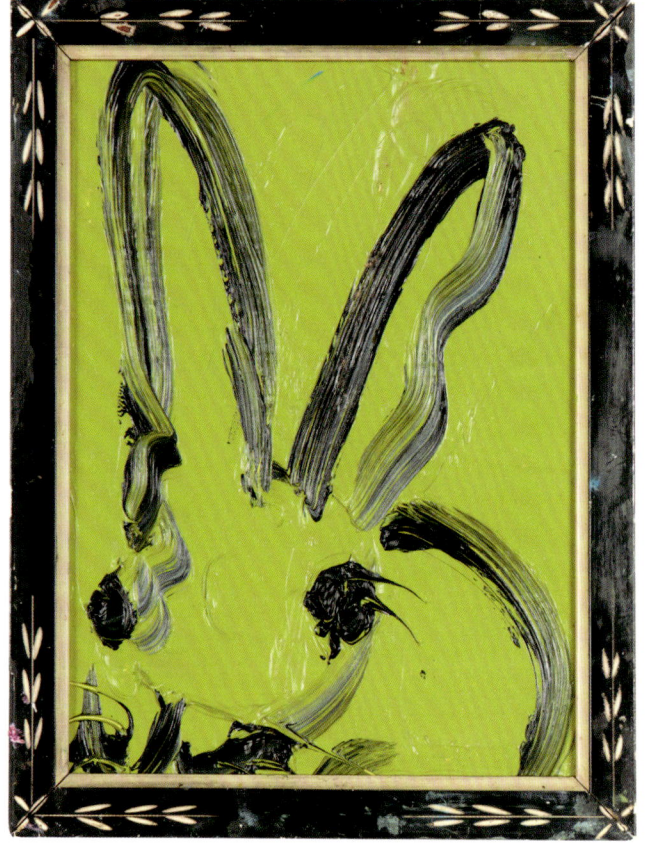

CHARLES
2012
OIL ON WOOD
10" X 8"

MORGANZA SPILLWAY
2012
OIL ON WOOD
31.5" X 27"

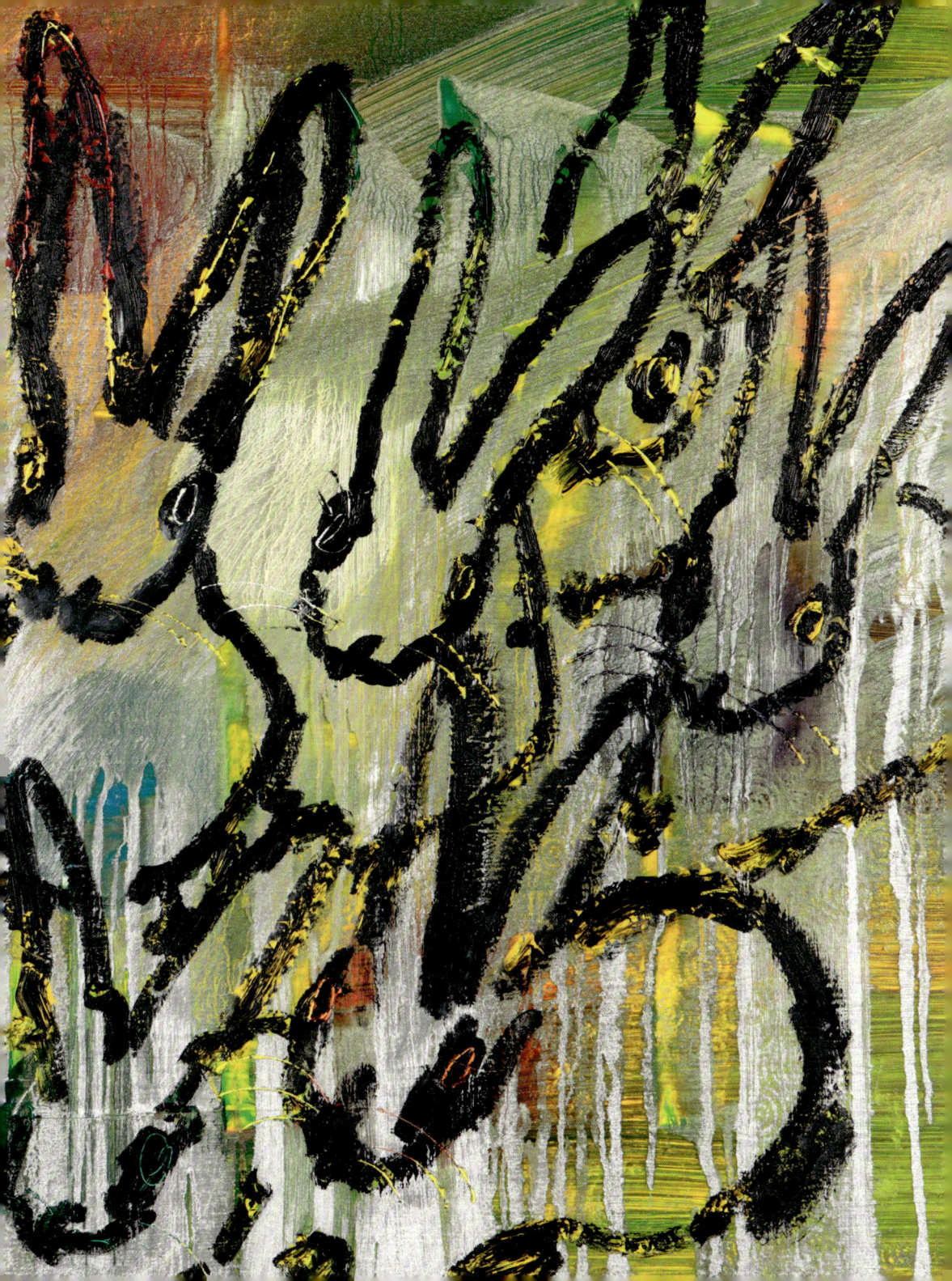

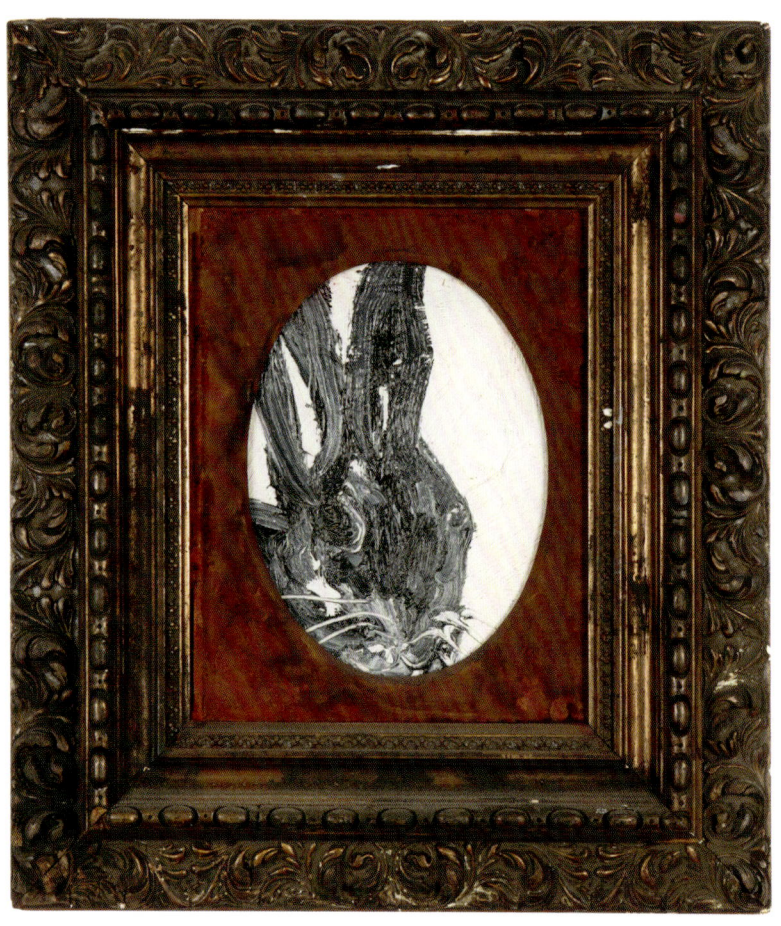

THE WITNESS
2011
OIL ON WOOD
10" x 8"

ALL EARS
2013
OIL ON WOOD
16" x 12"

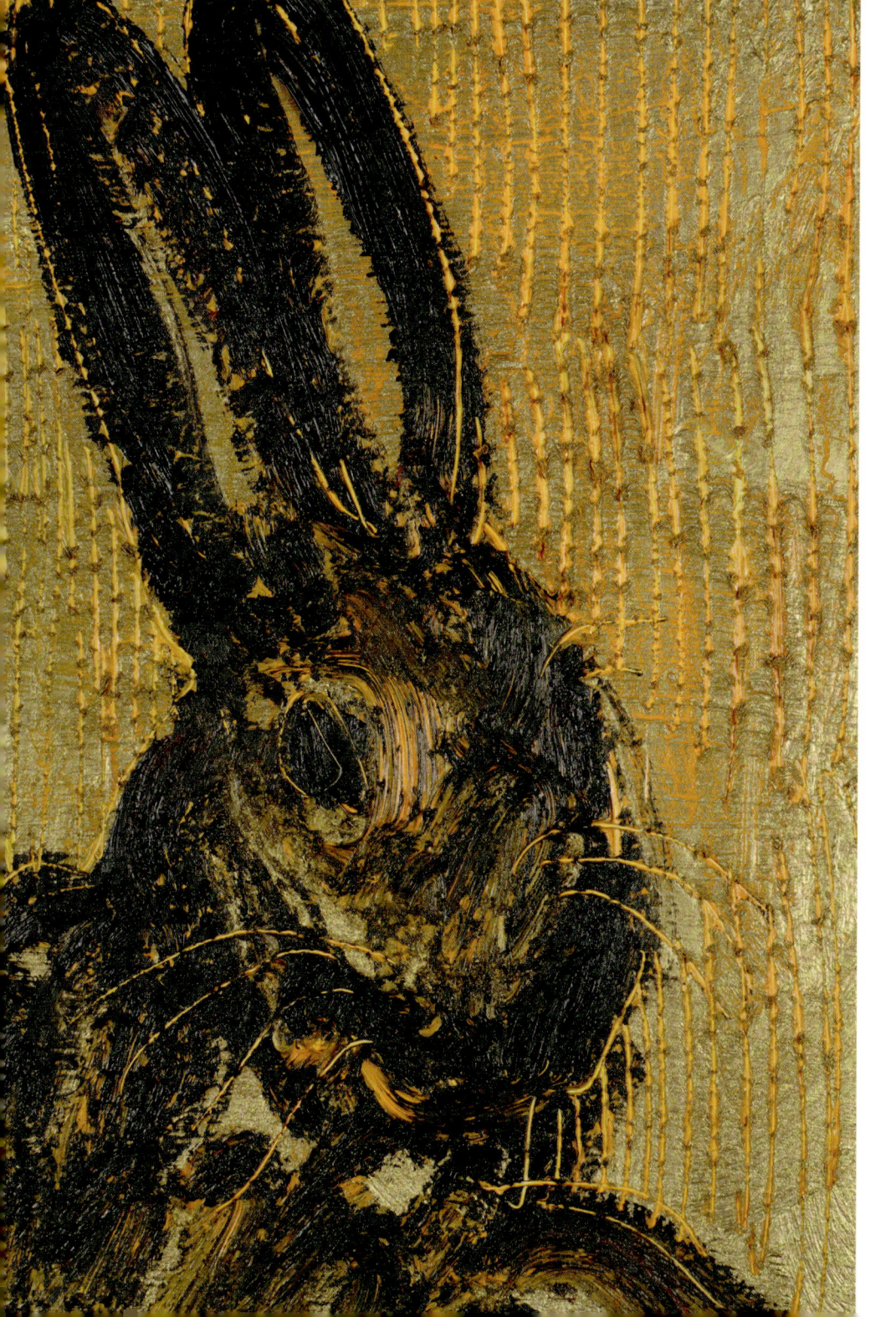

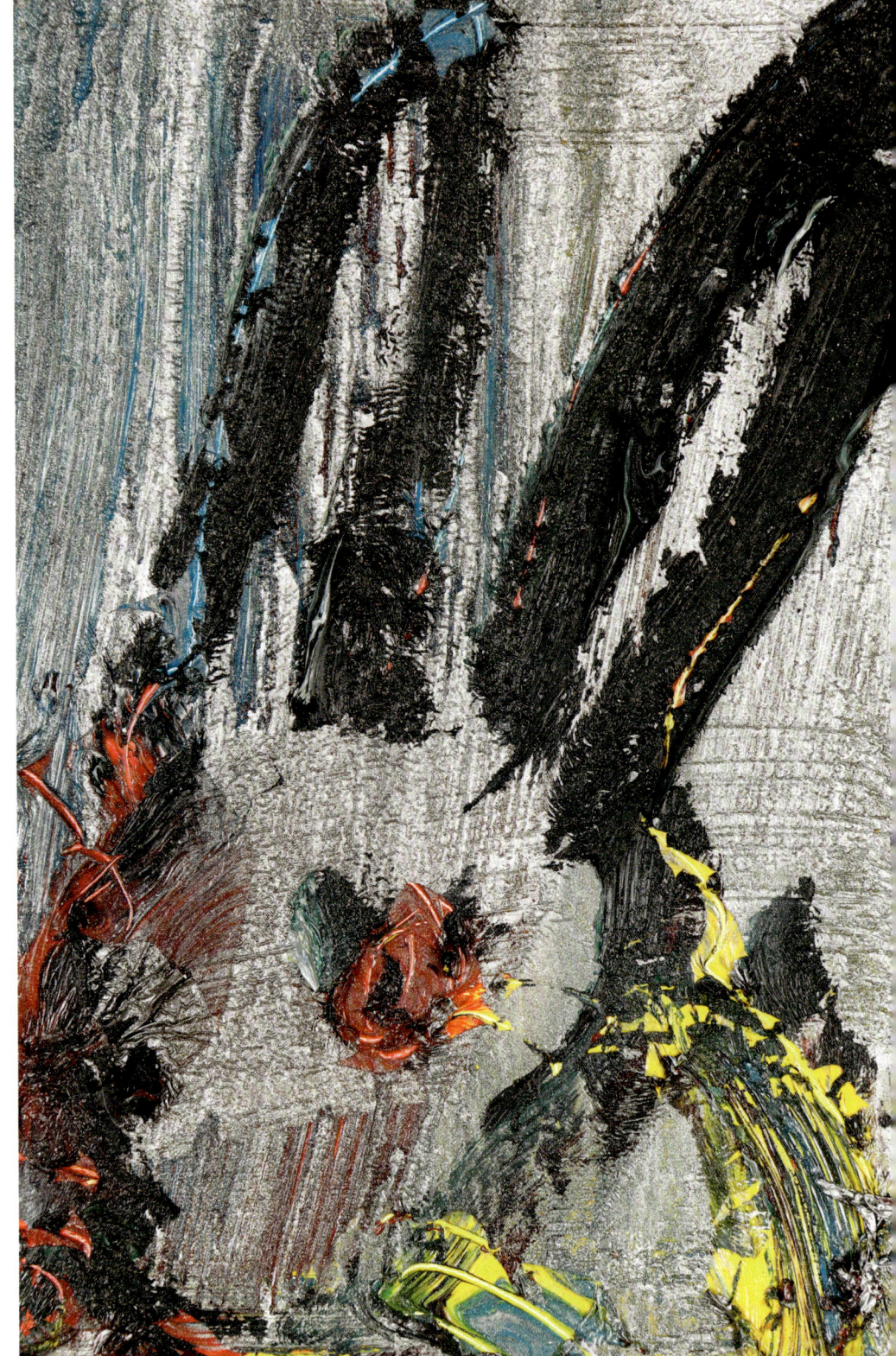

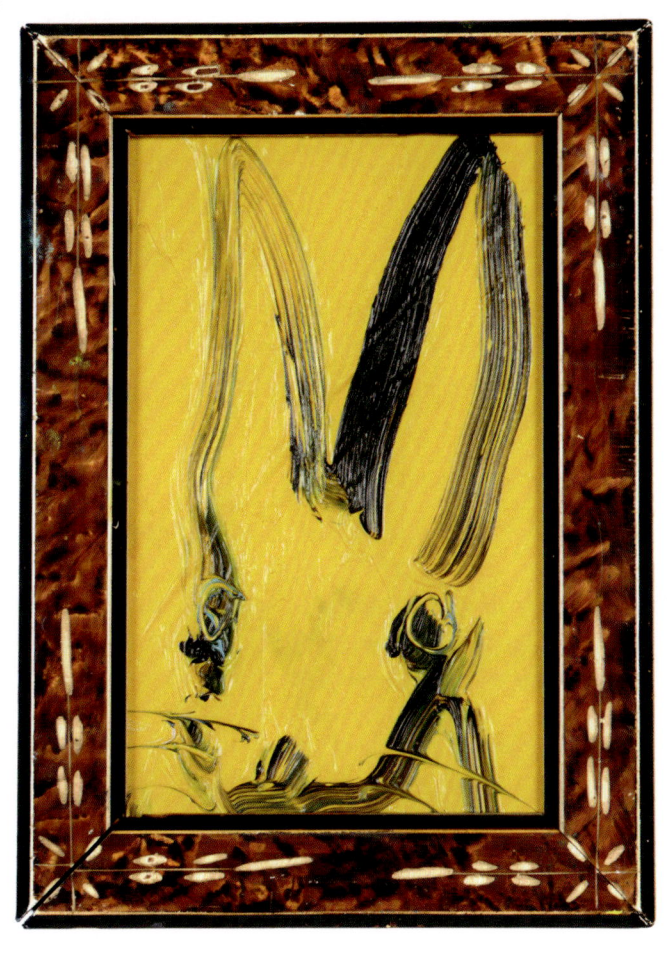

GABRIELLE
2012
OIL ON WOOD
10" X 8"

DUANE
2013
OIL ON WOOD
8" X 5"

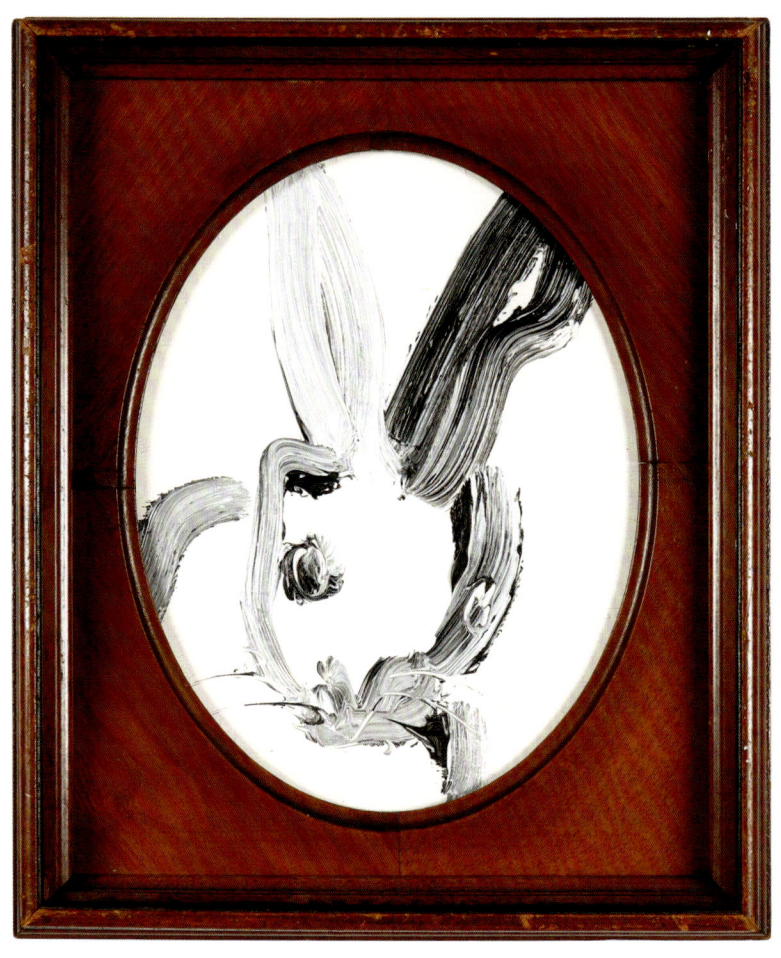

MAUREEN
2013
OIL ON WOOD
10" X 8"

DOUBLE METAL BUNNYS
2013
OIL ON WOOD
28" X 22"

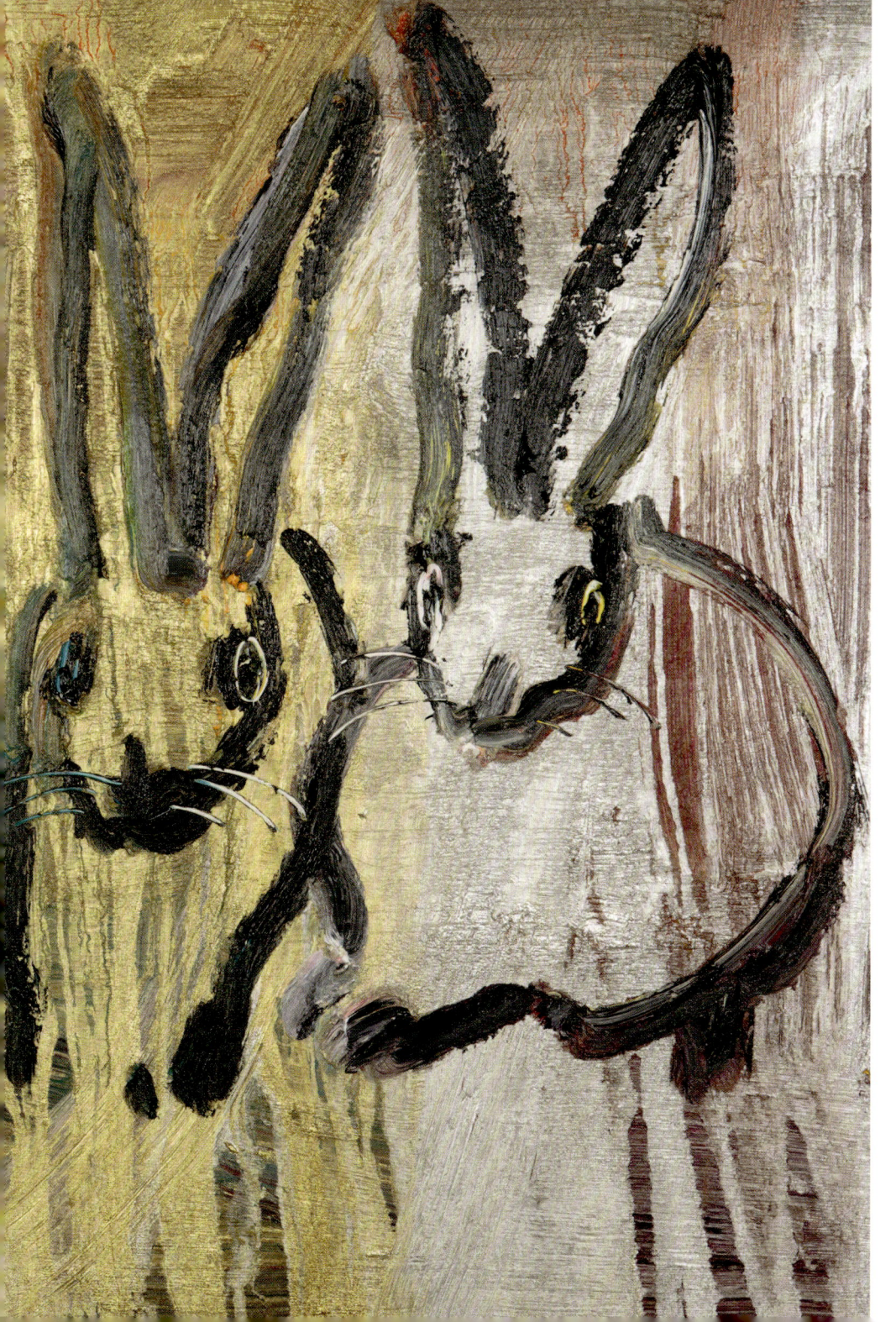

212

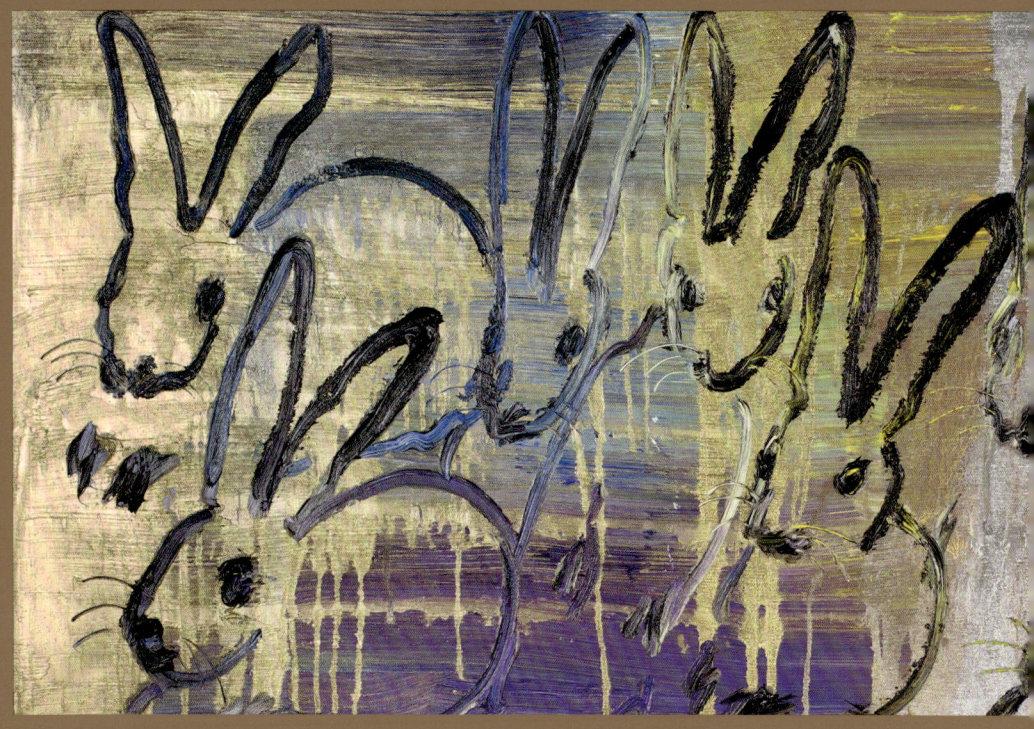

Chinensis #4
2013
OIL ON CANVAS
27" X 72"

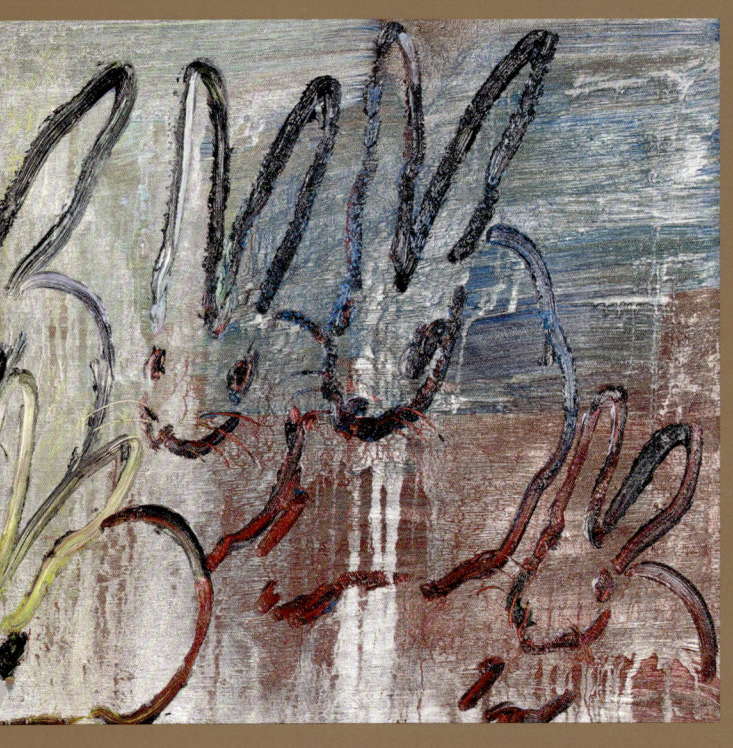

214

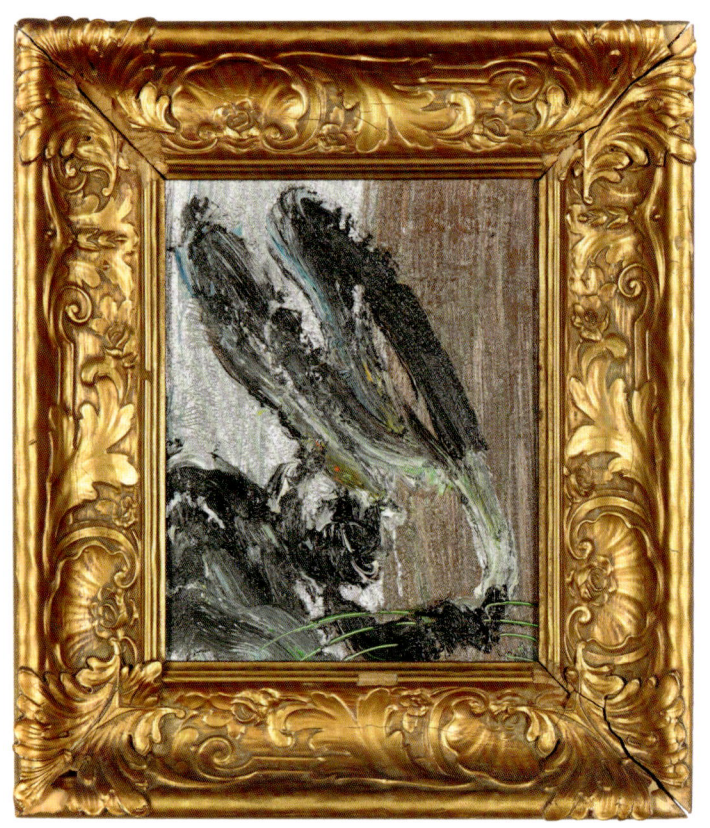

MARILYN
2013
OIL ON WOOD
10" X 8"

LISA
2012
OIL ON WOOD
10" X 8"

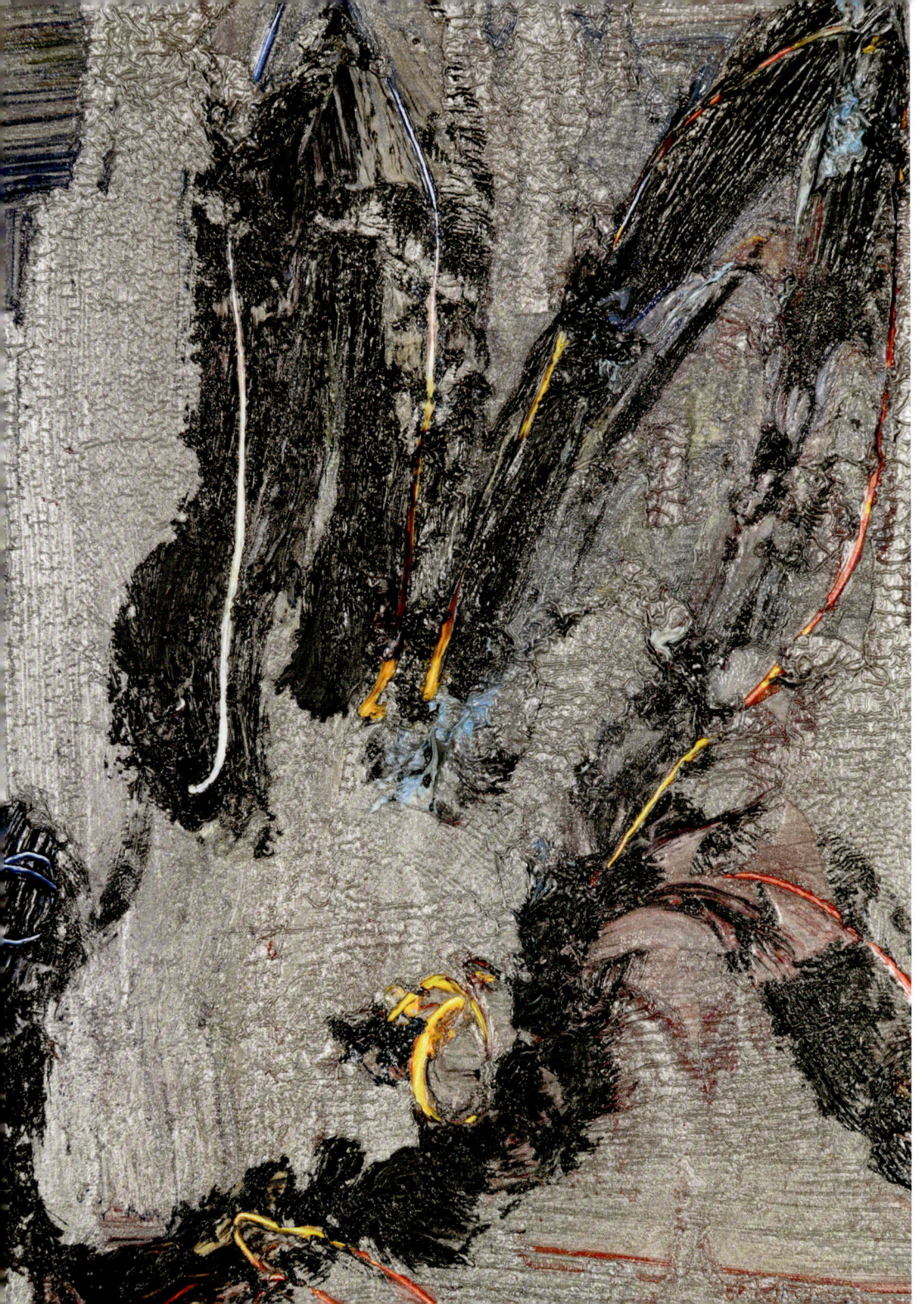

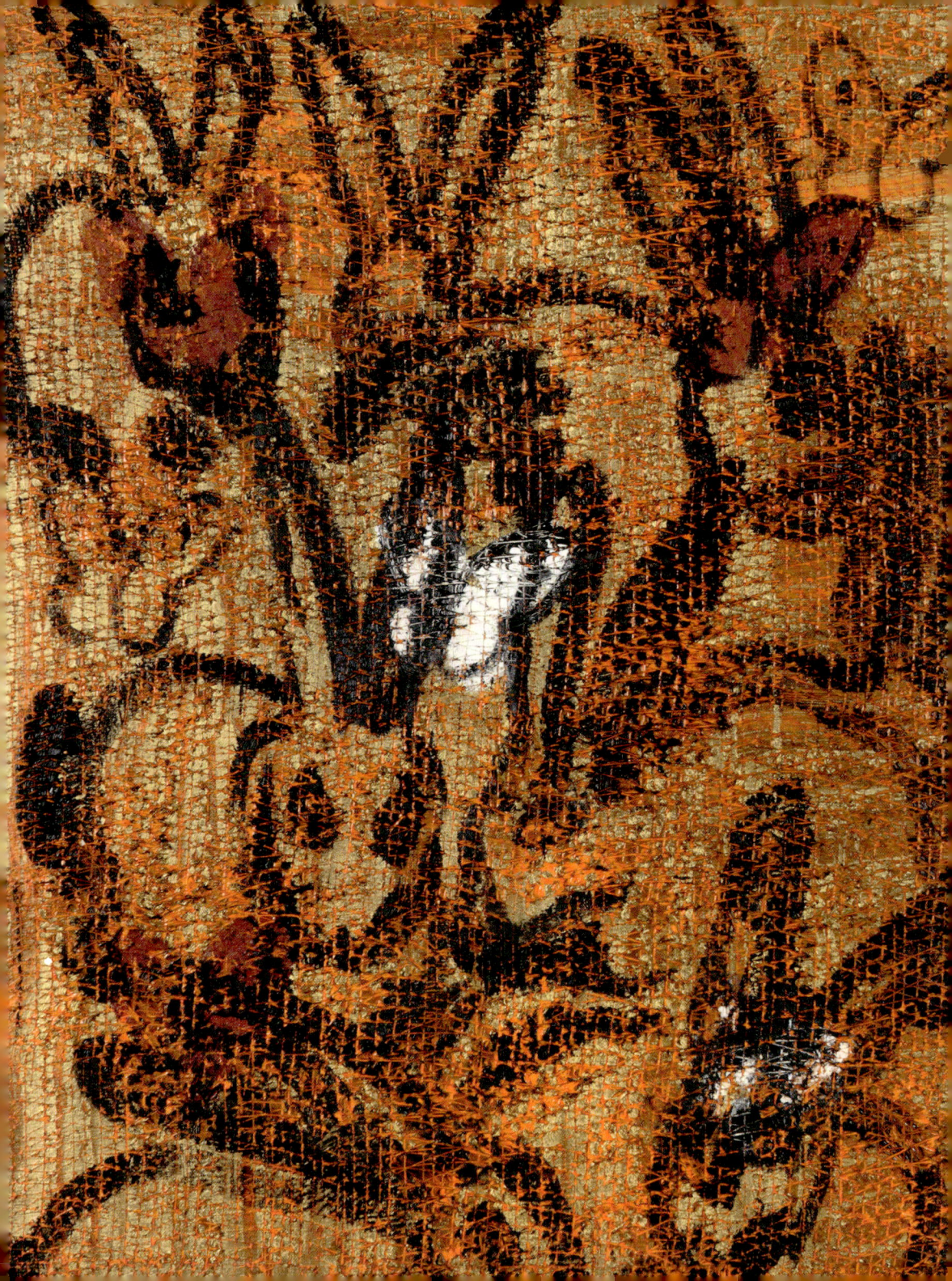

SULE'S CIRCLE
2007
OIL ON CANVAS
40" X 30"

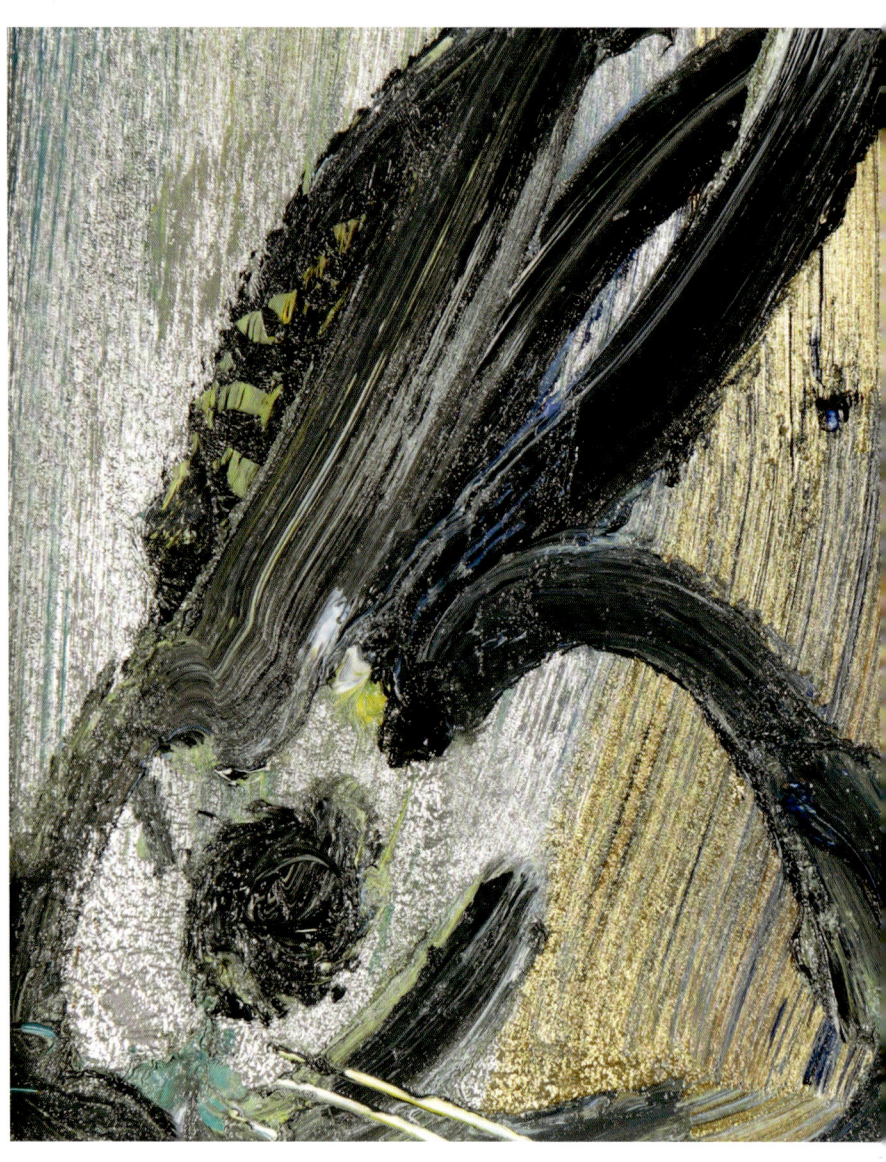

218

ANTHONY
2013
OIL ON WOOD
10" X 8"

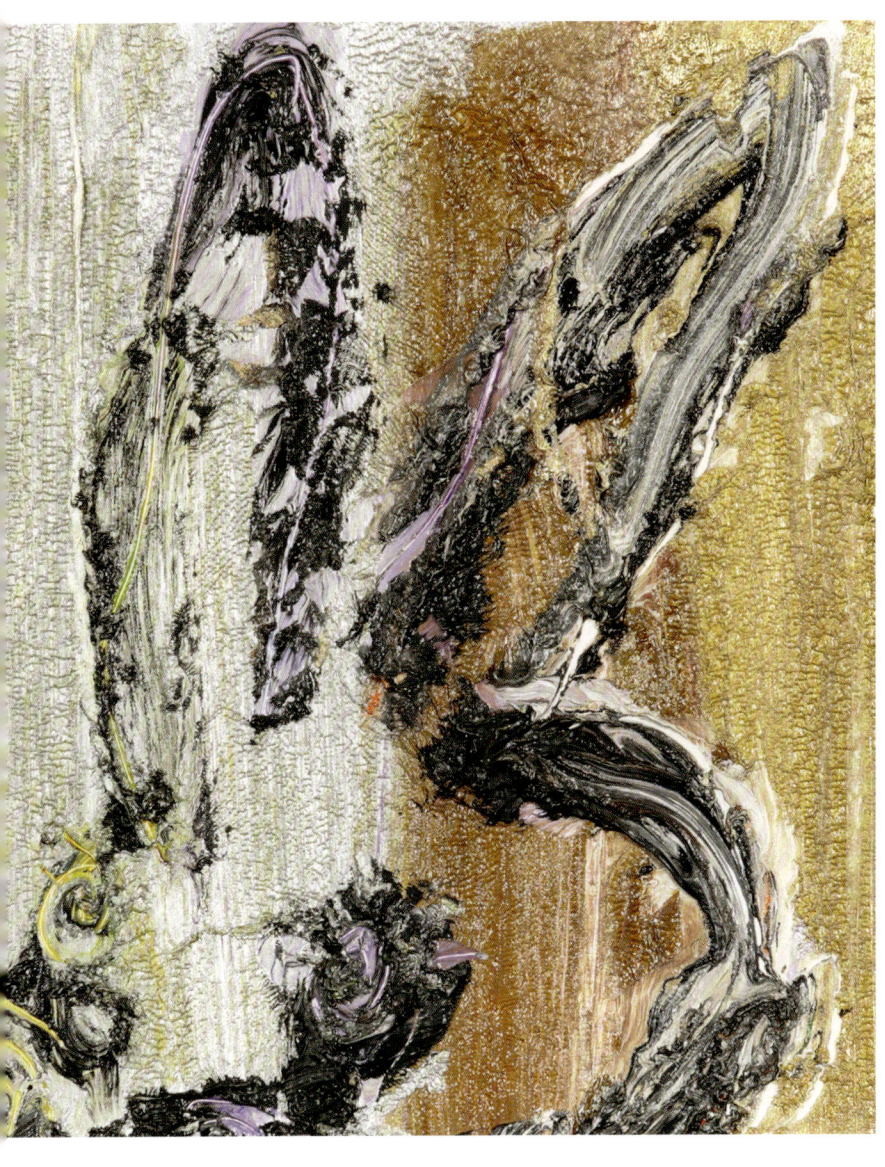

TIMOTHY
2013
OIL ON WOOD
10" X 8"

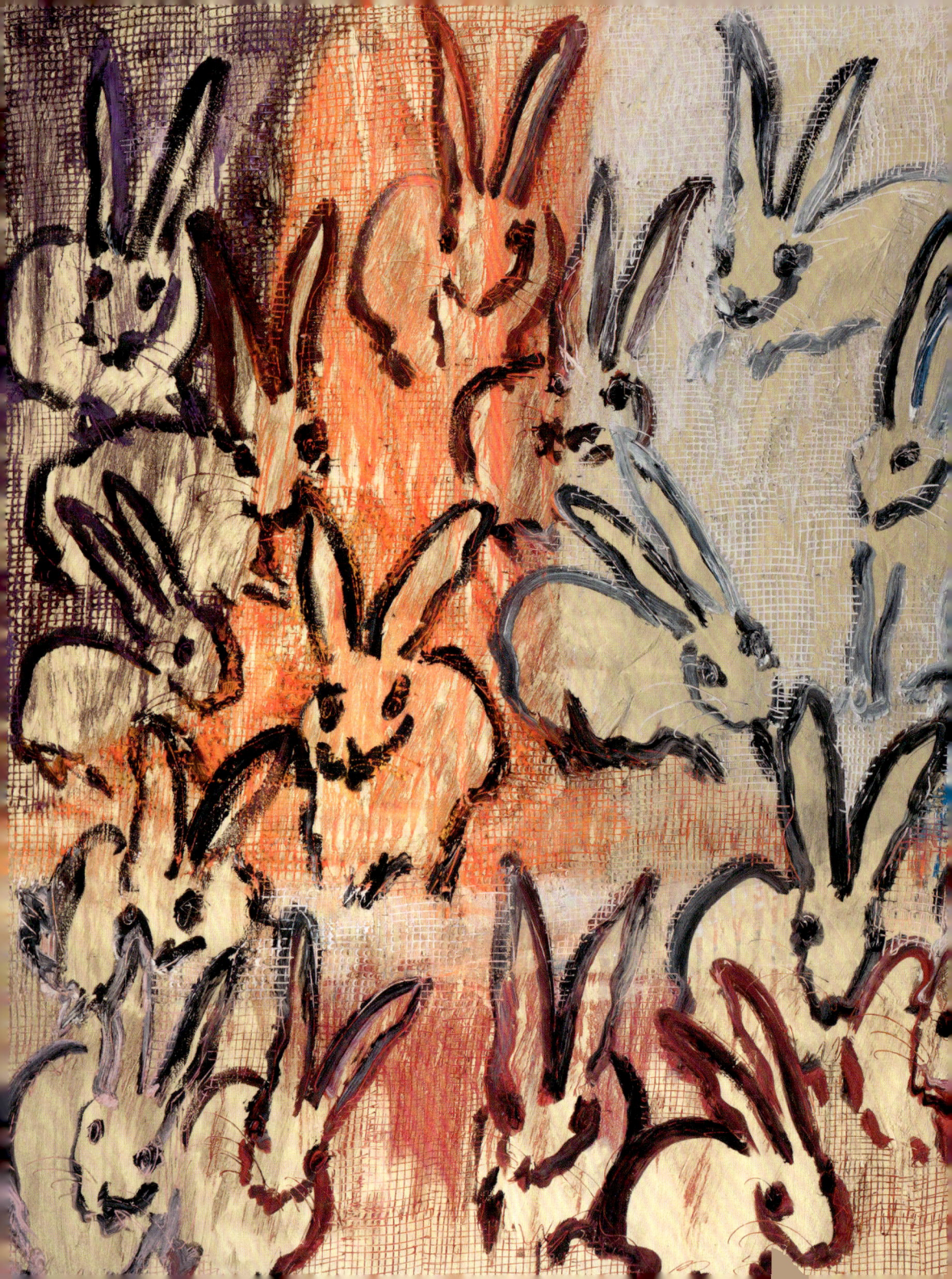

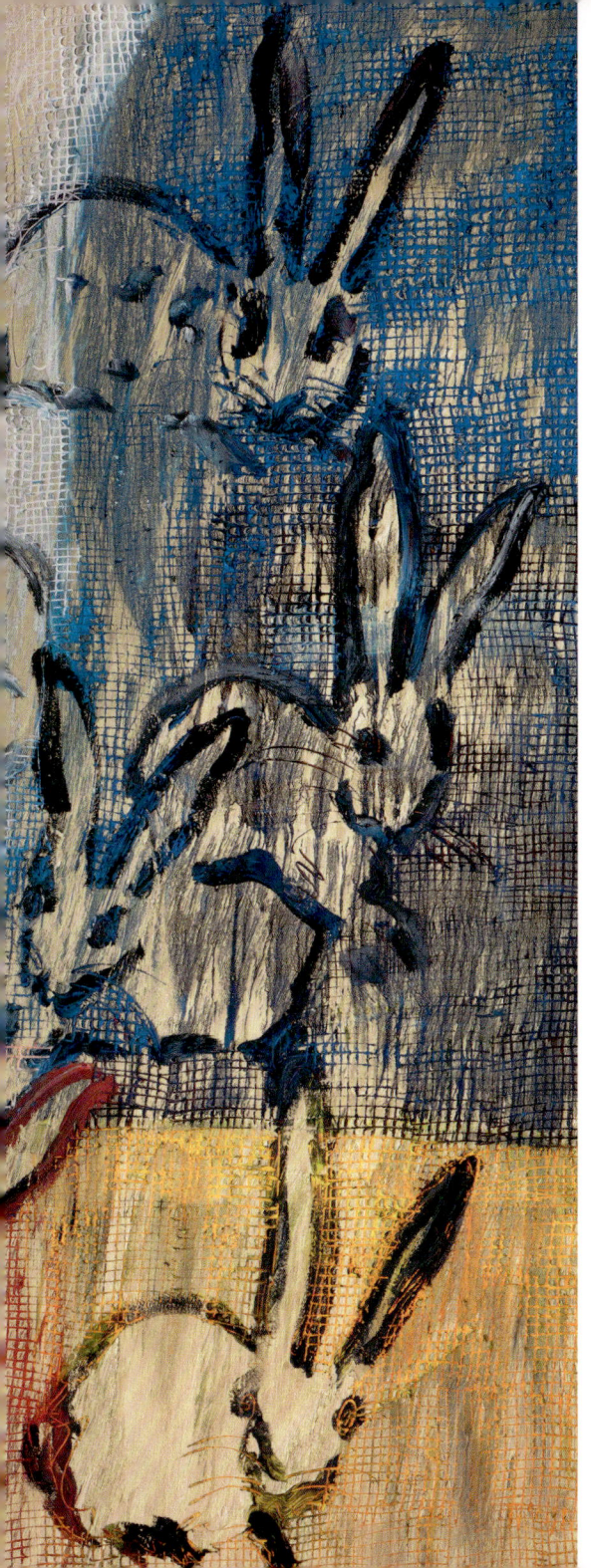

THREE METALS #2
2010
OIL ON CANVAS
72" x 84"

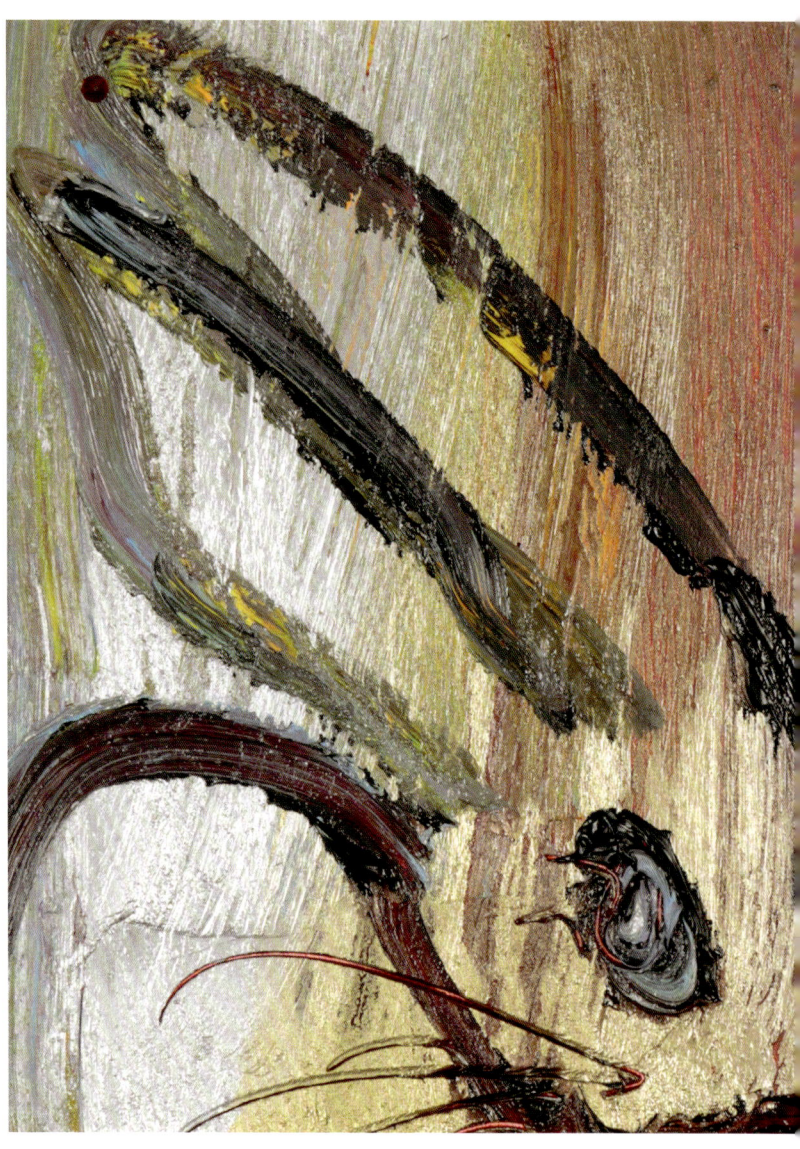

CORNER
2012
OIL ON CANVAS
10" x 8"

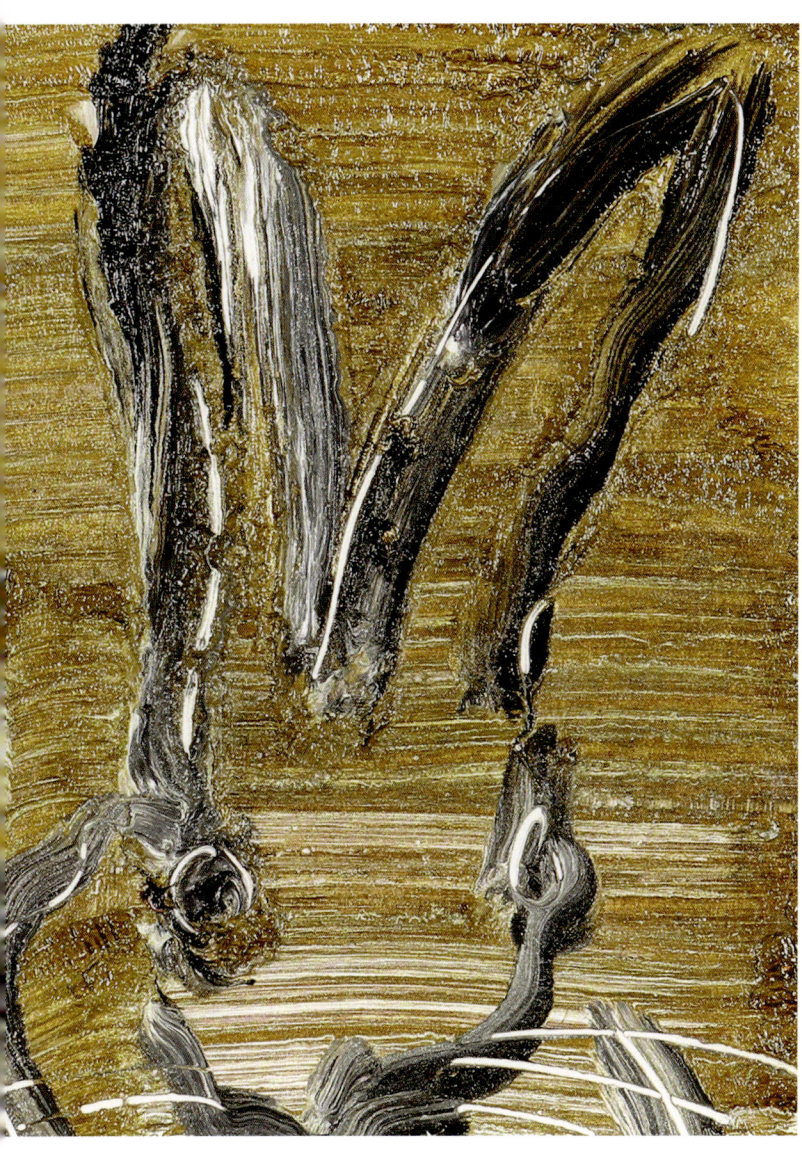

KEITH
2013
OIL ON WOOD
10" x 8"

MOTHER
2012
OIL ON WOOD
22" X 18"

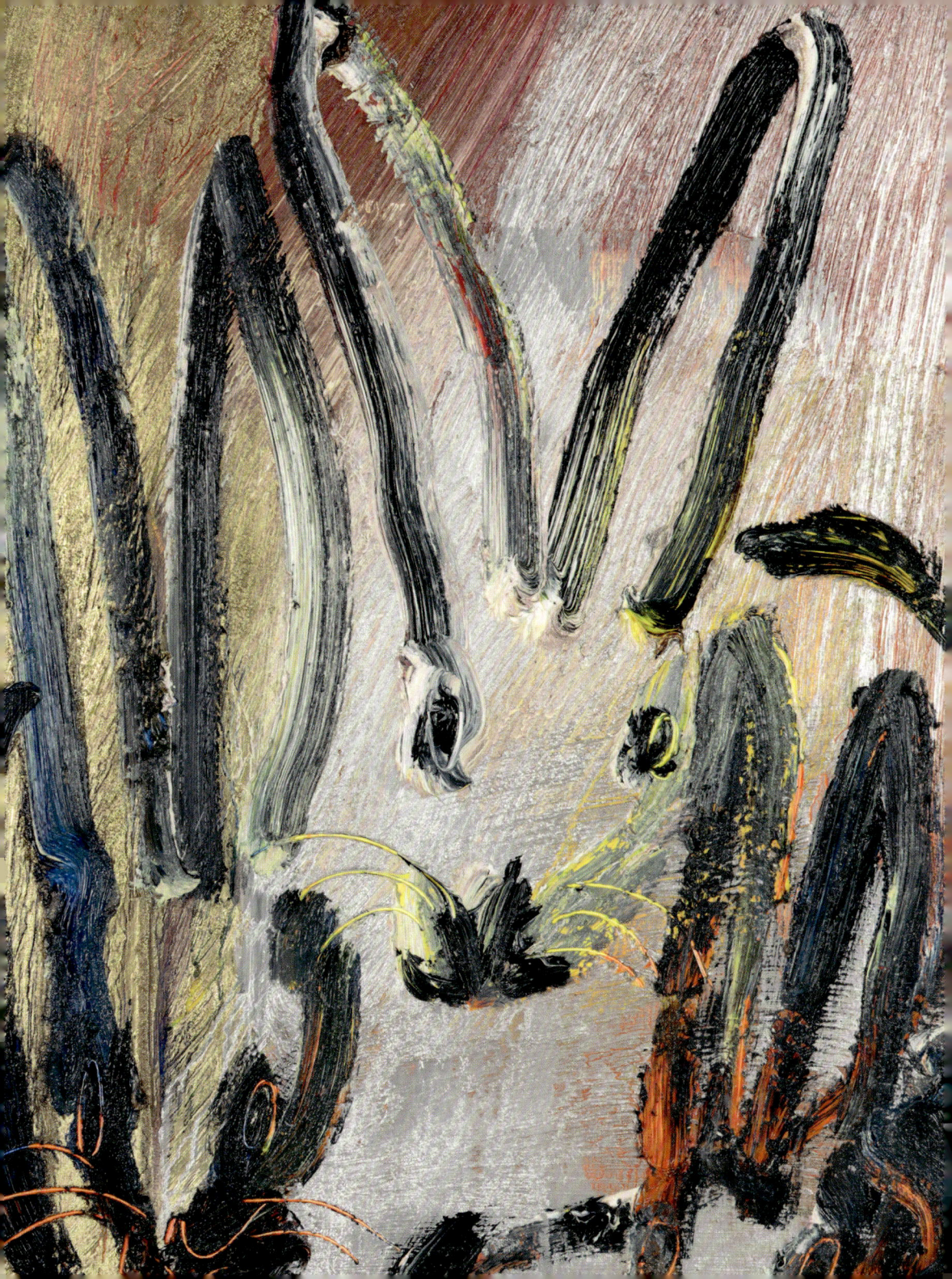

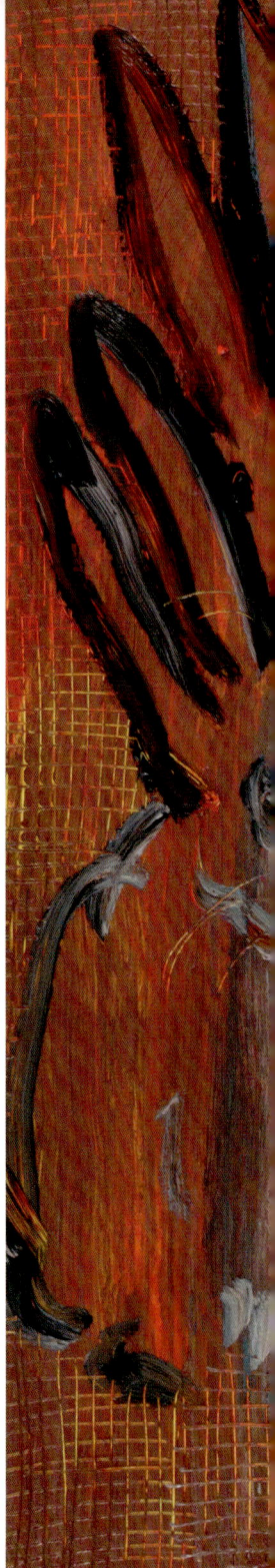

THREE METALS #1
2010
OIL ON CANVAS
48" x 48"

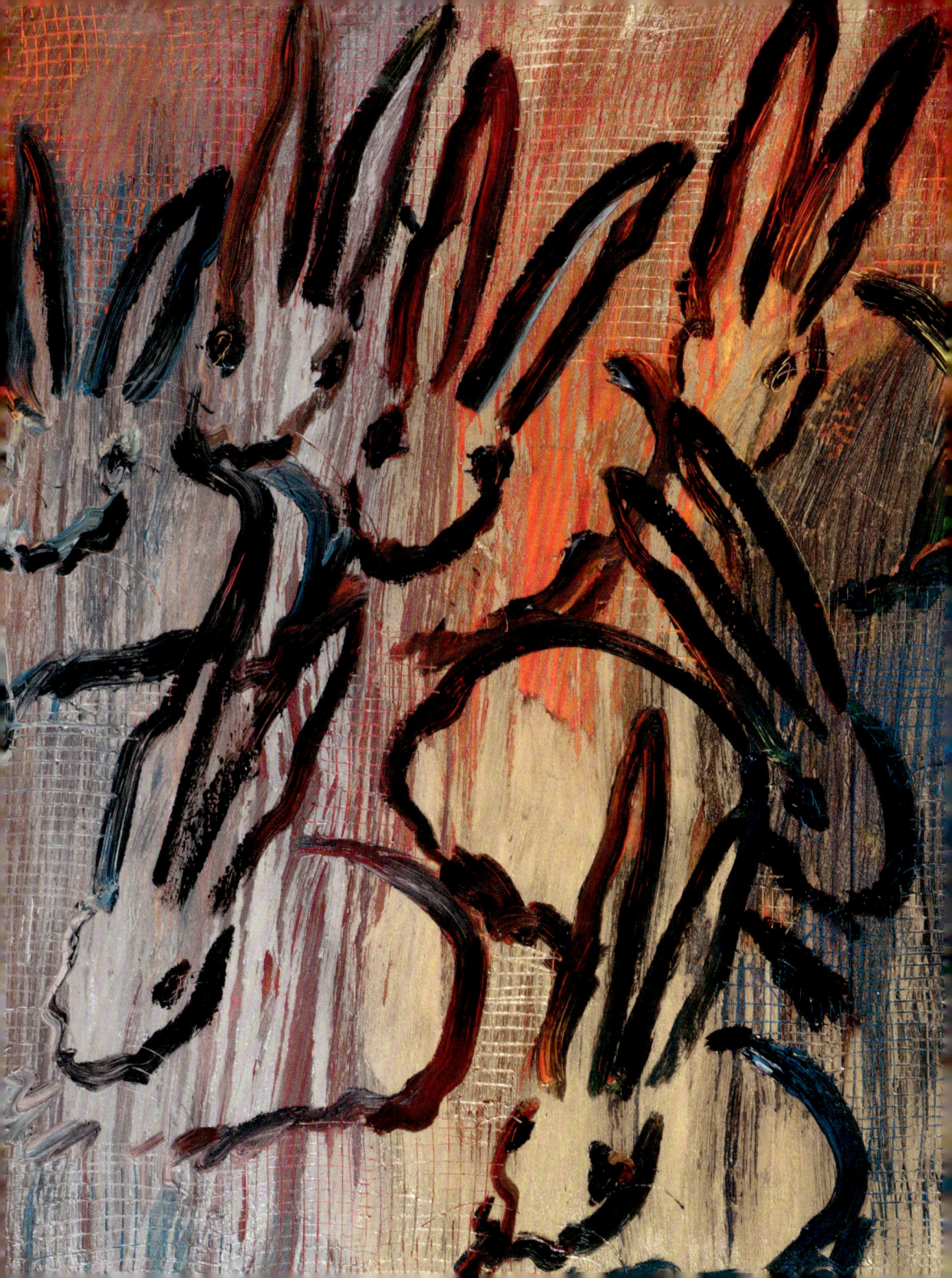

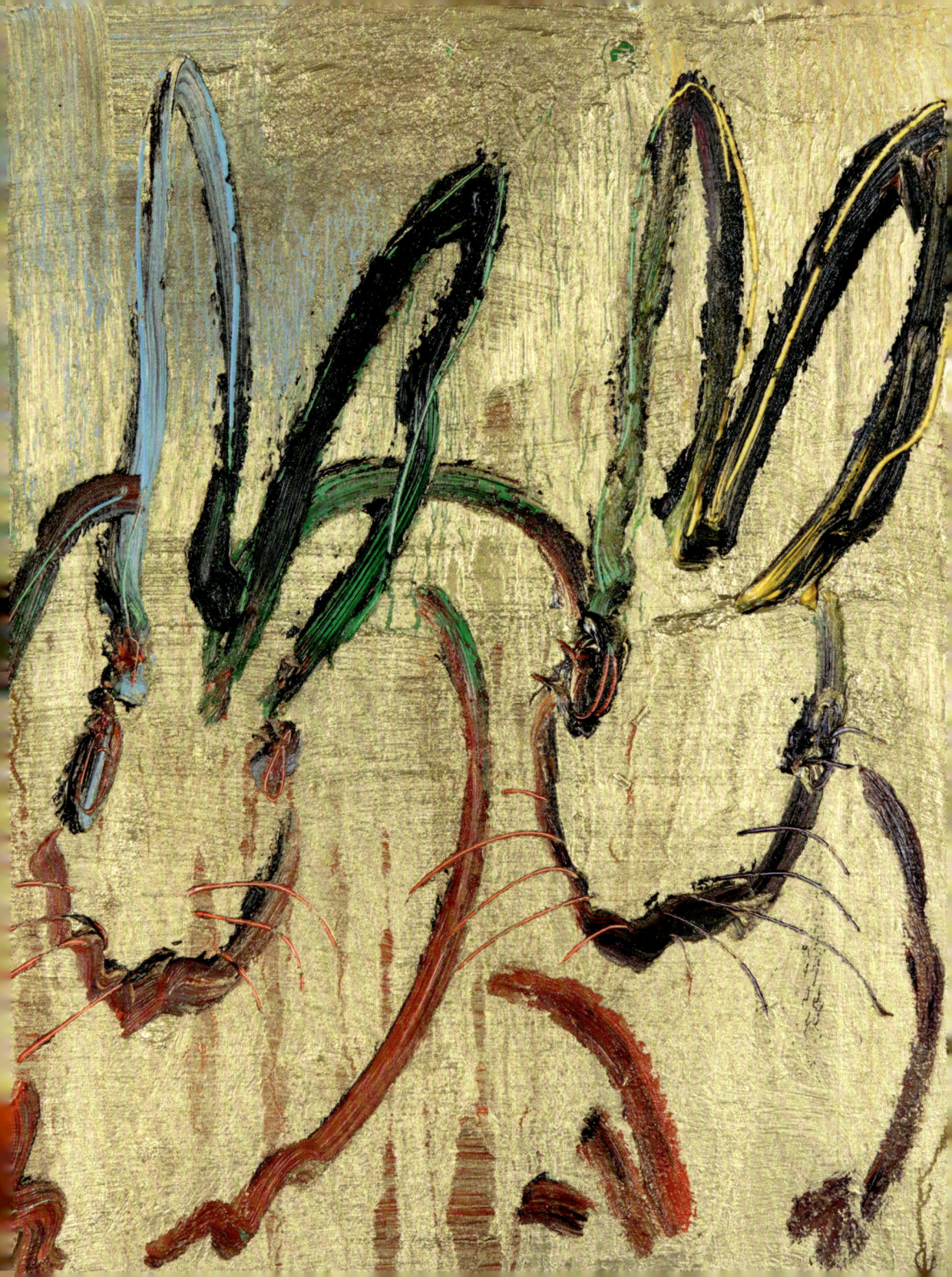

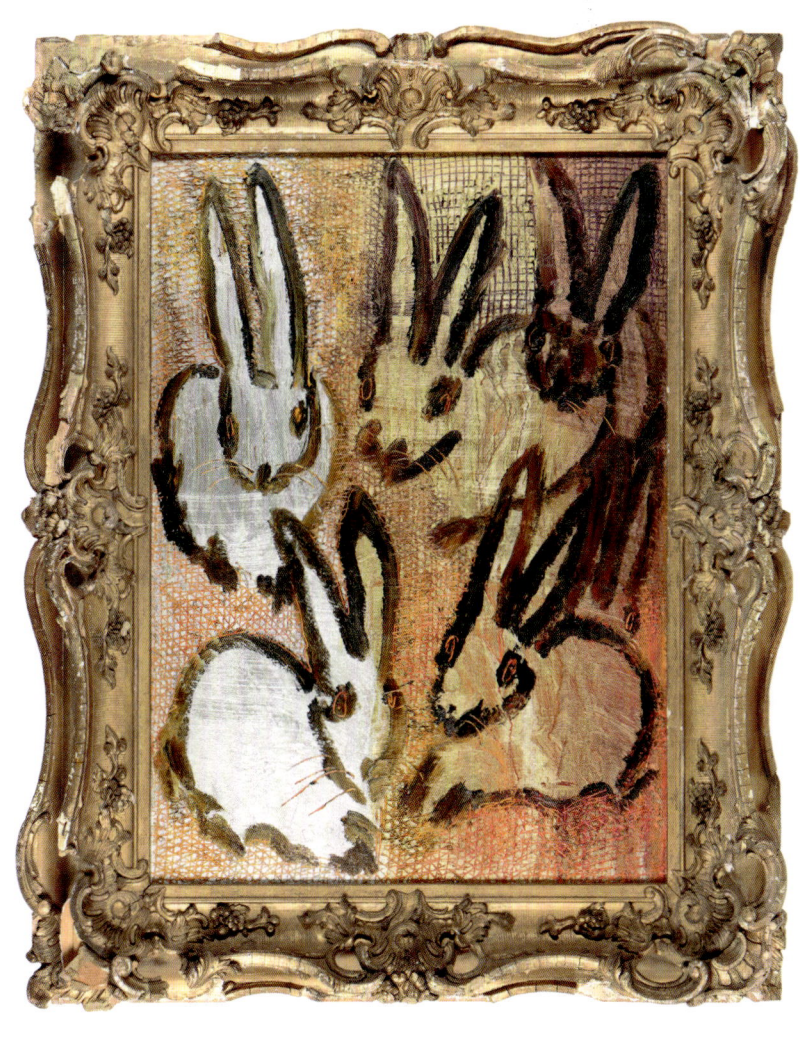

AUTUMN
2013
OIL ON WOOD AND METAL
24" X 20"

FIVE PLAY
2012
OIL ON WOOD
39" X 37"

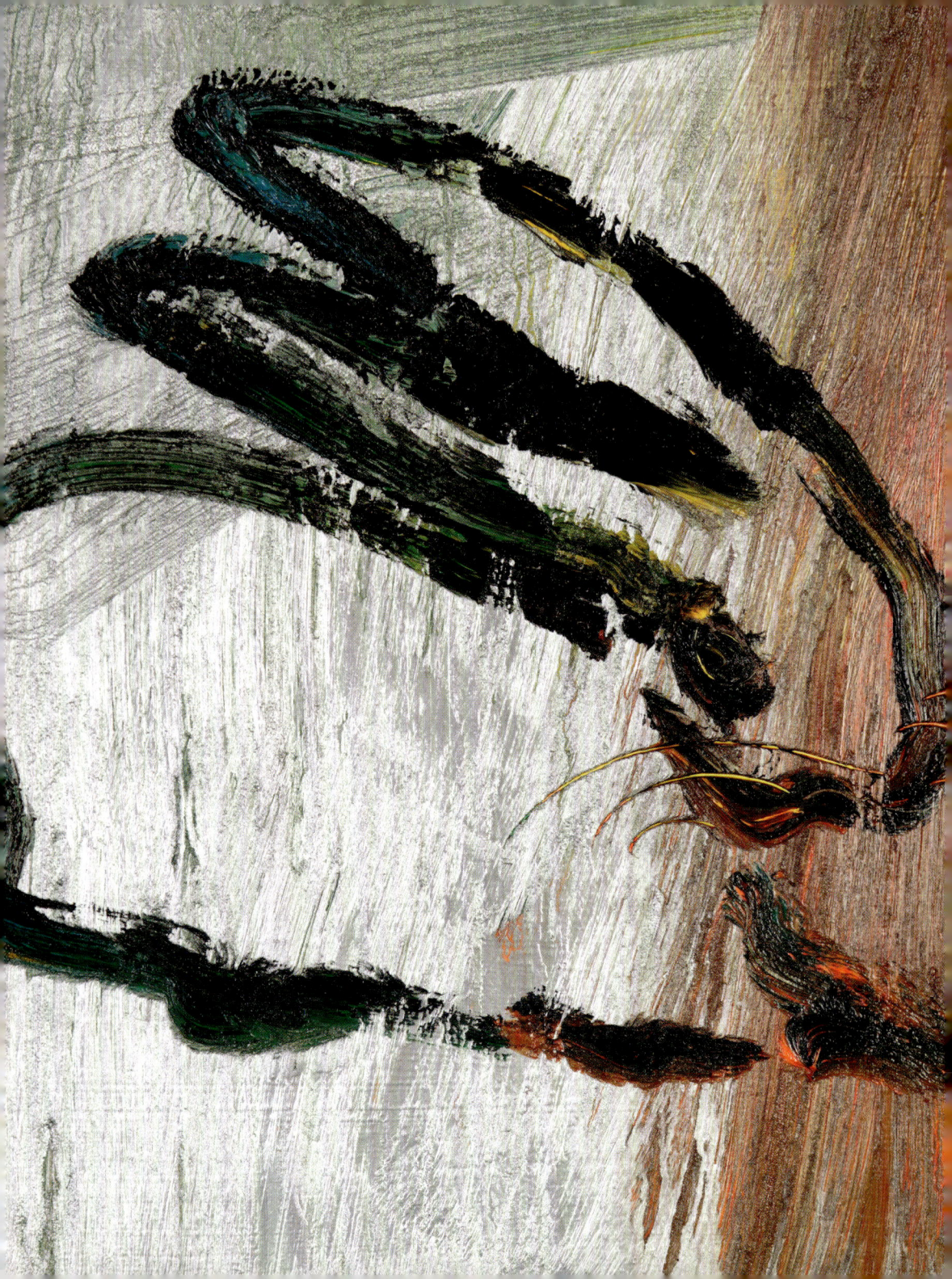

Scarlet
2013
OIL ON WOOD
16" x 18.75"

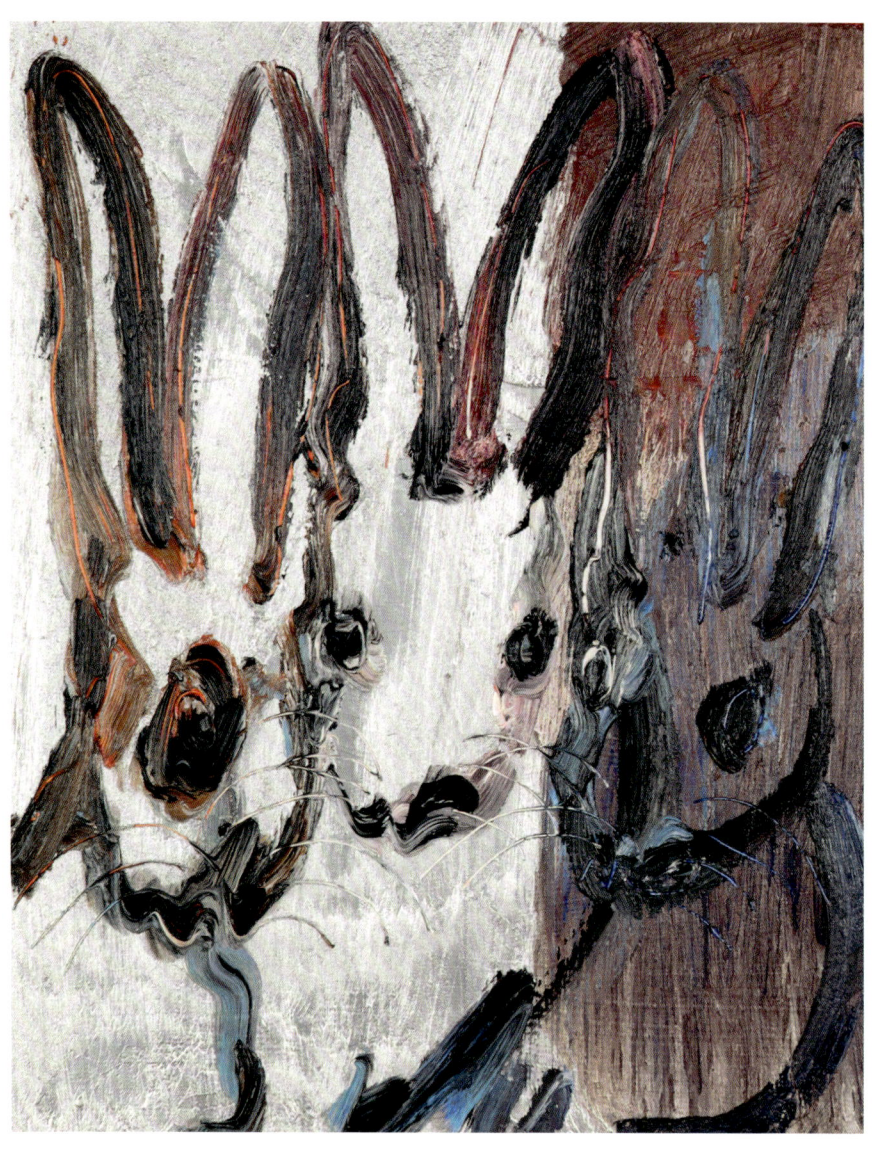

EXAGGERATION
2013
OIL ON CANVAS AND METALLIC
20" X 16"

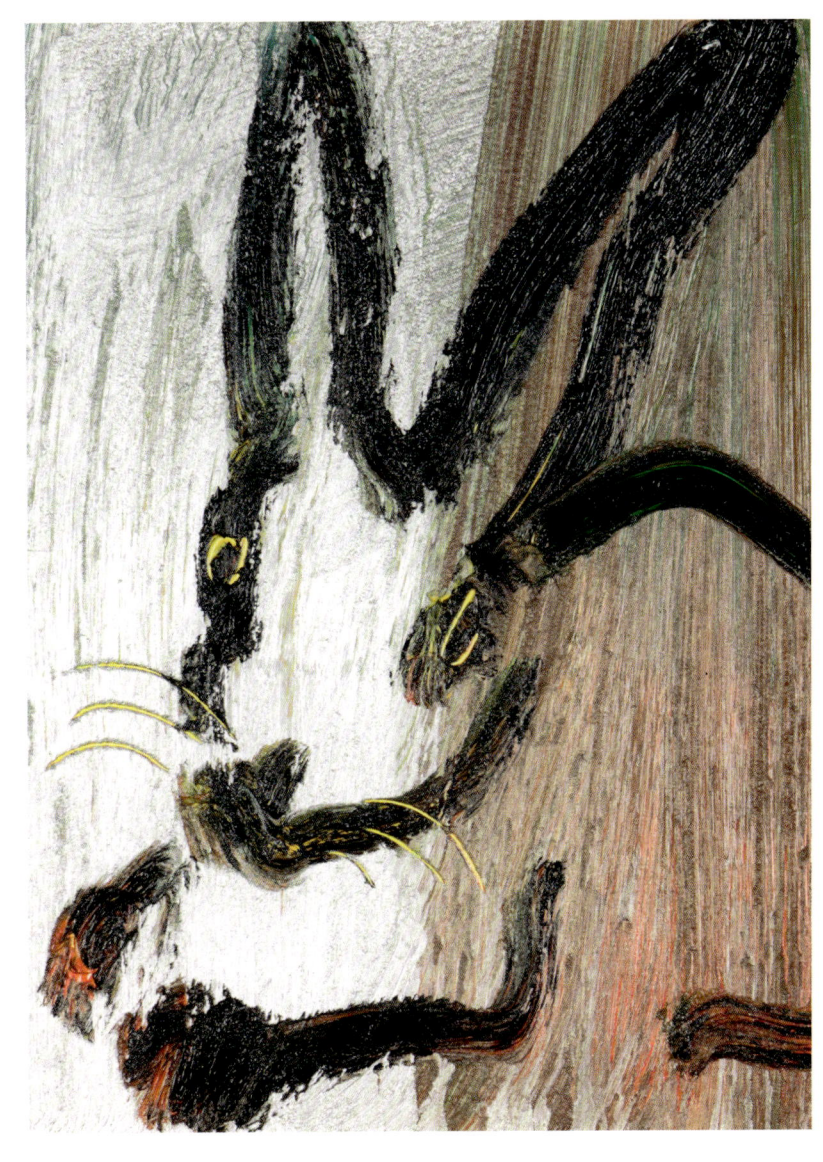

CAMPION
2013
OIL ON WOOD
16" X 12"

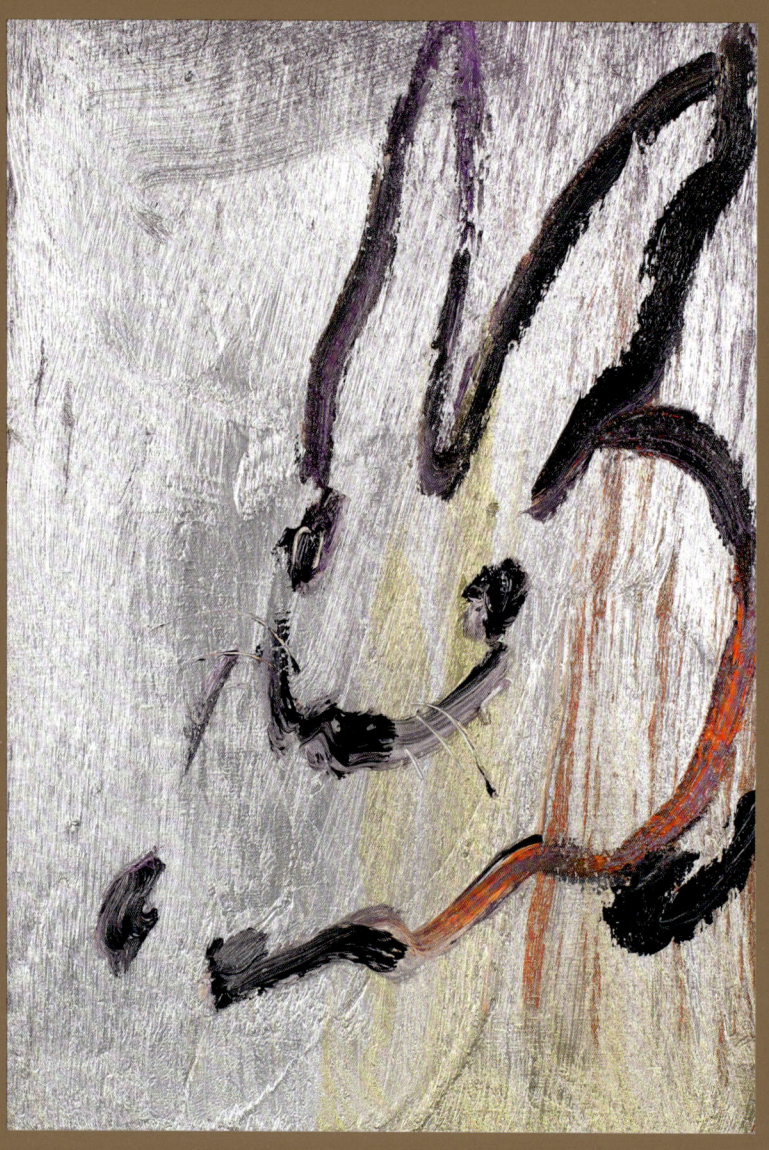

234

RALPH
2013
OIL ON WOOD
20" x 14"

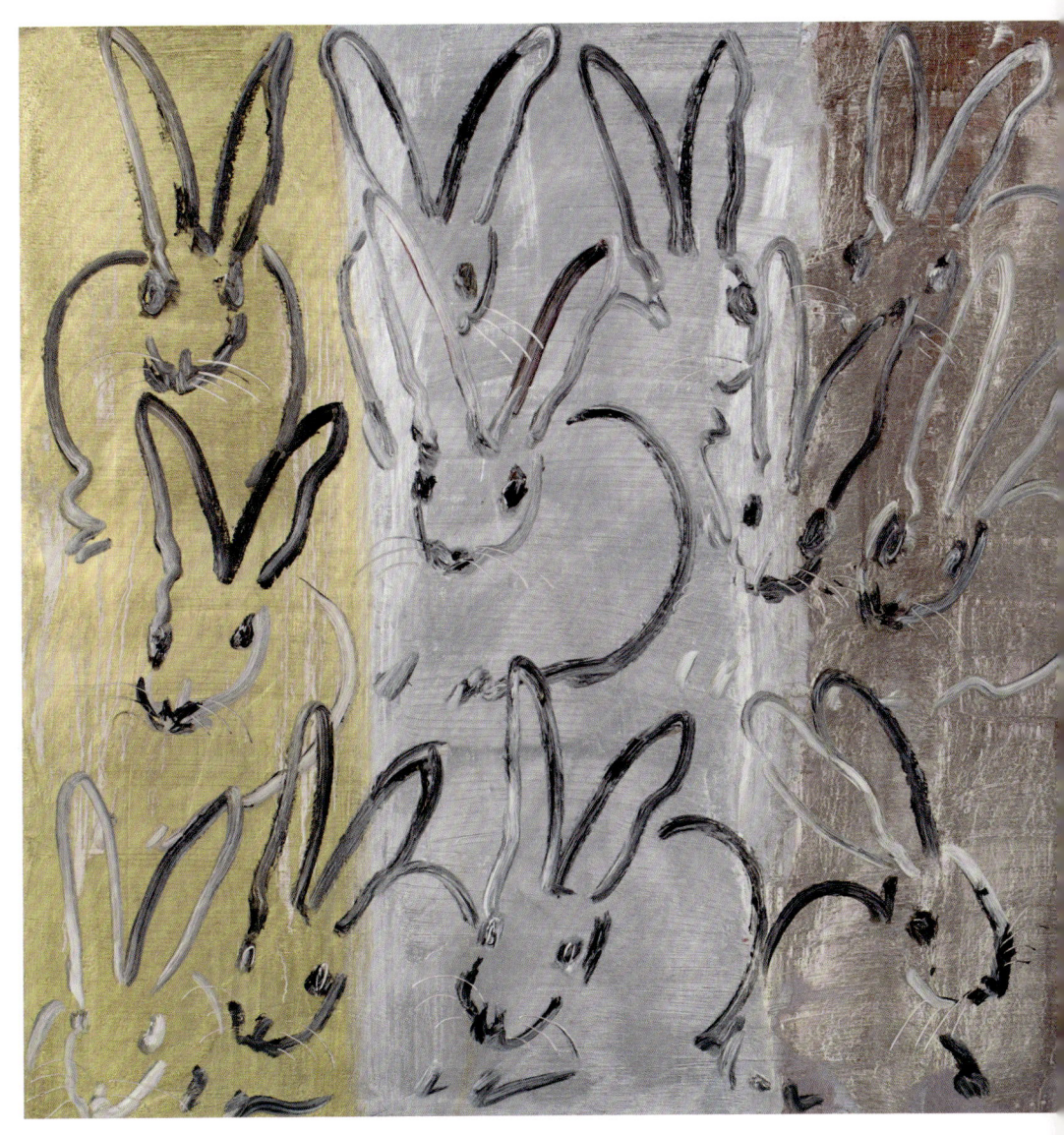

THREE METALS #4
2013
OIL ON CANVAS
48" x 48"

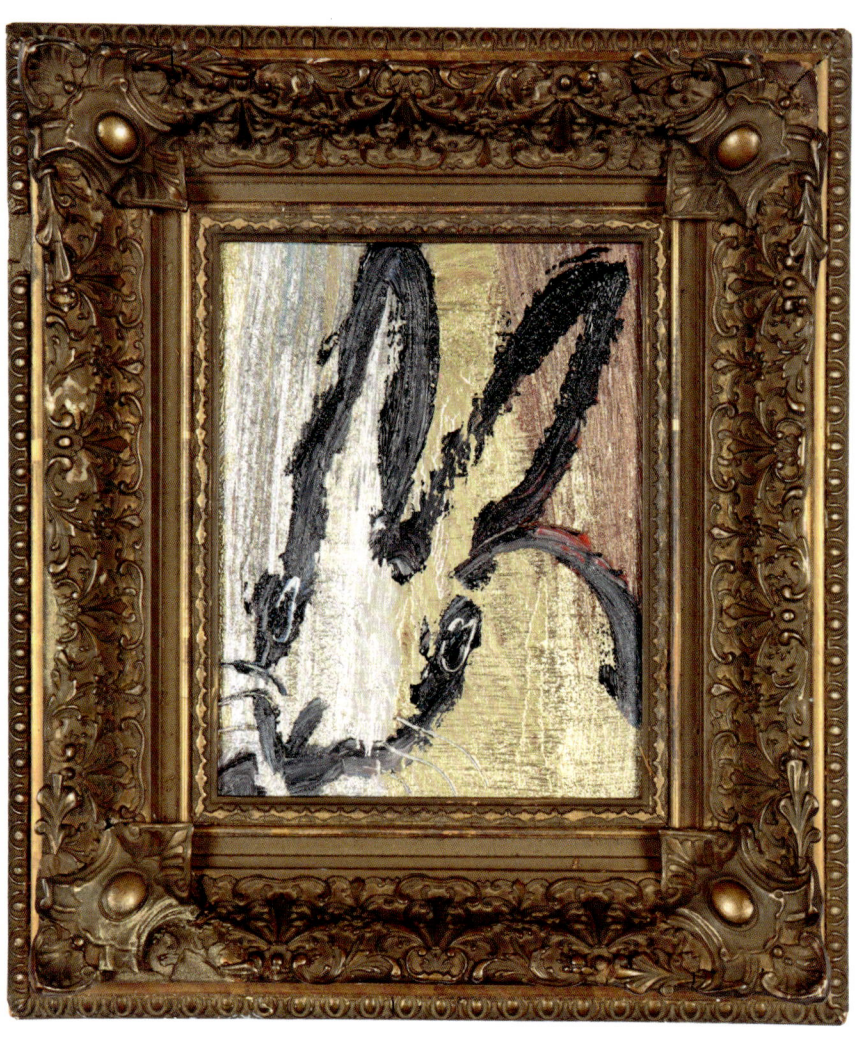

236

WILLY
2013
OIL ON WOOD
10" X 8"

SANDRA
2013
OIL ON WOOD
10" X 8"

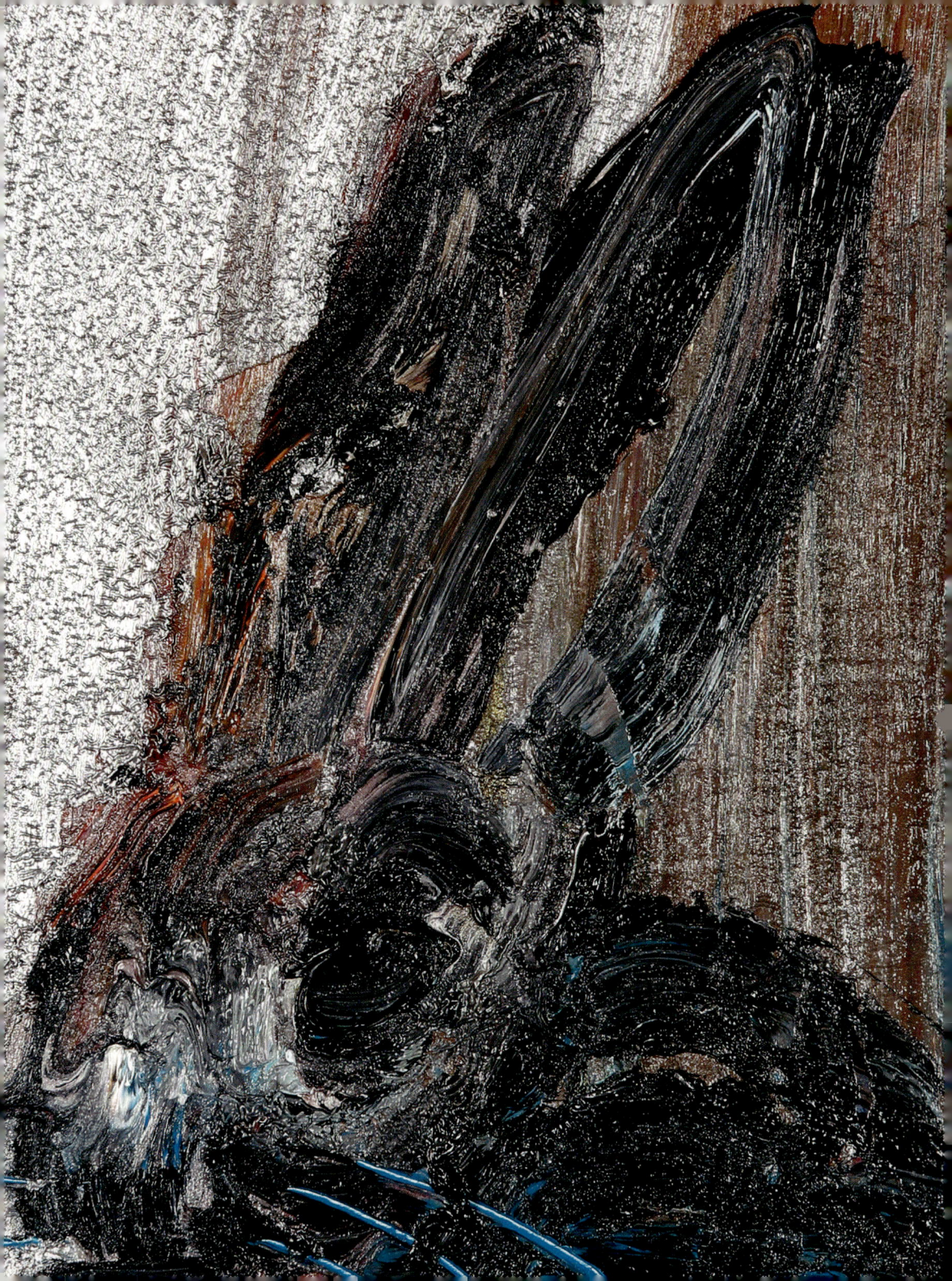

238

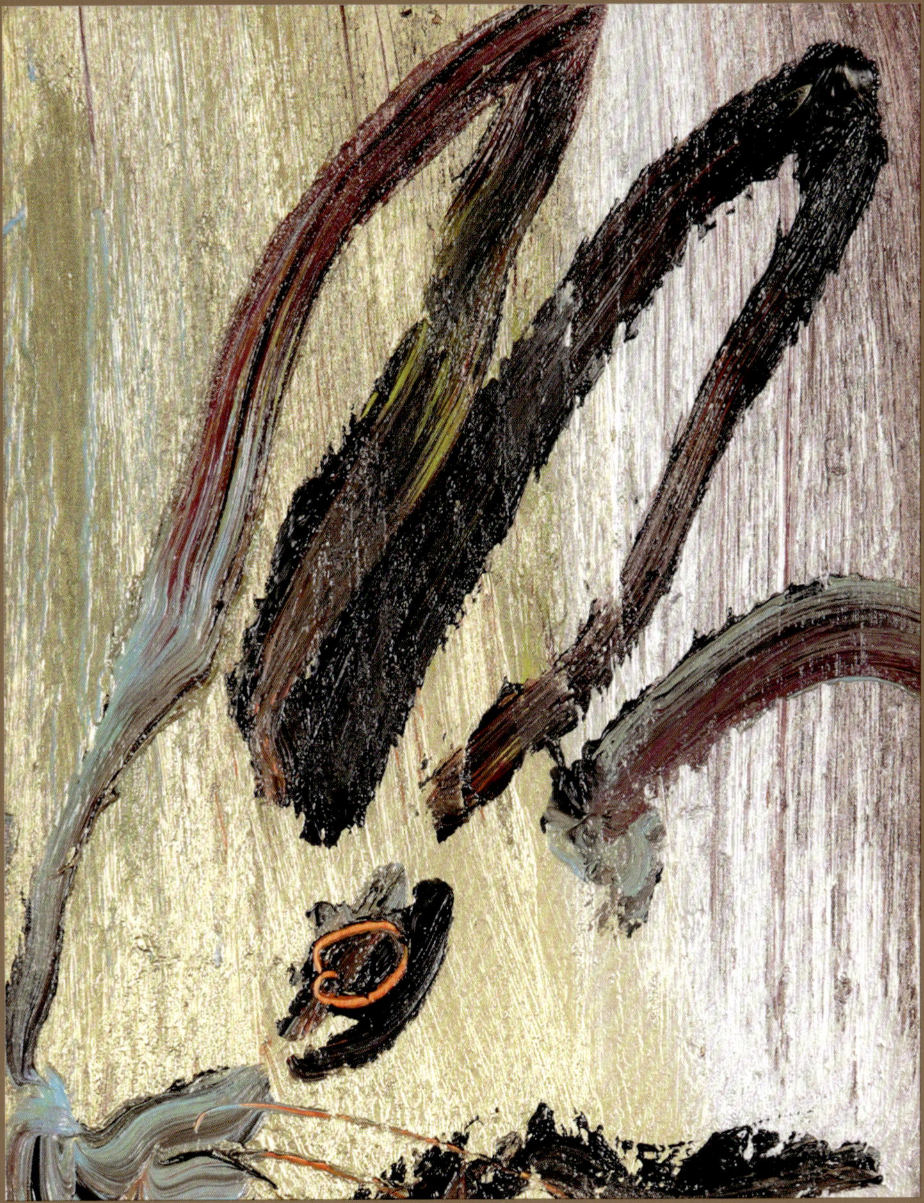

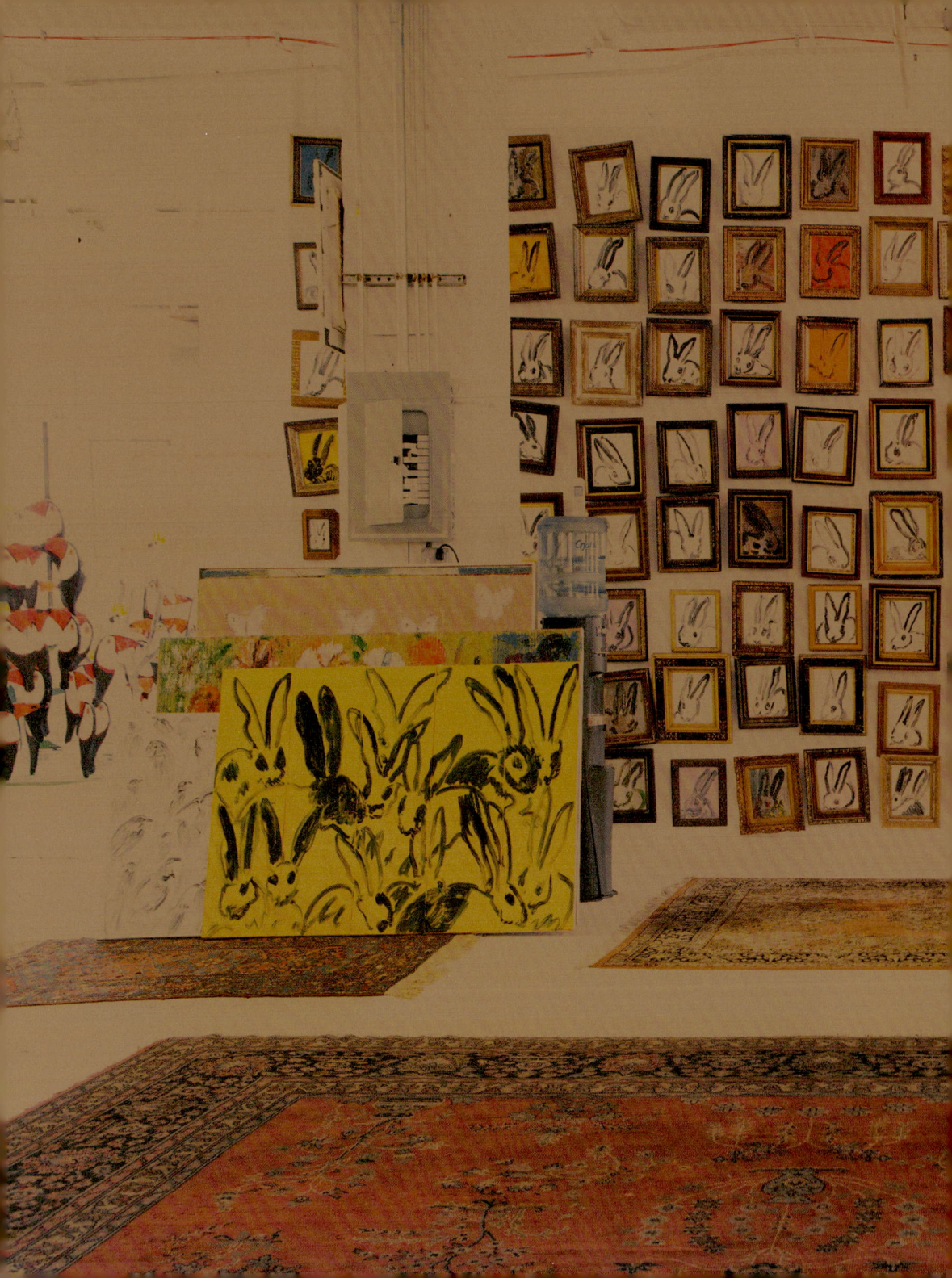

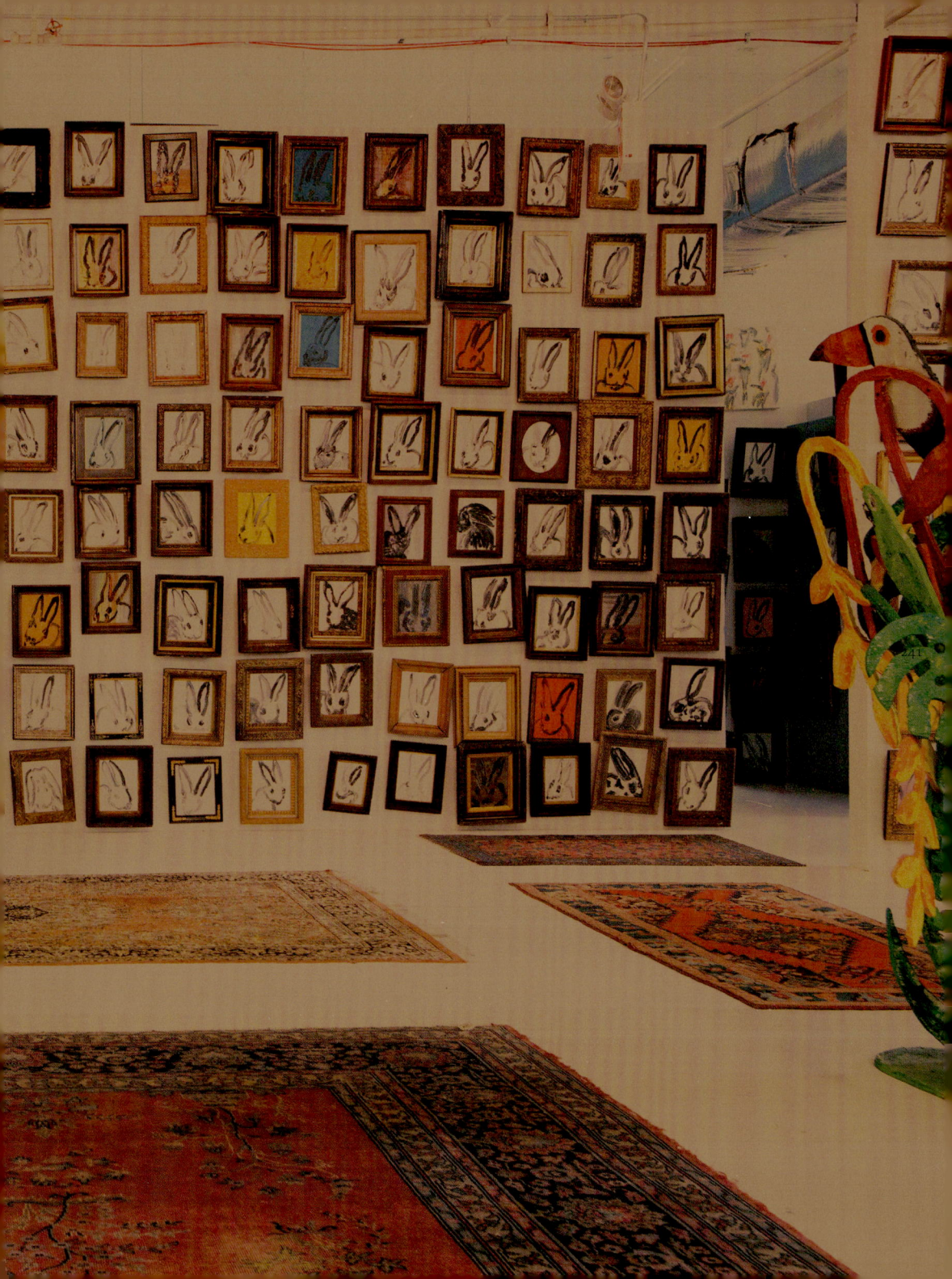

Author
Chronology

HUNT SLONEM

1951   Born July 18, Kittery, ME

69-70   Vanderbilt University, Nashville, TN

70-71   Universidad de las Americas, Cholula, Mexico

1972   Skowhegan School of Painting & Sculpture, Skowhegan, Maine

1973   Tulane University, New Orleans, LA, Bachelor of Arts

1973   Banff School of Fine Arts, Alberta, Canada

SOLO EXHIBITIONS (2000-CURRENT)

2000   Marlborough Gallery, New York, NY
Marlborough Gallery, Boca Raton, FL
Centro Cultural Recoleta, Buenos Aires, Argentina
Vanier Gallery, Scottsdale, AZ
Harmon-Meek Gallery, Naples, FL
Heriard-Cimino Gallery, New Orleans, LA

2001   Robert McClain Gallery, Houston, TX
Harmon-Meek Gallery, Naples, FL
Marcel Sitcoske Gallery, San Francisco, CA
Vered Gallery, East Hampton, NY
Jean Albano Gallery, Chicago, IL
Mariella Gonzalez Lerena Galeria de Arte, Punta del Este, Uruguay
Marlborough, Anguilla, British West Indies
Vanier Gallery, Scottsdale, AZ

2002   Marlborough Chelsea, New York, NY
Vanier Gallery, Tucson, AZ
Robert McClain Gallery, Houston, TX
Heriard-Cimino Gallery, New Orleans, LA
Jean Albano Gallery, Chicago, IL
Paula Brown Gallery, Toledo, OH

2003   Morgan Gallery, Kansas City, MO
Ten High Street, Camden, ME
Alva Gallery, New London, CT

Harmon-Meek Gallery, Naples, FL
Handsel Gallery, Santa Fe, NM
Harmon-Meek Gallery, Naples, FL

2004   Marlborough Chelsea, New York, NY
Vanier Galleries, Scottsdale, AZ
Jean Albano Gallery, Chicago, IL
Heriard-Cimino Gallery, New Orleans, LA
Harmon-Meek Gallery, Naples, FL
Pensacola Museum of Art, Pensacola, FL
Louisiana Museum of Art & Science, Baton Rouge, LA
Millenia Gallery, Orlando, FL

2005   Evansville Museum of Arts, History, & Science, Evansville, IN
Gebert Contemporary, Scottsdale, AZ
Pensacola Museum of Art, Pensacola, FL
Galerie Barbara Von Stechow, Frankfurt, Germany
Vered Gallery, East Hampton, NY
Don O'Melveny Gallery, Los Angeles, CA
The Armory Art Center, West Palm Beach, FL

2006   Miriam Shiell Gallery, Toronto, Canada
Heriard-Cimino Gallery, New Orleans, LA
Elaine Baker Gallery, Boca Raton, FL
Gebert Contemporary, Santa Fe, NM
Harmon-Meek Gallery, Naples, FL
Vered Gallery, East Hampton, NY

2007   The von Liebig Art Center, Naples, FL
Vero Beach Museum of Art, Vero Beach, FL
Olin Gallery, Roanoke University, Salem, VA
Harmon-Meek Gallery, Naples, FL
George Billis Gallery, Los Angeles, CA
Opelousas Museum of Art, Opelousas, FL
Wasmer Gallery, Ursuline College, Pepper Pike, OH
Heriard Cimino Gallery, New Orleans, LA
Ogden Museum of Southern Art, New Orleans, LA
Gebert Contemporary, Santa Fe, NM

2008   Marlborough Chelsea New York, NY
Galerie de Bellefeuille, Montreal, Quebec, Canada
DTR Modern, Boston, MA
Heriard-Cimino Gallery New Orleans, LA
Jean Albano Gallery, Chicago, IL
Cuadro Fine Art, Dubai, United Arab Emirates
Gebert Contemporary, Scottsdale, AZ
Seaside Gallery/Ogden Museum, Seaside, FL
Elaine Baker Gallery, Boca Raton, FL

2009   DTR Modern, Palm Beach, FL
        Gallerie Barbara Von Stechow, Frankfurt, Germany
        Harmon-Meek Gallery, Naples, FL
        Louisiana State Archives, Baton Rouge, LA
        Rymer Gallery, Nashville, TN
        Gallerie de Bellefeuille, Montreal, Quebec, Canada
        DTR Modern, Boston, MA
        PG Art Gallery, Istanbul, Turkey
        Gettysburg Festival, Gettysburg, PA

2010   Museo de Arte de El Salvador, San Salvador, El Salvador
        12 Gallagher Lane, San Francisco, CA
        Gebert Gallery, Venice, CA
        Coral Springs Museum, Coral Springs, FL
        Galerie de Bellefeuille, Montreal, Quebec, Canada
        DTR Modern, Boston, MA
        Thomas Masters Gallery, Chicago, IL
        Museum Gallery of Modern Art, Sofia, Bulgaria
        National Gallery of Foreign Art, Sofia, Bulgaria
        Paul & Lulu Hilliard University Art Museum, Lafayette, LA
        Meadows Museum of Art, Shreveport, LA
        Martine Chaisson Gallery, New Orleans, LA
        DTR Modern, Palm Beach, FL
        Varna City Art Gallery, Varna, Bulgaria
        ARC Fine Art, Fairfield, CT
        Gebert Contemporary, Santa Fe, NM
        Harmon-Meek Gallery, Naples, FL

2011   Marlborough Gallery, New York, NY
        Polk Museum of Art, Lakeland, FL (through March 2012)
        Alexandria Museum of Art, Alexandria, LA
        DTR Modern, Boston, MA
        Harmon-Meek Gallery, Naples, FL
        DTR Modern, Palm Beach, FL
        Weinberger Fine Art, Kansas City, MO
        New Gallery of Modern Art, Charlotte, NC
        Martine Chaisson Gallery, New Orleans, LA
        Couture Galleri, Stockholm, Sweden

2012   Mabeyn Gallery at the Chamberlain House, Istanbul, Turkey
        Brenau University, Gainesville, GA
        Miami Art Fair (Dean Project), Miami, FL
        DTR Modern, Palm Beach, FL
        Gremillion & Co., Houston, TX
        Galeria Espacio, San Salvador, El Salvador
        Martine Chaisson Gallery, New Orleans, LA
        McHugh Gallery, Aspen, CO
        DTR Modern, Boston, MA

Imago Galleries, Palm Desert, CA
New Gallery of Modern Art, Sofia, Bulgaria
Harmon-Meek Gallery, Naples, FL
Paula Brown Gallery, Toledo, OH

2013   "Birds and Bayous: Paintings by Hunt Slonem," Manship Theatre,
        Shaw Center, Baton Rouge, LA
Vered Gallery, East Hampton, NY
Gilman Contemporary, Ketchum, ID
Martine Chaisson, New Orleans, LA
McHugh Gallery, Aspen, CO
Serge Sorokko Gallery, San Francisco, CA
Harmon-Meek Gallery, Naples, FL
Bradbury Gallery, Arkansas State University, Jonesboro, AR
Ruiz-Healy Gallery, San Antonio, TX
Galerie de Bellefeuille, Montreal, Quebec, Canada
Gallerie Von Stechow, Frankfurt, Germany
DTR Modern, Boston, MA
Weinberger Fine Art, Kansas City, MO
DTR Georgetown, Washington, DC
New Gallery of Modern Art, Charlotte, NC
Madison Gallery, La Jolla, CA
"Playscapes," Children's Museum of Indianapolis, Indianapolis, IN
Gremillion & Co., Dallas, TX
DTR Modern, Palm Beach, FL
Cuadro Fine Art Gallery, Dubai, United Arab Emirates
Museum of Art DeLand, DeLand, FL
Morris Museum, Augusta, GA

2014   National Art Gallery, Sofia, Bulgaria
Hungarian National Museum, Budapest, Hungary
Martine Chaisson Gallery, New Orleans, LA
McHugh Gallery, Aspen, CO
Serge Sorokko Gallery, San Francisco, CA
DTR Modern, Boston, MA
Harmon-Meek Gallery, Naples, FL
DTR Modern, Palm Beach, FL
Galerie Barbara von Stechow, Frankfurt, Germany
Galerie de Bellefeuille, Montreal, Canada
Gremillion & Co., Houston, TX
Allison Sprock Fine Art, Charlotte, NC
Louisiana Arts & Sciences Museum, Baton Rogue, LA
Flint Institute of Arts, Flint, MI
Galerie Sono, South Norwalk, CT
Miller Gallery, Cincinnati, OH
Quidley & Company, Nantucket, MA
Madison Gallery, La Jolla, CA
Weinberger Fine Art, Kansas City, MO
Pensacola Museum of Art, Pensacola, FL

2015 Vogelsang Gallery, Brussels, Belgium
Sultan Gallery, Kuwait City, Kuwait
Hawk Galleries, Columbus, OH
Jean Albano Gallery, Chicago, IL
Coats-Writght Art & Design, Carmel, IN
Imago Galleries, Palm Desert, CA
Gerbet Contemporary, Scottsdale, AZ
Rarity Gallery, Mykonos, Greece
DTR Modern, Boston, MA
Moscow Museum of Modern Art, sponsored by Imperial Academy of Arts, Moscow, Russia
Galerie de Bellefeuille, Montreal, Canada
Serge Sorokko Gallery, Montreal, Canada
Galerie Sono, South Norwalk, CT
Miller Gallery, Cincinnati, OH
TEW Galleries, Atlanta, GA
Madison Gallery, La Jolla, CA
Harmon-Meek, Naples, FL
NaPua Gallery, Grand Wailea, HI
Marjorie S. Fisher Gallery, Center for Creative Education, West Palm Beach, FL

2016 Shaw Center for the Arts, Louisiana State University, Baton Rogue, LA
Cuadro Fine Art Gallery, Dubai, United Arab Emirates
Arsenal Contemporary Art, Montreal, Canada
Mattatuck Museum, Waterbury, CT
Elizabeth Leach Gallery, Portland, OR
Weinberger Fine Art, Kansas City, MO

2017 Harmon-Meek Gallery, Naples, FL
Galerie Von Stechow - Frankfurt, Germany
Rosenbaum Contemporary Art, Boca Raton and Miami, FL
Galerie Sono, Norwalk CT
Pop-UP Bunny Wall, Miller Gallery, Cincinnati, OH
Gallery 21, Bahrain
Martine Chaisson Gallery, Opening/ Book Signing
DTR Modern Gallery, Boston, MA
Rarity Gallery, Mykonos Greece
Tew Galleries, Atlanta, GA
The State Russian Museum, St. Petersburg, Russia
Contemporary Art Museum, Krasnoyarsk, Russia
Quidley & Co, Nantucket, MA
Missouri State University, Springfield, MO
The Ware Family Art Gallery of West Virginia University
Miller Gallery, Cincinnati, OH
Russell Collection, Austin, Texas
Weinberger Fine Art, Kansas City, MO
VW Contemporary Art, Greenwich, CT
Madison Galleries, LaJolla, CA
New Gallery of Modern Art, Charlotte, NC

2018	Laura Rathe Fine Art. Houston, TX

2018   Laura Rathe Fine Art. Houston, TX
        Diehl Gallery, Jackson Hole, WY
        Gilman Contemporary, Ketchum, Idaho
        Galerie Sono, Norwalk, CT
        Laura Rathe Fine Art, Dallas, TX
        Galerie de Bellefeuille, Montreal, QC
        Galerie de Bellefeuille, Toronto, ON
        DTR Modern, Boston, MA
        Central State Museum of Kazakhstan, Almaty, Kazakhstan
        Quidley & Company Fine Art Galleries, Nantucket, MA
        National Museum of the Republic of Kazakhstan, Astana, Kazakhstan
        Exhibit by Anberson, Tulsa, OK
        Martine Chaisson Gallery, New Orleans, LA
        Weinberger Fine Art, Kansas City, MO
        Everhart Museum, Scranton, PA
        Cuadro Fine Art, Dubai, UAE
        National Gallery - Sofia, Bulgaria
        McHugh Gallery, Aspen, CO

GROUP EXHIBITIONS (2000-CURRENT)

2000   Marlborough Gallery, Monte Carlo, Monaco
        Robert McClain Gallery, Houston, TX
        Kurt Lidtke Gallery, Seattle, WA
        Handsel Gallery, Santa Fe, NM

2001   *XXXV Prix International D'Art Contemporain de Monte Carlo*, Salle des Arts, Monte Carlo,
            Monaco
        Best of Tennessee, Tennessee State Museum, Nashville, TN.
        Myers School of Art, University of Akron, Akron, OH
        Marlborough Gallery, Monte Carlo, Monaco
        McClain Gallery, Houston, TX
        Kurt Lidtke Gallery, Seattle, WA
        Handsel Gallery, Santa Fe, NM

2002   Smith Andersen Editions, Stewart & Stewart, Palo Alto, CA
        A Public Trust: Recent Acquisitions at the Museum of Art, University of Arizona Museum of Art,
            Tucson, AZ
        Shared Pleasures: Vero Collects II, Holmes Gallery, Vero Beach Museum of Art, Vero Beach, FL
        Jean Albano Gallery, Chicago, IL
        Barbara Krakow Gallery, Boston, MA

2003   *Louis Cane, Israel Hershberg, Hunt Slonem*, Marlborough Gallery, Monte Carlo, Monaco
        Inaugural Exhibition, Ogden Museum of Southern Art, New Orleans, LA
        Art in the Chambers, Orange County Arts & Cultural Affairs, Orlando, FL
        Contemporary Art from the Tennessee State Collection, Tennessee State Museum, Nashville, TN
        Where Fashion Meets Art, Givenchy, New York, NY
        Selections from the Collection, von Liebig Art Center, Naples, FL

Marlborough Gallery, Monte Carlo, Monaco
The Bold 1980s: A Collector's Vision, Chrysler Museum of Art, Norfolk, VA
Ochi Gallery, Ketchum, ID

2004　*Out of the Blues*, Jean Albano Gallery, Chicago, IL
IV Centuries of Birds in Paintings, Sculptures & Fine Prints, Clarke Galleries, Stowe, VT;
　　Palm Beach, FL; New York, NY
Selections from the Permanent Collection, Orlando Museum of Art, Orlando, FL
Birdspace: A Post-Audubon Artists Aviary, traveled to Contemporary Art Center, New Orleans,
　　LA; Norton Museum of Art,West Palm Beach, FL; Hudson River Museum, Yonkers, NY;
　　McDonough Museum of Art, Youngstown, OH

2005　*Art and the Garden: Post-war and Contemporary Paintings of the Garden*, Spanierman
　　Gallery, East Hampton, NY
New York Beasts on the Bench, Salt Queen Foundation, Southampton, NY
The Long View: Selections from the Norma B. Marin Collection of Maine Art, University of
　　Maine, Bangor, ME
The Art of the Screenprint, Detroit Institute of Arts Museum, Detroit, MI
200 Years of American Portraits, Harmon-Meek Gallery, Naples, FL
Recent Acquisitions, Tampa Museum of Art, Tampa, FL
Summer Show, Marlborough Gallery, New York, NY
Winter Show, Robert Kidd Gallery, Birmingham, MI
Post Malcolm Modern, Forbes Galleries, New York, NY (through February 2006)

2006　*Summer Group Show*, Marlborough Gallery, New York, NY
Imago Galleries, Palm Desert, CA

2007　Wit and Whimsy, Marlborough Gallery, New York, NY
Summer Exhibition, Marlborough Gallery, New York, NY
Modern Momentum, Wally Findlay Galleries, Palm Beach, FL

2008　*Political Animals*, Harmon-Meek Gallery, Naples, FL
Ornithology: Looking at Birds, University of Connecticut, Storrs, CT
American Menagerie, Portland Museum of Art, Portland, ME
The Big Gift, Glenbow Museum, Calgary, Canada

2009　*Summer Exhibition*, Marlborough Gallery, New York, NY
Near & Far: Contemporary Fine Print, Birmingham-Bloomfield Art Center, Birmingham, MI
National Gallery of Foreign Art, Sofia, Bulgaria
Museum Gallery of Modernism, Sofia, Bulgaria
The Art of the Bird, Blue Hill Arts & Cultural Center, Piermont, NY (through April 2010)
New York, Gebert Contemporary, Scottsdale, AZ
Ruckschau 09, Galerie Barbara von Stechow, Frankfurt, Germany
Winter Show, Marlborough Gallery, New York, NY

2010　*Think Pink*, Gavlak Gallery, Palm Beach, FL (curated by Beth Rudin DeWoody)
Galerie Vomel, Dusseldorf, Germany

2011   Etra Fine Art, Miami, FL

2012   *Bayous & Ghosts* (with Margaret Evangeline) & Treasures From The Vault, Hollins
            University, Roanoke, VA
        Defrost in Time, Weinberger Fine Gallery, Kansas City, MO
        Wings of Whimsy (with Damien Hirst), DTR Modern, Boston, MA
        Conference of the Birds, Mana Contemporary, Jersey City, NJ
        Assemblage: An Exhibition Featuring Recent Works from the United States & Europe,
            Gremillion & Co., Dallas, TX
        Imago Galleries, Palm Desert, CA
        The Morris at Twenty, Morris Museum of Art, Augusta, GA
        Collection of Master Lee, Guilin Art Museum, Guangxi, China
        Treasures of Pointe Coupee, Julien Poydras Center, New Roads, LA (curated by Arts
            Council of Pointe Coupee)
        Galeria Espacio, San Salvador, El Salvador
        L'Amour du Vin, Knoxville Museum of Art, Knoxville, TN
        Summer Exhibition, Marlborough Gallery, New York, NY
        Rarity Gallery, Mykonos, Greece
        A *Collection of Prominent Works*, Collectors Contemporary, Singapore
        Butterfly World (with Damien Hirst), New Gallery of Modern Art, Charlotte, NC
        Corzine Fine Art, Los Angeles, CA
        Exposition de Groupe, Marlborough Gallery, Monte Carlo, Monaco
        Winter Group Show, Etra Fine Art, Miami, FL
        4th Annual FIA Print Fair, Flint Institute of Arts, Flint, MI
        Impressions: Selections from Stewart & Stewart, Ann Arbor Art Center, Ann Arbor, MI

2013   Marlborough Gallery, Monte Carlo, Monaco
        Gallery Espacio, San Salvador, El Salvador
        Art Miami, Dean Project, Miami, FL
        Art Palm Beach, Dean Project, West Palm Beach, FL
        ARC Fine Art, Fairfield, CT
        Fantasy, Fiction, or Fact, Memphis Brooks Museum of Art, Memphis, TN
        Lafayette Museum, Lafayette, LA
        Paula Brown Gallery, Toledo, OH
        Diehl Gallery, Jackson Hole, WY
        Customs House Museum and Cultural Center, Clarksville, TN
        Vered Gallery, East Hampton, NY
        Garden Party, Nassau County Museum of Art, Roslyn, NY
        Mabeyn Gallery, Istanbul, Turkey
        Harmon-Meek Gallery Goes Green, Harmon-Meek Gallery, Naples, FL
        Mint Museum of Craft and Design, Charlotte, NC
        Weinberger Fine Art, Kansas City, MO
        Galerie Von Stechow, Frankfurt, Germany
        Gallery Espacio, San Salvador, El Salvador
        Cloud 9, Sultan Gallery, Kuwait City, Kuwait
        Tweet, Children's Museum of the Arts, New York, NY

2014   National Art Gallery, Sofia, Bulgaria
        Marlborough Gallery, Monte Carlo, Monaco
        St. Moritz Art Masters, St. Moritz, Switzerland
        Unnatural Supernatural, Honolulu Museum of Art, Honolulu, HI
        Weinberger Fine Art, Kansas City, MO
        Small Works of Art, Harmon-Meek Gallery, Naples, FL
        Marjorie S. Fisher Gallery, Center for Creative Education, Palm Beach, FL

2015   *Artisti Italiani E Non 2*, Spazio Soncino, Soncino, Italy
        Aviarium, Diehl Gallery, Jackson, WY
        10th Anniversary Show & Celebration, Jessica Hagen Fine Art, Newport, RI
        Love/Paint, Madelyn Jordon Fine Art, Scarsdale, NY

2016   Phases of Faces, Jean Albano Gallery, Chicago, IL
        Contemporary Redux, Taubman Museum of Art, Roanoke, VA
        Art Palm Beach: Galerie Bellefeuille
        LA Art Fair: Dean Project, Coats Wright
        Palm Springs Fine Art Fair: Jean Albano Gallery
        The Nest: An Exhibition of Art in Nature, Katonah Museum of Art, (Katonah, NY)
        Welcome to Spring, Galerie Sono, Norwalk, CT
        Arts Alive, Sandra Ainsley Gallery, Toronto, ON
        Art New York: Galerie Bellefeuille, Galerie Von Stechow
        Spring Group Show, Galerie Sono, Norwalk, CT
        Summertime Sometime, Gilman Contemporary, Sun Valley, ID
        Imminent Ascent, Laura Rathe Fine Art, Dallas, TX
        Ave of the Americans, Galerie Von Stechow, Dusseldorf, Germany
        The Conference of the Birds, Shirley Fiterman Art Center, New York, NY
        Fourth of July, Harmon Meek Gallery, Naples, FL
        Art Southampton: Dean Project, Vered, ARC Fine Art
        Art Salon, New Gallery of Modern Art, Charlotte, NC
        Summer Exhibition, Clark Gallery, Banner Elk, NC
        Group Show Rarity Gallery, Mykonos, Greece
        Summer Group Show, Galerie Sono, Norwalk, CT
        Tenth Anniversary Show & Celebration, Jessica Hagen Fine Art, Newport, RI
        Feast for the Eyes, Nassau County Museum of Art, Roslyn, NY
        Summer Group Show, Miller Gallery, Cincinnati, OH
        San Moritz Art Masters, San Moritz, Switzerland
        Artisti Italiani E Non 3, Spazio Soncino, Soncino, CR, Italy
        Black & White: Modern & Contemporary Positions, Jason McCoy Gallery, New York, NY
        Art Chicago: Galerie Bellefeuille
        Cleveland Print Fair: Stewart & Stewart
        Art Silicon Valley: Dean Project
        Art Toronto: Galerie Bellefeuille
        IFPDA Print Fair: Stewart & Stewart
        Art Miami: Galerie Bellefeuille, Dean Project

2017   Boston Fine Art Print Fair: Stewart & Stewart
        Gallery 21, Bahrain

Blue Nights , Sultan Gallery, Kuwait City, Kuwait
TBC Heirloom Seed and Pollinators Corazon Contemporary, Santa Fe, New Mexico
Other Voices, Farnsworth Museum, Rockland, Maine
Cheryl Hazan Gallery
Fool the Eye,Nassau County Museum of Art

2018   Cornell Art Museum, Delray Beach, FL
Frederic Got Gallery, Paris, France

CORPORATE AND PUBLIC COLLECTIONS

Academy of the Arts, Easton, Maryland
American Banaco, New York, NY
Art Gallery of Nova Scotia, Halifax, Nova Scotia, Canada
Artbank Program, United States Department of State, Washington D.C.
Bahrain National Museum, Bahrain UAE
Bass Museum of Art, Miami, FL.
Bates College Museum of Arts, Olin Art Center, Lewiston, ME
Bergen Museum of Art and Science, Paramus, NJ
Birmingham Museum of Art, Birmingham, AL
Boca Raton Museum of Art, Boca Raton, FL
Borough Hall, Brooklyn, NY
Bowdoin Museum of Art, Brunswick, ME
Brandeis University Rose Art Museum, Waltham, MA
Alexander Breast Gallery, Jacksonville University Museum, Jacksonville, FL
Children's Museum of Naples, Naples, FL
Chrysler Museum, Norfolk, VA
Cincinnati Art Museum, Cincinnati, OH
Colegio de Architecto, Quito, Ecuador
Colby College Museum of Art, Waterville, ME
Columbia University Libraries, new York, NY
Columbus Museum of Art, Columbus, OH
Coral Springs Museum, Coral Springs, FL
Currier Gallery of Art, Manchester, NH
Customs House Museum, Clarksville, TN
Danville Museum, Danville, VA
Daum Museum of Contemporary Art, Sedalia, MO
Davenport Museum of Art, Davenport, IA
Dayton Art Institute, Dayton, OH
Delaware Art Museum, Wilmington, DE
Delgado University, New Orleans, LA
Detroit Institute of Arts Museum, Detroit, MI
Drury Univ., Springfield, MO
Eastman School of Music, Rochester, NY
Evansville Museum of Arts and Science, Evansville, IN
Everson Museum, Syracuse, NY
Farnsworth Library & Art Museum, Rockland, ME
Ford's Theatre, Washington, DC

Fort Wayne Museum of Art, Fort Wayne, IN
The Flint Institute of Arts, Flint, MI
Florida International University Art Museum, Miami, FL
Fundació Joan Miró, Barcelona, Spain
Grey Art Gallery, New York University, New York, NY
Guilin Art Museum, Guilin Guang XI P.R. China
Solomon R. Guggenheim Museum, New York, NY
Henie-Onstad Kunstsenter, Hovikodden, Norway
Hofstra Museum, Hofstra University, Hempstead, NY
Housatonic Museum, Bridgeport, CT
Human Systems Technology, Baltimore, MD
Hunter Museum of Art, Chattanooga, TN
Jedco, Jefferson Parrish, LA
The Kemper Museum of Contemporary Art & Design of Kansas City Art Institute, MO
J. Patrick Lannan Gallery, Palm Beach, FL
Community College Museum of Art, Lake Worth, FL
Le Musée d'Art Haitian, Port au Prince, Haiti
The Von Liebig Art Center, Naples, FL
Long Island Historical Society, Brooklyn, NY
Louisiana Arts & Science Museum, Baton Rouge
Maier Museum of Art, Randolph-Macon Women's College, Lynchburg, VA
Memphis Brooks Museum, Memphis, TN
Metropolitan Museum of Art, Manila, Philippines
The Metropolitan Museum of Art, New York, NY

Miami-Dade Community College South Campus, Miami, FL
Miami University, Oxford, OH
Michener Museum of Art, Doylestown, PA
Mills College Art Museum, Mills College, Oakland, CA
Mint Museum of Art, Charlotte, NC
Miro Foundation, Spain
Mississippi Museum of Art, Jackson, Miss.
Missouri State University, Springfield
University of Missouri, Columbia
Mita Corporation, Fairfield, NJ
Museum of Fine Arts, Houston, TX
Museum of Fine Arts, St. Petersburg, FL
The National Gallery of Art, Washington, DC
Neuberger Museum, Purchase College/State University of New York, Purchase
Newcomb Art Gallery, Tulane University, New Orleans, LA
New Museum of Contemporary Art, New York, NY
New Orleans Museum of Art, New Orleans, LA
New York Academy of Art, New York, NY
New York Historical Society, New York, NY
Newark Museum, Newark, NJ
Northfield Nt. Hermon School, Mt. Hermon, MA
Ogden Museum of Southern Art, New Orleans, LA
Ohio Wesleyan Univ. Delaware, OH
Olin Gallery, Roanoke College, Salem, VA

Oklahoma Art Center, Oklahoma City, OK
Orlando Museum of Art, Orlando, FL
Ozark Community Technical College, Springfield
Port Authority, One World Trade Center (Mural), New York, NY
Portland Museum of Art, Portland, ME
Pulitzer Collection, Amsterdam, Holland
Queens Museum of Art, Queens, NY
Saint Louis University, Cupples House & McNamee Gallery, St. Louis, MO
Saint Mary's College, Saint Mary City, MD
Saint Petersburg Museum of Fine Art, St. Petersburg, FL
Samford University, Birmingham, AL
San Antonio Museum of Art, San Antonio, TX
Salt Queen Foundation, Southampton, NY
Sidney Art Gallery and Museum, Port Orchard, WA
Smithsonian Institution, Washington, D.C.
Syracuse University Art Collection, Syracuse, NY
Stamford Museum and Nature Center, Stamford, CT
Tampa Museum of Art, Tampa, FL
The Taubman Museum of Art, West Virginia, Roanoke, VA
Tennessee State Museum, Nashville, TN
Tel Aviv Museum, Tel Aviv, Israel
Telfair Museum of Art, Savannah, GA
The Contemporary Museum, Honolulu, Hawaii
United States Department of State, Washington, D.C.
University of Arizona, Museum of Art, Tucson, AZ
University of Maine at Machias Art Galleries, Machias, ME
University of Michigan, Art Museum Project, Dearborn, MI
University of Oklahoma, Fred Jones Art Center, Norman, OK
Vanderbilt University, Nashville, TN
Vero Beach Museum of Art, Vero Beach, FL
Virginia Commonwealth University, Richmond, VA
Virginia Museum of Fine Arts, Richmond, VA
Von Leibig Art Center, Naples, FL
Wasmer Gallery, Ursuline College, Pepper Pike, OH
Whitney Museum of American Art, New York, NY
Wichita Art Museum, Wichita, KS
Wurth Museum, Kunzelsau, Germany
American Banaco, New York, NY
American Bar Association, Washington, D.C.
ARK Restaurant Corporation
Best Products, Richmond, VA
Chase Manhattan Bank, New York, NY
Children's Hospital, New Orleans, LA
Citibank, N.A.
Clifford Russell, Inc., New York, NY
Continental Airlines
Crummy, Del Deo, Dolan, Griffinger & Vecchione, Newark, NJ
E.I. Dupont De Nemours, New York, NY

2018   Forbes, New York, NY
Forgman Co., Louisville, KY
Goldman Sachs Co., New York, NY
Hamilton Restaurant, Washington, DC
Hilton Hotels, Guam
HRH Headquarters, Washington, DC
Human Systems Technology, Baltimore, MD
IBM Corporation
Intercontinental Hotel, Miami, FL
Jewish Home & Hospital for Aged, New York, NY
L'Ermitage Hotel, Hollywood, CA
Loews New Orleans Hotel, New Orleans, LA
Marsh & McLennan Companies, Inc., New York, NY
Marriott Corporation
Miller, Anderson & Sherrerd, Conshohocken, PA
Mita Corporation, NJ
NY American Telephone & Telegraph
Nieman-Marcus, Dallas, TX
Paine Webber, Inc., Lincoln Harbour, NJ
Pierce, Atwood, Scribner, Allen, Smith & Lancaster, Portland, ME
Primavera Systems, Bala Cynwyd, PA
Princess Cruise Lines
Readers Digest Inc., Pleasantville, NY
Relume Corporation, Troy, Michigan
Roger Ogden Company, New Orleans, LA
Royal Caribbean Quantum of the Seas
Saint Agatha's Children's Home, New York, NY
Sanco General Corporation
Silvestri Corporation, Chicago, IL
Simpson & Thatcher, New York, NY
Sonesta Corporation, Boston, MA
Takashima Corporation, Hawaii
TRW Corporation, Lyndhurst, OH
Tucker Anthony, Inc., New York, NY
UBS Paine Webber, Inc., Lincoln Harbour, NJ
U.M.K.C. John & Maxine Belger Family Foundation, Kansas City, MO
Zale Corporation, Dallas, TX

SPECIAL HONORS

2012   Louisiana Governor's Inaugural Painting and Poster for Inaugural Ball

AWARDS

1968   Rotary International Exchange Student, Managua, Nicaragua

1976   Elizabeth T. Greenshields Foundation, Grant for Painting, Montreal, Canada
Cultural Council Foundation Artists Project, New York, NY

1982	Millay Colony for the Arts, Austerlitz, NY
1983	MacDowell Fellowship, Peterborough, NH Ragdale Foundation, Lake Forest, IL
1984	MacDowell Fellowship, Peterborough, NH
1986	MacDowell Fellowship, Peterborough, NH
1991	National Endowment for the Arts
2006	Urban Stages Award for Fine Art, New York, NY
2007	ARTrageous Children's Expressions Project, Gala Dinner and Art Auction Honoree, New York, NY
2009	D&D's Stars of Design, Award in Art, New York, NY
2013	Louisiana Lieutenant Governor's Inaugural Lifetime Cultural Achievement Award The Horticultural Society of New York Award of Excellence, NYC
2015	Russian Academy of Art Medal of Merit

MONOGRAPHS

2002	Kuspit, Donald. *Hunt Slonem: An Art Rich & Strange*. New York: Harry N. Abrams.
2007	Katz, Vincent. *Pleasure Palaces: The Art and Homes of Hunt Slonem*. New York: powerHouse Books.
2011	Nahas, Dominique. *The Worlds of Hunt Slonem*. New York: Vendome Press.
2014	Helander, Bruce. *Bunnies*. New York: Glitterati Editions. Slonem, Hunt. *When Art Meets Design*. New York: Assouline Publishing.
2017	Slonem, Hunt. *Birds*. New York: Glitterati Editions.
2018	Costello, Sarah. *Gatekeeper Work of Folly by Hunt Slonem*. New York: Assouline

255

BIBLIOGRAPHY (1990-CURRENT)

1990	Raynor, Vivien. "Art: Birds Behind Bars (And Some Are Real)." *The New York Times*, Sunday, November 18, p. 20, ill. Zeaman, John. "Art: A Schema of Themes." *The Record*, October 12, p.11, ill. Watkins, Eileen. "Environmental Concerns Inspire Sculptor, Painters at William Paterson." *The Sunday Star Ledger*, October 14, ill. Rafferty, Carole. "Nature Backdrop for Artistic Passion." *The Beacon*, October 1. Adams, Brooks. "Art." *Vogue*, July, pp. 94-99. Bernard, Jami. "Hunt Slonem." *Hamptons*, July, p.38, ill. Katz, Vincent. "A Jury of Our Peer's Ears." *Interview*, July, p.42.

Schwan, Gary. "Art." *Palm Beach Post,* June 1, p. 27.

Cyphers, Peggy. "New York in Review." *Arts Magazine,* April, p. 111.

Murphy, Jay. "New Orleans." *Contemporanea,* February, p. 32.

1991   Martin, Douglas. "About New York: This Artist Draws Inspiration from His Birds,
        All 72 of Them." *The New York Times,* December 25, p. 35, ill.

Kokkin, Dan. "Rimelig Fugleesker [Reasonable Birdlover]." *Dagens Naeringsliv,*
        December 7.

Sokolov, Raymond. "Style." *The Wall Street Journal,* December 3, p. A13.

Flor, Harold. "Kultur, Fugler I Fabrikhallen." *Dagbladet,* November 23, p. 27.

Copeland, Irene. "Object of Desire." *Cosmopolitan,* October, p. 209, ill.

Nash, Jesse. "Law of The Jungle." *New Orleans Art Review,* March/April, p. 24.

Green, Roger. "Exotic Birds, Thoughtful Art." *Times-Picayune Lagniappe,* p. 21, ill.

Segerstrom-Sato, Rebecca. "Hunt Slonem and His Birds." *Idea Magazine,* vol. 225, Tokyo,
        February, pp.118-121, ill.

Beldegreen, Alecia. *The Bed Book.* New York: Stewart, Tabori & Chang, pp.110-111, ill.

"Hunt Slonem: My Life-People in New York." *Travel Information Satellite,* January 1,
        p. 9, ill.

Lamarre, Paul, and Melissa Wolf. *The Starving Artists' Cookbook,* New York: Edia Books,
        p. 55, ill.

Mitrotti, Roberto. "Hunt Slonem." *Next: Arte e Cultura,* p. 80, ill.

1992   Pener, Degen. "Egos & Ids: Crazy for Birds, but No Birdy." *The New York Times,*
        November 1, p. B4.

Anon. "Running Out of Time." *South China Morning Post,* October 14, p. 3

Auty, Giles. "Weighty Implications." *The Spectator,* September 5.

Slonem, Hunt. "Birds in Spirit." Bir*d Talk,* August, pp. 8-10, ill.

Princenthal, Nancy. Untitled review. *Art in America,* June, p. 104, ill.

Vallongo, Sally. Untitled review. *ARTnews,* June, p. 144, ill.

Vallongo, Sally. "Flying Off in a New Direction—Hunt Slonem Opts for Softer, More
        Reflective Works." *The Blade,* April 23, p. 43.

Findsen, Owen. "Final Friday Becomes the Main Event." *The Cincinnati Enquirer,*
        April, p. B4.

Hampton, Howard. "On Heavy Metal." *Artforum,* April, pp. 13-14, ill.

Seville, Kaede. "Hunt Slonem." *Nikkei Woman,* April, pp. 52-54, ill.

Liebmann, Lisa. Untitled review. *The New Yorker,* March 9, p. 10.

Servin, James. "Spectator Sport: Inspirational Squawks Fill Artist's Bird Land Loft."
        Associated Press, March 6.

Slonem, Hunt. "Self Portrait, Hunt Slonem." *The New Yorker,* March 2, p. 12, ill.

Cembalest, Robin. "Safety Net." *ARTnews,* March, p. 18.

Thorson, Alice. "Initial Interest Lures You Deeper." *Kansas City Star Journal,* January 19,
        p. J4, ill.

Schwan, Gary. "New York Exhibition Inventive, Cheeky." *Palm Beach Post,* January 9,
        p. J4, ill.

Elton, Lars. "Eksotisk og Fargerikt [Exotic and Colorful]." *Tique* (Stockholm), January.

Guccione, Antonio. "Faces of New York." New York: The Time Is Always Now
        Gallery, 1992.

1993   Geldzhaler, Henry. *Hunt Slonem (forward)*. New York: Kunst Editions.
        Herrmann, Ralph. "Sinnlig Abstrakt Fogelkonst." *Dagens Industri*, December 6.
        Slesin, Suzanne. "Modernism and Mysticism; Coverage in a New York Loft." The New
            York Times, July 29
        Dorance, Scott, photographer. "The Fashionable Eye." New York, March 29, p. 61, ill.
        "Shells." Interview, February.
        Edmondson, Anthony. "Hunt Slonem, In the Realm of the Spirit." Central and Western Virginia
            Arts and Entertainment, January, pp. 20, 46.
        Altabe, Joan. "Birds of a Feather Flock to Mira Mar Gallery." Sarasota Herald Tribune,
            January 8, p. 18, ill.

1994   Slonem, Hunt. "For the Birds." Living With the Animals, Indiana, Gary, ed. Winchester,
            MA: Faber & Faber, pp. 141-148.
        Parish, Betsy. "Sunday Style". Houston Post, December 18.
        Chadwick, Susan. Review: "Hunt Slonem, Robert McClain & Co." Houston Post,
            December 16.
        Brody, Jacqueline. "Review of Toucans Print by Stewart & Stewart." The Print Collector's
            Newsletter, vol. XXV, no. 5, November/December.
        Thorson, Alice. "Hunt Slonem Tribute is a Fine-Feathered Way to Honor Artist." The
            Kansas City Star, August 14, p. J3, ill.
        Cohn, Edie. "Lembo Bohn." Interior Design, May, pp. 232-233, ill.
        Anon. "Art Spotlight: What's Happening in the Arts." The Tennessean, March 20, p.13, ill.
        Katz, Vincent. Review: "Hunt Slonem at Helander Gallery." Art in America, February,
            pp. 101-102, ill.
        "Der Amerikaner Hunt Slonem im Kunstchalter." Kölner Stadt-Anzeiger, no. 14,
            January 18, p. 15.

1995   Woolley, Robert. *Going Once: A Memoir of Art, Society, and Charity*. New York: Simon &
            Shuster, pp. 136-37.
        Lorenz, Lee. "Portrait by Hunt Slonem." *The Art of the New Yorker, 1925-1995*. New York:
            Alfred A. Knopf, p. 158, ill.
        Cadena, Joseph M. *El Periodico de Catalunya*, November, p. 27.
        Slonem, Hunt, Vincent Katz, Ronny Cohen, and John Ashbery. *Hunt's Place*. Turin,
            Italy: Tipostampa.
        Anon. "La Vanguardia." *Goya*, November 17, p. 49.
        Siytangco, Deedee M. "US Painter Slonem at Manila Pen for Exhibit and Charity
            Auction." *Manilla Bulletin*, November 18, p. 30.
        Cohen, Ronny. "Lannon Gallery Show." *Artforum*, November 18, p. 30.
        Anon. "Bryant Park Grill." *Interior Design*, October, pp. 108-111, ill.
        Finch, Charles. "Bird Man of Bryant Park." *Hamptons*, July 28.
        Bernard, Jami. "Exhibit." *Daily News*, July 22. ill.
        Anon. "Galeristin bringt Kunst aus USA nach Stendal." *Volksstimme*, (Germany), July
        Edelman, Robert. "Hunt Slonem Abstracts the Aviary." *Cover*, Summer, pp. 18-19, ill.
        Greene, Gael. "Forget Paris." *New York*, June 5, p. 91, ill.
        Gill, Brendan. "Miracle on 42nd Street." *The New Yorker*, June 19, pp. 31-32.
        Young, Lucie. "Two Roads to Splendid: One Long, the Other Short." *The New York Times*,
            May 25, p.C3.
        Krell, Olga. "Gothic Cage." *Arte e Design*. (Brazil), May, ill.

Sato, Susumu. "Hunt Slonem Beyond Audubon." *Replan* (Tokyo), March, pp. 74-79.

Holiday, Kate. "Inside the Flight Cage." *New Orleans Art Review*, January/February, pp. 18-19, ill.

Waddington, Chris. "Bold Bird Painter." *The Times-Picayune*, January 20, p. 14, ill.

Szabo, Julie. "Predicting Greatness: Henry Geldzahler's 14 Favorite Artists." *New York*, January 16, pp. 42-47.

Waddington, Chris. "There Is Art Beyond Monet." *The Times-Picayune*, January 1, p. 17.

1996   Delehanty, Randolph. *Art in the American South: Works from the Ogden Collection.* Baton Rouge and London: Louisiana State University Press, p. 96, ill.

Mitrotti, Roberto. "Hunt Slonem." *Next: Arte e Cultura*, p. 80, ill.

Nichols, Ann. "Painting Donated to Chattanooga Theater." *Chattanooga Free Press*, December 15, p. N6.

Cesbron, C. "Hunt Slonem at KNA Studio" *Ou-est France*, December 2.

Nahas, Dominique. "Art and Sensual, Drive/Energizer 2." *Review Art*, December 1.

Waddington, Chris. "Abstractions Take Wing Under Colorful NY Artist." *The Times-Picayune*, "Lagniappe" sect p. 28.

Osborne, Lawrence. *The New York Scene 1996.* Visby, Sweden: Gotlands Konstmuseum, p. 14, ill.

Cosper, Darcy. "Urban Remedy Ritual Healing." *Metropolis*, October.

Slivka, Rose C.S. "'From the Studio': Hunt Slonem's Birds." *The East Hampton Star*, October 24.

Gargiulo, Gerald J. "Art Byte." *The Independent*, October 23.

Kean, Amy. "Follow Your Nose." *New York Post*, July 27.

"Hunt Slonem Cockatoo Prints." *Journal of the Print World*, Summer.

Sokolowski, Tom and Bill Arning. "Curating the '80s." *Village Voice*, April 30, pp. 93-94.

Compère, Rita. "Le Paradis de Hunt Slonem." *Décor*, March/April, pp. 132-139.

Janowitz, Tama. "Bird Man of Houston Street." *Elle Decor*, February/March, pp. 158-163.

Colborn, Marge. "Hunt Slonem." *The Detroit News*, February 10, cover ill.

Anon. "Osadia y temeridad." *El Pais*, January, p. 8.

1997   *Hunt Slonem: Exotica.* Turin: Edizioni d'Arte Fratelli Pozzo.

Cohen, Ronny. *Forces of Nature.* New York: Taipei Gallery, pp. 12-13.

Esser, Kevin. *Streetboy Dreams.* New York: Ariel's Press, cover ill.

Gower, Christopher. "New York Profile: Hunt Slonem: Birds! Birds! Birds!" *Antique Interiors International*, p. 35.

Sato, Susumu. "Photography, New York City. A Portrait, Hunt Slonem." *Graphis Creative Showcase*, July/August, p. 150.

Peretti, Alberto. "A Featherland. Hunt Slonem. 'Featherwall.'" *Vogue Italia*, July, ill.

Ribar, David. "A Slingbrush." *Nashville Scene*, May 8.

Slonem, Hunt. "'Lucky Charm II, 1997', New Works by Three Screen Print Artists." *Journal of the Print World*, Fall, p. 45.

Slonem, Hunt. "Lucky Charm and Lucky Charm II." *On Paper*, September/October.

Schlesinger, Toni. "Art Houses, Hunt Slonem, Painter." *The Village Voice*, September 30, pp. 3-4.

Russell, Jenna. "Excess as an Art Form." *Bangor Daily News*, September 4, p. C4, ill.

Reef, Pat Davidson. "Slonem's Flights of Fancy." *Central Maine Newspaper*, August 17, p. D2, ill.

Crane, Darrin. "Forces of Nature." *Taipei Gallery Review*, vol. II, no. 4, p. 45, ill.

Vallongo, Sally. "Chairs of Design." *The Blade*, April 24, p. 33, ill.

Wibking, Angela. "Slonem Exhibit Features Exotic Art on Massive Scale." *Nashville Business Journal*, March 31, p. 16, ill.

Anon. "Our Critic's Picks." *Nashville Scene*, March 20, p. 43, ill.

Bostick, Alan. "The Birdman of SoHo." *The Tennessean*, March 20, p. D3, ill.

Chappell, Susan. "NY Painter Flying High in 'Exotic' Area Exhibit." *Nashville Banner*, March.

Mahoney, Robert. "Hunt Slonem, Jeffrey Coploff." *Time Out New York*, February 13-20, p. 44, ill.

Scott, Whitney. *New York Post*, January 25, p. 28.

1998   Tolley, Emelie, and Chris Mead. *Flea Market Style: Decorating with a Creative Edge*. New York: Clarkson Potter, pp. 38-39, 96-97, 140.

Katz, Vincent. "Animal, Vegetable, Mystical." *Art in America*, October, pp. 126-129.

Coleman, David. "Chelsea Ring." Elle Décor, Summer, p. 108.

Johnson, Ken. "Hunt Slonem; Marlborough Chelsea." *The New York Times*, October 9, p. E38.

Hogrese, Jeffrey. "Hunt Slonem's Awakening." *New York Observer*, September 14, p. 30, ill.

Nahas, Dominique. Review: "Hunt Slonem, Marlborough Chelsea." *Review, The Critical State of Visual Arts in New York*, October 1, p. 21.

McMullen, Patrick. "The Scene." *New York Magazine*, October 5, p. 14, ill.

Weld, Jacqueline. *Rara Avis*. Books & Company, October, cover ill.

Waddington, Chris. "Slonem Walks Line Between Abstraction, Representation." *The Times-Picayune Lagniappe*, May 22, p. 15.

Kahlil, Sean and Frank Sepe. *Playgirl*, January, pp. 150-151, ill.

1999   Edney, Andrew. *Cat: Wild Cats and Pampered Pets*. New York: Watson-Guptill, pp. 292-93, 371, ill.

Williams, John. *Sex: Portraits of Passion*. New York: Watson-Guptill, pp. 58, 114, 170, ill.

Battistini, Matilde. *Ovazione*. Milan: Electa, p. 153, ill.

Steinberg, Claudia. "Paradise-Vogel." *Architektur & Wohnen*, March, pp. 72-79.

Garbarino, Steve. "Birds of a Feather." *Details*, April, pp. 126-131.

Slonim, Jeffrey. "The Absurdists." *Manhattan File*, January, p. 58.

Goren, Manuela Cerri. "Birds Land." *L'Uomo Vogue*, February.

2000   Bacot, H. Parrott, Barbara SoRelle Bacot, Sally Kittredge Reeves, John H. Lawrence, and John Magill. *Marie Adrien Persac: Louisiana Artist*. Baton Rouge: Louisiana State University Press, pp. 24-25.

Adams, Brooks. "Treasure Hunt." *Elle Decor*, January, pp. 204-211.

Harrison, Lorraine. *Horse: From Noble Steeds to Beasts of Burden*. New York: Watson-Guptill, pp. 225, 259, 277, ill.

Slonim, Jeffrey. "Birds of a Feather." *Madison*, March/April, pp. 64-70.

Scobie, Ilka. "Pantheistic Painter." *Artnet*, March 6.

Cook, Cindi. "He Dreams in Technicolor." *Manhattan Style*, November/December, pp. 219-222.

Bouchez, Hilde. "het huis van de artiste." *De Standaard*, June 16, no. 24, p. 22.

Badessi, Laurent Elie. *Skin*. Zurich: Edition Stemmle, New York: Abbeville Press, pp. 126-127.

MacDonald, Mary. "Their Hawaii." *Avenue*, May, vol. 4, no. 9, p. 73.

Bane, Carolyn. "All for the Birds." *Flatiron Magazine,* vol. 6, no. 1, Spring.

Schwan, Gary. "Exhibits Showcase 3 Artists." *Palm Beach Post*, April 23.

Anon. "Artist Hunt Slonem Prints in Michigan While He Paints in His New York Lofts." *Journal of the Print World*, vol, 23, no. 1, Winter.

Jenkins, David. "American Booty." *The Sunday Telegraph Magazine*, March 5.

Past Present Future. DKNY catalogue, ill.

2001   Szabo, Julie. *Animal House Style: Designing a Home to Share with Your Pets*. Boston, New York, and London: Bulfinch, pp. 61, 63. ill.

Anon. "Quirky Art." *Arizona Republic, October 13, Scottsdale sect.*

Donohue, Jewel. "Hunt Slonem: Birds of a Feather." *Animal Fair*, Summer, pp. 28-31.

"Birds of a Feather." *Art & Antiques Weekly*, June 8, p. 47.

Szabo, Julia. "Pets, Works of Art." *New York Post*, May 6, p. 48.

Calloway, Stephen. "Divinely Decadent." London: Mitchell Beazley, p. 48, ill.

Weld, Jacqueline. "Society: Out & About." *On the Avenue*, May 3, p. 2.

Claridge, Laurann. "Social Show." *PaperCity*, April, p. 4.

Sloley, Emma. "On the Hunt." *Harpers Bazaar Australia*, January/February, p. 79.

Rozensztroch, Daniel. "Un Loft Flamboyant." *Marie Claire Maison*, December/January, pp. 164-173.

2002   *Unframed: Artists Respond to AIDS*. New York: powerHouse Books, p. 124, ill.

Kuspit, Donald. *Hunt Slonem: An Art Rich and Strange*. New York: Harry N. Abrams.

Slava, Laima. "Like Children in a Candy Store." *Studija* (Latvia), December, p. 68-69, ill.

Osadchaya, Irina. "Art as an Instrument of Diplomats." *Architecture & Design* (Russia), October, p. 24-29, ill.

Clifton-Mogg, Caroline. *A Passion for Collection*, Aurum Press 2002, p. 96-97, 102-103, 121, 159, 180-181, ill.

Dinerman, Barbara. "Winged Victory." *Arts and Antiques*, Contemporary Showcase, December, p. 68-70, ill.

Woods, Vicki. "Brillo de Estrella." *Vogue en Español*, November, pp. 100-105, cover, ill.

Woods, Vicki. "Sparkling Star." *Vogue*, September, pp. 16,-17, cover, ill.

Stefánsson, Páll, "Hunt's World." *Atlantica*, Icelandair, July-August 2002, p. 16-17, ill.

Art in the Embassies, exh. cat, Regional Program Office, Vienna, p. 6, ill.

Stewart & Stewart, *Works on Paper*. Palo Alto: Smith Anderson Editions.

Batiste, Janice. "The Rainforest on the River: Hunt Slonem in His Studio." *New York Living*, October.

Violette, Robert. "Stitch and Pixel: 21st Century Voices on Renaissance Tapestries at the Met." *Tate Magazine*, September/October, p. 42.

Katz, Vincent. "Finches, Ferns and Fantasies." *The World of Interiors*, July, p. 106-113, ill.

Vallongo, Sally. "Slonem's Winged World." *The Blade*, June, pp. 1-2, ill.

Miebach, Bärbel. "Le Bonheur est dans les couleurs." *Maison française*, no. 517, April/May, cover, pp. 101-107, ill.

Kino, Carol. "Hired Hands." *Art & Auction*, February, p. 102-11, ill. p. 103.

Szabo, Julia. "Animal House." *Traditional Home*, March, p. 66-68, ill.

Byrne, Chris. "The Original Print: Understanding Technique in Contemporary Fine Printmaking." *Madison, Wisconsin: Guild Publishing*, p. 106-107, 116, 117, 124, ill.

Lo Vetro, Gianluca. "Le Collezioni di Massimo Osti." *IO Donna*, January, p. 124-27.

Kino, Carol. "Hired Hands." *Art & Auction*, February, p 102-111, ill.

Kalogerakis, George. "Mind Games." *New York*, February, p. 66-73.

Duran, Tony. "Each Day is Valentine's Day." *GQ*, February, p. 123-127.

Barnes, Brooks. "The Hot New Subject: You." *The Wall Street Journal*, February 8, pp. w1, w12, ill.

Sellards, Jason. "Portfolio." *Genre*, March, pp. 42-43.

Johnson, Richard. "Body of Work." *New York Post*, March 9, p. 10.

Slonim, Jeffrey. "Grace Notes." *New York Post*, March 17, p. 38.

McMullan, Patrick. "Scene." *New York*, March/April, p. 20.

Geddes-Brown, Leslie. *The Color Design File*. New York: Ryland Peters & Small, p. 30, ill.

2003   Anon. "Bench Impressed." *The Washington Post*, October 2, sec. H3

Slonim, Jeffrey "The Manor Reborn." *Elle Décor*, November, pp. 226-33, ill.

Anon. "The Benches of Central Park." *New York Daily News*, September 30, pp. 43-45, ill.

Curd, Barbara. "The Birdman of Chelsea." *Trump World*, May, pp. 48, 50, ill.

Anon. "Exposition: Galerie Marlborough." *l'Essentiel* (France), May 10, p. 21, ill.

Anon. "Marlborough Goes Natural." *Cote* (France), June, ill.

Ceber, Gundega. "American Art in Riga." *Maksla Plus* (Latvia), February, p. 10-13, ill.

Bernard, S. and D. Schoeneman. "The Dish on Dinner." *New York*, May 5, p. 25, ill.

Watts, Ben. "Cargo Class." *Elle*, January, p. 138, ill.

Bolton, S. and G. Kessler. "Let's Shop." *Gotham*, February, p. 40, ill.

Ballentine, Sandra. "Footnotes." *New York Times Magazine*, February 23, pp. 62-63, ill.

2004   Calloway, Stephen. *Obsessions: Collectors and Their Passions*. London: Mitchell Beazley, pp. 50-53, ill.

Steinberg, Claudia and Bärbel Miebach. *Kunst 1st Essen 1st Kunst*. Munich: Knesebeck, pp. 148-153.

Gallo, Peter. *IV Centuries of Birds in Paintings, Sculptures & Fine Prints*. Stowe, VT: Clarke Galleries, pp. 17, 78, ill.

Gabetti, Christina. "Stephanie Seymour: Un Eden a Manhattan." *Elle* (Italy), December, p. 150-154.

Steinberg, Claudia. "Spukschloss am Hudson." *Architektur & Wohnen*, December, pp. 82-90, 188.

Steinberg, Claudia. "Ganz schön exzentrisch." *Madame* (Germany), November, p. 74-79.

Price, Anne. "For the Birds." *Advocate* (Louisiana), October 27, Arts sect.

Weinstein, Elizabeth. "Hunt Slonem." *LASM Quarterly* (Louisiana), Fall, pp. 4-5.

Keeps, David and Tony Duran (photographer). "Jennifer Lopez: It's Hard to Be Me." *Marie Claire*, September, p.114-120.

Camper, Fred. "Critics Choice." *Chicago Reader*, July 30, sect. 2.

Steinberg, Claudia. "For a New York Artist, a Canvas of 100 Rooms." *The New York Times*, July 22, sect. F.

Anon. "Where Fashion Meets Art." *The New York Times*, May 5, p. B6.

Deitch, Dr. Lew. "Flights of Fancy." *Art Book of the New West*, March, pp. 34 -35.

Wadler, Joyce. "Boldface Names." *The New York Times*, February 20, p. B2 .

Craig, Caroline Torem. "Cultural Sushi." *Paper Magazine*, November, p. 20.

2005   Meek, J. William, III. *185 Years of Women as a Subject in American Art (1820-2005)*. Naples, FL: Harmon-Meek Gallery, pp. 77, 137, ill.

Sojka, Nancy. *Collaboration in Print: Stewart & Stewart Screenprints 25th Anniversary.* Detroit: Detroit Institute of Arts, pp. 92-105, ill.

Robinson, Walter. "Hurricane Katrina and the Arts." *Artnet*, September 15.

Streetman, John W., III. *Hunt Slonem.* Evansville, IN: Evansville Museum of Arts, History & Science.

Wexler, Kathryn. "Fashion World Does Its Part for Storm Aid." *Miami Herald*, September 16.

Roberts, Mike. Pensacola News Journal Weekender, June 17-23.

Hinojosa, Cassandra. "Slonem's Art Goes Coastal." *Caller Times* (Corpus Christi, TX) August 11.

Cook-Romero, Elizabeth. "His Caged Birds Sing." *Pasatiempo*, September 2-8.

McBain, Roger. "Slonem Finds Spiritual Side of Exotic Life, Art." *Evansville Courier & Press*, June 9.

McRoberts-Mitchell. *Rainforest Foundation US 2005 Calendar.* Quotes by Elton John, Brad Pitt, Robin Williams.

Tom Hanks, et al.*Rainforest Foundation US*, all ill.

Serrell, Allison. "Cordt's Mansion: At Home in the Hudson Valley." Chronicle Books, ill. p. 72-9.

Roversi, Paolo (photographer), "Flights of Fancy." *W Magazine*, April, pp. 183-205, ill.

Leffingwell, Edward, "Hunt Slonem at Marlborough Chelsea." *Art in America*, March, pp. 140-141.

Wadler, Joyce. "Boldface Names." *The New York Times*, March 3, sect. B2.

Helander, Bruce. "Bird's Eye View." *Art of the Times*, February, pp. 16-17, ill.

Afanador, Ruven (photographer). "Day Dreams." Elle, February, ill.

Atwood, Tom. *Kings in Their Castles: Photographs of Queer Men at Home.* Madison: University of Wisconsin Press, pp. 34-35, ill.

Henderson, Stephen. "Dixie Dreaming." *Palm Beach Cottages & Gardens*, pp. 72-79, ill.

Calloway, Stephen and Katherine Sorrell. "Neo-Gothic Furniture." *Obsessions*, London: Mitchell Beazley, pp. 50-53, ill.

2006   Frank, Peter. "Review of In Flight, by Hunt Slonem, Don O'Melveny." *Art News*, November 4-30.

Anon. "Two Extraordinary Works of Art." *Art & Antiques Magazine*, September.

Nixon, Jason Oliver & Mackenzie Dawson Parks. "Guess Who's Coming to Dinner." *Gotham*, Summer.

Anon. "Albania Restored." *St. Mary & Franklin Banner Tribune* (Louisiana), May 12.

Shi, Jim. "Carolina's Madison Avenue Fiesta." *The Daily Scene*, April 26.

Ricapito, Maria. "A House Called Albania." *InStyle Home*, Fall/Winter 2006, pp. 129-137.

Tutwiler, Mary. "Ageless Beauty." *The Independent Weekly* (Lafayette, LA), October 18.

Carlson, Contance. "Gloriously Gothic." *Hudson Valley Magazine*, September 2006, pp. 54-59.

Devlin, Ryan and Danielle Levitt. "Parker's People." *Premiere Magazine*, November 2006, p. 86, ill.

Gill, Kathryn. "Completed in 1874, Kingston's Cordts Mansion has Rich History." *Daily Freeman* (Kingston, NY), July 31.

Pospischil, Doris. "Poison Yellow and Pink: The Exotic Worlds of Hunt Slonem." *Drive Magazine*, pp. 55-59, ill.

Sugliano, Claudia. "Colore a tutti I costi." *Antiquariato*, March, pp. 62-69, ill.

Linda, Sara. "Special Features: Hunt Slonem." *Florida Design*, March, pp. 416-418, ill.

Champagne, Karma. "Albania Mansion Rescued from Decay." *The Daily Iberian* (New Iberia, LA), May 24, p. 1.

Tropiano, Dolores. "Gallery to Host Artist at Reception for Current Show." *Scottsdale Republic*, March 16.

Nichols, Kimberly. "The Tropical World of Hunt Slonem." *The Bottom Line*, March 17, pp. 92-93.

Christopher, Valerie. "Where the Wild Things Are." *Desert Post Weekly*, March 2-8, pp. 26.

"Limelight: Out & About." *Los Angeles Confidential*, March/April, p. 332.

2007   Gearson, Tierney. "They Really Are a Scream: A Hudson River Victorian Manse is the Backdrop for a Kooky Tweed-clad Family Outing." *New York*, August 27, pp. 92-99, ill.

Wadler, Joyce. "Southern Gothic: Ghosts Welcome." *The New York Times*, May 31, ill.

Warren, Bonnie. "An Artist & His Mansions." *Louisiana Life*, Summer 2007, pp. 22-24, ill.

MacCash, Doug. "Hunt Slonem's Art Tickles His Fancy." *The Times-Picayune*, Aug 3, ill.

Gruber, Rick. "Hunt Slonem: Artist & Collector." *Country-Roads Magazine*, September, ill.

Schillinger, Liesl. "Runway or Hallway, It's a Matter of Flair." *The New York Times*, September 9, ill.

McMullan, Patrick. *Glamour Girls*. Patrick McMullan Company, Henry N. Abrams, p. 223.

Bancroft, Debbie. "Seasonal Treats." *Avenue*, December, p. 18, ill.

Coleman, Mary. "Ready for the Season." *Connecticut Cottages & Gardens*, December, p. 125.

Hale, Lara. "The Art of the Party." *Kansas City Spaces*, Holiday 2007, pp. 168-177, ill.

Santelices, Manuel. "Laberinto de pasiones." *Casas*, December pp. 22-26, ill.

Anon. "Fall Leaves." *Papercity*, October, p.

Guarnieri, Anne-Marie. "Books." *Gotham*, October, pp. 140, ill.

LaFarge, Brian. "Birds of Paradise in a Self-Contained World." *Times of Acadiana*, November 21, p. 40, ill.

Stern, Paul. "Pull Up a Chair." *Black Book*, June/July, p. 34, ill.

Essex, Sara. "Style." *New Orleans Homes & Lifestyles*, July, p.12, ill.

Anon. "Above the Store." *Louisiana Life*, Autumn, p. 25, ill.

"Books." Gotham, October, p. 140, ill.

Breakstone, Stephanie. "Fully Booked." *Elle Décor*, December, pp. 54-55, ill.

Peck, Renee. "Shelf Help: Homes Sweet Homes." *The Times-Picayune*, September 15, p. 3.

Robinson, W. "Hunt Slonem in the House." *ArtNet*, August 9.

Gogol, Ariella. "Books: Pleasure Palaces: The Art and Homes of Hunt Slonem." *Nylon.com*, November 11, ill.

Doyle, Alice Welsh. "Holiday Gift Guide." *SouthernAccents.com*, October 29, ill.

2008   Helander, Bruce. *Learning to See: An Artist's View on Contemporary Artists from Artschwager to Zakanitch*. StarGroup International, p. 86-89, ill.

Siegel, Fern. "Get Your Groovy On." *Neiman Marcus: The Book*, April, pp. 24-27, ill.

Musso, Michael. *Plantation Homes of Louisiana and Historic Buildings*. Library of Congress, p. 3, 65.

"Benefit Takes Wing." *Palm Beach Daily News*, April 2, p. B4.

Vandewal, David and Alexei Hay. "Metanoia." *10 Men*, Spring, pp. 154-171, ill.

Kennedy, Eleanora. "A Well Lived Life: The Sondes." *Palm Beach Cottages & Gardens*, February/March, pp. 66-67, ill.

Peveto, Ryland Holmes. "Painting the Town With Hunt Slonem." *PaperCity*, February p. 10, ill.

Karni, Anne, "Living: Om Sweet Om!" *Page Six Magazine*, March 9, p. 42.

"Best Buddies Artists." *Palm Beach Society*, March 14-20, p. 23, ill.

Cohen, David "Birds of a Feather Flocking Together." *New York Sun*, June 12, p. 22, ill.

"Meet Famed Artists." *The Walton Sun*, (Santa Rosa Beach, FL) July 26, p. B3.

"Ogden Opens Florida Satellite." *New Orleans City Business*, July 14, p. 11, ill.

Wheeler, Deborah. "A Southern Culture Debut at Watercolor." *The Walton Sun*, July 5, ill.

Spaulding, Clint and Patrick McMullan Company. "The Flash." *Hamptons Magazine*, June 20-26, p. 37.

Bancroft, Debbie. "Good Will Hunting: Birds of a Feather Fete Together." *Hamptons Magazine*, June 13-19, p. 128, ill.

Thurman, Judith, Durston Saylor, and Geoffrey Bradfield. "Glamorous Gesture in London." *Architectural Digest*, February, p. 184, ill.

Cohen, David. "Arts: Hunt Slonem." *New York Sun*, June 12, p. 22, ill.

Gist, Taylor. "Pet Project." *The Times-Picayune: Inside/Out*, March 1, pp. 24-26, ill.

McMullan, Patrick & Jeffrey Slonim. "Society Pages." *Interview Magazine*, August, pp. 134-136, ill.

Frois, Jeanne. "Batchelor's Resident Artist." *Louisiana Life*, Autumn, pp. 97-98, ill.

"A Cubist Approach to Art." *Canvas Magazine: Art and Culture from the Middle East and Arab World*, November, p. 108-113, ill.

Scott, Gray and Kate Stukenberg. "Clueless." *PaperCity*, October, pp. 22-25, cover, ill.

Bonnar, Karen Doss. "Opening Minds to the Power of Art." *Roanoke College Magazine*, Issue One, p. 12-17, cover, ill.

Hackett, Kathleen and William Waldron. "Living Large." *Elle Décor*, September, p. 172, ill.

Abramovitch, Ingrid and Simon Upton. "Global Impact." *Elle Décor*, December, pp. 144-146, ill.

"Cuadro Museum Inaugurated." *The Gulf Today: Home* (Dubai, UAE), p. 2, ill.

2009   Bradfield, Geoffrey with Jorge S. Arango. *Geoffrey Bradfield: Ex Arte*. Plano: Panache Partners, p. 249, 282-283, 306, ill.

Steinberg, Claudia, & Miebach, Barbel. *The Art of Living*. Monacelli Press, pp. 184-195, ill.

Rushdie, Salman, Julianne Moore, Bob Colacello. Indochine: Stories Shaken & Stirred. Rizzoli Publishing, pp. 42-43, ill.

Sully, Susan. "The Southern Cosmopolitan: Sophisticated Southern Style." Rizzoli, p.32.

Constanza, Rusty. "Toucan Play This Game." *The Times-Picayune*, December 12, p. A14, ill.

Russell, Margaret. "Style and Substance: The Best of Elle Décor." Filipacchi Publishing, p. 214, ill.

Jackson, Ted. "Toucan Talk." *Times-Picayune*, December 22, p. B1, ill.

Yuan, Jada. "Party Lines." *New York*, November 12, p. 22, ill.

Bronston, Barry. "An Art Collector Goes Public." *The Times-Picayune: NOLA.com Art & Stage News*, December 21, ill.

Eichner, Steven. "City Slickers." *WWD* (Friday), May 23, p. 14, ill.

Lowe, Catherine. "Brush With Nature." *Prestige Magazine*, September, p. 46-47, ill.

Bartlett-Hines, Emily. "Best Solo Art-Show: Hunt Slonem at the Rymer." *Nashville Scene: Best of Nashville*, October 15-21, vol. 28, no. 36.

Henderson, Stephen. "Haute & Spicy." *Town & Country*, October, pp. 130-139, ill.

Bronston, Barry. "Henry Shane Likes to Put Art Where the People Are." *Times-Picayune*, December 21, pp. A-1, A-8, ill.

Scelfo, Julie. "Newly Married, In Search of Style." *New York Times: Home*, December 3, pp. D1 and D8, ill.

Kahn, Eve. "A Collector of Houses Unloads Some Gothiana." *The New York Times*, October 23, pp. C30, ill.

Clarke, Gerald. "Designers Own Homes: Campion Platt." *Architectural Digest*, September, pp. 174-179, ill.

D'Annunzio, Grazia. "Kaleidoscopic: Hunt Slonem." *L'Uomo Vogue*, July/August, ill.

"Arikonmaz ile Sanat Konusmalari: Hunt Slonem." *In Style Home: Turkey*, p. 149, ill.

"Diary of the Week: Hunt Slonem." *Hello, Turkey*, May 13-10, p. 30, ill.

Peveto, Ryland. "You Look Like Someone I Know." *PaperCity*, March, p. 10, ill.

Miller, Robin. "Archives Show Offers Lincoln Portraits, More." *The Advocate*, February 22, p. 6E, ill.

Schmidt, Esther & Franklin. "Jewel of the Hudson Valley: Hunt Slonem Follows an Artistic Legacy." *Victorian Homes*, March, p. 36-46, ill.

Heines, Jessica. "Lincoln Painting Set for Display Through November." *Gettysburg Times*, October 28, p. C1, ill.

Pitzer, Scot Andrew. "Blue Lincoln." *Gettysburg Times*, December 23, p. C1, ill.

Hirst, Arlene. "Word. The Goods." *Metropolitan Home*, April, p. 34, ill.

"175 Ways Tulane Has Rocked the World." *Tulanian*, Fall, p. 16.

2010   *Hunt Slonem on the Bayou*. Lafayette: Paul and Lulu Hilliard University Art, University of Louisiana at Lafayette.

Feen, Diane. "Painting With Passion." *Art New Orleans*, Summer pp. 30-35. Ill.

Kim, John. "Hunt Slonem: Stroke of Genius." *7x7 San Francisco*, January 20, http://www.7x7.com/blogs/hunt-slonem-stroke-genius, ill.

Mills, Michael. "Check Out Slonem's Rabbit Art at the Coral Springs Museum." *New Times Broward/Palm Beach*, January 28, http://browardpalmbeach.com/content.

Bronston, Barry. "New Orleans-Area Collector Goes Public New Sculptures." *The Advocate*, January 4, p. 3B, ill.

Paskin, Murray. "Top Pick: Flora, Fauna, Faces & Feathers." *San Francisco Examiner*, January 28, p. 24, ill.

Cheema, Sushil. "House of the Day." *The Wall Street Journal*, January 28.

Raiser, Jennifer. "Dish, Dance & a Bit of Romance." *Nob Hill Gazette*, February, pp. 14- 15, ill.

Goodman, Wendy. "Living With a Thousand Best Friends." *New York Magazine*, March 8, pp. 44-47, ill.

Willie, Jill. "Streets Boast More Than Blooming Flowers." *Jefferson Life*, Spring, pp. 34-35, ill.

Platt, Campion. "Made to Order." Monacelli Press, pp. 15-16, 23, 29, 68-70, 75.

Campion, Freddie. "Hunt Slonem." *Acne Paper*, Winter 2010/2011, no.11, pp. 36-37, ill.

Morrisey, Cedric. "Zoo In My Luggage." *Architectural Digest Russia*, December/January 2011, pp. 184-189, ill.

Weiss, Lois. "Between the Bricks." *New York Post*, March 30, p. 34, ill.

Morrison, David. "The Kindness of Strangers." *Brenau Window*, Winter, cover, p. 12-15, ill.

DiGiacomo, Frank. "Gatecrasher." *New York Daily News*, June 8.

Shepard, Sherry P. "Exotic Inspiration." *Shreveport Times*, August 17, p. C1, ill.

2011   Crow, Kelly. "Hunt Slonem's Oddball Menagerie." *The Wall Street Journal*, November 19, 2011.

Benson, Harry and Hilary Geary Ross. *New York New York*. powerHouse Books, p. 120-121, ill.

Art on the Hill: Works from the OHSU Collection. Portland: Oregon Health & Science University, p. 113, ill.

Owens, Mitchell. "Manhattan Transfer." *Architectural Digest*, October.

Stein, Clare. "Lincoln is Hunt Slonem's Marilyn." *InterviewMagazine.com*,
    http://www.interviewmagazine.com/art/hunt-slonem-acadian-dreams/.
Nasitir, Judith. "Tudor Triumph." *Elle Décor*, February/March, p. 153, ill.
Lipsky-Karasz, Elisa. "Diandra Douglas Defends Herself." *Harper's Bazaar*, April, p. 174, ill.
"Multiple Choice." *Elle Décor*, November 2011.
"Petal Pusher." *Lilly Pulitzer Catalogue*, Spring, pp. 26-39, insert, ill.
"Mary Bird Perkins to Auction Hunt Slonem Artwork to Benefit its Five Cancer Centers."
    The Pointe Coupee Banner, April 7, p. 3.
Kususto, Lauren. "Colorful Hunt Slonem Lands Near 10th." *The New York Observer*,
    April 26.
"Amuse Bouche Limited Edition." *Napa Valley Home*, Summer, p. 14, 18.
Menke, Anne. "Half Their Age." *People*, April 25, pp. 6, 71, ill.
Moore, Holly. "Booked & In Person." *PaperCity* November, p. 6, ill.
O'Grady, Megan. "Words of Wonder." *Vogue*, December, p. 233, ill.
Davies, Roger. "Kathryn Ireland: Inside My Home." *People Magazine*, October 17, p. 100, ill.
Needleman, Deborah. "Three and a Half Billion Men." *WSJ Magazine*, October, Editor's
    Letter Masthead, p. 18, ill.
Weidner, Elyse. "On the Town: Artful Living." *Kansas City Spaces*, Holiday, p. 190, ill.
"Hunt Slonem." Art Interview, issue 014, November.
Akar, Serra Yazi. "Ruya Apartmanda." *InStyle Home*, October, p. 231-233, ill.

2012   Artunc, Nilufer. "Tuy Oyunlai." *Maison Francaise*, April/May, p. 79, ill.
Alanson, Biricik Suden. "Hunt Slonem: Hepimiz kafeslerde yasariz." *Alfa Magazine*, April 9.
Allen, Libby. "Artist Profile: Hunt Slonem's Work." *New Orleans Living Magazine*, October, ill.
Allen, Mike. "New Art at Hollins." *The Roanoke Times*, January 8, ill.
Anspon, Catherine D. "Birds & Butterflies." PaperCity, October.
Ates, Ertugrul. "'Mabeyn Gallery' De Iki Sergi." *Artam*, April/May, p. 96, ill.
Bell, Zach. "Antebellum Oz." *Artlog*, July 6.
Gates, Tom. "Manhattan." *Palm Beach Society*, February 10-16, p. 37, ill.
Hass, Nancy. "Hamptons Classic." *ELLE Décor*, December, p. 121, ill.
Ireland, Kathryn M. *Timeless Interiors*. Layton: Gibbs Smith, pp. 146-147, ill.
"Modern Art Matters." *Mandarin Hotel Book* (Editorial), ill.
"The Morris at Twenty, Closes September 16, 2012" in "Exhibitions." *Morris Museum of Art*
    Quarterly Newsletter, Fall 2012, p. 4, ill.
Özaytekin, Merve. "Bird Painter Living in the Wild." *Posta.com.tr* (Turkey), April 15.
Powell, Jennifer. "Introducing the World of Hunt Slonem." *Kravet Inspired News*, Fall 2012,
    vol. 4, issue 3, pp. 10-11, ill.
Siegler, Mara. "Hunt Slonem's Wonderland." *Avenue*, May, p. 52-61, ill.
Thurman, Judith. "Personal History." *Architectural Digest*, March, p. 79, ill.
Trebay, Guy. "In Constant Motion, With an Elusive Point." *The New York Times*,
    September 16, "Styles" section, p. 12.
Shetty, Deepika. "An Hour @the Museum," *ST Life!* (Singapore), Sept 12.
Utkan, Hatice. "Discovering a Cabinet of Curiosities." *Hürriyet Daily News* (Istanbul, TR),
    April 9. p. 53, ill.

2013   Walther, Gary. "The House That Roger Built." *Boston Common*, Spring 2013, p. 96, ill.
    & p. 101.

Cobb, Kellie. "Slonem Work Donated to ASU's Permanent Art Collection." *The Jonesboro Sun*, March 31, C1, C7, ill.

Finnigan, Sean. "Butterfly Effect." *Interior Living Trends*, Volume 28 No.10, Cover, p. 10, ill.

Parr-Moody, Karen. "Hunt Slonem: Collection Arrives at Customs House." *Nashville Arts*, January, p. 40-41, ill.

Miller, Robin. "Painter Hunt Slonem Never Happier Than When He's Winging It." *The Advocate*, February 10, p.5E, ill.

Meek, J. William, III. *Images of America*. Charleston, SC: Arcadia Publishing. pp. 96,102, 106, 108, 112-115, 124, ill.

Brenner, Douglas. "A Cut Above." *Architectural Digest*, September, p.202, ill.

Bradfield, Geoffrey. *Artistic License*. Smallwood & Stewart, pp. 206, 234-235, ill.

Vilensky, Mike. "Butterflies, Birds, and Black Streaks." *Wall Street Journal*, July 27-28, p. A21, ill.

Kogevinas, Vanessa. "Villa de Luxe," *Luxe Interiors*, Spring, vol. 11, issue

Gannon, Suzanne. "Artful Dodgers." *Luxe Interiors*, Winter vol.11, issue1, pp. 175-178, ill.

Fox-Smith, James. "Variations on a Theme." *Country Roads* August, Cover, p. 36-39, ill.

Hackett, Kathleen. "Creating A Scene:Cameron Diaz's Ultra Glam Apartment." *Elle Décor*, October, p. 213, ill.

"Seen." *Naples Illustrated*, October, p. 157, ill.

Bergstrom, Anders. "Artist Hunt Slonem." *Journal of the Print World*. October, p.27, ill.

Rodrigue, Wendy W. "The Other Side of Painting." Lafayette, LA: University of Louisiana at Lafayette Press. P. 119,165, ill.

Le, Vanna. "Art of the Deal," *Forbes Life*, October, p.86, ill.

Safavi, Charlotte. "Going Homes," *Home&Garden*, July/August, ill.

Stinson, Carter. "Crown Heights," *Room 101*, Spring, p. 40-47, ill.

"Designer Project: Art & Space in Montreal Loft," *Kravet InspiredNews*, Summer, pp.32-33

2014   Helander, Bruce. *Bunnies*. New York: Glitterati Incorporated, March.

MacAdam, Barbara A. "Birds of a Feather," *ARTnews*, January, p. 18, ill.

Schink, Carole. "L'Art d'agencer l'art," *Decormag*, January/February, p. 63-67, 74, ill.

Godfrey-June, Jean. "The Beauty Closet," *Lucky*, February, p. 84, ill.

Siegler, Mara. "Alec and Hilaria Baldwain Make Appearance at Book Launch," *Page Six NY Post*, March 27th, ill.

Ludewig, Joachim. "Vogel, Autos, Schmetterlinge," *Drive*, Winter 60-61, ill.

Palazzi, Helena. "Art & Musing," *Modern Luxury*, Manhattan, Miami, Dallas, Scottsdale, Houston, Atlanta), March/April, pp. 102-109, ill.

Tomaine, Gina. "Hop to It," *Boston Magazine*, Spring, p.28, ill.

Cull, Deborah. "Luxe Living: Harmon-Meek Gallery Hosts Hunt Slonem Reception," *Florida Weekly*, March, p.16.

Von Unwerth, Ellen. "Masterpiece Theater," *Numero* (Tokyo, Japan), April. Ill.

Feitelberg, Rosemary. "Bird's Eye View: Talking Art with Hunt Slonem," *WWD*, March 25, ill.

Bruno, R. Stephanie. "All Ears," *The Advocate*, April 20. Ill. p. 1D

Johnson, Robert. "Heartbreak Hotel," *NY Post*, May 11. Ill. p.17

Hoffman, Barbara. "In My Library: Hunt Slonem," *New York Post*, April 20, p. 32, ill.

Park, Mimi Chloe. "The World According to... Hunt Slonem," *Avenue*, May. Ill. p. 116

Huang, Grace. "One Week in New York," *Elle Japan*, May ill.

Anspon, Catherine D. "Through the Rabbit Hole," *PaperCity*, April, p.46, ill.

Engebrecht, Julie. "City Hosts Painter with Vibrant Persona," USA Today /// The Enquirer, May 25, p. D8, ill.

"Great Reads: Bunnies," *Kravet InspiredNews*, Summer, p. 32, ill.
"Quintessential: Design Monographs That Are Required Reading for Fall," *Veranda*.
    September-October p. 66, ill.
"Where to Buy: Hunt Slonem," *The Week*, September 5, p./24, ill.
Fertig. Judith. "My Blue Heaven," *Kansas City Spaces*, August, p. 105, ill.
Assouline, Prosper and Martine. *Assouline: 20 Years!*, Fall, p. 89, ill.
Goldfarb, Brad. "The Life Eclectic," *Architectural Digest*, October, p. 175, ill.
Sullivan, Maureen. "Must-Do List Q & A: Hunt Slonem," *Kansas City Spaces*, September,
    pp. 86-87, ill.
Cook, Cindi. "Spreading the Love," *New York Cottages & Gardens*, Holiday, p. 87, ill.
Eerdmans, Emily. "A Colorful Life," *House Beautiful*, December/January, pp. 68-75, ill.
"Wishlist: The Artist," *Modern Luxury Manhattan*. November, p. 51, ill.
Benson, Harry. *Palm Beach People*, powerHouse Books, pp. 128, 186, 243, ill.
Sinclair, Leslie. *Segreto Style*. Segreto Publishing, Houston, TX

2015   Mauk, Laura. "House Of Style." *Luxe Interiors Houston* November/December. Cover,
            & P. 236 Ill.
        Terrebone, Jackie. "Inside Artist Hunt Slonem's Magical New Brooklyn Studio."
        Architectural Digest Online. November 5th. Video Produced By Marcus Jones.
        Morse, Trent. "Out Of The Studio, Onto The Wall." *1stDibs.Com*. June 8th. Ill.
        Kennedy, Kerry. "Hunt Slonem's Richly Layered Life." *Art & Design*. Winter. P.64-73. Ill.
        Schultz, Kimann. "Kindred Spirits: Hunt Slonem & Carmelo Blandino." *Huffington Post*.
            May 28. Ill.
        Oller, Julia. "Prolific Painter To Appear At Hawk Galleries." *Columbus Dispatch*. July 24. Ill.
        Katz, Anita. "Hunt Slonem Inspired By Birds, Butterflies And Bunnies."
        San Francisco Examiner. May 28. Ill.Grossnickle, Jacqueline Z. "Strokes Of Genious"
        Modern Luxury. January/February P.26. Ill.
        Quinlan, Adriane. "Art For Art's Sake: Jefferson Given A Dozen Louisiana Landscapes"
        Jefferson: *The Times-Picayune*. April 1st. P. B-1 & B-2. Ill.
        Bradford, Amy. "Thrill Of The Hunt." *Elle Decoration*. May. P. 27-29. Ill.
        Cook, Cindi. "Life Of Reily" *Hamptons Cottages And Gardens* July 15. P. 92 & 95. Ill.
        MacCash, Doug. "The Shapes Of Things To Come" *The Times-Picayune* August 9.
            P. A-1 & A-10. Ill.
        Traweek, Lance. "Beauty Before Business" *New Orleans City Business* July 8.
        "Teamworks @ Stewart & Stewart" Journal Of The Print World July. P. 7 & 20. Ill.
        Rossbund, Krissa. "New Season". *Traditional Home* September. P. 114. Ill.
        Rozhin, Alexander. *Hunt Slonem Paintings: Moscow Museum Of Modern Art*, Glitterati
        Editor's Choice. *Harper's Bazaar Russia* September P. 4 Ill.
        Annett, Carole. "Out And About: Rabbiting On.", *House & Gardens UK*, October. P. 88 Ill.
        Bale, Lindsey. "Bunnies, Butterflies, And Mantras." *Adornomag.Com* November 23. Ill.
        Barman, John. *Interior Design*. The Monacelli Press: New York, 2015. P. 108 And 113. Ill.
        Poole, Ed And Susan. "Albania Plantation." *Louisiana Plantations: Real To Reel*. Ed And
            Susan Pool: Middletown, DE, 2015. P. 3-8.
        Rozhin, Alexander. *Hunt Slonem Paintings: Moscow Museum Of Modern Art*, Glitterati.
            New York.
        McLean, Virginia. *Journey To The Beginning Of The World*. Rapscallion Press: Enfield,
            England, 2015. P. 22. Ill.

2016   The Martin Z. Margulies Collection Of Painting And Sculpture
        Seipel, Joseph H. Anderson Gallery, *45 Years Of Art On The Edge*. School Of The Arts,
            Virginia Commonwealth University. P. 80 Ill.
        Cregan, Lisa. "House Call", *House Beautiful*. February. P. 68 & 71. Ill.
        Laneri, Raquel. "The Ringmaster", Alexa: *New York Post*. April 16. P. 16 & 17. Ill.
        Loos, Ted. "Host With The Most", *Traditonal Home*. May. P. 56-60. Ill.
        Miller, Robin. "Pop Art Life", *Louisiana Advocate*. May 4. P. 1D-2D. Ill.
        Yoder, Kaci. Inside The Stunning Design Of LSU MOA's Hunt Slonem Exhibit. 225 Baton
            Rouge.May 24.
        Thompson, Helen. "French Refresh", *Luxe Magazine*. May/June. P. 211 & 215. Ill.
        Beuershausen, Allen. "All He Ever Wanted To Do", *Influential Magazine*. May/June.
            P. 81-85 2D. Ill.
        Slonim, Jeffrey. "Seen & Heard" *Hamptons Magazine*. June 1.
        Stephens, AnnaMaria. "Contemporary Appeal." *Modern Luxury Interiors*.
            Spring/Summer. P. 46. Ill.
        Stephen, AnnaMaria. "Treasure Hunt." *Modern Luxury: San Diego*. May. P. 73 Ill.
        Carlino, Nicole. "Floss Barber." Hotel Business Design. May/June. Ill.
        Kendrick, Isabella. "Selected New Editions." Art In Print. July. Ill.
        Fonk, Hans. "Hunt Slonem's Worship Of Colorful Repetition." *Objekt Canada*. May.
            P. 24-31. Ill.
        "The Alchemy Of Art." *Singapore Tatler Homes*. February. P. 148-155. Ill.
        Achara, Esther Adams. "This Just In: Major Style News From Jason Wu And His Chic
            Bestie Diane Kruger." *Glamour.Com* April 13. Ill.
        Iredale, Jessica. "Jason Wu Launches Sibling Collection Grey Jason Wu." *WWD.com*
            April 12. Ill.
        Rodulfo, Kristina. "Get A Sneak Peek At Jason Wu'd New Sister Line, Grey Jason Wu."
            Elle.Com April 14. Ill.
        Heinzinger, Kristen. "Jason Wu Launches Sister Label, Grey Jason Wu." *FashionWeek
            Daily.Com* April 12. Ill.
        Tortura, Laura. 'Grey Jason Wu." *Vogue.It & Vogue.Ru* April 13
        "Jason Wu Lance Grey Jason Wu, Sa Nouvelle Marque." *Elle.Fr* April 13.
        Plummer, Todd. "Grey Jason Wu Launches With Martha Hunt, Zosia Mamet, Constance
            Jablonski, And Miroslava Duma." *Vogue.Com* June 9. Ill.
        Bass, Erin. "Antebellum Pop!" *Deep South Magazine*. May 3. Ill.
        Seipel, Joseph H. Anderson Gallery: 45 Years Of Art On The Edge. *School Of The Arts,
            Virginia Commonwealth University*. P. 80 Ill.
        "Another New Sculpture Installed On Power Boulevard." *Kenner Star*. August Cover &
            P.19 Ill.
        Gunnerson, Tate. "Forever Young." *Luxe Interiors* July/August. Cover & P. 339 Ill.
        Bozeman, Kelli. "Hunt Slonem:Antebellum Pop!" *InRegister*. June. P. 44. Ill.
        Helander, Bruce. "Pooling Our Resources." *Art Hive*. Summer. P. 61 & 62. Ill.
        Bernard, Shane K. Teche: "A History Of Louisiana's Most Famous Bayou". *University
            Press Of Mississippi*, Jackson, Miss., 2016. P.4 & 172.
        Biggs, Caroline. "Bark Before Entering." *The New York Times*, October 29. P. RE1.

2017   *Russian State Museum, St. Petersburg Exhibition Catalogue/ Author Hunt Slonem,
            Essays by Anthony Haden-Guest and Anton Uspensky, Palace Editions*
        Baycrest Foundation. "The Brain Project" *Baycrest Foundation*, Toronto, 2017. P. 94. Ill.

Artsy Editors. "Inside Hunt Slonem's Studio, a Peaceful Kingdom of Animals and Art"
 Artsy.net February 17, 2017
"Behind Artist Hunt Slonem's Obsession With Birds". *Galleriemagazine* May 12 2017
Carreon, Blue. "The Artist Hunt Slonem And His Fascination With Birds",
 Forbes.Com May 13, 2017
Bozeman, Kelli. "Hunt Slonem:Antebellum Pop!", *InRegister*. June. P. 44. Ill.
Editors Of *New York Magazine*. "High Brow, Low Brow, Brilliant, Despicable: 50 Years
 Of New York". Simon & Schuster: New York, 2017. P. 249. Ill.
Gunnerson, Tate. "Forever Young". *Luxe Interiors* July/August. Cover & P. 339 Ill.
Helander, Bruce. "Pooling Our Resources", *Art Hive*. Summer. P. 61 & 62. Ill.
"In Birds, An Acclaimed Artist Finds Both Companions And Muses", Meghan
 Bartels. *Audubon.Org*. April 25, 2017.
Vogl, Sydney. "Hunt Slonem: A Force Of Nature", *Art Of The Times*. Winter 2017.
 Cover & P. 2-5. Ill.

MOVIES IN WHICH WORKS APPEAR

1989 *Slaves of New York*. Dir. James Ivory. With Bernadette Peters, Chris Sarandon,
   Mary Beth Hurt, and Steve Buscemi. TriStar Pictures.

2006 *The Namesake*. Dir. Mira Nair. With Irrfan Khan, Kal Penn, and Jacinda Barrett.
   Fox Searchlight Pictures.
   All the King's Men. Dir. Steven Zaillian. With Sean Penn, Jude Law, Kate Winslet,
   James Gandolfini, Patricia Clarkson, and Anthony Hopkins. Columbia Pictures

2009 *In the Electric Mist*. Dir. Bertrand Tavernier. With Tommy Lee Jones, John Goodman,
   Peter Sarsgaard, Kelly MacDonald, and Mary Steenburgen. Ithaca Pictures.

2013 *Beautiful Creatures*. Dir. Richard LaGravenese. With Alden Ehrenreich, Alice Englert,
   Jeremy Irons, Viola Davis, Emmy Rossum, Thomas Mann, and Emma
   Thompson. Warner Bros. Pictures.
   Broken City. Dir. Allen Hughes. With Mark Wahlberg and Russell Crowe. Regency
   Enterprises.
   Fading Gigolo. Dir. John Turturro. With Sofia Vergara, Woody Allen, Sharon Stone,
   Liev Schreiber, and Vanessa Paradis. Antidote Films.

2015 *Get Hard*. Dir. Etan Cohen. With Will Ferrell, Kevin Hart, T.I. and Alison Brie.
   Warner Bros. Pictures.

TELEVISION

1990 "BNN Spotlight." Bombay Broadcasting, 1697 Broadway, New York City.
"Hunt Slonem Report." Daiwa New York View, Japan.

1991 Antonio Guccione. *Hunt Slonem: The Movie.*

1992 Amy Atkins. Fox 5 News, New York City, January 1
"What's Up New York?" PVE/NHK, Japan, show 73, January 11
Jeanie Moos. "Prime News," CNN, February 12
The Marty Antoinette Show. Channel 16, New York City, September 24.

1993 *Good Day New York.* WNYW TV, Channel 5, Nov 1

1995 "New Yorkers: Hunt Slonem." NHK.

1996 *Good Day New York,* WNYW TV, Channel 5, March 15.

2008 *CBS Sunday Morning,* April 13.

2010 "Hunt Slonem." Louisiana Public Broadcasting, May 14.

2011 "Plantations and Spirits." Louisiana Public Broadcasting, October 28.

2012 "Hunt Slonem's Artist's Aviary." *Studio 360*, Public Radio International, February 24.
"Artist's Exotic Loft Provides Oasis of Inspiration." *Whipples's World* NY1 April 4.

2015 Stephanie Simon. "Artist Hunt Slonem's New Brooklyn Studio Mixes Art, Interior
Design and Aviary," NY1, New York City, September 28.
Utro Rossii. "With Exotic World Hunt Slonem Introduces the Exhibition in
Moscow," Russia-1 TV, September 30.
"Today's Guest of the 'Arts Council': The Artist and Sculptor Hunt Slonem," TV
Kultura Studio, Russia, September 30.

2016 "Art is now the new gold: Hunt Slonem," CNBC, New York, January 27

2017 "Artist Hunt Slonem is out with a new book, 'Birds,'" Good Day New York, New York
City, March 2

ACKNOWLEDGMENTS

Catherine Johnson, Angele Parlange, Bruce Helander, Susan Hau, John Berendt, Pablo García Pérez, Claire Lachow, Natasha Quam, Ted Vassilev, Mark Millene, Wilson Kidde.

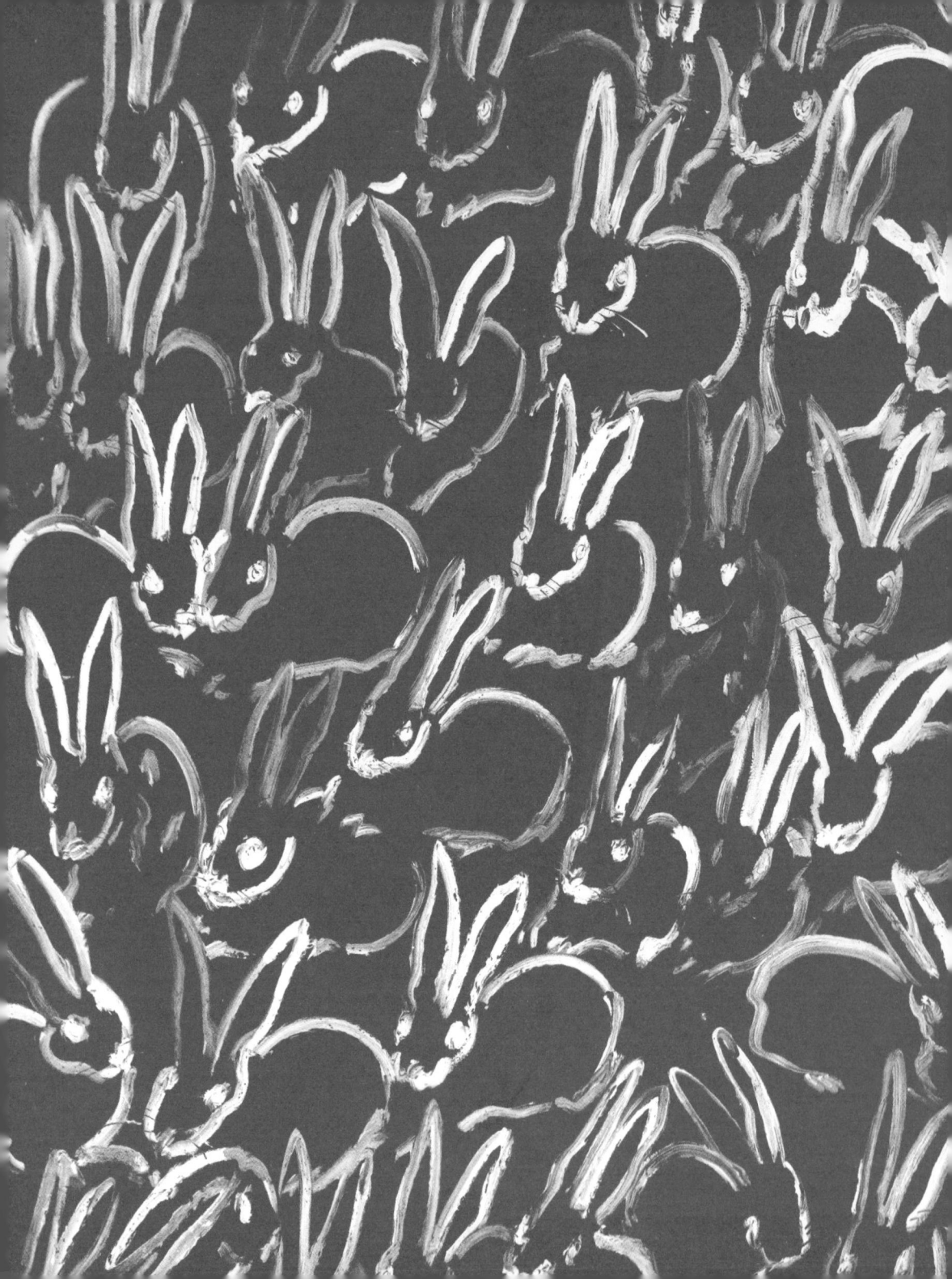